CONNECTED

CONNECTED

How Trains, Genes, Pineapples, Piano Keys, and a Few Disasters Transformed Americans at the Dawn of the Twentieth Century

Steven Cassedy

STANFORD UNIVERSITY PRESS
Stanford, California

Stanford University Press
Stanford, California

Printed in the United States of America on acid-free, archival-quality paper

Library of Congress Cataloging-in-Publication Data

Cassedy, Steven, author

Connected : how trains, genes, pineapples, piano keys, and a few disasters transformed Americans at the dawn of the twentieth century / Steven Cassedy.

pages cm.

Includes bibliographical references and index.

ISBN 978-0-8047-6372-1 (cloth : alk. paper)

1. United States—Civilization—1865–1918. I. Title

E169.1.C298 2014

973.8—dc23 2013010533

ISBN 978-0-8047-8841-0 (electronic)

Typeset at Stanford University Press in 10/14 Minion

To my family

Contents

A Note on Usage ix

Acknowledgments xi

Preface xiii

Part I: Body and Mind

1 "To Push Back the Shadow upon the Dial of Time": The Astonishing New Facts of Life and Death 3

2 The Biological Self 17

3 Sex O'Clock in America 45

4 The Neurophysiological Mind—or Not 66

Part II: The New Physical World

5 The Network of Spatialized Time 95

6 The Networked House and Home 116

7 The Globalized Consumer Network: From Pineapples to Turkey Red Cigarettes to the Bunny Hug 142

Part III: The Secular, Ecumenical Collective

8 Race Goes Scientific, Then Transnational 177

9 Religion Goes Worldly, Ecumenical, and Collective 218

10 Citizen, Community, State 246

Conclusion: Who You Are 267

Notes 277

Index 305

A Note on Usage

In this book, I've made a practice of adhering to word usage that was conventional during the period I'm examining. For that reason, I've chosen to use the word "Negro" throughout, instead of "African American." I trust this will give no offense.

Acknowledgments
(in no particular order)

Patrice Cassedy, San Diego, Calif.; Michael Schudson, University of California, San Diego (UCSD); Howard Pollack, University of Houston; Alain J. J. Cohen, UCSD; the late James H. Cassedy, National Library of Medicine, National Institutes of Health; Brian J. Cudahy, formerly of Department of Transportation; Charles Lester, vacuum cleaner historian; David Phillips, UCSD; Donald Glassman, Wollman Library, Barnard College; Noraleen A. Young, Staff Archivist, Kappa Alpha Theta Fraternity; Mary Edith Arnold, Kappa Alpha Theta Fraternity Archivist; Jocelyn K. Wilk, Assistant Director, Columbia University Archives; Steve Laise, Chief of Cultural Resources, Manhattan Sites, National Park Service; John Mullarkey, University of Dundee, Scotland; Andrew Dolkart, Columbia University; James C. Riley, Indiana University; Peter Uhlenberg, University of North Carolina, Chapel Hill; Philip L. Fradkin, author of *The Great Earthquake and Firestorms of 1906*; Michael Parrish, UCSD; Debra Feiger, piano technician, San Diego, Calif.; Karl Hagstrom Miller, University of Texas, Austin; Carey Stumm, Archivist, New York City Transit Museum; the late Beth M. Howse, Special Collections Librarian, John Hope and Aurelia E. Franklin Library, Fisk University; Lin Chao, UCSD; Edwin DeLeon, New York & Atlantic Railway; Paul Victor, New York & Atlantic Railway; Jason Wood, Simmons College Archives; Donna Webber, Simmons College Archives; Tony Rinaldo, Concord, Mass.; Peter Galison, Harvard University; James Morrison Sr., town historian, Gloversville, N.Y.; Joan and Bill Loveday, Fulton County Museum, Gloversville, N.Y.; Jodie Mattos, Hawaiian Collection, Thomas Hale Hamilton Library, University of Hawaii at Manoa; Michael O'Malley, George Mason University; Peter Muir, Institute for Music and Health, Verbank, N.Y.; Michael Cassedy, Brooklyn, N.Y.; Meghan Finn, Brooklyn, N.Y.; Don Malcarne, town historian, Essex, Conn.; Gabriele Wienhausen, UCSD; Eva Cassedy, Nashville, Tenn.; Stephen D. Cox, UCSD; Seth Lerer, UCSD; Ronald Berman, UCSD; E. S. Cassedy Jr., Polytechnic Institute of New York (Emeritus); Kim Barrett, UCSD; the late Henry Z. Steinway, Steinway & Sons; Douglas Di Carlo, La Guardia and Wagner Archives, La Guardia Community College, City University of New York (CUNY); Rosemarie Rinaldo, San Diego, Calif.; the late Joseph A. Rinaldo Jr., San Diego, Calif.; Tim Cassedy, Southern Methodist University, Dallas, Tex.; Richard Elliott Friedman, University of Georgia, Athens; Roger Newman, Riverdale, N.Y.

Preface

I stood at a grade crossing in Del Mar, California, where I used to live. With me was cousin Ugo from Italy. The single-track line that runs along the Pacific Coast serves the local commuter trains between San Diego and the city of Oceanside, twenty miles north. It also serves Amtrak. If your eye follows the tracks south from the crossing, you can see almost nothing, for they bend sharply to the left and are immediately lost to view behind the steep bluffs over the beach. We stood silently, looking north. Past the abandoned beachside passenger station, a siding splits off from the main line, allowing one train to pull off while another one passes through. A half-mile or so from the split, the entire road bends to the left, once again out of sight. I waited for Ugo to speak, because I knew he would get it. "You see," he finally said, squinting into the distance, "the beauty is it can take you *anywhere*." Meaning *these rails*, right here, under our feet, in this crossing.

Just think: if I had a HiRail (one of those pickup trucks with both rubber tires and train wheels that servicemen use to perform track inspection and maintenance), and if I had the ability to throw switches wherever I wanted, I could start right here at the grade crossing in my hometown and head to Los Angeles. From Los Angeles, I could travel far north, to Vancouver, where my sister Amy lives. Or I could set out east for Chicago, go south, then east again toward Detroit. Until a few years ago, just west of the passenger station in Ann Arbor, Michigan, where I was an undergraduate in the early 1970s, I could back up and switch off the Amtrak line, onto the tracks of the Ann Arbor Railroad.

Following this line south, I could pass within a mile of where my daughter-in-law's parents live and, many miles later, end up in Toledo. Following it north, where it turns into the Great Lakes Central Railroad, I could switch off near Durand onto the Lapeer Industrial Railroad and cross over the rural highway we used to take through the town of Lapeer as we drove to a vacation spot on Lake Huron. The Lapeer Industrial would take me to Port Huron, way in the east of Michigan, across the Saint Clair River from Canada. From Port Huron, I could veer south and head to Detroit, where my wife, Patrice, grew up. Detroit is connected to Windsor, Ontario, via the Michigan Central Railway Tunnel (no longer used by passenger trains), and from Windsor it's an easy matter to cross through that tongue of Canada that protrudes downward from Toronto, separating Michigan and western New York, to Niagara Falls and Buffalo. From Buffalo, Amtrak runs on the tracks of the former New York Central, along the Mohawk River, to Albany. Until 1990, I could have taken a short jog north at the town of Fonda, up the tracks of the Fonda, Johnstown & Gloversville Railroad, to Gloversville, where both my paternal grandparents were born and raised. Returning from Gloversville to the main road, I could have followed the line to Schenectady, where my first cousin, father, grandfather, great uncle, and great-grandfather all attended Union College. From Schenectady, I would head to Albany, and from there I could follow the route that my grandmother Edna Muddle took when she traveled to Simmons College in 1917 to begin her college studies. In Boston, it would be an easy matter to make my way onto the tracks of the Commuter Rail and ride the Fitchburg/South Acton Line out to West Concord, passing through Waltham, where my daughter Eva attended college. There I would switch onto a lonely abandoned line running through wooded terrain and photographed in stunning black and white by Boston photographer Tony Rinaldo (my brother-in-law). The photo hangs by my desk. I'm looking at it right now, as I write this. In it, the solitary track recedes into an unseen, dimly lighted distance.

And then it would be back to the main Amtrak line that serves the Northeast corridor. It would be a straight shot through New York, past Baltimore, where I lived from the age of 2 till the age of 7, and down to Washington, D.C. There I could switch off to the Metropolitan Subdivision (formerly of the B & O) and pass through Silver Spring, Maryland, where my father grew up, not far from where I was born and not far from where my sisters Ellen and Susannah live. Before 1986, I could have switched off this line to a spur that would have taken me directly through a country club in exclusive Chevy

Chase, Maryland. In the late 1960s, Edward Spencer ("Mike") Cassedy (originally from Gloversville) attempted without success to teach his grandson to play golf there. I could then thread my way back up the Northeast Corridor, to New York, through Penn Station, and onto the tracks of the Long Island Railroad, Port Washington line. That would take me to Great Neck, where I lived from age 8 through high school. If I headed back toward the city, at Sunnyside Yards in Queens (just this side of the tunnel into Manhattan) I could switch onto the tracks of the New York & Atlantic Railway, a freight company, heading south and east toward the company's main yards in Glendale, Queens. Just before hitting the yards, I'd switch south onto the company's Bay Ridge branch. This would take me into Brooklyn. That's where my son Michael and his wife Meghan live, where my maternal grandparents lived, where my mother grew up, where my father spent his career as a professor, and where my Uncle David used to live. I would proceed to a spot where the tracks, above grade level, run parallel to an elevated stretch of the BMT Canarsie subway line (known nowadays as the L train) on the left and, on the right below, Junius Street, just south of Riverdale Avenue in Brooklyn's Brownsville neighborhood . . .

So, could I go *anywhere?* Not really: only anywhere the tracks go, as long as there are connections. *That's* the real essence: it can take you anywhere *it* goes, not just anywhere *you* want to go. It's not the same as a driveway or a dirt path. Sure, the driveway leads out onto a surface street, and the surface street leads to other surface streets, and those streets lead to interstate highways, and those interstate highways lead back to other surface streets, which lead to dirt paths and driveways. But with the proper vehicle, you can steer off the road and drive in open fields, through deserts, on the beach, across rocky flats. You can go pretty much *anywhere.*

But the tracks confine you. They have rules. The engineer never gets to steer the locomotive off them and keep traveling *ad libitum.* And yet the arbitrarily chosen entry point—a lonely, deserted line of track in the woods someplace, a pair of half-buried rails dug into the asphalt in some grubby urban wasteland—makes you potentially at one with any number of fabulously distant points, in the sense that all those points are accessible to you. If you connected light bulbs to them and touched a *very* high voltage cable to your entry point (while somehow forming a circuit, of course), those bulbs would light up—almost immediately.

So the tracks form a *network*, in the modern sense of the word. Networks consist of pathways and nodal points (switches, circuits, barriers). They can be entered from numerous places, and they offer both promise and constraint. Once you're in, you're potentially connected with all destinations in the system. At the same time, like me in my imaginary HiRail or a real engineer in a locomotive, you're confined to the pathways and nodal points. The route I described forms the network—or at least *one* network—of my own life.

By the end of the nineteenth century, if you were an American, you increasingly lived in networks, most of them the result of developments in science and technology. This world was staggeringly different from the one that your ancestors inhabited earlier in the century—that is, if you *had* ancestors that lived in the United States. Alexis de Tocqueville had brilliantly evoked what he regarded as an essential quality of the Americans he observed when he visited the young United States in the early 1830s. The quality, as he described it, was a capacity to overcome a lamentable tendency that he associated with fledgling democracies, a tendency that he called "individualism" (effectively introducing the word, in this sense, into the English lexicon through the translation of his work). He defined this novel concept as "a mature and calm feeling, which disposes each member of the community to sever himself from the mass of his fellows and to draw apart with his family and his friends, so that after he has thus formed a little circle of his own, he willingly leaves society at large to itself." Americans had defied the demon of individualism not only through their free institutions, which, as de Tocqueville wrote, "remind every citizen, and in a thousand ways, that he lives in society," but above all through a peculiar character trait: the natural inclination to form associations. "Americans of all ages, all conditions, and all dispositions, constantly form associations," he wrote. Civil associations, political associations—these are the stuff of American life and democracy.[1]

Of course, de Tocqueville was describing a *tension*, not a simple quality. The love for associations was there to counteract a native individualism, and each existed only in struggle with the other. The celebrated French traveler never really told us where the love for associations came from; it was just there, and he saw it. It functioned sometimes on an astonishingly grand scale, as when, by his report, a hundred thousand men joined up to forswear alcoholic beverages (he was referring to the American Temperance Society, which was founded in 1826 and which, by the early 1830s, had attracted an even higher number of followers than what de Tocqueville stated).[2] But, the temperance movement notwithstanding, the associations de Tocqueville described (if you accepted his account), by later standards, were small and local. He was seeing what a much later historian would call "island communities," groups that were usually, of necessity, confined to towns.[3] After all, when de Tocqueville visited the United States, the telegraph did not exist and railroads elicited from him merely the comment that this nation had the longest ones in the world—not that they had transformed life by helping to join the citizens together in a giant network. How could they? By the time de Tocqueville went home, there were still only a handful of railroads: the Baltimore & Ohio, a couple in New York, and a few short lines in the South.

But by the end of the century, networks—and not just railroads—were everywhere. This was especially true if you lived in a town or city, which is why I'll speak mostly about town and city life in this book. It was also especially true if you had access to what we call "media" nowadays—which was very likely if you lived in a town or city. In the pre-radio and pre-television era we're looking at here, this means mostly books, newspapers, magazines, posters, lectures, and eventually movies. If you were an ordinary American with such access, you were exposed to conditions and ideas that placed you in networks. You did not need to be a member of the educated elite.

There were transportation networks, of course, such as railroads. There was the mass of pipes and wires that poked out through the bottom of your house or apartment building (especially if you lived in a city) and stretched into vast systems of commercial and municipal services. There was the array of consumer products—gastronomic, cultural, recreational—that, in order to reach you, had followed established routes from distant shores or from sources close to home. There was standard time, a network that swept into its structure everyone who owned a timepiece (as virtually everyone did) and even those who didn't. There were networks composed of other human beings, past and present. The Public Health Movement made you responsible for your own health so that you could also be responsible for the health of others. You carried the genes of your ancestors (as you began to learn sometime after 1900) and were connected with them in your appearance and even in your everyday actions. You were connected to yet more primitive forebears in your species but also, through your unconscious life, to your own primitive self. You were socially bound to your fellow human beings by a spirit of cooperation and collective action that you learned was a scientifically explicable fact of nature. As a religious believer, you heard you were enjoined by God to act in that same spirit. The kingdom of God was here, right now, in your city, country, and world, and you were inextricably connected to it.

Not only that: by the end of the nineteenth century, you learned that *you yourself* were a network. Your body and mind were now so conceptualized. Your body was a network of cells, tissues, organs, and circulatory vessels. It dwelt in a world of predatory microscopic enemies that, in the absence of proper countermeasures, could invade it, travel its inner pathways, pass through critical nodal points, and carry it off to an early death. Your mind was a system of chemical and electrical impulses traveling along segmented filaments, through circuits and switches. Or it was simply an internally governed structure of thoughts, desires, and impulses that (investigation appeared to show) interacted in relatively predictable ways, traveling along established "pathways." Your entire conception of your individual self was something that earlier generations would have found incomprehensible. The more you thought about it (if you took the time to think about it), the more you realized that, if seen from above by some creature endowed with supernatural powers of vision, you would appear as a tiny network moving along the filaments of several dozen external networks that overlapped and intersected with each other in hopelessly complicated ways.

We can see how pervasive the concept was by how frequently the network of the human self was used as a metaphor for the network of the outside world—and vice versa. In explaining the latest dazzling discoveries in neurophysiology and biology to ordinary educated readers, popular science writers often used the image of a transportation network. Conversely, the celebrated high priest of electrical technology, Nikola Tesla, looking ahead as early as 1904 to "The Transmission of Electrical Energy without Wires" (that is, radio, as it would come to be called), fell back on neurophysiology and the integrated nervous system for his vision of the future: "Thus the entire earth will be converted into a huge brain, as it were, capable of response in every one of its parts."[4]

. . . But I stopped above Junius Street in Brooklyn. Here, as it happens, is a place where, via the tracks of the New York & Atlantic, the nation's larger rail system intersects with the New York City subway system—one of the *anywheres* that cousin Ugo spoke of. And so, in three switching maneuvers—from the main southbound track of the Bay Ridge line to a side track, from the side track onto a connector track, from the connector track onto a track owned by the Metropolitan Transit Authority, which leads south into the Linden Shops (where they make switches and weld rails for the subways) or north, I could ride my HiRail north, onto the Wye trackage connecting the Linden Shops with the IRT New Lots line (today the 3 train).[5] Curving up and around to the west, in no time I'd merge onto that line (elevated here), heading into Manhattan. There, following the tracks of the 3 train, I'd proceed straight up Seventh Avenue and Broadway (staying under Broadway after 96th Street by following the tracks of the local 1 train, as the 3 train tracks veer off east toward Lenox Avenue).

Here is the nerve center of my adolescent adventures in New York City: 14th Street, where I used to surface from the underground station to wander the streets of Greenwich Village; 34th Street/Penn Station, my point of entry into the city from Long Island; 42nd Street/Times Square, where I would gawk at the seamy attractions of the city's illicit and semi-licit trades; 66th Street/Lincoln Center, where I spent much of my senior year of high school at the piano; and finally 116th Street/Columbia University. That's where, from 1965 to 1969, I used to get off the subway on Saturdays and walk up the west side of Broadway to 122nd Street for my trumpet and composition lessons.

Up 122nd Street to the left a couple of blocks was Riverside Park, where a fellow music student and I, between classes, would scramble down the steep slope toward the Henry Hudson Parkway, open an iron grating on the hillside, and crawl into an underground wonderland: here were the train tracks that (as I learned years later) hugged the west side of the island, peeking out from time to time between cross streets and then surfacing by Penn Station to proceed downtown to the city's meatpacking district as the famous High Line (now a park and major tourist attraction). Here was another *anywhere*, for if you went north along these tracks (today an Amtrak passenger line), you intersected with the New York Central on its way along the Hudson River to Albany—and thus destined for wherever trains or my imaginary HiRail could take you in the United States and Canada.

But back at the corner of 122nd Street and Broadway, if you crossed the street onto the Broadway median and faced north, you found yourself standing right over the place where the subway tracks (after the 116th Street station) emerge from underground onto a viaduct spanning Manhattan Valley. From this spot, with the smell of creosote and wooden railroad ties in your nostrils, you could peer up the tracks before they reenter the netherworld ten blocks later. You could use your imagination to picture the lurid attractions and enticing dangers of precincts beyond, where, back then, a short, slight 14-year-old from the suburbs had never set foot.

But my story begins downtown, a short walk east (or a short ride on the Shuttle train) from the Times Square station . . .

PART I: BODY AND MIND

1 "To Push Back the Shadow upon the Dial of Time"

The Astonishing New Facts of Life and Death

AT THE END OF 1921, New York City hosted an extraordinary event. Mayor John F. Hylan declared November 13–19 "Health Week." Two floors of New York's premier exhibition hall, the Grand Central Palace (right next to Grand Central Terminal), were given over to what was billed as "the largest health exposition ever attempted." Thousands attended the exposition. To help draw in crowds, organizers offered a "Health Clown" and "Health Characters." There was a Harbor of Child Health, where the Child Health Family resided. "Happy," a member of that family, appeared as a sailor. Baseball great Babe Ruth and heavyweight boxing champion Jack Dempsey were on hand to sign autographs (though it's hard to see how either could have served as a model for healthy living, even in those days). Visitors had a chance to gawk at "fat men and women" who for the past three weeks had participated in a weight-loss competition. The winner of the "perfect baby contest" was announced (William Yarnias, eighteen months old).[1] And of course no health exposition would be complete without a finalist in the quest for the perfect woman's foot—to demonstrate, as the reporter for the *New York Times* put it, "that the world is as romantic as in the days of Cinderella and the Prince."[2] The honor went to Miss Elizabeth Doyle, nurse.[3]

The United States Public Health Bureau and other New York City departments participated, as did social service, charity, and business organizations.[4] There was a plan to set up educational displays and activities throughout the city: "diet squads," blood pressure machines, and nutritional demonstrations, including animals.[5] Proceeds from ticket sales were to be used to fund public health organizations and activities at the local, national, and international levels.

But none of this was the big news. "Health Week" was actually just the middle segment of an entire "Health Fortnight." It had been preceded by an international conference, called the "Health Institute," and it was followed by the Fiftieth Annual Meeting of the American Public Health Association. The big news came at that meeting.

The APHA had been founded in New York City in 1872. It was the first public health organization in America, at a time when the very concept of "public health," with its emphasis on sanitation, preventive medicine, and collective responsibility, was a novelty. In November of 1921, at the Hotel Astor, the association was celebrating its fiftieth anniversary. The Jubilee meeting brought together some of the most distinguished figures in the field. On the program were dozens of speeches, including some with such deadening titles as "Sanitation of Bath-Houses at Public Bathing Beaches," "Proper Size of Sand for Rapid Sand Filters," and "The Prevention and Cure of Rickets by Sunlight." But two caught the attention of the press. Dr. Mazÿck P. Ravenel gave the Presidential Address, titled "The American Public Health Association, Past, Present, Future." Like other top officials of the association, the president was partly interested in boosting the achievements of his organization—and why not? This *was* a celebration, after all. But he also used the occasion to give a capsule history of medicine over the previous half-century, speaking above all of Louis Pasteur and Robert Koch. Each achievement he listed—the discovery of a pathogenic microorganism (staphylococcus, streptococcus, pneumococcus, the Asiatic cholera spirillum, the tuberculosis and diphtheria bacilli)—represented a victory, imminent or current, over an illness that had threatened populations for centuries.

One passage in his speech was particularly striking. Telling his audience about the journals the APHA had published during its fifty-year history, Dr. Ravenel was moved to say this:

> In comparing the earlier volumes with those of to-day, one is struck by the fact that the most important topics discussed in the early years are scarcely ever mentioned now. The first volume, published in 1873, is given up largely to yellow fever and cholera. One finds it hard to believe that cholera was at that time widespread in the United States, and that it existed in more than two hundred towns and cities of the Mississippi Valley.[6]

The other presentation that found its way into the newspapers was the keynote speech at the opening banquet. Dr. Stephen Smith was a founder of the association, and on the evening of November 16, 1921, his topic was "A Half Century of Public Health." While Ravenel and others celebrated the concrete achievements of medicine and public health over the previous, extraordinary half-century, Smith looked at the larger ramifications. Let's say you believed that European and American medicine had practically obliterated the ravages of infectious disease. What did that mean for *you*? It's a simple question, and Dr. Smith had a simple answer: a longer life—a *much* longer life.

Smith spoke specifically of the drop in the death rate, making an astonishing observation. "The steady fall of the death-rate," he said, "until it has nearly reached the vanishing point, suggests the possibility of its passing that point. What a tremendous result!" "Vanishing point"—meaning immortality? Well, almost. "We have too long been content with the false code of the Mosaic law," he said a little later, "that limits life to three-score years and ten, with a possibility of reaching four-score years." Thanks to modern science, however, we know what the limit should be. "Biology teaches that the normal and potential life of man is one hundred years; that every child born is adapted in physical construction and function to live a century."[7]

In honor of the Jubilee celebration, the APHA published a volume of essays, titled *A Half Century of Public Health*. Included in that volume was an expanded version of Smith's Jubilee speech, in which the association's elder statesman explained the scientific basis for his extravagant claim. It was this: the normal life span of any vertebrate, he believed (drawing on the work of famed British paleontologist Richard Owen), is five times the number of years it takes for that vertebrate's bones to develop fully. Human bones take twenty years to develop, so the normal human life span is a century.[8] What the past fifty years have shown, he maintained in the speech, is that "all deaths occurring at an earlier age are due to conditions existing which are not compatible with the construction and functions of the human organisms." And so he proposed that, to mark the anniversary, the APHA should dedicate itself to raising "the standard for the length of life" by thirty years. Maybe he wasn't talking *literally* about immortality; he was talking about "life that suggests immortality."[9]

No one could have been a better spokesman for this cause. Smith was almost 99 years old when he gave this speech. An editorial in the *New York Times*, titled "All in a Lifetime," picked up the veteran doctor's fondness for Biblical reference. "What preventive medicine and sanitation have done in the span of that one life to push back the shadow upon the dial of time—as the shadow receded on the dial of King Hezekiah of old—so that there is prospect for a longer enjoyment of that birthright, is one of the brightest chapters of science," and all thanks to the scientific advances that Smith and Ravenel had mentioned in their speeches. Dr. Smith "happily illustrates" his own theory of longevity, the editor said.[10]

The editor jumped the gun on this point, as it turned out, for Stephen Smith died the following August, about a half-year short of his biologically allotted century. Still, his achievement was impressive, and the press celebrated him, both before and after his ill-timed demise. How had he made it to such an advanced age? He had plenty of advice for whoever would listen: lots of milk, not too much meat, plenty of sleep, no spirits or stimulants. He even recommended short skirts for women—not, heaven forbid, because he found them eye-catching (which in 1921, with hemlines almost up to the knee, they certainly were), but because he thought they were less likely than long skirts to carry dirt and bacteria from the street into the home.[11]

At the first annual meeting after Smith's death, the APHA adopted a resolution to honor its founder. It noted that, in many parts of the world, over the previous seventy-five years, fifteen years had been added to the average life. It noted, too (though without statistics to support the claim), that the gains in the most recent twenty years had outstripped those of the previous fifty, adding that these gains were continuing "at an accelerated rate." It reiterated the claim that modern science had overturned "the scriptural ideal of three score years and ten." And finally it issued the prediction "that within the next fifty years as much as twenty years may be added to the expectancy of life which now prevails throughout the United States." The resolution pledged the efforts of the association to the attainment of this goal, slightly more modest though it was than the one Dr. Smith had issued at the Jubilee meeting.

Unhappily, both Dr. Smith and the association were wide of the mark, and by a fair amount. According to much more recent figures, expectation of life at birth in 1922 was indeed approaching 60, but fifty years later, in 1972, it had risen only to slightly over 70 (71.1, to be precise, averaged for both genders): a single decade instead of two or three. How disconsolate Dr. Smith and the APHA members would have been, with their fondness for scriptural allusion, to know that "three score years and ten" was pretty much what the average American would get (at birth) a half-century in the future.

Still, as more recent figures also show, the assessment of the fifty years leading up to the Jubilee was essentially correct. Beginning around 1880, life for the average American—*physical* life—changed dramatically for the better. People in the United States began to live longer, and fewer died in childhood. The pace of change was especially pronounced between 1880 and 1930, though it was not precisely moving "at an accelerated rate," as the APHA resolution in 1922 had held; it began to slow about ten years after the resolution was passed.

Nowhere was the transformation in human life more eloquently and forcefully expressed than in an essay written for the same Jubilee volume by Dr. Charles V. Chapin (1856–1941), one of the most influential figures in the history of public health. Chapin had spent virtually his whole career in Providence, Rhode Island, where he served as superintendent of health from 1884 until his retirement in 1932. He looked back at the movement he had led, describing its various phases and his own participation in those phases. The essay is considered a classic, succinct history of the Public Health Movement in American cities. In the concluding section, Chapin announced the movement's achievements. The section is worth quoting at length, because it's difficult to imagine a more eloquent and stirring testimony to the transformation that American society had undergone in a mere half-century. Chapin restricts his discussion to the public health work of cities and states.

> Thus have cities and states sought to control disease. The yellow fever nightmare will terrify no more. There has been practically no cholera since 1873. Smallpox, which in former epidemics sometimes attacked half the population, is a negligible cause of death. Typhus fever is a very rare disease. Plague has not been able to gain a foothold. . . .
>
> Typhoid fever is a vanishing disease. The diarrheal diseases caused four times as many deaths fifty years ago as now. Scarlet fever mortality has fallen ninety per cent. Diphtheria has decreased nearly as much, and the mortality from pulmonary tuberculosis has been cut in two. Infant mortality in our better cities has dropped fifty per cent. Not all this, it is true, is due to conscious community effort, but is in part, dependent upon economic and other unknown causes. Nevertheless, if only one half of this life-saving is to be credited to health work the dividend on the money and energy employed indicates good business.
>
> Figures do not measure the terror of epidemics, nor the tears of the mother at her baby's grave, nor the sorrow of the widow whose helpmate has been snatched away in the prime of life. To have prevented these not once, but a million times, justifies our half century of public health work.[12]

This was all good news. Dazzling news, if you had been around for over fifty years and could remember an era when the conditions that Dr. Chapin and others were now describing were *not* present—when life on average was significantly shorter, when many children died in infancy, when the next outbreak of infectious disease could occur without apparent cause at any moment. Dr. Smith had emphasized personal responsibility as the key to a long life. Chapin emphasized the network: collective, public action directed by (in this case) municipal authorities. Both were right: collective action was essential, but so was individual responsibility, as we'll see.

What Statistics Show Today

Were the celebrants at the Jubilee right?

Let's consider just two rudimentary measures of a population's health: expectation of life at birth and infant mortality, using only averages and leaving out variations based on gender, ethnic group, geography, income, and educational level. Expectation of life at birth is the average number of years people who are born in a particular year can expect to live. Infant mortality is the number of children born in a particular year (usually reckoned per thousand) who die before their first birthday. According to figures from the 1990s, the trend in life expectancy and infant mortality from the late eighteenth century to the early twentieth century looks something like this: modest improvement (greater life expectancy, lower infant mortality) through the early nineteenth century, a setback from about 1840 until about 1870, "sporadic" improvement until about 1880, and then truly dramatic improvement.[13]

Expectation of life at birth rose from 38.3 in 1850, to 39.4 in 1880, to about 54.1 in 1920. The largest jump over a single decade (for years ending in zero) between 1850 and the end of the twentieth century occurred from 1880 to 1890. That jump was 5.8 years. The largest jump over a twenty-year period (for years ending in zero) from 1850 till well into the twentieth century occurred between 1880 and 1900. It was 8.4 years.

Infant mortality fell from 229 per thousand in 1850, to 225 per thousand in 1880, to 86 per thousand in 1920. By the end of the twentieth century, it stood at 7 per thousand. The largest decline over a single decade (for years ending in zero) between 1850 and the end of the twentieth century occurred from 1880 to 1890. It was 64.7 per thousand. The largest decline over a twenty-year period (years ending in zero) during the same century-and-a-half occurred between 1880 and 1900. It was 96.1 per thousand.[14]

In sum, the averages tell us this: starting sometime around 1880, whether you lived in the city or the country, whether you were rich or poor, well educated or illiterate, male or female, white or nonwhite, you were likely to live longer—even *significantly* longer—than your parents; you were more likely—even *significantly* more likely—to survive infancy than your parents had been; and, finally, your children were more likely—even *significantly* more likely—to survive infancy than you yourself had been. Those are essentially the transformations in American life that Stephen Smith and others were vaunting in late 1921 at the meeting of the American Public Health Association.

So the question is, how did the public come to know the good news? We today know that ordinary people in 1921 had a solid foundation for the belief that they themselves stood a good chance of living to a substantially more advanced age than their parents and grandparents, and for the belief that their children were much more likely than children of previous generations to survive to adulthood. But what were the sources of these beliefs *in that era*?

There appear to be three principal sources. One is vital statistics produced in the era we're discussing. The second is the public health campaign, which I'll describe in the next chapter. The third is path-breaking scientific research in the early twentieth century that promised either to extend human life *for more people* to conventionally recognized limits or to extend human life *generally speaking* beyond all conventionally recognized limits. I'll describe this, too, in the next chapter.

What Statistics Showed at the Time

Shortly before the conclusion of his essay on the history of the municipal Public Health Movement, Dr. Chapin devoted a short paragraph to vital statistics. "The proper registration of births, marriages and deaths may not seem to the public to have any very close connection with stamping out smallpox, or the prevention of typhoid fever," he wrote, "yet it is the first and most important health work that any community can do. Sanitary science will never progress," he continued, "and even the knowledge we have cannot be intelligently applied, without a fairly accurate system of vital statistics."[15] *First and most important?* More important than even the disease prevention measures Chapin had championed during his entire professional career? To take him at his word, yes. In 1908, the APHA had recognized the importance of this field by forming a Vital Statistics section.[16] While vital statistics was hardly a new field, having been around in roughly its modern form since the late seventeenth century, little effort seems to have been made to bring it to the attention of the public in the United States until the early twentieth century.

Chapin, in fact, was pointing to not one but two fundamental flaws in the condition in which vital statistics found itself when he wrote these words. The first has to do with the creation and reliability of statistics. In order for figures purporting to show trends in mortality and life expectancy to give an accurate picture of a population's health, those figures need to reflect as much of the population as possible. That means that births and deaths need to be registered as widely as possible. A major part of the public health campaign at the time that Chapin made his plea for improved vital statistics was aimed at increasing the size of the "registration areas," that is, the areas in which births and deaths were recorded. The objective, of course, was to make registration mandatory nationwide, but since public health measures of this nature were generally left up to the states, champions of vital statistics faced the daunting task of persuading state legislatures to pass measures that would create the appropriate mechanisms for registering births and deaths. In the year 1900, only ten states, plus the District of Columbia, registered deaths, and there was no birth registration to speak of. Birth registration began, in a limited way, in 1915, but it was not until 1933 that there was mandatory nationwide registration of births and deaths.

The other flaw, implicit in Chapin's complaint, was the limited extent to which existing information was made available to public health officials and to the general public. In order for vital statistics to be effective, people need to *know* about them: public health officials, in order that they might take proper measures to confront the threat of infectious disease, and members of the general public, so that they might take the appropriate personal measures to protect themselves from the same threat.

But one shouldn't infer from Chapin's comments that *nothing* had been done in recent years to improve the gathering of vital statistics and to make those statistics available to professionals and the general public. In the late nineteenth century, the primary source for vital statistics, which meant little more than general mortality rates, was the life insurance industry. Starting in 1868, the industry published the American Experience Table, which presented statistics gathered from the "experience" of some thirty life insurance companies. But because the Experience Table was based only on data drawn from insurance policyholders, it could not pretend to give a comprehensive picture of the larger population.[17] In the 1880s, there were some attempts to establish statistics from census data. These figures were possibly more useful than the life insurance figures, but they were still tainted by the small number of registration areas in the country.

It was not till the end of the first decade of the twentieth century that the field of vital statistics really began to come into its own. The APHA's formation of a vital statistics section in 1908 is part of this story. The following year, in February, the National Conservation Commission brought out a report titled *National Vitality, Its Wastes and Conservation*. The author was Irving Fisher, a Yale professor of economics (in fact, one of the towering American figures in the field) who, after a bout with tuberculosis in the 1890s, turned his attention to public health. Fisher was primarily a mathematician, and statistics had a particular appeal for him. The first two chapters of the report cover length of life and mortality, so they are rich with tables and figures. The statistical material, by today's standards, is strikingly unhelpful. Because of the limited number of registration areas, Fisher's figures cover only small and selected parts of the country (in addition to a number of European cities). When it comes to infant mortality, all he can say is that it "is probably falling."[18] That statement is bound to surprise us today, because, after all, *we* know that infant mortality had dropped quite significantly, that, in fact, it was less than half what it had been sixty years earlier. But the figures available to Fisher in 1909 were not sufficiently solid to support a judgment about infant mortality.

Naturally Americans were not exactly thronging bookstores to purchase copies of *National Vitality*. Still, as dry as the subject was and as imperfect as the book's findings were, Fisher and his work captured the attention of the press and, as a result, the public. *The New York Times* ran an article on him in March of 1909, under the title "Working to Lengthen the Span of Man's Life." The central visual image was a chart showing the percentage of American men still alive, by decades, starting at age 50. To each decade there corresponded a picture of a man whose size was proportional to the percentage figure provided for him. If you looked closely, you saw, in addition to the caption that the *Times* editors placed under the chart, one that formed part of the chart itself. This caption read, "American Experience Table of Mortality." Oddly, despite the emergence of more sophisticated statistics based on census figures, the author of this article chose to fall back on the standard life insurance table.[19]

Later that same year, journalist Allan L. Benson (who would enjoy a brief period of notoriety as the Socialist Party's candidate for president in 1916) wrote an article for the Sunday magazine section of the *New York Times* titled "Learning the Length of Life." Benson described the current scientific work that held out the prospect of longer life for the human species and, unlike many journalists writing in the popular press, included a number of Census Bureau charts and tables on causes of death at various ages. In fact, it would hardly be an exaggeration to say that the entire article serves as a tribute to the value and power of vital statistics. Virtually every claim Benson made about health and longevity was based directly on statistics. In addition, he made an observation significant to the social historian, namely that one source of statistical information available to members of the general public (who did not spend their time studying census charts) was the material that life insurance companies assembled in an effort to educate prospective clients. The idea presumably was that by this time the life insurance companies themselves were using data beyond just those gathered from their own clients. Insurance companies "pretty nearly know from a man's height, weight, and occupation what kind of a disease is destined to carry him off," Benson wrote. "This is a point worth considering, for if a man know wherein lies his weakness he can, if he choose, take steps to postpone the inevitable." The visual impact of the article must have been quite dramatic to contemporary readers. Benson included, in the midst of his charts, cartoon-like images of Death (with Sickle), Old Age (with flowing beard and crooked walking stick), and a terrified Youth (with curls and cherubic, plump cheeks).[20]

One of the era's most striking notices to the public that things had changed quite dramatically in recent decades was a tiny article in the *New York Times* that most readers probably did not even see, because it was oddly tucked away on page 13 of the first section. But if you read your newspaper thoroughly and turned to that page on May 23, 1913, you would have seen this arresting headline at the top of the fourth column: "Young Live Longer Now," with this underneath: "But Those Above 40 Have a Decreased life Expectancy." And here's what you would have read:

> A life table measuring the health conditions in this city, based on the mortality in three years, 1909 to 1911, inclusive, has been prepared by the Department of Health. In 1882 a similar life table was prepared under the direction of the late Dr. John S. Billings, who supervised the construction of the table for New York City on behalf of the Federal Census authorities, and was based upon the triennium 1879 to 1881.
>
> The compilation shows that thirty years ago a child under 5 years could ex-

> pect to live 41 years, while a child at that age at present may look forward to a future lifetime of almost 52 years, an increase of almost 11 years. The life of a child between 5 and 10 years has been prolonged from 46 to 51. A person of 25 to 30 years had an expectancy of life 30 years ago of almost 32.6 years. At present the expectancy is 34.3, an increase of 1.7 years.[21]

There were figures to show that life expectancy for people over 40 years of age had dropped in the previous thirty years, the decline being attributed to an increase in the incidence of "cancer, heart diseases, and kidney diseases." The author finished by reporting the Health Department's findings that the rise in incidence of non-infectious illnesses has been accompanied by "an increase in the consumption of spirituous liquors and nitrogenous articles of food," in other words, "too much drink and too much meat."

Clearly this was mixed news. Although the figures applied only to New York City, the author of the article appeared to generalize the findings to all Americans. It would have been disappointing to learn that the odds of reaching 40 were better than ever, but that after 40 the odds of reaching a truly advanced age were worse than they had been thirty years earlier. Still, one fact would have stood out. To believe what was reported in the article, in the preceding thirty years the expectation of life in the first five years of life had jumped over 25 percent, thanks to a reduction in the effects of a group of infectious illnesses. If infectious illnesses had been brought under control, then there had certainly been a decline in deaths among young children.

The document referred to in the article (but not cited there) was a table published by Dr. William H. Guilfoy, a great champion of vital statistics in this era and the Registrar of Vital Statistics of the New York City Department of Health from 1901 to 1927. It contained life expectancy figures for New York City in the two triennia, 1879 to 1881 and 1909 to 1911. The earlier figures were compiled from census data in the 1880s. The source of the figures for 1909 to 1911 was information contained in a vital statistics report for the Department of Health in 1912.[22]

The remainder of the second decade of the twentieth century saw the publication of additional work in vital statistics. In 1916, the Census Bureau issued a publication with the title *United States Life Tables 1910*, because 1910 had been a year that brought particularly good statistical news about the health of the American people.[23] In 1919, George Chandler Whipple, professor of sanitary engineering at Harvard, published a book titled *Vital Statistics: An Introduction to the Science of Demography*. Whipple was widely known in the Public Health

Movement for his role in promoting water purification, and in 1921 he would contribute to the APHA's Jubilee volume a lengthy, authoritative essay on the topic. He was not a statistician or a demographer, and it served his purposes to say so in the preface to his book.[24] The idea was not only that vital statistics were necessary for the promotion of public health but that even a nonspecialist such as Professor Whipple himself could learn the field well enough to write a textbook about it.

It would be a great exaggeration to say that all ordinary people in the early decades of the twentieth century frequently came across vital statistics and that these vital statistics alone served as a foundation for widespread optimism about longevity. As we've seen, on several occasions writers in the popular press presented their readers with statistical evidence for the rise in life expectancy and the drop in infant mortality (mortality in general, for that matter) that had been occurring since the final decades of the nineteenth century. And of course if you were in the market for life insurance, the salesman who sold you your policy was likely to produce a table that showed you your own expectation of life.

The Spirit of Cooperation, the Will to Optimism, and the Network

Still, it's hard to imagine that access to such statistics would have served members of the American public as the primary basis for optimism about how old they'd be when they died.[25] But the optimism was there, and the question is, where did it come from? Of course there's no reliable method for uncovering the source of the feeling that life will last longer for *me* than for my parents and grandparents—even on the assumption that such a feeling was widespread. If we do accept the claim that attitudes about life expectancy took a turn for the more favorable around 1900, we have to recognize that there are countless truly immeasurable factors. If casual empirical observation led ordinary people to judge that fewer children were dying in, say, 1920 than had died forty years earlier (1880) or that fewer children *and* adults were dying of infectious disease today than forty years earlier, then perhaps those ordinary people extrapolated the view (however vaguely formulated) that everyone had a better chance of living longer in 1920 than in 1880. But no amount of casual empirical observation could offer a 30-year-old in 1920 solid, unassailable evidence that a large proportion of people just like him or her would live to a ripe old age.

What is clear, however, is that optimism about life expectancy was widely expressed in this era. Let's return to that Jubilee meeting of the APHA. Think for a moment about the year in which this big celebration took place: 1921. Two major mortality crises were, respectively, a mere three years and a mere two years in the past: the Great War and, far more significant for the United States, the great influenza epidemic of 1918–19. Admittedly the Great War took the lives of far fewer Americans than it did Europeans, and admittedly it would not qualify as a *health* crisis. The flu, however, carried away over a half-million American souls. And yet, to listen to the speeches given at the celebration and to read the articles printed for the occasion, you'd never guess that an infectious illness had recently created one of the worst health crises in recorded history. In the Jubilee volume that the APHA published, there are but three passing references to the recent pandemic, though the association's journal had printed numerous articles on the topic during the crisis. When Charles V. Chapin exultantly told his audience in 1921 of the drop in overall mortality figures in the United States, the *recent* year he used for purposes of comparison was 1919. He somehow forgot to mention that the flu had just taken out its final cohort of Americans in the winter and early spring of that year: close to a quarter-million, according to figures from the era (figures, incidentally, that more recent historians consider to be quite low).[26] During the Paris Peace Conference, in the early months of that same year, President Woodrow Wilson himself was taken gravely ill and thought to have contracted influenza. Many participants in the conference were stricken, and some died.[27] And yet somehow people believed that infectious disease had been *conquered*—and had been for some time (never mind the influenza pandemic). That's why members of the medical profession and the general public could legitimately turn their attention to humankind's next big goal: extending the span of life, either so that more people could reach an already recognized natural limit or so that the limit itself could be extended far beyond what had ever been considered possible.

Chapin was focusing on *results*. But results were only one part of a much bigger story that observers might have told in 1921. The bigger story included a transformation in the entire conception of the physical person that had taken place during roughly the same period as the transformation in health that the APHA Jubilee celebrated—a transformation in how Americans thought of themselves as physical beings. That's the subject of the next chapter. The story included, as well, a transformation in how individual people saw themselves in relation to their fellows. As members of the public came to know beyond a shadow of a doubt, reductions in mortality and rises in life expectancy came about as a result of cooperation, and cooperation took place once individual citizens understood that looking after their own personal health was not only an end in itself but also a means to promoting the health of the larger public. It had to start with choice: you could *choose* to cooperate—or not. And yet individuals were networked whether they liked it or not, for the obvious reason that the state of the community's health was always possibly linked to the state of their own health. It's just that in this era, individuals came to know not only *that* they were networked but, to a considerable extent, *why* and *how* they were networked.

2 The Biological Self

ON SEPTEMBER 4, 1912, Edward A. Schäfer gave an address in Dundee, Scotland, on the occasion of his installation as president of the British Association for the Advancement of Science. The title was hardly modest: "The Nature, Origin and Maintenance of Life." On September 15, the *New York Times* ran an article about it under the sensational title "Are We Near the Chemical Creation of Life?"[1] In the short time between the speech and the publication of the article, the remarks of Edinburgh's esteemed professor of physiology ignited a fierce debate both inside and outside the scientific community. During those eleven days, the *Times* reported on it every single day.

Two passages from the article show what sparked the controversy. Here's the first, printed under the heading (supplied by the *Times*) "Life Is Not Soul":

> For the problems of life are essentially problems of matter; we cannot conceive of life in the scientific sense as existing apart from matter. The phenomena of life are investigated, and can only be investigated, by the same methods as all other phenomena of matter, and the general results of such investigations tend to show that living beings are governed by laws identical with those which govern inanimate matter.

Here's the second passage:

> The elements composing living substance are few in number. Those which are constantly present are carbon, hydrogen, oxygen, and nitrogen. . . . The presence of certain inorganic salts is no less essential, chief amongst them being

> chloride of sodium and salts of calcium, magnesium, potassium, and iron. The combination of these elements into a colloidal compound represents the chemical basis of life; and when the chemist succeeds in building up this compound it will without doubt be found to exhibit the phenomena which we are in the habit of associating with the term "life."

The statements are breathtaking—and would be breathtaking in any era—for their uncompromising materialism and their rigidly mechanistic view of organic life. The reduction of life to what is denoted in the glib phrase "colloidal compound," with its implicit but unmistakable denial of any spiritual element in human experience, was guaranteed to discomfit even the most secular readers.[2]

And there was more.

If the methods for studying organic substances are the same as those for studying inorganic substances, Schäfer thought, it's because organic substances arose from inorganic matter. He believed that the transition from one condition to the other happened gradually, as the result of many separate events. Evolutionary theory was so fundamental to his approach that he didn't see the need even to argue for it. Dismissing a host of recent and contemporary theories about the origin of life, Schäfer declared that "the evolutionary hypothesis" offers the best solution. "I assume," he said in a part of his speech not reported in its entirety in the *Times*, "that the majority of my audience have at least a general idea of the scope of this hypothesis, the general acceptance of which has within the last sixty years altered the whole aspect not only of biology, but of every other branch of natural science, including astronomy, geology, physics and chemistry."[3] The evolutionary hypothesis, as Schäfer explained in a passage that *was* printed in the *Times*, offered the most plausible explanation for the transition from nonliving to living substance.

Evolutionary change led to the differentiation of matter into individuals, and it led to sexual reproduction. Since complex organisms are composed of aggregates of cells, evolutionary pressures favored the development of means by which activities in the aggregate could be coordinated—thus the emergence of the nervous system, which developed the ability to "convey the effects of stimuli" from the outside to "distant parts" of the organism. From this system there arose its loftiest product, the "human intellect."

In addition, Schäfer spoke of two closely related topics that had recently attracted attention among both professionals and members of the public: the maintenance of living cells after the death of the host organism and the prospect of extending the "natural" lifespan of human beings. In connection with the first topic, he cited a number of the era's most eminent researchers, including French-born Alexis Carrel, who won a Nobel Prize that year and who only months earlier had made big news by announcing the possibility of "indefinitely" extending the life of tissues outside the body. In connection with the second, he cited the work of Russian-born biologist Elie Metchnikoff, also a Nobel laureate and hugely famous in this period for suggesting that humans should be able to live for more than a century.

Finally, Schäfer spoke about "the principles of preventive medicine and hygiene." Though he raised the subject in connection with lengthening human life, he might have added that preventive medicine and hygiene functioned only in a climate in which people are educated so as to take responsibility for their health. In Schäfer's era, that meant familiarity with many of the trends and fundamental concepts he was discussing in his address.

Response to Schäfer's remarks was immediate. British scientist Oliver Lodge disputed the notion that life is reducible to material that can be produced in the laboratory, arguing that "vitality" will continue to evade the reach of human knowledge.[4] Charles Darwin's famous associate Alfred Russel Wallace, by this time a hoary eminence, agreed with Lodge but expressed himself in much stronger terms. He utterly rejected the notion that life can exist without some sort of "directive power" and insisted that Schäfer and like-minded "agnostics" had failed to give this power any sort of plausible explanation.[5] The debate continued for months after Schäfer's speech, not only in the *New York Times* but in other publications as well. But what emerged from all the turmoil surrounding the speech was not unanimity of opinion among writers or members of the public; it was a common awareness of principles that, like it or not, appeared to be here to stay. Schäfer's views, as presented in the press, might very well have stunned lots of readers, but only because of their absoluteness. No reasonably informed reader in 1912 would have been surprised to hear that living organisms are composed of cells, that there is a connection between the mind and the nervous system, that higher forms of life evolved from lower forms of life—or for that matter, from inorganic matter.

Which means, when it comes right down to it, that the debate the public heard was about niceties, not fundamentals. The *biological self* was an undisputed reality. You could believe all you wanted in God, in a "directive power," in what Schäfer contemptuously referred to as "vital force" (a hugely common phrase in the era)—or *not* believe in any of this, if that was your pleasure.[6]

Either way, cells, germs, chemical forces, electrical impulses, and evolution were now irrevocably the actors in a new living universe that would have been unrecognizable to ordinary readers of the *New York Times* even thirty years earlier.

How did members of the public come to know this universe? Perhaps a better question is "why?" The order in which they came to know its constituent parts gives a partial answer, especially when it came to cells and germs, because the order was different from the order in which these constituent parts arose in the world of scientific research. *That* order was cells, then germs. And, although there was considerable overlap and experiences differed from person to person, the order for the American public generally was germs, then cells (including chemical forces and electrical impulses). Why? The simple answer was that the public's education on each topic came along only when that topic had something concrete to promise. The effect was to build in the public mind a conception of the physically networked individual. But for now, let's look at how each topic came into popular consciousness.

Germs

Here are three snapshots from American life at about the time that Schäfer gave his speech.

(1) Two young women in a fashion drawing are carrying parasols and wearing enormous, lavishly decorated hats. Their figures are slender and their dresses tight-fitting, with hemlines high enough to expose delicate pointed shoes, a striking look for that era. The title: "Off the Ground Walking Skirt." The year is 1910.

(2) Four dapper young men in a drawing from a fashion catalogue are dressed to the nines for winter. A pretty young woman looks attentively at one of them from behind. The scene appears to be a park. Three of the men are clean-shaven; the fourth sports only a mustache. Dimly seen in the background is an older gentleman wearing a top hat, in clear contrast to the shorter headgear of the young men. The older gentleman wears a goatee. The year is 1910.

(3) A group of children, probably between the ages of 7 and 9, are working at school desks, wearing cape-like cloaks with pointed hoods pulled over their heads. They are outside. The caption reads "Open Air Class." The year is 1913.[7]

Explanation?

The short skirts. Some twenty years earlier, T. Mitchell Prudden, an American bacteriologist who had made public health education one of his life's missions, wrote a little book called *Dust and Its Dangers.* Respected health professionals would soon abandon the notion that dust *was* terribly dangerous, but on the basis of what medical science held in 1890, Dr. Prudden told his readers how to reduce their exposure to this substance. Why was it dangerous? Because it carried bacteria, and the public was just beginning to learn that microscopic organisms cause many of the most dreaded infectious illnesses. Most dust is found indoors, but in one particularly impassioned passage, Prudden warned his readers of the presence *in the street* of tuberculosis bacilli, most of them emanating from our "mongrel immigrants," who are in the habit of spitting. Spit turns to dust, and dust gets carried indoors by women's skirts. Prudden even invoked Darwin to support his case against both immigrants and unsanitary women's attire: "The spectacle of the well-dressed, filthy brutes, whom natural selection has most unkindly left but a few degrees higher than their congeners in the sty, wallowing in their expectoration, about certain hotels and theatre entrances, may well impress the sensitive onlooker with the colossal task which Nature undertook when she set to work to evolve man, and the lamentable failures which are so often but half-concealed in fashionable attire."[8]

Prudden wasn't solely responsible for the change, of course, but before long hemlines began to rise as women became aware that their skirts were dragging millions of microbes into their homes, exposing themselves and their families to the dangers of tuberculosis and countless other infectious illnesses.

The clean-shaven faces. By the middle of the first decade of the twentieth century, it had become established wisdom—or established hearsay—that whiskers were havens for infectious organisms. *Harper's Weekly* ran an article as early as 1903 in which the writer explained the belief (without citing any evidence or authority), while also implicitly offering us a clue to a relatively recent change in public knowledge and attitude: "Now that consumption is no longer consumption, but tuberculosis, and is not hereditary but infectious, we believe that the theory of science is that the beard is infected with the germs of tuberculosis, and is one of the deadliest agents for transmitting the disease to the lungs."[9] In April of 1907, a state assemblyman in New Jersey introduced a bill that would have imposed a tax on facial hair, the amount being pegged to the overall quantity (from five dollars for "ordinary whiskers" to fifty dollars for "billygoat" whiskers). The proposed bill was partly responsible for prompting a two-page satirical piece in *Harper's Weekly* titled "The Revolt Against the Whisker," complete with grossly caricatured drawings of such styles as "Birds' Nesting-grounds" and "Mormon Elders' Face Mats." It's clear to the author that the fundamental issue is health: he jocularly refers to beards as "capillary microbe-carriers" and their enemies as "enthusiasts for hygiene."[10]

The hooded children. Once again it was the anti-tuberculosis movement that was behind the practice. Even before 1913, the medically supported belief had become widespread that maximum exposure to open air is helpful for both the prevention and the treatment of "the White Plague." Contemporary science apparently saw several benefits from open air, though the literature on the subject seldom offered any sort of physiological explanation. In 1907, the economist Irving Fisher was advocating outdoor sleeping not only for the treatment of tuberculosis but also for its prevention, on the grounds that fresh air somehow keeps us "in condition" so that we can resist the tubercle bacilli.[11] Even as late as 1917, in a pamphlet titled "Sleeping and Sitting in the Open Air," the National Association for the Study and Prevention of Tuberculosis took it as a given that fresh air helps promote good health and that everyone should get as much of it as possible. As to the treatment of tuberculosis, the idea was to strengthen resistance in order "to conquer the germs" of this dreaded illness.[12] The expression "sleep out," frequently heard in the first three decades of the twentieth century, was a reference to the salubrious powers of fresh air. When we first meet the fatuous, molly-coddled hero of Sinclair Lewis's *Babbitt* (1922), he is awakening on the "sleeping-porch" that had become commonplace in suburban middle-class American households.

When it came to open-air schools, tuberculosis authorities offered two arguments, both based on the germ theory of disease. The first and more common one was that, because tubercle bacilli are everywhere (including the mouths of healthy people), the tendency to contract the illness must have to do less with exposure to the germs than with our capacity to resist them. Fresh air builds resistance (how, no one seemed to know) and therefore helps in the prevention of tuberculosis. The second argument was that, given the presence of bacilli in the air, a proper rate of air exchange in the environment will lessen one's exposure. In open-air schools, for example, there was a lower concentration of human beings per unit of space, plus (in an era when such things were conscientiously measured and frequently discussed) a rate of air exchange suitable for reducing the concentration of microbes in any one place. The photograph of hooded children, incidentally, was taken on the roof of Teachers College of Columbia University in New York City, where the Horace Mann School held its open-air classes.[13]

In *The Gospel of Germs*, Nancy Tomes tells the story of how ordinary Americans came to embrace the germ theory of disease and changed their lives in accordance with that theory (or to be more precise, with their understanding of it at the time). What emerges from the book, though this is not Tomes's central point, is a story with at least two chronologies. The first is the chronology of events by which the modern understanding of germs was established in the scientific community. The second is what Tomes's title suggests: the chronology of events that made the new theory into a "gospel" for the public.

The first chronology runs from the mid-1860s to roughly the end of the nineteenth century. It begins with Louis Pasteur, Robert Koch, and the articulation of a germ theory in the early 1870s, continuing to the emergence of bacteriology as a field and the establishment of academic departments of bacteriology. The second chronology differs substantially from the first. The conscientious researcher will certainly find references to bacteria and the germ theory of disease in publications intended for the general public as early as the 1870s. But as best I can tell, for roughly twenty years these references were few and far between, and many of them were likely to go right over the heads of even an educated reading public.

It's impossible to assign a precise beginning to "the era when ordinary Americans generally knew about germs," but it's safe to say that the era had begun by the turn of the century. In 1897, Herbert W. Conn, Wesleyan University professor of biology and author of numerous popular works on medicine and science, published a little book called *The Story of Germ Life*. As Conn explained at the outset, awareness of bacteria and of their association with illness was so widespread at this time that he could afford to write a book designed to correct the common misapprehension that all bacteria are harmful.[14] At this point the public knew in a general way of the connection between bacteria and illness. Within less than a decade, the connection was so firm that it would have been hard to find a moderately informed American who did not know about it in some detail. The question is why the public came to know about this connection so much later than doctors and scientists. The answer turns out to be fairly simple: ordinary Americans learned what was useful to them (as might be expected), and a major reason they were able to do so was the Public Health Movement. I'll return to that movement shortly.

Cells, Tissues, and Organs

In 1899, Herbert W. Conn published another of his short science books for the general public. This one he called *The Story of the Living Machine.* Conn believed that an individual organism could be likened to a machine and that the living machine ultimately boils down to the cell. His "cell doctrine" was impressively detailed. He offered a description of protoplasm, including its known chemical properties, and, in a passage that anticipated Schäfer's remarks in 1912, said that "the formulation of the doctrine of protoplasm made it possible to assume that *life* is not a distinct force, but simply a name given to the properties possessed by the highly complex chemical compound that is protoplasm."[15] Conn, it turns out, believed that this extreme chemical theory had been superseded, but only because the complexity of protoplasm had come to be better understood. Life is not reducible to a simple set of chemical compounds, but this is because protoplasm presents a more delicate "machinery" than a chemical compound does. "Protoplasm is a machine and not a chemical compound," he declared.[16] Conn went on to describe the cell nucleus, cell division, and the function and behavior of chromosomes (as they were understood just before the turn of the century).

Much of what Conn presented as the "cell doctrine" was not at all new in 1899. As in the case of germ theory, we're looking at two stories: the story of how the scientific community developed the cell doctrine and the story of how the informed public came to know about it. In simplified form, the first story (some of which Conn tells in his book) goes like this: By the 1830s, microscopy had advanced sufficiently to allow investigators to see not only cells themselves (Robert Hooke had seen these in cork as early as 1665) but two essential components of cells: nuclei and the streaming (therefore living) substance that was later (in 1846) named protoplasm. By the end of the 1830s, German researchers Theodor Schwann and Matthias Schleiden had enunciated the fundamental theory, namely that cells are the basic constituents of every living thing, plant or animal. By the mid-1850s, thanks to the work of pioneering pathologist Rudolf Virchow, the phenomenon of cell division had led to the conclusion that cells are formed not freely (from nothing) but only from other cells. And by the early 1880s, German biologist Walther Flemming had observed mitosis, the process by which somatic cells, but not germ cells, divide into two. By the 1890s, members of the scientific community understood enough about the role of chromosomes in fertilization and thus in heredity to infer that the basic processes of life are essentially cellular. The application of "Mendel's laws" to the cell doctrine and the emergence of genetics would follow shortly after the turn of the twentieth century.

Little of this appears to have been known to the general public until the early years of the new century. In 1896, *Popular Science Monthly* had published an article titled "Some Modern Views of the Cell," but, like most articles that appeared in that magazine, this one was technical and probably beyond the reach of ordinary readers.[17] When we look at life science textbooks for high school and college students, we find that cell doctrine begins to appear in rudimentary form in the mid-nineteenth century and in more thorough form in the last two decades of the century.[18] But in the world of life science textbooks from our era broadly speaking, the most complete statement of doctrine, combined with the most thorough presentation of the state of knowledge as of the date of publication, came in 1914, in George William Hunter's *A Civic Biology* (which, incidentally, made it into the history books as the text that a formerly unknown high school teacher named John Scopes, later of "Scopes Monkey Trial" fame, was indicted for using in his classes in Dayton, Tennessee, in 1925). Hunter covered the doctrine from more to less complex: organs, tissues, cells, then protoplasm.[19]

Hunter was on to something when he chose the order of his topics. He appears to have predicted that his pupils, learning biological concepts perhaps for the first time, would find it easier to begin with what they knew and what could be observed—bodily organs and the tissue constituting those organs—and move on from there to what we can experience almost exclusively in a laboratory—cells and their constitutive substance. It made sense that not only Hunter's pupils but also members of the informed public should grasp cell doctrine organs—and tissues—first. As in the case of germ theory, they came to the doctrine in the first place because there was a powerful incentive: as members of the public experienced it, illness, borne by microbial agents, attacked organs (lungs, for example) and tissues (mucous membranes, for example).

With the terminology of cells, tissues, and organs, it became possible, more precisely than ever before, to present the living organism as a network of interconnected component parts. In fact, the network image had occurred in the field of anatomy even before Schwann and Schleiden, but it became particularly frequent after the emergence of cell doctrine. Virtually every anatomy textbook written in the nineteenth century from the 1840s on included the term "network" in connection with the circulatory system, if not in other connections as well. George Henry Lewes, the British critic, philosopher, and popular science writer, was moved to use the image in a popular book called *The Physiology of Common Life* (1859). In a chapter on the function of blood, Lewes wrote, "The body is like a city intersected by a vast network of canals, such as Venice or Amsterdam; these canals are laden with barges which carry to each house the meat, vegetables, and groceries needed for daily use; and while the food is thus presented at each door, the canal receives all the sewage of the houses."[20] In *A Civic Biology*, Hunter described the veins on a leaf as a network and went on to explain that they are made up of "the smallest units of building material," called cells. It's the first occurrence of "cells" in his book.[21] Following the established tradition, he described the circulatory system as a network of tubes traversing tissues and organs.[22]

So it's safe to say that, by the end of the nineteenth century, at least some high school students and many college students in the United States had encountered cell doctrine in their science courses. Let's not forget, of course, that in the period we're examining a much smaller portion of the high school–age population (defined as those between the ages of 14 and 17) attended high school than today, and a still smaller portion attended college. But textbooks are not the only place to search for the source of the public's familiarity with the terms that Schäfer used in his speech. The Public Health Movement was aimed through popular education at *everyone*, not just those who had studied biology in high school or college, and the scientific movement to prolong life was guaranteed to attract the attention of ordinary Americans. Both were firmly founded in the conception of the biological self.

The Public Health Movement Networks the Network

For our purposes, a brief account of the Public Health Movement will be sufficient. The movement can be broadly defined as the aggregate of efforts in the United States to treat the health of the population collectively rather than individually. Its beginnings can be dated to the middle of the nineteenth century. Before that, medicine in the United States was largely a local affair. Training varied widely from region to region. Medical knowledge in the early United States was far behind what it was in France, Great Britain, and the German lands. Licensure was patchy and regulation almost nonexistent. The number of medical practitioners did not begin to grow dramatically till the 1830s. In a nation where the bulk of the population still lived outside cities, where the best medical care available was concentrated in urban areas, and where that medical care was primitive even by comparison with what it would become by the end of the nineteenth century, the profession could hardly be seen as a collective enterprise.[23]

The Public Health Movement, when it came along, consisted of two overlapping phases. The first was based on false science that paradoxically yielded favorable results. The second was based on "good" science that not only yielded better results but did so by altering the behavior of ordinary people. The first phase rested on the theory that filth in and for itself has the mysterious ability to cause illness. Filth takes many forms, from the dust in your house, to the noxious gases (miasmas, as they were called) emanating from outhouses and sewers (a recent invention themselves), to whatever might cause drinking water to look and smell nasty. Because this sanitarian phase of the Public Health Movement arrived on the cusp of a truly modern understanding of disease, it mingled empirical evidence with a hefty dose of superstition. Empirical evidence showed that constructing sewers (*carefully*, of course, so as to prevent the release of miasmas) and purifying drinking water significantly reduced the incidence of certain infectious diseases. It was thought, by extension, that cleanliness, generally speaking, would further contribute to the prevention of disease. And so, in a public education campaign that successfully combined what passed for science with an old-fashioned moral/religious attitude toward cleanliness and disease, sanitary authorities persuaded the public to focus on the environment, both municipal and domestic.

The solution was a network, and a very physical one, at that. The sanitarian phase caught the public's attention and introduced the concept of a collective, communitarian approach to health. From the 1870s through the 1890s, and even into the early years of the twentieth century, ordinary citizens were reading household manuals that urged them to rid their surroundings of "dirt"—anything that seemed foul. But they also witnessed the translation of this spirit of collectivism into the physical construction of gigantic urban networking projects—primarily sewers, aqueducts, and water treatment plants—projects that linked ordinary citizens through a web of pipes and conduits to services and products remote from their homes.[24]

While the sanitarian phase helped make the public mindful of the connection between their environment and their health, it offered them almost no scientific understanding of either the identity of the agents of death in the environment (even after the identity of those agents had been discovered by

Pasteur, Koch, and others) or the manner in which those agents *caused* illness in the human body. That understanding came to the public only after the fledgling field of bacteriology began to make inroads in the Public Health Movement, and only after that movement had shifted its focus from the environment to the individual. In fact, as historian Robert H. Wiebe claimed, the success of the movement was responsible for the dramatic and permanent rise in prestige of the entire medical profession in our era.[25]

The man who championed the shift—and who probably deserves more credit for it than anyone else—was Charles V. Chapin, who served as superintendent of health in Providence, Rhode Island, from 1884 till 1932. The early decades of his career followed the progress of the Public Health Movement from the sanitarian phase to the newer, scientific phase. By the end of the 1890s, he had become fully convinced that a municipal policy based on the filth theory, despite the modest improvements in health this policy had brought about, needed to be abandoned in favor of a policy based on solid, experimental, bacteriological science. In 1901, Chapin wrote an article for *Popular Science Monthly* titled "The End of the Filth Theory of Disease." The approach was simple: he needed do little more than list the bacteria, recently identified, that caused the illnesses that had been attributed to filth in its many varieties (chief among them sewer gas). At the very end of the article, he merely hinted at the practical program that would make all the difference—for both the success of the Public Health Movement and the public's understanding of the science underlying it. The sanitarian phase of the movement, he allowed, had been well worth the effort, if for no other reason than that cleanliness is an essential component of a civilized society. But a new emphasis was needed. The key phrase was "cleanliness of person."[26]

Chapin's next campaign was to shift the focus in public health dramatically from the environment—that is, from *outside* the human body—to the individual person. His argument was sound and was based on the most recent and authoritative scientific findings, chief among which was that the primary mode of transmission for microbial pathogens is direct physical contact with an infected person (whether or not that person is actually ill). Thus the new approach to public health was to promote personal hygiene. The desired result was to make individuals responsible for their own health. The means to that result was education. So the secondary results were (a) to establish in the mind of ordinary citizens the idea of the biological self, (b) to instill the sense that taking responsibility for one's own health meant at the same time taking responsibility for the health of the larger community, and therefore ineluctably (c) to make the biological self part of a social network.

In 1901, Chapin formed the Committee on Diphtheria Bacilli in Well Persons, whose most important legacy was a list of health rules that were not specific to diphtheria at all but, in the view of the late medical historian James H. Cassedy, "became the virtual catechism of twentieth-century hygiene."[27] The list, apparently written by Harvard University pathologist Theobald Smith but distributed and made famous by Chapin, bore the title "REMEMBER THESE THINGS" and came to be popularly called "the don'ts." The list and variants of it soon became widely displayed in schools, so if you attended a public school in the first decades of the twentieth century, there's a very good chance you saw this or something like it:

> REMEMBER THESE THINGS.
>
> Do not spit if you can help it. Never spit on a slate, floor, or sidewalk.
>
> Do not put the fingers into the mouth.
>
> Do not pick the nose or wipe the nose on the hand or sleeve.
>
> Do not wet the finger in the mouth when turning the leaves of books.
>
> Do not put pencils into the mouth or wet them with the lips.
>
> Do not put money into the mouth.
>
> Do not put pins into the mouth.
>
> Do not put anything into the mouth except food and drink.
>
> Do not swap apple cores, candy, chewing gum, half-eaten food, whistles or bean blowers, or anything that is put into the mouth.
>
> Never cough or sneeze in a person's face. Turn your face to one side.
>
> Keep your face and hands clean; wash the hands with soap and water before each meal.[28]

As Nancy Tomes relates in a chapter called "Antisepticonscious America" (borrowing the title of a magazine article from the 1930s), reminders for the public were everywhere: paper cups (rather than glass "common cups") at public drinking fountains; the disinfection of Pullman cars; new sanitary policies in hotels; the anti-kissing campaign—the list goes on.[29]

The true glory years for bacteriological consciousness in the United States, however, were from roughly 1910 to 1920. These are the years when hygiene entered the public schools with a vengeance. Schoolchildren looking at enormous windows might not have made the connection with tubercle bacilli in the atmosphere, and even those attending open-air schools might have thought simply that fresh air is "good for your health." But instruction in hygiene became routine and included references to the causes of illness. To cite one isolated example: in the Gardner School in Valparaiso, Indiana, starting in 1910, teachers regularly treated pupils in all grades to "health hints" on the subject of sunshine, air, personal cleanliness, care of the eyes, care of the teeth, and flies. A health hint titled "Air" began, poetically, like this:

> Night air is purer and more wholesome than day air.
> Night air is charged with health and strength.
> Let night air into your bedroom abundantly.
> Night air contains less smoke, less dirt and fewer microbes than day air.[30]

If first-graders in Valparaiso, Indiana, knew about microbes, it's a safe bet that almost everyone in the country with any education did too. Microbes could make you sick, but once you were sick, you could make others sick too. If you were a Valparaiso schoolchild, you knew you were looking out not only for yourself but for your friends, teachers, neighbors, and family members as well. You were in the network.

Growing the American Methuselah— Or at Least the American Moses: Old Age as Disease

Members of the public learned about science when they had a stake in doing so. Preventing familiar communicable diseases reduced infant mortality and increased the expectation of life, so clearly it was in everyone's interest to practice the hygienic habits that the modern science of bacteriology was teaching. Thus science offered solid grounds for optimism that longer life was possible. But an increase in the "expectation of life" (whether or not members of the public thought about it in those words) simply meant a better chance of making it to an age that, in human history, had always been attainable—just not by a very high percentage of any known population. But what if "old age" itself was a kind of disease, one that modern science could identify and promise at least partially to cure? Then what the public was looking at was the chance not just to make it to a preconceived limit, say 75, or for the extremely rare and lucky, like Stephen Smith, (almost) 100, but to push that limit beyond what had ever been recorded (outside of the Hebrew Scriptures, of course). Talk about optimism! And so the public came to know the name "Metchnikoff."

Elie Metchnikoff (1845–1916) was a distinguished biologist and bacteriologist who had worked in Odessa, Russia, and in Medina, Italy, before moving to a prestigious post at the Pasteur Institute in 1888. For the last thirteen years of his life, Metchnikoff was practically a household name. That's because the great biologist began to take an interest in a topic tangentially related to his research but guaranteed to attract public attention: the prolongation of human life beyond its traditionally recognized limits. In early 1903, he published *Études sur la nature humaine: Essai de philosophie optimiste* (Studies in human nature: Essay in optimistic philosophy). The impact of the book was apparently immediate, for his publisher, George Haven Putnam, engaged an English translator by June, and before the end of the year *The Nature of Man: Studies in Optimistic Philosophy* was already on the shelves in Great Britain and the United States. Four years later, in 1907, Metchnikoff published *Essais optimistes* (Optimistic essays). Putnam brought out an English translation the following year, under the title *The Prolongation of Life: Optimistic Studies.* Also that year, for his earlier work Metchnikoff shared the Nobel Prize for Physiology or Medicine with famed German medical researcher Paul Ehrlich.

I've been unable to find a single reference to Elie Metchnikoff in the popular press before 1900. Once *The Nature of Man* came out, however, his name was all over the place—both for what he was alleged to have said and for what he really said. The extravagantly optimistic notions he inspired were based on what he was alleged to have said, and yet what he really said provided ample grounds for optimism to those inclined to take him seriously. And many, many people did.

Here, in summary, is the science underlying his philosophy. Metchnikoff was a learned man of his generation, and so he accepted evolutionary theory in its broad outlines. Resistance to this theory, in his view, was simply a dead letter. As Metchnikoff understood it, a species evolves according to the principle of natural selection, but at any given moment in its development we are likely to see anatomical features that have not kept pace with the real conditions in which members of that species live. Thus we have what Metchnikoff calls "disharmonies" in the organization of certain species—or, simply put, features that serve (or served) a function in lower (or earlier) life forms but that now have become harmful. Everyone knows one or two classic examples of such features. The vermiform appendage (or as we call it today, the appendix) at one time served a digestive purpose, but today all it does in humans is sit there, at best doing nothing and at worst threatening the life of the individual by becoming infected. Wisdom teeth served a function in a lower species, but today in humans they erupt in early adulthood, at best serving no function and at worst wreaking havoc with the placement of other teeth.

In Metchnikoff's view, these are minor examples. In humans, the feature that presents far and away the most significant disharmony is the entire large intestine. This organ apparently developed by natural selection in such a way as to favor the survival of mammals that needed to travel long distances without stopping to void their waste. But it in no way contributes to the process of digestion (Metchnikoff believed), serving instead purely as a space in which food collects, putrefies, and thus generates substances toxic to the organism. In an animal whose survival depended on traveling long distances, the detriments of the toxins were outweighed by the benefits of endurance and mobility. But modern humans survive primarily by their wits, which is to say by their highly developed brains, and not by their ability to travel.[31]

Here's where Metchnikoff's earlier work enters the picture. Phagocytes (*phago*-, "eat"; *cyte*, "cell") are cells that promote immunity by devouring dangerous foreign organisms before such organisms cause infection. In the large intestine, however, they collect and begin to eat *healthy* cells. With the contents of the large intestine stagnant, bacterial poisons form and strengthen the harmful phagocytes. Misplaced phagocytosis, by which healthy cells are destroyed and replaced with hypertrophied connective tissue, is the central cause of "senility" (by which Metchnikoff simply meant "old age"). In the large intestine specifically, this act of nature gone awry is "the greatest disharmony of the constitution of man"[32]—thus the contention, picked up again and again by Metchnikoff's lay contemporaries, that old age is a form of "chronic malady."[33] Metchnikoff did not pretend to have a cure for old age, but he had a partial remedy for phagocytosis in the large intestine: "yahourth." This milk product, common in Bulgaria but virtually unknown in the United States and the rest of Europe at that time, contains large amounts of lactic acid.[34] Today we generally spell it "yogurt." Kephir, also rich in lactic acid, will do the trick too. The thinking was that, because the microbes that cause putrefaction multiply in alkaline (base) media, the consumption of large quantities of an acidic medium produces conditions unfavorable to the survival of such microbes.[35] In any case, microbial pathogens—*germs* to the general public—were the ultimate culprits in the aging process.

The message was clear and explicit. There may well be a natural limit to human life, but there's nothing natural about death at ages that people of Metchnikoff's era considered natural. If modern medicine has shown some success in its efforts to diminish the impact of communicable diseases, then why should it not turn its attention to other life-shortening diseases—such as old age itself? And if it should find success in its attack on this target, then why should we not be able to prolong life to its truly natural limits? The distinctive feature of the message was that, unless you had a basic knowledge of bacteria, cells, tissues, and organs, this promising theory made no sense at all. If you believed it would be possible for humans to live longer, you had to understand the underlying biology—even if only at the most rudimentary level.

But what *is* the natural limit of life? That was the big question for Metchnikoff and members of his generation. Once we've eliminated the threat of all illness and accident for a particular individual, at what age would a truly "natural death" come? Metchnikoff was fond of Biblical allusion in his discussions of this issue, and so were lots of his contemporaries. He was rational enough to know that no one could live to the age of Methuselah (969) or Noah (950), but the 120 years that Moses attained didn't seem entirely unreasonable.[36] Still, those were just ancient stories. What was needed was *science*, and that's what the public got. It was rather heavily distorted by journalistic optimism, to be sure, but then again Metchnikoff's entire message *was* optimism.

Even before Metchnikoff began speculating on the possibilities of life prolongation, there already was some science on the subject. The idea was to establish a numerical value for a "normal life," by which was apparently meant a life luckily untouched by illness or fatal injury. From the middle of the eighteenth century to the end of the nineteenth, scientific estimates ranged between 70 and an even 100.[37] Metchnikoff was more sanguine than his precursors. He thought a century was probably on the short side. So what everyone wanted to know was . . . how many years *do* we get? Metchnikoff's answer was disappointing. "Probably in the human race," he wrote, "the duration of life varies and cannot be expressed by a definite figure. In most cases it ought to be more than a hundred years, and only in rare cases ought it to be much less than that term."[38] No precise figures, no evidence, nothing truly substantial for a contemporary reader, beyond the thought that life could probably be extended well beyond its current apparent limits.

Everything turned on the idea of a "natural death." Having established that old age is an illness, and having suggested that it could one day be cured, Metchnikoff imagined a fascinating possibility: that there might be individuals for whom the threat of *all* illness, including old age, has been completely eliminated. No one will live forever; everyone must die. But with illness out of the way, we will finally get to see what a completely *natural* death is—and at what age it comes. Individuals who have escaped the effects of "senility" will no doubt live a very long time, and, if other fields of medicine advance as much as preventive medicine, such individuals will be not only very old but also very wise and productive.

Metchnikoff came up with a rather odd and undemocratic vision of an ideal future, and yet it promoted a version of the network that we find in the entire Public Health Movement and linked that idea of network with the optimism that infused his vision. For him, science, specifically biology, was the foundation for proper living, not only in the practical, physical sense (as in the Public Health Movement) but in the moral sense as well. Such was his faith in his own sub-branch of biology that he was moved to say, "Bacteriology has placed hygiene on a scientific foundation, so that the latter is now one of the exact sciences. It has now become necessary to give it the chief place in applied morality as it is the branch of knowledge that teaches how men ought to live." His books—*popular* books, that is—were positively brimming with references to bacteria, cells, tissues, and organs. He used the term "orthobiosis" ("right living") for the way he thought "men ought to live," which included a long period of healthy advanced age and the wisdom that comes with it.[39] He clearly held out high standards for the ideal society he envisioned. In that society, only competent, knowledgeable persons, not "the ignorant masses," would make important decisions.[40] And yet what it all added up to for him was a future prevailing morality that somehow (he finds himself unable to explain exactly how) would be characterized by a minimum of "mutual damage" and a maximum of "mutual help."[41] Society was thus doubly networked: public health, based on public knowledge of the germ theory and the sense of collective responsibility that knowledge fosters, leads to the prolongation of life and the emergence of individuals who attain the wisdom of old age; those individuals provide moral leadership, which expresses itself in the network of mutual aid. And this is a powerful foundation for the optimism referred to in the titles of his books.

Members of the public no doubt cared more about longevity than about orthobiosis or any other philosophical-sounding words and phrases. Metchnikoff was the larger-than-life scientific authority who gave them the hope they sought—especially when the press misrepresented and distorted his views. Metchnikoff was credited with the claim that human life could be extended indefinitely, though he never said any such thing. Also attributed to him was the figure 140 as the age at which natural death ought to occur in humans. He never said this either, but if you read about him in the press between 1905 and about 1910, you would encounter this figure again and again.[42]

Metchnikoff's ideas came up in popular fiction around this time, suggesting that they had found a wide audience among the reading public. Arthur B. Reeve, a science writer and a third-rate author of detective fiction, invented the character Craig Kennedy, a science professor at a university in New York City—Columbia, no doubt (to judge from the descriptions of its location), though it is never named. This "American Sherlock Holmes," with unlimited time off from his academic duties, solves criminal cases through the application of his boundless knowledge of the most recent scientific discoveries. Reeve published his first Craig Kennedy story in *Cosmopolitan* in 1910 (the magazine in those days, under William Randolph Hearst, was a far cry from the cleavage-sporting fare that Helen Gurley Brown introduced in the 1970s). In 1913, *Cosmopolitan* brought out a series of stories under the name "Dream Doctor," published the following year in book form. Kennedy is working on a case of murder by poisoning. His sidekick comes to Kennedy's lab to find a large gathering of animals. Here's the professor's explanation:

> I'm making a little study of intestinal poisons . . . poisons produced by microbes which we keep under more or less control in healthy life. In death they are the little fellows that extend all over the body and putrefy it. We nourish within ourselves microbes which secrete very virulent poisons, and when those poisons are too much for us—well, we grow old. At least that is the theory of Metchnikoff, who says that old age is an infectious chronic disease. Somehow . . . that beautiful white kitchen in the Pitts home had really become a factory for intestinal poisons.[43]

Reeve and his character were clearly betting that the name Metchnikoff required no identification. They were also betting that "microbes which secrete very virulent poisons" needed no explanation and that readers would grasp, no matter how imprecisely, the process by which such poisons attack the tissues and organs of living things. After all, what members of the public now knew, namely the optimistic truth that before long life would be extended beyond any expectations that had ever existed outside the Hebrew Bible, had been brought to them courtesy of biology and the fledgling science of bacteriology—or, to put it more precisely, courtesy of *their knowledge of* bacteriology (and the consequent changes in their behavior). No wonder Metchnikoff was an outsized celebrity in his day. So it was probably a lucky thing for him that, as a product of the era preceding the one in which his predictions were supposed to come true, he failed to live long enough to see that they didn't.

The Immortality of Tissues: Why Stop at Methuselah When We Can Live Forever?

What interested the public about cell doctrine was the prospect of immortality, and it was tissues (aggregates of cells) that came to inflame the popular imagination. The key figure in this field was Alexis Carrel (1873–1944), especially after he won the Nobel Prize for Physiology or Medicine in 1912. The work for which Carrel was honored ("vascular suture and the transplantation of blood vessels and organs") bore little relation in the public's mind to the work that established his reputation. *That* work was much more exciting, because, as interpreted in the popular press, it held out the possibility of immortality.

Carrel had moved from his native France to the United States in 1904, working first at the University of Chicago and then at the Rockefeller Institute for Medical Research in New York. In May 1912, he made a stunning announcement in the *Journal of Experimental Medicine*. The title of his article pointed to the possibility that his research had raised: "On the Permanent Life of Tissues Outside of the Organism." Of course, he wasn't saying he'd actually achieved the permanence his title hinted at, but his results led him to make claims well beyond what Metchnikoff had been willing to hazard. Carrel's aim was not modest: "The purpose of the experiments described in this article was to determine the conditions under which the active life of a tissue outside of the organism could be prolonged indefinitely."[44] Carrel took several types of live tissue and passed them through a variety of media: Ringer's solution (distilled water containing sodium chloride, potassium chloride, and calcium chloride), plasma (in blood), and serum. In each case, the media not only arrested the process of degeneration that would normally lead to the death of the tissue but permitted the tissue to continue growing. The results inspired Carrel to express his confidence that experiments based on more perfect techniques "may lead to the solution of the problem of permanent life of tissues *in vitro*."[45]

Permanent. That meant the conquest of death. Commentators in the press took note, and before long the reading public came to know not only that immortality was somehow in the cards but that death itself had become a multivalent concept. One type of tissue particularly excited reporters. Carrel had taken a fragment of the heart of a chick and had found that he could keep it alive and pulsating for more than two months. It's easy to imagine what a sensation this created. The *New York Times* jumped on the story immediately, with an article titled "Heart Tissue Beats Long After Death."[46] If various *tissues* could be kept alive indefinitely, why not entire organisms?

Such speculation had already led to a distinction easily integrated into the conversations about life prolongation and death that Metchnikoff's work had been sparking for several years. It was the distinction between *general death* and *elemental death*. Dr. Carrel had brought it up in November of 1908, at a meeting of the American Philosophical Society in Philadelphia. In his talk titled "Further Studies on Transplantation of Vessels and Organs," his aim was to show that, with proper surgical techniques of the sort that he himself had been developing (this was the tie-in with the work that would win him his Nobel Prize), it was possible to keep vessels and organs alive for the purpose of transplanting them. It was a purely practical matter—how long you can keep tissue alive between extirpating it from one organism and transplanting it into another—that led him to a speculative discussion of death:

> There are two kinds of death, general death or death of the whole organism, and elemental death or death of the tissues and organs. It is impossible to give a definition of general death. Everybody understands what it means. Nevertheless, we are as ignorant about it as about life. General death can occur suddenly, while elemental death is a slow process. A man, for instance, is stabbed through the heart and killed. His personality has disappeared. He is dead. However, all the organs and tissues, which compose the body, are still living. The life of every tissue and organ of the body could go on if a proper circulation was given back to them.[47]

Carrel's topic was keeping tissue alive outside the body, initially for surgical purposes, but his work had led him to establish a temporal and causal relationship between general death and elemental death: general death precedes and causes elemental death. This meant that our constituent parts, cells, tissues, and organs, are more durable than we ourselves are. So, as the public began to consider the prospect of indefinite life for tissues and organs, the prevention or forestalling of "elemental death" came to be seen as a first step toward the prevention or forestalling of "general death." Nowhere would this have been clearer to members of the general public—those not in the habit of turning to the *Proceedings of the American Philosophical Society* for their reading fare—than in an article by Burton J. Hendrick for *McClure's Magazine* in January 1913.

Hendrick was widely known in the Progressive Era as a muckraking journalist, and *McClure's* was one of the primary muckraking publications. In 1913, he turned his attention to science and wrote "On the Trail of Immortality: An exclusive and authorized article describing in full the revolutionary discoveries of Dr. Alexis Carrel—the first authentic account of the marvelous experiments for which the young American scientist was awarded the world-famous Nobel Prize."

Hendrick mentioned the elemental-general distinction, but he pursued the discussion beyond the boundaries of Alexis Carrel's work. He brought in Metchnikoff and another distinction relating to death: that between accidental and natural death. If, as Metchnikoff had taught, whole organisms tend to die accidental deaths and science holds out the hope that, by avoiding accidental death, an organism may find its way to a purely natural death, may we not speak of accidental and natural death at the level of the tissues and organs that Carrel was studying? And that question led to the bigger question that Carrel's research raised in the minds of his contemporaries, one that served as the subtitle in Hendrick's article: "Can the Body as a Whole Be Rejuvenated?" The answer Hendrick gave is only partly based on the words of Carrel. He rightly acknowledged that different media would be required to keep different tissues alive. He also acknowledged that the current state of knowledge on the subject was inconclusive. "As the body contains an almost endless variety of cells, an almost endless variety of media would have to be injected. Even though other difficulties did not present themselves, as they unquestionably would, the human mind would soon get lost in the complexity of this problem."[48]

From 1910 through 1914, American newspapers and magazines regularly carried stories about Alexis Carrel. The *New York Times* ran dozens in that period. Cells, tissues, and organs were discussed in these stories without ever a definition. In order for members of the public to grasp the magnitude of the miracles that might one day be attributed to the celebrated French doctor, they needed to know what those words meant. Carrel's distinction between the "personality" of a dead man and the organs and tissues that compose that man's body would appear at first to contradict the more starkly materialistic view of Edward Schäfer. But Carrel did not explicitly weigh in on the question of whether there is a soul or whether there is a mind that is independent of our physical organism. What he did, however, was unequivocally define the biological self, the thing made up of cells, tissues, and organs, as the undisputed substrate of any other self we might like to picture. Cells, tissues, and organs, at least for the time being (in 1908 and thereafter), are more durable than *we* are. And if *we* are ever to attain immortality, it will not be thanks to some ineffable, metaphysical self but thanks to the survival of those cells, tissues, and organs—the biological self.

Carrel did not use the word "network" in his discussions of general and elemental death, but the notion is implicit. If not only individual tissues and organs but entire aggregates of tissues and organs can survive on their own while the organism as a whole ceases to exist, then the organism is necessarily a network that depends on a certain minimal set of interconnected functional components. General death occurs not because an immaterial soul suddenly flies out of the body, but because some vital group of connections has failed. Carrel never isolated any minimal set (or sets) of components, but it's obvious from his model that the death of *certain* elements precedes general death. To use Carrel's own example, the man who is stabbed dies because the organism cannot survive the death of the element of the heart (whereas it often *can* survive the removal of an element such as the gall bladder or the amputation of elements such as arms and legs). Using the railroad image again, picture a modern-day scenario in which a malign foreign power bombs all the bridges that span the Mississippi River over its entire length. Amtrak, as a larger national network or "organism," would cease to exist, since every route between the eastern states and western states would be severed. But its regional services, "tissues," on either side of the Mississippi would continue to function.

A Frenchman Offers a Seductive and Optimistic Alternative to Darwinism

Let's not forget that, not long before the era we're examining, biological science had undergone the most dramatic change in its history owing to the publication of *On the Origin of Species* in 1859. The reception of evolutionary theory in the United States is a long and complicated story, one that has been told in numerous ways. I'm not going to tell or retell that entire story here. But there's a curious little subplot that sheds considerable light on attitudes toward science and the biological self in the American public.

As with other scientific fields, the chronology of the public's reception of Darwinism differs from that of developments within the scientific community. By most accounts, what controversy there had been in the scientific community over Darwin's theories in the early years following the publication of *On the Origin of Species* (1859) and *The Descent of Man* (1871) had largely settled down before the turn of the twentieth century. Consider just two of Darwin's most vocal and distinguished opponents in the United States. Louis Agassiz, the renowned Swiss-born naturalist who had become a fixture of American science at Harvard, was intransigent in his rejection of Darwinism, but he died in 1873, and his most prominent disciples went on to champion the theory. Yale geologist James Dwight Dana had attacked evolutionary theory on geological grounds as early as 1862 and continued to do so for over a decade. But in 1874 he declared publicly that he had been converted to the cause.[49]

There is no thorough, systematic study of *public* attitudes toward Darwinism and evolutionary theory in the United States before the turn of the twentieth century—or for that matter, before the decade of the teens. To the extent that it's possible to gauge such attitudes from the popular press and from brief references in scholarly works on related topics, it appears safe to say that there was no significant, active, public opposition to Darwinism and evolutionary theory in the last two decades of the twentieth century. In the first decade of the new century, however, Darwinism and evolutionary theory enjoyed a bumpy ride both inside and outside the scientific community.

The year 1905, for example, saw the publication of a pamphlet titled *Collapse of Evolution*, by Luther Townsend, a Methodist pastor, former divinity professor, and member of the Bible League of North America. Townsend, who to his credit showed some familiarity with evolutionary theory, attacked it almost exclusively on religious grounds.[50] But most of the criticism in the era came from within the scientific community, and it arose not because scientists had come to doubt the fundamentals of Darwin's theories but because the rise of modern genetics at the turn of the century had forced some significant revisions to those theories. The press often reported the criticism as if it were directed against the theories themselves. In 1911, for instance, the *New York Times* ran a full-page article in the Sunday magazine about Dr. William Hanna Thomson, former president of the New York Academy of Medicine. A text box at the top of the page included the statement that "the Darwinian theory is now rejected by the majority of biologists as absurdly inadequate."[51] But anyone who took the time to read the article carefully would have seen that it did not challenge every detail of Darwin's findings, let alone evolutionary theory in general. It merely presented aspects of Darwin's theories that had been superseded by the findings of subsequent research.

Then, in early 1913, a story under the following headline appeared on the front page of the *Chicago Daily Tribune*: "Man Came from Ape, Scientists Tell Christians." The reporter's mildly sarcastic tone came through loud and clear in the first paragraph of the article: "Famous scientists went on record yesterday to uphold the Darwinian theory of man's evolution from the lower animals. A symposium of opinion of leading savants of the United States gathered on behalf of the Christian people of the universe by Dean Shailer Mathews of the University of Chicago was published in his magazine, the *Biblical World*."

Progressive Christian leader Shailer Mathews, dean of the University of Chicago Divinity School, thought the American public had been convinced that evolutionary theory had collapsed. So he conducted a poll of "the leaders of American science," asking each of them to respond to the question, "Does modern science still believe in evolution?" This was a naïve way of posing the question, perhaps intentionally so—how could you say no? The "men of science" whose views were sought were hardly inconsequential figures. Among them were physiologist/biologist Jacques Loeb, a true national and international celebrity in the scientific world of this era; renowned zoologist and embryologist Frank R. Lillie; and Henry Fairfield Osborn, president of the American Museum of Natural History in New York City. The response was a unanimous "yes," and Mathews published the results in *Biblical World*, the official journal of the Divinity School.

This was big news. The *New York Times* ran a short article on the *Biblical World* symposium on the same day as the *Chicago Daily Tribune* and then, a few weeks later, published Mathews's entire article under the original title, "Has Evolution Collapsed?"[52] Not only did all "men of science" allegedly accept the validity of evolutionary theory, but a devout Christian had used the occasion to argue that evolutionary theory is fully consistent with Christian belief. Mathews even published, in the same issue of *Biblical World*, an article by John M. Coulter, professor of botany at the University of Chicago. Coulter's piece was intended to show readers that a man of science could at the same time be a man of fervent religious belief.[53] Mathews's article and the coverage it received in the press should not be construed as evidence that the American public had abandoned all doubts about Darwin and evolutionary theory, but it shows that, at least in some quarters, the controversy that had been sporadically reported in the previous decade had once again died down.

And yet the situation was by no means stable. Within a couple of years, with the emergence of Fundamentalism and the charismatic figure of William Jennings Bryan, the controversy heated up and has not abated since.

Into this ever-changing landscape stepped the French philosopher Henri Bergson (1859–1941). I'll have much more to say about Bergson, who was widely celebrated in his era but is largely forgotten today, when I take up the topics of mind and time in a few chapters. In February 1913, the month when Shailer Mathews's survey came out, Columbia University presented two series of lectures by Bergson. One series, in French and open to the general public, bore the title "Spiritualité et liberté." The other, in English and restricted to an invited audience of students and professors, was called "The Method of Philosophy, an Outline of a Theory of Knowledge."[54] The lectures were anticipated in the press for over a year. During the month of the series, Brentano's, G. P. Putnam's, and Henry Holt & Co., all major publishing houses, took out large ads in the *Times* featuring English translations of Bergson's works. Havemeyer Hall on the Columbia campus was filled to capacity each time Bergson lectured there, crowds of people had to be turned away, and upper Broadway was the scene of a major traffic jam as members of New York's intelligentsia flocked to hear this star academic widely famed for his electrifying speaking style—whether he spoke in French or in the polished and fluent English he'd learned from his mother.

It might come as a huge surprise to you today that New Yorkers turned out in droves to hear someone speak on topics as dry as Bergson's titles might suggest—and half the lectures were in *French*. But there had been plenty of opportunities to learn about Bergson in the press. For years, this French philosophy professor, with a face "of the most spiritual Jewish type," featuring a pair of penetrating eyes that stare out at you arrestingly, yet somehow gently, from the portrait most commonly reproduced in the papers, had been drawing enormous, standing-room-only crowds to his lectures in Paris.[55] To judge from reports in American newspapers and popular magazines, what appeared to be attracting audiences in Paris and elsewhere, in addition to Bergson's formidable talent as a public speaker, was a collection of faintly mystical ideas noteworthy for their antagonism toward modern science. Even someone who had never taken a philosophy course could easily grasp that the *intuition*, the *vital impetus*, and the *freedom* the Frenchman was promoting in his writings and lectures somehow represented a powerful form of resistance to forces that were trying to reduce us all to laboratory animals, bundles of tissues and impulses, creatures whose every movement science might someday render entirely predictable.

One intriguing thought that emerged from the Columbia lectures was that humans could possibly survive after death, though Bergson conceded that immortality, in the strict sense of endless life, could not be proved. To judge from what Bergson was reported to have said in one of his French lectures in Havemeyer Hall, the thought sprang from reflections on the mind, specifically on the independence of the mind from the brain and nervous system (and the haunting possibility that the mind might survive the death of the body).[56] But the conquest of death was something that obviously fascinated Bergson, and he famously wrote about it in another context. In 1907, he had published a book titled *l'Évolution créatrice*. It was translated into English as *Creative Evolution* and released in Great Britain and the United States in 1911, two years before the Columbia lectures. It had an enormous impact. The periodical press was filled with reviews of it and references to it. Newspapers carried countless advertisements for it. The great French apostle of intuition and freedom did not set out to attack Darwinism at its foundations. In fact, he sought to assure his readers that he understood and accepted the basic science underlying evolutionary theory. He sought to *revise* Darwinism. What he objected to was the idea implicit in Darwinism that evolutionary change *among humans* occurs in the absence of any participation from the very individuals (and eventually populations) that it affects. And so he suggested that humans, individually and collectively, through the exercise of free will, can alter the future course of variations in such a way as to benefit the species as a whole.

Nowhere in the era do we find evolutionary theory more flagrantly placed in the service of optimism. In perhaps the most famous passage in the book, often quoted in the popular press, Bergson spoke about the possible conquest of death: "The animal takes its stand on the plant, man bestrides animality, and the whole of humanity in space and in time is one immense army galloping beside and before and behind each of us in an overwhelming charge able to beat down every resistance and clear the most formidable obstacles, perhaps even death."[57] This represents a stunning revision of Darwinism. Apart from the rapturous suggestion that we can somehow overcome the most formidable opponent that living things face in Darwin's Struggle for Existence, Bergson explicitly turns that struggle into a kind of enterprise with two characteristics that would be anathema to Darwin: it is purposeful, and, at least in this passage, *collective*.

Bergson was not the first person ever to suggest that evolutionary processes operate at the level of both the individual and the group. In chapter 7, I'll have much more to say about this. But no one to my knowledge gave the idea a more seductive image—and without so much as a shred of scientific evidence to support it. But that's why the image has more to tell us about the American reading public (I won't speculate about the French) than about Bergson himself. If any members of that reading public, newly and widely educated in the life sciences, were seduced by this idea, it must have been because they were now married to the idea of collectivity. As we'll see shortly, Bergson thought that modern life had networked people together through standardized time, but to his mind lamentably so, because standardized time suppressed the precious autonomy of the individual's free will. That was the idea that had made him famous in France two decades earlier. So, perhaps by 1907, when he wrote *Creative Evolution*, he had come to find consolation, even joy, in the thought that, if collectivity or the network is an inescapable condition of modern life, then that collectivity (a) can be seen as representing the aggregate of the individual wills of its members, and (b) can be an immense force for progress.

3 Sex O'Clock in America

THAT'S RIGHT: "Sex O'Clock in America." William Marion Reedy, a bad boy of American journalism, ran the St. Louis-based *Mirror* from 1891 till 1920. In August of 1913, the recently founded New York-based *Current Opinion* fairly bellowed the jocular phrase to the reading public as the title of an unsigned editorial piece in its "Religion and Ethics" section. "A wave of sex hysteria and sex discussion seems to have invaded this country," the article began. "Our former reticence on matters of sex is giving way to a frankness that would even startle Paris."[1] Yes, *Paris*. When it came to sex, what could be more shocking than to call someone more candid and open than the French?

From the Law of Continence to Sex as "One of the Strongest Human Impulses"

If Reedy was right, then things had changed in a truly dramatic fashion since a generation or two earlier. If you were a young or middle-aged woman in the last two decades of the nineteenth century and you had more than a superstitious knowledge of sexuality, there's a good chance you learned some of what you did know in *Tokology: A Book for Every Woman*, which served numerous educated young American women as a sex manual from its publication in 1883 into the twentieth ("tokology" being constructed from *tok*, a Greek verbal root for "to bear"). It was written by Alice Bunker Stockham, M.D. A reader today, thinking back on the Victorian era in which this book appeared, will probably be surprised by its candor, though it was not a sex manual in the twentieth-century understanding of the phrase. It did not explain how to discover the joys of healthy and fulfilling sexual activity. Dr. Stockham promoted the "law of continence," which held that "the sexual relation should never be sustained, save for procreation." Its corollary was that "the procreative element" (she meant seminal fluid), when retained in the (male) body, "is in some way absorbed and diffused throughout the whole organism, replacing waste, and imparting a particular vivifying influence." The precious substance, when not uselessly expended for purely physical gratification, could even be absorbed into the brain and "coined into new thoughts."[2]

In support of the law of continence, Dr. Stockham quoted two predecessors: Dr. John Cowan, author of *The Science of a New Life* (1869), and John Harvey Kellogg (of corn flake and Battle Creek Sanitarium fame), author of *Plain Facts for Old and Young: Embracing the Natural History and Hygiene of Organic Life* (1877). That Dr. Cowan and Dr. Kellogg were *men*, not "women, with some fancied wrongs to redress," strengthened Stockham's case.[3] Like *Tokology*, *The Science of New Life* presented a remarkably frank discussion of sexual matters from the physical standpoint, while featuring as its central doctrine the law of continence. Dr. Cowan had offered definitive proof of the claim that "sexual connection was intended only for the propagation of the species" and urged married couples to abstain from sexual activity for a full three years after each impregnation.[4] He was convinced that semen, "reabsorbed into the blood of the individual," possessed the capacity to renew life, just as he was convinced that a "licentious life" could lead to a host of ailments and calamities, from dyspepsia and rheumatism to premature old age and deformed offspring.[5] The book included in the back matter testimonials of support from such eminent, credentialed feminists as Elizabeth Cady Stanton, William Lloyd Garrison, and Robert Dale Owen (son of the famed British proto-socialist Robert Owen and founder of the utopian New Harmony community in Indiana).

Dr. Kellogg, for his part, largely agreed with Cowan. He was equally convinced that excessive sexual activity led to physical infirmities in the guilty parties and to deformities in their offspring. And like so many others of his era, he saw the problem as stemming largely from male behavior. In support of the claim that sexual desire exists in women only at the time of "periodical development" (a later generation would say "ovulation"), he quoted what has since become the *locus classicus* of Victorian thinking about sexual desire—actually its absence—in women. The eloquent statement belongs to William Acton, the British author of a surprisingly early sex manual bearing the ungainly title *The Functions and Disorders of the Reproductive Organs in Childhood, Youth, Adult Age, and Advanced Life, Considered in Their Physiological, Social, and Moral Relations* (1857). Here are Dr. Acton's words on the subject: "I should say that the majority of women (happily for society) are not very much troubled with sexual feeling of any kind. What men are habitually, women are only exceptionally. . . . As a general rule, a modest woman seldom desires any sexual gratification for herself. She submits to her husband's embraces, but principally to gratify him; and, were it not for the desire of maternity, would far rather be relieved from his attentions."[6]

Such, in brief, was the state of professional knowledge about human sexuality, as transmitted to the general public, at the time that *Tokology* was first published. Not that everyone was following the advice of Stockham, Cowan, and Kellogg: in her study of the Gilded Age, Rebecca Edwards includes an entire chapter on the emergence of liberated sexual behavior even as early as the 1880s.[7] But such behavior at the end of the nineteenth century hardly reached the proportions that led Reedy to make his wry comment, and the press certainly did not comment much on the subject back then. Still, whether the message in this early era was to avoid as much as possible or, among bohemians, to indulge, the topic was now out in the open in a way that, at least in the United States, was without precedent. Even if a finger-wagging medical moralist was cautioning you to stay away, you could have, as never before, a fairly vivid idea, complete with detailed descriptions and in some cases even drawings, of what you were supposed to stay away *from*. In its own limited way, sex was now a publicly acknowledged and candidly discussed activity. And even though the medical experts who wrote about it issued statements any reasonably educated reader today would dismiss as completely unscientific, the simple fact that "science" was now shining a light on this most intimate of subjects made it inevitable that sex would soon find its way into increasingly respectable conversation—between doctors and patients, wives and husbands, and also between journalists and their readers.

If we jump ahead to August 1913, when *Current Opinion* published "Sex O'Clock in America," we'll find in that same month Arthur Reeve's fictional story "The Dream Doctor" in *Cosmopolitan*. Because the story's protagonist,

Professor Craig Kennedy, follows the latest developments in science of all sorts, he is familiar not only with Elie Metchnikoff's theory of old age (which I mentioned in the previous chapter) but also with the most recent theories about sexuality. Kennedy and his sidekick are investigating a case of apparent suicide. Not surprisingly, the suicide turns out to be murder, but among the clues that lead Kennedy irresistibly to his conclusion is the behavior that Mrs. Maitland, widow of the dead man, exhibits. As a "specialist in nerve diseases" observes to the sleuth-professor, Mrs. Maitland "belongs to a large and growing class of women in whom, to speak frankly, sex seems to be suppressed . . . she is really frigid, cold, intellectual . . . a consciously frigid but unconsciously passionate woman."

Kennedy has been reading the work of a certain "Dr. Sigmund Freud, of Vienna" and, as a result, has been drawn to take seriously what others involved in the case are inclined to dismiss—a "dream of fear" that Mrs. Maitland had recounted at her dying husband's hospital bedside (the venom that killed Mr. Maitland had at first inconveniently robbed him of the ability to speak, so even in his final moments he had been unable to reveal the truth about his condition). In the dream, several days before the actual death, Mrs. Maitland had seen her husband in a casket, dead. Once Kennedy solves the case, he explains the theory: "Now, the dream is not an absurd and senseless jumble, but a perfect mechanism and has a definite meaning in penetrating the mind. . . . Freud says that as soon as you enter the intimate life of a patient you begin to find sex in some form. In fact, the best indication of abnormality would be its absence. Sex is one of the strongest of human impulses, yet the one subjected to the greatest repression." Mrs. Maitland's dream was a dream of fear and thus represents "the fulfillment of a suppressed wish." Fear, Kennedy declares, "always denotes a sexual idea underlying the dream. In fact, morbid anxiety means surely unsatisfied love." Mrs. Maitland's dream represented a wish that her husband should die, so that she could be united with the man to whom she was truly drawn (by her repressed sexual instinct, no doubt). *That* man, of course, was the murderer, who had carefully (but not carefully enough) given Mr. Maitland's death the appearance of suicide.

In a prefatory paragraph, the editors of *Cosmopolitan* sought to pique their readers' interest, before insisting that Reeve was a brilliant author. "Do you dream? Have you ever heard of Dr. Sigmund Freud, of Vienna?" they asked.[8] Reeve could safely bet that at least some readers had. As in at least some other Craig Kennedy stories, when the time comes for the great science professor to explain the recent scientific discoveries that have helped him solve a case, Reeve lifted text verbatim from newspaper articles, without attribution, and turned it into his character's speeches. For example, the passage with the phrase "absurd and senseless jumble" was stolen from one of two *New York Times* articles. Both were about Dr. A. A. Brill, the Columbia University neurologist who applied Freud's theories to his work with patients at the Institution for the Insane on Ward's Island.[9] Dr. Brill was also the first to translate Freud's *Interpretation of Dreams* into English, just months before Reeve's story was published.[10]

Whether or not readers had been following the career of "Dr. Sigmund Freud, of Vienna," Reeve seemed certain that they would not be completely shocked to hear that the sex drive *in a woman* had been unnaturally suppressed, which suggests that it is naturally *there*, and that sex is "one of the strongest human impulses," in women as well as in men. In fact, Reeve must have believed too that the use of the word "sex" by itself, in the sense of "sexual activity" instead of "gender" (as we say today) would not surprise his readers.

What had happened in the previous thirty years?

The Law of Sex (Gender) and the Law of Sex (Sexual Activity)

One part of the story is remarkably simple. Until the very end of the nineteenth century, no one really understood how characteristics of individual members of a species, including gender, were passed along to the next generation. The good doctors who wrote the best-selling marriage manuals in the second half of the nineteenth century continued to believe, for example, that the behavior of parents during intercourse, or for that matter, simply in everyday life, was by some mysterious process transmitted to their children. A continent life for men was a particularly urgent necessity, not only because "excessive venery" was believed to be harmful to the health of both partners but also because sexual congress carried out in the heat of animal passion could lead to a host of character flaws and physical defects in the resulting offspring.[11] As to what determined the sex (gender) of a child, there were a number of theories. Dr. Cowan listed some of these in *The Science of a New Life*: "that the parent possessing the greatest amount of vital force will confer the sex of the offspring"; that it is a matter of the time during the menstrual cycle when coition takes place; that it depends on whether the impregnating sperm originated in the left or the right testicle.[12] To later generations of professional scientists or just moderately educated lay readers, the lack of compelling evidence (or any evidence at all) to support many of these theories is surprising, but members of those generations need to keep in mind that modern standards of laboratory research were beginning to emerge just as the era of these Victorian marriage manuals was drawing to a close.

Be that as it may, the answer to the question, once it emerged, was decisive in overturning the earlier theories, and if you were among those who came to know the answer (incomplete though it might appear to us today), there was no longer any use trying to influence gender selection by any of the means that earlier nineteenth-century science had proposed. With the more sophisticated and accurate knowledge that arose between about 1899 and 1913, it became apparent that gender selection was essentially beyond your control—and for reasons that were pretty easy to understand, even if you didn't have a medical degree or a Ph.D. in one of the biological sciences. As we'll see, some members of the public—even some highly educated members—were not so ready to give up the idea that certain traits besides gender, especially those having to do with personality and intelligence, are passed along to succeeding generations by a process that either has or requires no scientific explanation.

But the key to the scientific conception was *chromosomes*, to be specific, or *modern genetics*, more generally. As usual, there are two timelines.

The discovery of chromosomes, together with their connection to heredity, had been made in the 1880s by German biologist Theodor Boveri, though few particulars of the process by which traits are passed from generation to generation were understood. Nonetheless, in 1899, Herbert W. Conn was able to include in *The Story of the Living Machine* a fairly detailed description of the cell nucleus, complete with chromosomes and centrosomes, cell division, and fertilization. Conn reported that "the chromosomes form the part of the cell which contain[s] the hereditary traits handed down from parent to child," though he had to acknowledge that no one yet understood exactly how the process worked.[13]

One good measure of the timeline on the professional science side is a book by Columbia University zoologist Thomas Hunt Morgan titled *Heredity and Sex*. Morgan was one of the key figures in the burgeoning biological study of heredity, and this book, which came out in 1913, was the published version of a series of lectures he gave at Columbia that same year. While *Heredity and Sex* contains a fair number of technical terms as well as references to specialized publications in the field, it is written in a style that makes the

material accessible to lay readers. On the question of sex determination, the story is straightforward. In fact, Morgan describes its basic components in a simple paragraph. As of 1913, the precise details of the process by which X and Y chromosomes determined sex in offspring remained to be worked out, but Morgan felt confident telling his listeners and readers this: "The facts that we have considered furnish, I believe, demonstrative evidence in favor of the view that sex is regulated by an internal mechanism. The mechanism appears, moreover, to be the same mechanism that regulates the distribution of certain characters that follow Mendel's law of inheritance."[14]

Not everyone was convinced, nor did the public come to embrace this exclusive view at this early date. Competing theories lived on briefly in the scientific world, and the public continued to be exposed to them. In October of 1912, the *New York Times* ran an article by Scottish naturalist J. Arthur Thomson. Thomson had written a number of popular books on evolution and other scientific matters, including *The Evolution of Sex*, in 1889, with his compatriot, the biologist Patrick Geddes. For readers of the *Times*, Thomson offered a survey of then-current wisdom on the question of sex determination. He rejected the antiquated theories that sex is determined exclusively by environmental influences or that it is determined by the relative strength of the "germ cells." Yet he was also oddly skeptical of the chromosome theory, finally settling on the rather vague explanation that sex is determined by a "rhythm of bodily changes," an "initial difference in the balance of chemical changes" between male and female.[15]

But even though this explanation, whatever it means, would soon finally yield (and among many scientists had already yielded) to the overwhelming power of the chromosome theory, it was distinctly different from the explanations that the public might have taken from nineteenth-century marriage manuals. Thomson's account at least sounded scientific and left little room for the essentially moral foundation of earlier sex determination theories. It would be difficult to name a precise date by which a substantial segment of the public came to know and accept chromosome theory, but by the beginning of the second decade of the twentieth century, sex determination (not sexual activity in general) appeared to lie safely outside the realm of behavior, thus of human agency (and morality), and within the realm of chemical and biological forces. Sex determination sprang from the networks within the nuclei of "germ cells," themselves part of the larger network of cells, tissues, and organs that made up the individual human being.

By 1913, the word "genetics" was increasingly making appearances in the press, alongside the more frequently used "heredity." A professorship of genetics had been established in 1912 at Cambridge University.[16] Americans who were reasonably perceptive would have recognized that if sex (gender) is determined in some way by chromosomes (even if they didn't quite understand what these were), then it is subject to the same forces, recently brought to light by the science of genetics, that determine other characteristics in individual members of species. To those perceptive Americans around 1913, sexual activity, as connected with reproduction and specifically gender determination, now had a credible scientific theory behind it. That theory accorded the activity a central position in a vast evolutionary network, linking the activity as well as each individual (including that individual's internal networks), *by scientifically explicable means*, with the past and the future.

The Black Plague, or How Germ Theory Helped Spread the Word about Sex

Nineteenth-century marriage manuals had taken a modest but significant first step toward bringing sex into the public eye. Venereal disease and a Public Health Movement specifically dedicated to it finished the job and changed the world forever.

In 1905, a dermatologist named Prince A. Morrow (1846–1913) founded the American Society of Sanitary and Moral Prophylaxis, whose aim was "to limit the spread of diseases which have their origin in the Social Evil." "Social evil" meant prostitution. The diseases in question were "social diseases," which meant "venereal diseases." The use of euphemisms stemmed from one of the conditions that the society was formed to combat: the "conspiracy of silence" regarding venereal disease. The other was the "double standard of morality" for men and women. Over the next decade and a half, the conspiracy of silence was smashed to pieces, and the American public was given a crash course in sex hygiene and sexuality itself.

It's probably accurate to say that the days of a *purely* moral and superstitious approach to "social disease" were already numbered in 1905, even without Prince Morrow. The gonorrhea bacterium, *gonococcus*, had been identified as long ago as 1879. The syphilis pathogen, *Spirochaeta pallida* (as it was first called), was identified by two German researchers in the same year that Morrow founded his society, though there were strangely few references to

it in the press or even to the fact of its discovery until about five years later. But there was no doubt in the mind of any health professional that the two primary social diseases were caused by microbial agents and that, just like yellow fever, cholera, typhoid fever, and tuberculosis, these diseases were public health problems.

Morrow and his fellow crusaders in the sanitary and moral prophylaxis movement recognized that an important and very obvious factor set social diseases apart from other infectious diseases: their association with sex. Enlightened as the new understanding of the subject might be, science could not afford to abandon morality altogether. What was needed was a morality specifically informed by science. In a campaign against social disease, Morrow thought, public health could not reasonably be separated from public morality. Such a campaign therefore could not rely exclusively on methods that had come to serve the campaign against other infectious diseases, above all public education that emphasized personal hygiene. For tuberculosis, it was fine to advise members of the public to refrain from spitting, to wash their hands, and to avoid common drinking glasses. But if the disease was syphilis, the corresponding advice would have been to avoid promiscuous sexual activity (before and during marriage) and especially the services of prostitutes. The conspiracy of silence that Morrow's society attacked was the tacit agreement among people of all classes to avoid speaking about sexual matters in general and to turn a blind eye to the habits of *men*—even those of the most exalted social standing—who sought extramarital gratification in brothels, contracted venereal diseases, and then infected their unsuspecting wives. What was the use of advising men not to visit prostitutes if their activities were so carefully wrapped in protective secrecy?

A different sort of education was called for, one that brought the offensive behavior into the open, recognized it for what it was, and surrounded *it*, not sex in general, with shame. Here was a sexual morality free from superstition and ignorance. Morrow, an enlightened physician writing after the turn of the twentieth century, found himself endorsing continence—or attacking *in*continence. But there was a great difference between the approach he took and the one we find in the nineteenth-century marriage manuals, and this difference signals the dramatic shift in attitude toward the very topic of sexuality. "All thinking men must recognize that the development of the sex function is intimately associated with the physical, mental, and moral growth of the individual," Morrow wrote in 1907. "Sex is the physical basis of love, of

the family sentiment, of the existence and prosperity of society."[17] For Morrow, continence meant a kind of restraint, "clean living," so as to protect the "essential dignity" of the sex function. The education campaign that would strike a blow at venereal disease would be a "socio-sanitary movement" that would enlighten people—even the very young—about the physical dimension of sexuality. The point was to liberate it from the "system of shame" that a code of silence had helped create, while also raising a moral awareness of the value of sex *in its proper place.*[18]

Dr. Morrow was no advocate of free love, and he unapologetically believed the proper place for sex was in a marriage founded on mutual affection and respect. Like the marriage manual authors who preceded him, Morrow regarded himself as a champion of women's rights and dignity. But for him, women's rights meant acknowledging a role for women in the sexual act, recognizing them as responsible agents, and protecting them from irresponsible behavior rather than from the act itself. As he put it, the young man today must "unlearn the ethical heresy that one-half of humanity has imperious duties which the other half may repudiate or disclaim."[19] So Dr. Morrow, the members of his society, and many others went forth to educate the American public—about hygiene and morality.

There were publications. A bibliography compiled for *Educational Review* in 1913 listed, as recommended reading for teachers, eighty-eight books and journal articles, three periodicals, and pamphlets printed by eight different organizations.[20] Much more, of course, was published in the era. There were additional organizations. In 1910, the American Federation for Sex Hygiene was founded in St. Louis, with Prince Morrow as its first president. The founding members of the federation made a very wise public relations move: they chose Charles W. Eliot, who had retired the previous year after serving as president of Harvard University for forty years, as their honorary president. Eliot had decided to devote a hefty portion of his energy in retirement to the cause of sex hygiene and sex education in America, and wielding the clout of his former position, he attracted considerable public attention. In 1913, the federation merged with the American Vigilance Association (an anti-white-slavery organization) to form the American Social Hygiene Association. The following year, the organization was renamed American Social Health Association, which remains today a primary force for education and research in sexually transmitted diseases. There were conferences. The Fourth International Congress of School Hygiene, held in Buffalo in August

of 1913, featured an entire section on sex hygiene. President Eliot spoke at that meeting.

And there was the campaign for education in sex hygiene. A clear sign that the topic attracted widespread public attention is that *Good Housekeeping* magazine ran a series on it between 1911 and 1913. While *Good Housekeeping*, relative to other wide-circulation periodicals in this era, leaned heavily in the progressive direction, championing pure food and drug regulation, promoting public hygiene, and generally adopting a strongly pro-consumer stance, it was hardly a bastion of free-love anarchism. What it all added up to was what the editors clearly regarded as a common-sense approach to sex hygiene and education: frank, open discussion, together with support for the view that an informed public—even a *young* public—was a healthy public. It offered an admirably balanced set of views, featuring, among others, a contribution by a clergyman, one by British sexologist Havelock Ellis, one by Prince Morrow himself, and one by the immensely popular advice columnist Dorothy Dix (Elizabeth Meriwether Gilmer).[21] If the *Good Housekeeping* series shows anything about the subject, it is that educators and the public were talking about it often and loudly in 1913 and had been doing so for a number of years.

For most of the decade, however, sex education was talked about more than it was actually implemented in schools.[22] One famous/notorious experiment threatened to derail the movement for a very long time. It happened in Chicago, and it was in the national news as the final installments of the *Good Housekeeping* series were appearing. In 1913, Ella Flagg Young, superintendent of public schools in Chicago, persuaded the city's Board of Education to add instruction in sex hygiene to the public high school curriculum. To make the idea palatable to the public, the board changed the name of the topic from "sex hygiene" to "personal purity." The course of instruction would consist of four lectures for boys, to be delivered by male physicians, and three for girls, to be delivered by female physicians. By the end of the fall semester, some twenty thousand students in Chicago had attended the lectures. Initial reports were favorable. The *Chicago Daily Tribune* reported in October that both the students and the sponsors of the instruction were pleased with the results.[23]

And yet by January, it was all over. In November, the League of Medical Freedom, an anti-sex hygiene organization, successfully lobbied to have the contents of the lectures declared obscene and therefore, under federal law, unmailable.[24] In December, a few members of the board began to express their opposition to the personal purity lectures, drawing support from Chicago's Catholic community. Over a chaotic thirteen-day period that month, Mrs. Young was ousted from her post, replaced, and then reinstated.[25] Nonetheless, in early January, the school board voted to discontinue the program.[26]

If the lectures truly reached twenty thousand students, then we can safely say that many students ended up at least a little bit the wiser about matters sexual. You could hardly say, however, that this number represented any significant portion of the American youth population. Yet the discontinuation of the program probably did not impede the progress of the movement. After all, the episode achieved a grand *succès de scandale.* Sex hygiene and sex education were all over the Chicago papers for several years leading up to the public school experiment and remained there for months afterwards (though by 1915 there were only a handful of references to sex hygiene or the public school episode). Between 1909 (when superintendent Young first appointed a committee to look into the possibility of offering sex instruction) and January of 1914, the *Chicago Daily Tribune* ran close to two hundred articles containing references to sex hygiene or sex education. The *Los Angeles Times* and *New York Times* both covered key events in the controversy. The movement had gathered support from a pantheon of respected authorities, in the scientific, educational, and even religious communities, among them John M. Coulter, whom we met in the previous chapter as a supporter of reconciling religion and science.[27]

By a few years later, the approach to sexual hygiene instruction used in the Chicago experiment came to have a name: *emergency sex education*, meaning specially designated presentations and printed materials that focused on sexual activity as an immediate health problem. "Personal purity" was not simply a euphemism; it accurately described the emphasis in the lectures, which aimed to encourage behavior—through the dissemination of real knowledge, of course—that would help young people avoid the pitfalls of sex outside marriage. The phrase came along at a time when a different method had emerged, one from which the emergency method needed to be distinguished. The new method was called "integrated sex education," meaning the topic was included in the regular school curriculum—for example, in biology or physical education courses. Integrated sex education would have to wait for the end of the Great War. As American young men were sent overseas and exposed to both military and "social" perils, it was considered the better part of wisdom to instruct them in sexual matters in order to protect them from venereal infection. But after the war it became possible to shift the focus and actually address the possibility that sexual activity was something that could be incorporated into a normal life as a healthy and desirable source of fulfillment.[28] By 1920, it was reported, at least one-fifth of American high schools (or two-fifths of those responding to the survey on which the results were based) were offering some form of sex education. Within that group, roughly two-fifths were offering the emergency instruction and three-fifths the integrated instruction.[29]

But whether instruction in the 1920s was "emergency" or "integrated," a great change had already taken place years earlier. Read what President Eliot said to participants at the Buffalo Congress in 1913, looking back with astonishment at a mere decade's worth of history: "During my somewhat recent active life," he said, "I have never seen such a change of public opinion among thoughtful people as has taken place among them within the last 10 years on the subject of sex hygiene, using that term in its broadest sense. The policy of silence on all the functions and relations of sex, whether normal or morbid, was almost universally accepted for centuries by physicians and clergymen, and in family life." Interest in sex hygiene, Eliot said, had arisen in recent years partly because of the new scientific understanding of sexuality and venereal disease but partly, too, because, in light of this understanding, young people were being confronted with a highly personal question. As Eliot put it, "How can I best regulate my own conduct in order to win the normal satisfactions of family life? . . . In short, how can I steer a safe course through the swirls and tumults of the sexual passion, which seems to be a principal source not only of the normal satisfactions and delights of human life, but also of its worst anxieties and afflictions?"[30] Eliot was still very much attached to the idea that sex *hygiene*, the prevention of venereal disease, should be a dominant topic, but consider how he framed the issue. "Normal satisfactions and delights of human life": this meant that, at least in certain circumstances, sexual activity was something healthy and normal. Eliot spoke only generally about "family life" and did not further qualify "normal." Language like this would have been hard to find in the nineteenth-century marriage manuals unless it was explicitly associated with the sacred virtues of procreation.

Even with its strong moral tinge, the topic was now firmly grounded in science. Sexuality was part of the biological self, and new knowledge of it overlapped considerably with new knowledge that formed the basis of that self. Germ theory had brought awareness of the *actual* causes of illness arising from sexual activity. But as we saw in the previous chapter, germ theory was in large part responsible for a conception of the networked self. As the public health campaign taught, thanks to germs, no individual could live in isolation. Disease and the necessity of preventing it created a social network founded in the most basic force: the desire to survive. If one big reason the public came to know about sex was that sex was sometimes responsible for the transfer of pathogens, then sex, like tuberculosis, created a social network based on the confluence of individual and public interest. Of course, personal choice played a greater role in the avoidance of venereal disease than in the avoidance of tuberculosis: you could abstain from sex (except in cases of rape) altogether or avoid contact with prostitutes (though if you were a woman you could not avoid having your husband secretly visit prostitutes), but you could not always abstain from contact with the tubercle bacillus. Yet by the early decades of the twentieth century, the idea that the law of continence could actually be obeyed was beginning more and more to look like fanciful thinking. To put it crudely, the minute you decided to play, you were part of the game. And it goes without saying that almost everybody played.

From Germs to Ideal Married Love

What was missing from the personal purity phase in the development of modern sexuality was explicit discussion of sex as its own sphere of activity with its own rewards, together with the sense that, in the right circumstances, those rewards were justifiable and deserved. We find plenty of this in Havelock Ellis's colossal seven-volume *Studies in the Psychology of Sex*, but few Americans had the opportunity to read any of the volumes of that work until the 1930s (in the United States, only members of the medical profession were legally permitted to read the work before then).

They read the Swedish feminist Ellen Key, whose *Love and Marriage* and *Love and Ethics* both came out in English translation in 1911. "The problem of sex," Key wrote in *Love and Ethics*, "is the problem of life, it is the problem of society's happiness, in comparison with which all other problems sink into insignificance."[31] You could hardly get more explicit than that. And, if they got their hands on her book before it was banned in the United States (the ban was lifted in 1931 by Justice John M. Woolsey, who two years later would gain notoriety for lifting the ban on James Joyce's *Ulysses*), they read Marie Carmichael Stopes, the Scottish-born proponent of family planning. Her *Married Love* (1918), like Key's *Love and Marriage*, was a plea for a freer sexuality and, above all, for recognizing the existence of women's desire and satisfaction in a sexual relationship. Stopes, a Doctor of Science with an impressive list of academic credentials, offered a scientific account of the "Law of Periodicity of Recurrence of desire in women," in part to destroy the Victorian myth that women have no desire.[32] She addressed the importance of the woman's "crisis" (orgasm), and she emphasized the necessity of a man's wooing his wife "before every separate act of coitus."[33] A small sign of her celebrity is her appearance in Virginia Woolf's *A Room of One's Own* (1929), where she is very thinly disguised as the writer "Mary Carmichael" (author of *Life's Adventure*, a thinly disguised reference to Stopes's novel *Love's Creation*, 1928).[34]

And, beginning in 1926, they read Theodoor H. van de Velde, the Dutch gynecologist who dazzled and shocked the world with the publication of *Ideal Marriage: Its Physiology and Technique.* Despite the inclusion of the word "marriage" in the title and the author's insistence that the activities he describes are ideally suited for married relationships, this book was a full-blown sex manual, in comparison with which Key's and Stopes's books look almost prudish. Van de Velde gave a full, detailed description of the anatomy and the physiology of sex. Fully one-third of the book is devoted to a detailed discussion of stages, techniques, and positions, including how-to advice for acts—regarded as well within the range of normal—that Key and Stopes would have blushed to mention. Van de Velde boldly declared sex "the foundation of marriage" and established as a premise what by now had apparently become clear to so many ordinary people in Europe and the United States: "I cannot doubt," he wrote, "that the sexual impulse is fundamentally an impulse to reproduce. But it is equally certain that the two impulses have become increasingly separate, distinct, and independent. . . . Thus, among civilised races, the urge to reproduce has ceased to 'play lead' among the components of the sexual impulse, which appears as a further stage of evolution; an advance in psychic power and complexity."[35]

Van De Velde firmly put to rest any notion that continence and the consequent preservation of secretions promoted physical and mental health. On the contrary, he found "discharge of seminal matter" to be essential to the relief of sexual tension.[36] He believed, furthermore, that disuse leads to atrophy, and so he urged men to exercise the sexual organs "*regularly and appropriately*" even into their 50s and 60s—beyond the age of fertility for their wives, if they and their wives were roughly the same age.[37] *Ideal Marriage* became a classic in the United States, going through over forty printings and, according to the publisher, reaching over a half-million readers by 1960.[38]

Anyone who had been through the personal purity phase of the sex education movement would have noticed in these new books two closely related, truly sensational shifts. The obvious one is the shift from a focus on disease prevention to a focus on sexual activity seen as something potentially independent from the need to reproduce. The related one is the shift to an exalted view of *human* sexuality as something genuinely sublime, as evidence of the superiority we enjoy as a species. Nowhere is this more evident than in Dr. Van de Velde's characterization of the sexual impulse as "a further stage of evolution," suggesting that the development of our species has brought us the gift of this impulse as something not exclusively tied to our own propagation. Just as we enjoy reason, conscience, and advanced psychic power, we enjoy the benefits of the sexual impulse as an end in itself. As the foundation of *all* marriage, sex is precisely what allows us to build the *ideal* marriage announced in Van de Velde's title.

Naturally there was a practical dimension to all this celebration of the sexual impulse as its own source of gratification and fulfillment. Enjoying the spiritual and emotional fruits of that impulse without the physical fruits, in the form of offspring, required reliable means for preventing conception. Perhaps the ability to develop such means is another signal gift of the evolutionary process. I don't mean to offer a detailed history of the birth control movement in the United States, but three details from that history are worth mentioning. The first is that, with the notable exception of the birth control pill, virtually all modern forms of contraception (devices and methods) had already existed, some of them in a relatively reliable form, since the middle of the nineteenth century—well before the revolution in sexual mores that would reach its apogee in the 1920s. What did not exist was either ready access to contraceptive devices or widespread social approval of their use. The birth control movement that Margaret Sanger, Marie Carmichael Stopes, Emma Goldman, Mary Ware Dennett, and others led, starting in the middle of the second decade of the twentieth century, did not directly generate any new technological developments. What it did do was create a climate of acceptance, no matter how hushed. That's the second detail from the story. Middle-class couples might have been uncomfortable with the ideological viewpoints of birth control proponents (everyone "knew" that Emma Goldman, for one, was a dangerous anarchist), but that did not mean they avoided using "articles for the prevention of conception." The third detail *is* technological, but it has to do not so much with innovation as with preference and effectiveness. The birth control movement can be statistically correlated (the usual caveats concerning correlation and causality apply here) with a significant rise in the use of the diaphragm over unreliable devices and methods (douching and withdrawal, for example). The diaphragm, requiring training and a doctor's prescription, was the consummate feminist contraceptive device, because (a) it was effective, when used properly, and (b) it placed birth control under the control of women.[39]

Presumably, if you embraced the idea that sexual pleasure, in the proper circumstances, was a wholesome and even beneficial thing, then there were plenty of grounds for celebration in the new ethos. In the absence of disease, infidelity, and, now, unwanted pregnancies, you could safely indulge an impulse that respectable professionals were assuring you was natural and salubrious—in fact, *necessary* for proper physical and mental health, according to some. What better news could there be than that?

From Ideal Married Love to Better Children: Sex for the Good of the Whole "Race"

There *was* better news, much of it belonging to the 1920s and later. It was that healthy sexual activity and a rational approach to reproduction via birth control would lead to improvements in the "race," where "race" was understood either as "species" or as the dominant race of a particular nation (such as the white race in the United States). Leaders in the birth control movement almost without exception advocated one form or another of eugenics—whether loosely construed as a method for improving the human species or more narrowly construed as the science of selection created by Sir Francis Galton, William Graham Sumner, and others. So all that wholesome and pleasurable activity, just like the measures designed to eliminate its *un*wholesome form, now curiously networked you to a much larger social unit of which you were one individual part.

In an untitled essay published in 1920, Marie Carmichael Stopes (whose *Married Love*, incidentally, was brought out by the Eugenics Publishing Co. in New York, beginning in 1927, and who left much of her fortune to the British Eugenics Society) addressed the issue of "what the human race may one day become."[40] Like other leaders in the birth control movement, Stopes saw widespread race degeneration as she looked around. The primary causes: crowding and venereal disease. That birth control could help retard the spread of venereal disease was obvious. But what about "crowding?" Stopes set out to convince her readers that crowding, by which she simply meant the production of too many offspring, was in itself an evil: that is to say, for *any* woman, numerous pregnancies, by damaging physical and spiritual well-being, can lead to inferior offspring. Why? "In my opinion," she wrote, "the truth of antenatal influence through the mother is certain, so that not only the bodily condition, but the mental and spiritual outlook, of the mother affects the child she is bearing." This view, she added, was "axiomatic," so there was no need to supply evidence in support of it. The goal for modern society must therefore be "the conscious elimination of all diseased and overcrowded lives *before* their conception, by planning only to conceive those for whom adequate provision of material necessities and a loving welcome are reasonably to be anticipated."[41]

That sounded like a worthy (if completely impractical and impossible) goal, as long as what Stopes had in mind was voluntary participation by an increasingly large number of people (increasingly large because such advocates of birth control as Stopes herself had trained the light of their reasonable opinions on a previously ignorant public). But in her conclusion, Stopes hinted at some of the darker schemes that the eugenics movement had concocted and would concoct, though it is difficult to say just how serious she was at this point:

> Alas! that the age of a beneficent autocracy has never been and is not here today! Instead of achieving in two generations the great result on the human race that could be achieved, it will be necessary to take the slower means of creating in every individual that intense consciousness of the race which will make it impossible for individuals ever to tolerate the coercion of enforced and miserable motherhood, with its consequent poison of the racial stream.[42]

Stopes certainly did her own legacy no great favor by going to Berlin in 1935, in her capacity as president of the Society for Birth Control and Progress of Race, to attend the International Congress for Population Science, sponsored by the regime of Adolf Hitler.[43]

Margaret Sanger was grander in her views. Her two books of the early 1920s were titled *Woman and the New Race* (1920) and *The Pivot of Civilization* (1922). When they turned to eugenics, birth control advocates all faced a powerful argument against their case: if only enlightened people practiced birth control, the world would soon be overrun by the offspring of the unenlightened, leading to the degeneration, rather than the uplift, of "the race." Sanger, like Stopes, believed that crowding produced inferior offspring and that birth control was the solution. But what to do with the already inferior population that used no birth control and thus threatened to degrade the future population by contributing a disproportionate number of "defectives?"

For Sanger took seriously the warnings of the harsher eugenicists, men such as H. H. Goddard and Robert M. Yerkes (the principal villains in the late Stephen Jay Gould's 1981 assault on the excesses and abuses of intelligence testing, *The Mismeasure of Man*): the population of the United States was showing an alarming and growing proportion of feebleminded people, defectives, and "morons" (H. H. Goddard had recruited this term from the Greek in 1910).[44] Sanger was not proposing any plan for mass extermination or sterilization. Deciding who's fit and who's unfit is a serious problem, she thought, and yet, she allowed, "The grosser, the more obvious, the undeniably feebleminded should, indeed, not only be discouraged but prevented from propagating their kind."[45] Still, the thrust of her message was radiantly hopeful: sex itself will lead to a "great spiritual illumination which will transform the world, which will light up the only path to an earthly paradise,"[46] and birth control will lead to a future in which children are "brought into the world because they are desired, called from the unknown by a fearless and conscious passion."[47] That's why birth control, as expressed in the title of Sanger's book, is "the pivot of civilization."[48]

But even before the rise of the birth control movement, Havelock Ellis had written of eugenics in connection with sexual hygiene and sexual selection. As early as 1906, in an article titled "Eugenics and St. Valentine," he likened enlightened sexual selection to the medieval St. Valentine's Day custom, by which (as Ellis described it) the townspeople in certain regions of England, France, and Austria playfully chose a mate for marriageable young women. In modern times, Ellis wrote, the equivalent would be the application of "ideals" to the process of mate selection, by which he meant simply that when we select a mate we should be mindful of producing the best possible offspring. Such a practice would represent an expansion of the notion of eugenics that Galton had introduced. Ellis was cautious. There was to be no program that would resemble "the artificial breeding of animals," nor could there ever be compulsion associated with the breeding he had in mind: no "legislative projects."[49] "It is a matter of accepting an ideal and of exerting our personal and social influence in the direction of that ideal," he concluded. "If we really seek to raise the level of humanity we may in this way begin to do so to-day."[50] "Eugenics and St. Valentine" was later reprinted (with minor modifications) as chapter 6 (retitled "Eugenics and Love") of *The Task of Social Hygiene* (1913).

Toward the end of the era when hygiene dominated the national conversation about sexuality, and on the cusp of the era when birth control would come to assume such an enormous part in that conversation, Ellis spoke grandly about progress and ideals, in connection with "social hygiene" and eugenics. All social hygiene, he wrote in the preface, "is but an increasingly complex and extended method of purification—the purification of the conditions of life by sound legislation, the purification of our own minds by better knowledge, the purification of our hearts by a growing sense of responsibility, the purification of the race itself by an enlightened eugenics, consciously aiding Nature in her manifest effort to embody new ideals of life."[51]

The eugenic element that later emerged in the birth control movement proper certainly had its flaws. It relied heavily on premises—worthy of the Victorian precursors whose views it sought to supplant—that were unscientific and arguments that were specious. No one ever bothered to explain *how* such factors as a woman's poor physical and mental health could be translated into defects in her children—and this, surprisingly, at a time when then-modern genetics was offering the public, especially such members of the highly educated public as *Doctor* Marie Carmichael Stopes, some fairly persuasive ideas about how traits are passed from one generation to the next. Sanger wrote ambivalently and ambiguously about "the modern Mendelian point of view" and yet fell back on a kind of mysticism when she needed to account for inferior and superior traits in offspring.[52] No one bothered to explain how the use of birth control and the consequent reduction in offspring among enlightened people (presumably of superior "stock") would offset the higher fertility rate among the less enlightened—apart from vague suggestions about the future universal practice of birth control methods. Nor did anyone bother to explain how love and sex—or *loving* sex—in today's generation would translate into a physically and spiritually exalted generation tomorrow.

But there can be no doubt that these new developments—a wider acceptance of birth control methods and products, the availability of increasingly explicit published material on sex, and the linking of birth control with a genetically bright future—turned sex into a networked and networking activity. The use of birth control products brought sexual activity into the commercial arena, making consumers of sexually active men and women. Sex manuals and tamer fare such as the works of Ellen Key created a set of shared images and values among people who, especially in the 1920s, appeared increasingly willing to discuss such matters openly. And the attention that Stopes and others brought to eugenics made sexual activity part of a large, collective enterprise, much like the fanciful "creative evolution" that Bergson envisioned early in the twentieth century. Sexual "connection," as the nineteenth-century experts sometimes called it, was now neither the illicit and dirty abuse of women by lascivious and "incontinent" men nor the idealized, pure act of procreation carried out at most once every three years. Represented in those ways, it was a hidden, isolated activity. In the new way of thinking, it certainly remained private, but it now took its place among any number of life's practices that bound individual actors, often through unseen forces, to the larger community of their fellows.

4 The Neurophysiological Mind—or Not

ON MARCH 13, 1912, Theodore Roosevelt, having declared his intention to challenge incumbent William Taft in the primaries for the Republican presidential nomination, was campaigning in Portland, Maine. As soon as he climbed the steps to the platform on which he was to give his speech, the structure collapsed, throwing him to the floor. Roosevelt joked that it was "the weight of intellect" that brought down the platform and punned on the word "platform" (the physical one and the collection of his political positions). The crowd loved the spectacle, shouting, "Bully for you, Teddy!" It goes without saying that the rugged outdoorsman, pugilist, and slayer of African game was completely unrattled by the experience. All very amusing—and terrific for the campaign. This was front-page news in the *New York Times* the following day (a Sunday).[1] Given the tone of the news article, you might well have thought the editorial board and reporting staff of the paper were made up of unswerving Roosevelt supporters. But if you turned to the Sunday Magazine section, you saw that a true indignity awaited the popular former president.

The cover story bore the title "Roosevelt as Analyzed by the New Psychology" and this subtitle: "Famous Neurologist Says the Colonel Will Go Down in History as One of the Most Illustrious Examples of the Distortion of Conscious Mental Processes Through the Force of Subconscious Wishes." The photos accompanying the article made "the Colonel" look positively regal. You saw him astride a horse and engaged in conversation with the German kaiser (also on horseback and wearing a spiked military helmet of the sort that would become notorious a few years later), riding in a motorcar with the king of Italy, in a parade receiving "the adulations of the people," and represented in a statue by sculptor Paul Noquet. And yet the article itself was hardly flattering. The author was Morton Prince, M.D., identified at the head of the article as professor of nervous diseases at Tufts College Medical School.

Dr. Prince appeared to have two aims. The first was to tell about the "New Psychology." The second was to shed some light on the personality of a widely known figure. What were the principles of the New Psychology? Dr. Prince generously cleansed his language of all forbidding technical terms, in order to make the science "intelligible to laymen." He listed three principles: (1) When we think we are putting something out of our minds, it doesn't actually leave our minds but instead becomes *subconscious.* (2) When we put into our subconsciousness wishes too shocking to think about, we *repress* them. (3) Repressed wishes come to the surface in a "disguised or veiled form."

According to Prince, Roosevelt, despite originally claiming he would never seek an additional presidential term, harbored a subconscious wish, one that was "intolerable," to do just that. A conflict developed "between the repressing moral conscience and the wish," but "the unacceptable wish to be an active candidate [was] unconsciously determining [Roosevelt's] conduct," leading to his willingness to accept his party's nomination. Dr. Prince was confident of his diagnosis: "I have no doubt Mr. Roosevelt will probably resent this interpretation and attribute it to all sorts of malignant motives on the writer's part," he wrote. "If so, it will be psychologically interesting because the greater his resentment the greater the probability of the truth of the analysis. So it is always."[2]

Some readers might have been surprised by the analysis of their former president's hidden motives, but Dr. Prince appeared to think they wouldn't. He never once said where the New Psychology came from. The name Freud never appeared in the article. Prince seemed to think everyone already knew about both Freud and the New Psychology. Two months later *Current Literature* published a review of Dr. Prince's article under the title "A Scientific Vivisection of Mr. Roosevelt." The unnamed author got right to the point: "The principles of the new psychology which perform this illumination for us are those developed by the famous Dr. Sigmund Freud, of Vienna," he explained. "Dr. Prince accepts Dr. Freud's principles and proceeds to apply them." Like

Prince himself, the author clearly assumed his readers already knew who Freud was.

If you were an attentive reader, you would have noticed in the introductory, editorial paragraph to "Roosevelt as Analyzed" that Dr. Prince had written a book titled *Mind and Human Automaton*. Let's say, in addition, you had a burning interest in the question and plenty of time on your hands to pursue it. Once you located a copy (no small feat, since even the New York Public Library did not own one), you would have discovered that the *Times* editors got it slightly wrong: the true title of Dr. Prince's book was *The Nature of Mind and Human Automatism*, and it had been published quite a bit earlier—in 1885, to be exact. Then, once you started reading the book, the content would have surprised you because of its stark contrast with the content of the article on Roosevelt.

Three decades earlier, a younger Dr. Prince had taken a view of the human mind very much at odds with the analysis he gave of President Roosevelt. Back then, it seemed, there was no separation between the mind and its physical foundation in the brain and nervous system. There was a basis for this hardline stance on the mind-body connection: a thoroughgoing commitment to *materialism*, which, as Dr. Prince unabashedly explained in 1885, had become the prevailing view of the world and had decisively defeated all *spiritualism*, at least among knowledgeable and intelligent people. "To-day the weight of authority is in favor of a material basis for all mental phenomena," he wrote. "It is generally conceded that mind depends upon the development of a peculiar matter, the brain, for its existence."[3]

So, what happened between 1885 and 1912 to change the views of a professional in the field so dramatically? And did the change in Dr. Prince's views correspond to a change in the views of ordinary Americans?

The Nature of Mind and Human Automatism was hardly a best-seller, so it would be wrong to suppose that lay readers received from its pages whatever education they had in psychology and the physiology of the nervous system. But if Prince's book reflected beliefs that were widespread at the time in professional circles, did the public know about them from other sources? At the other end of this stretch of time, the editors of the *New York Times* in March of 1912 clearly believed their readers would take an interest in what they called the New Psychology and were probably betting that some of them had already heard something about it. Six months later, of course, they would publish the series of stories on Edward A. Schäfer and the famous speech on the "chemical creation of life," a speech whose underlying philosophy was essentially identical to the one that Morton Prince had embraced in 1885. In his one brief reference to the field of psychology, Schäfer would seat the human intellect wholly in the nervous system. What did the public make of all this in 1912 and the surrounding years?

First, let's speak about the earlier era, the one in which "materialism" dominated, and see where the science of the mind had led before the New Psychology (and whatever might have led up to it) appeared on the scene—and how much the public new about *this*.

The Neurophysiological Mind and the Internally Networked Self

One path into the view of the human mind that had developed by the last decades of the nineteenth century may be found in yet another work published in 1912, this one by renowned psychologist G. Stanley Hall, under the title *Founders of Modern Psychology*. A couple of striking facts about this book, which was based on a series of public lectures the author gave at Columbia University in January of the same year: First, Hall, as president of Clark University in Worcester, Massachusetts, had attracted public attention three years earlier by inviting "Dr. Sigmund Freud, of Vienna" to his institution to participate in what became an historic conference on psychology—historic precisely because it included Freud, in the only visit the Viennese doctor ever made to the United States. That conference was in large part responsible for introducing and affirming the very trends in psychology that Morton Prince was following in his analysis of Theodore Roosevelt. So there appears to be little doubt that Hall was a champion of the new movement in psychology. And yet the man Hall considers to have had the most significant impact on modern psychology was Hermann von Helmholtz (1821–94), the arch-proponent of the view that the human mind is solidly based in the brain and nervous system. Hall regarded Helmholtz's works on psychology as "more important for psychology than the contributions of any individual thinker since [German philosopher Immanuel] Kant."[4]

It's true that Helmholtz made pathbreaking advances in both optics and acoustics and that his work remained authoritative and influential for decades after his death. His work in optics demonstrates both the magnitude of his accomplishments in the field of psychology and the view of the mind that emerged from his research. Here is a very short version of that view and how Helmholtz came by it.[5]

First, it is helpful to be reminded of two scientific achievements from earlier in the nineteenth century. By as early as 1802, there was already in place a neurophysiological description of the visual faculty—color perception, in particular—that, crude as it was, pretty closely resembles the one we have today. Credit goes to Thomas Young (1773–1829), a British medical doctor and natural philosopher (today we would probably describe him as a physicist). Though he lacked certain terms and concepts that would emerge during the ensuing century, Young nonetheless elaborated a wave theory of light and a trichromatic theory of color perception. No one knew about cells at this time, but Young proposed the hypothesis that color perception results from the interaction of light waves with three different types of "particle" in the retina, each one sensitive to a different color. The vibration of the light waves, Young thought, induced corresponding vibrations in the color-sensitive particles, and the various hues we perceive arise from the combination of different levels of intensity in each of the three particle types. Perception of a given color occurs after nerves from the retina transmit vibrations to the "sensorium," or brain. On this last point, Young simply followed a principle that Newton had established as early as 1675.

The second achievement was the law of *specific energy of sensory nerves*, formulated by German physiologist Johannes Müller (1801–58) and presented in a book on the visual sense that was published in 1826. A statement of the law in its simplest form would sound trivial today. It would go something like this: any sensory nerve can produce only sensations associated with its own type. The optic nerve can produce only visual sensations, the auditory nerve sound sensations, and so on. It's the corollary to this observation that was so important. A given type of perception, say, visual, occurs only in response to the interaction between a stimulus and a sensory nerve associated with that type of perception. All the nerve can do is switch on or not. The actual cause of the stimulation is a matter of indifference. Put more bleakly, our perceptual system communicates to us no firm knowledge of any real world. Just as a blow to the head that affects the optical nerve can cause us to "see stars," the impingement of light on our retina can cause us to think we "see" the object that reflected the light. But the nervous system is not designed in such a way as to communicate absolute knowledge. Here's how Müller himself, in a philosophical mood, expressed it: "For all material objects, all stimuli affecting the organism excite in that organism not what they themselves are but something distinct from themselves, namely the vital energies of the organism."[6] All we can study is the organism.

The legacy that Müller left for his pupil Helmholtz was a worldview with a physiological component and a philosophical component that were inseparably joined. The best term for the philosophical component is "idealism," in the very loose sense of a belief system in which the mind never holds any absolute knowledge of an external world. But the physiological component is what really mattered for the future of psychology. The foundation for Müller's idealism was a view of the mind as essentially a closed, wholly organic system. As luck would have it, the organic system includes components that react to various types of stimuli: chemical, physical, and "vibrational" (as wave energies were understood in Müller's day). Every time a certain something happens to these components, they spring into action and transmit their own peculiar type of "vibration" to the brain. The brain interprets the vibration as—well, any number of things but the true source of the vibration is the *nerve*, not an external object. So if the human mind exists in a condition of idealism, it is because its constitution ultimately is completely *physical*: nerves and a brain.

That was in the mid-1820s.

Helmholtz wrote his classic *Handbook of Physiological Optics* between 1856 and 1866. He divided the work into three sections, each devoted to its own topic: (1) dioptrics, or the physics of light and its interaction with the eye; (2) the theory of visual sensations, explained with reference to the "nerve apparatus"; and (3) visual perception—that is, how we understand visual sensations. The second and third sections are where we find Helmholtz's contributions to a psychology that is neurological and physiological. In an introductory portion of the book, Helmholtz told his readers that his aim in the second section was to discuss visual sensations "without making reference to the possibility of knowing external objects by means of those sensations."[7] How to do this? The key idea is the *stimulus*, generalized, as in Johannes Müller, to denote any object or event, "real" or illusory, that causes a sensory nerve to react.

In the third section of the *Handbook*, Helmholtz elaborated on the philosophical implications of his science of vision. The question is how we form *perceptions* from the visual sense, in other words, how the initial sensations that arise from the triggering of sensory nerves become what we regard as actual knowledge of the external world. The answer is that they don't. All we ever have are *representations* of whatever might or might not be outside us.[8] The reason is clear: sensory nerves bring to the brain the results of contact with stimuli, but the word "stimulus" needs to be defined in such a way that it loses any necessary suggestion of real existence. Stimulus is just a word for whatever-triggers-sensory-response. In this lonely view, we are essentially formed by the network of our nervous system. Helmholtz used the German word *Sehnervenapparat*, "visual neural apparatus," where "apparatus" means much the same thing as "network," and he introduced the term in connection with stimulation (*Reizung*).[9] We are also imprisoned within that network, since the hub of the network, the brain, can "know" nothing farther from itself than a sensory nerve that has been switched on. In the second edition of *Physiological Optics*, Helmholtz was moved to wax even more philosophical, and he put the point quite bluntly. Having referred to the "idealist hypothesis," he wrote this: "I do not see how one could refute a system of even the most extreme subjective idealism, one that considered life a dream. One might declare it to be as improbable, as unsatisfactory as can be—in this connection I would even agree with the most adamant expressions of rejection—but one could still implement it with full consistency; and it seems to me very important to keep this in mind."[10]

Helmholtz was not a household name in the United States at any time. The great scientist visited Columbia College (before it became Columbia University) in 1893 and was entertained by the institution's president, Seth Low (who later became mayor of New York City). The visit received modest attention in the press. A year later, when Helmholtz died (in part because of head injuries he sustained from a fall on the return trip to Germany), a number of American periodicals carried obituaries with detailed accounts of his scientific work. He was given credit for inventing the ophthalmoscope, for his work in optics and acoustics, for a number of contributions to physics, and even (later on) for the size of his brain.[11] Little was said about his contributions to psychology or to a theory of mind.

And yet, by the time Helmholtz died, neurophysiology had made, or was making, some of the most significant strides—quite possibly *the* most significant strides—in its entire history, and Helmholtz's work was fundamental to the field. Starting in the 1860s, French physician and neurologist Jean-Martin Charcot had studied a host of organic neuropathological conditions, such as multiple sclerosis, amyotrophic lateral sclerosis, and Parkinson's disease. By the early 1890s, Spanish researcher Santiago Ramón y Cajal had constructed a picture of the nervous system as a network of independent cells, disconnected from one another. The same decade saw the identification and naming of dendrites, the neuron itself, the axon, and the synapse.

A culminating point in this story is the publication of *The Integrative Action of the Nervous System* by British neurophysiologist Charles Sherrington, in 1906. The author devotes a considerable amount of space in the book to the specific topic of reflexes, but his reason for doing so is to assert his principal claim: that the entire nervous system, as discontinuous as it might appear once we take into account its separate neurons and the spaces between them, which Sherrington himself named, is fully integrated. What this meant was that no event in the nervous system, including the one that would appear to be the most independent, namely a reflex action, can occur in isolation from the rest of the system. For this reason, Sherrington believed, reflex actions are capable of being consciously controlled. At the same time, the idea of conscious control in no way suggested to Sherrington a human mind that was independent of the nervous system. He firmly denied the existence of "an informing spirit resident in the organism," just as he denied the possibility of access to real external things. Here's how he describes the way we establish our sense of a thing that involves more than one type of sensory input: "A reaction is synthesized which deals with the environmental object not merely as a stimulus possessing one property but as a 'thing' built up of properties."[12] In other words, the sense of a "thing" comes to us by way of the only possible channel, our nervous system as it responds to one or more stimuli.

Perhaps no one in the era expressed as forcefully and eloquently as Sherrington the idea that the nervous system, and by extension the entire organism, can be envisioned as a network. He used the terms "network," "net," and "web" dozens of times in his book. Toward the end of his chapter on compound reflexes, he said this:

> The central organ is a vast network whose lines of conduction follow a certain scheme of [*sic*] pattern, but within that pattern the details of connection are, at the entrance to each common path, mutable. The gray matter may be compared with a telephone exchange, where, from moment to moment, though the end-points of the system are fixed, the connections between starting points and terminal points are changed to suit passing requirements, as the functional points are shifted at a great railway junction.[13]

Sherrington was no more a household name in the United States in 1906 than was Helmholtz in 1894—or at any other time. *The Integrative Action of the Nervous System* represents a stage in the history of science among professionals that helps explain the materialist views of Edward A. Schäfer in 1912. The public had already been hearing details about the physiological theory for quite some time. To give just one example, in September of 1895, *Current Literature* reprinted an article on Ramón y Cajal from the *Pittsburg Leader*, titling it "Magic in the Brain" (original title: "The Geography of Thinking"). The author acknowledged the continuing mystery of consciousness and memory, but the topic of the article was *thought* and *thinking*, and everything in it was about physiology and system. The brain was like an "electrical battery," "thought cells" had been studied under the microscope, the operation of the nervous system was likened to machinery, every event in the organism is "telegraphed instantly to headquarters" (the brain, of course), and all nerve cells show a "general connectedness." Memory might be a mystery, but only because physiology had yet to investigate it adequately. For now, the author reported, we can be sure that its functions are carried out by "memory nerves" and that memory is located "all over the body."[14]

And yet, well before 1912, in fact, around the time that Sherrington's book came out, it was already clear that something major had changed in the field of psychology—at least as the public was likely to see it. When it comes right down to it, Schäfer's words about the nervous system might have surprised at least some members of the public (older ones who had heard something about the materialism of Morton Prince's youthful days) not because they represented such a radical and absolutist point of view but because they were now actually out of date.

The Independent Mind, Part I. Hypnotism Becomes a Tool of Science, "Functional" Replaces "Organic," and the Mind Is Divided in Two

One name does appear to have achieved household status in the late nineteenth century—at least to judge from how it was handled in the press: Charcot. From the 1870s on, the name of Jean-Martin Charcot appeared in the American press as simply M. Charcot, Dr. Charcot, or Prof. Charcot, with no additional identifying information. By the late 1880s, his name increasingly appeared in association with the word "hypnotism," and that's because, at the end of the previous decade, in his quest to determine a physical basis for the mysterious condition known as hysteria, Charcot had begun to think that hypnotism, because it produced a state similar to that of hysteria, would provide the investigator with a powerful tool for the study of the disorder. Hypnotism as a method of study and treatment came to be associated with a group of mental disturbances whose causes could not easily be traced to, say, lesions in the spinal cord or nerves themselves, as in many of the illnesses Charcot had studied earlier in his career. To make a long and complicated story short and simple, illnesses less susceptible of physiological diagnosis increasingly came to occupy their own independent realm. And as they came to occupy that realm, psychology, as the public saw it, increasingly paid attention to these illnesses and increasingly distanced itself from those that presented a simple, physical etiology. By the first few years of the twentieth century, the change had crystallized into the distinction between *organic* mental illnesses and *functional* mental (or nervous) illnesses.

The distinction was not new in the profession. As early as the 1860s, if you were a physician, you could read in the professional literature about such "functional nervous affections" as epilepsy, eclampsia, and delirium tremens.[15] In the 1870s and early 1880s, "functional nervous diseases" included hay fever, sexual exhaustion (caused, of course, by "sexual excess and disturbance"), and forms of disturbance closely allied with, but not identical to, "insanity."[16] The functional-organic distinction was fundamental to the work that helped introduce the term "neurasthenia" into the American lexicon (the world's lexicon, for that matter): George M. Beard's *American Nervousness: Its Causes and Consequences* (1881). In the late 1890s, even technical neurological literature continued to place functional nervous ailments in a separate category, characterizing their origins as "molecular."[17]

But these references were either obscure or intended primarily for professionals. A clue to the change that was about to come appeared in the last year of the nineteenth century in the *New York Times*. It was tucked away on page 12, so it's unlikely that many people saw it, but it looked ahead to what the public in a few years would be reading on a weekly basis. "Hypnotism the Cure-All," it was titled. The subject was Columbia University's Professor (emeritus) John D. Quackenbos, who had made what the article's author clearly regarded as rather extravagant claims for the capacity of hypnotism to treat a wide variety of ills, both moral and mental. Though the article didn't include many details about Quackenbos, the retired professor had had a rather unconventional career, receiving a medical degree in 1871 and then teaching rhetoric and English literature at Columbia for twenty-three years. In retirement, he had returned to the practice of medicine. The author reported that Quackenbos was now using hypnotism to cure not only "stammering, drug and alcoholic addictions, moral perversions, and excessive cigarette smoking," but also "functional nervous disease." The theory that served as a foundation for his method was as significant as his emphasis on hypnosis. "The phenomena of hypnotism are scientifically explicable on the supposition of a double ego, a duplex personality, implying two distinct states of consciousness—one called the primary consciousness, involving the mind's recognition of its own acts; the other, called the secondary consciousness, holding those mental processes and procedures of which we have no knowledge. That is, each human being is one individual with two distinct phases of existence."[18]

What definitively brought the functional-organic distinction to the attention of the lay American public was the Emmanuel Movement, begun at Boston's Protestant-Episcopal Emmanuel Church by its rector, Elwood Worcester, in 1906. Reverend Worcester described the origins of the movement two years later in *Religion and Medicine: The Moral Control of Nervous Disorders.* As he explained, there was a great religious revival going on at the dawn of the new century, one that represented a decided rejection of "the scientific materialism and the rational criticism in which we have grown up." As important as the simple fact that the Church had returned to the lives of Americans was the new emphasis it brought along with it: "the time is come," he wrote, "when the Church must enter more deeply into the personal lives of the people and make a freer use of the means modern science and the Gospel of Christ places at her disposal if she is to continue even to hold her own." And so, in July of 1905, he organized the Emmanuel Church Tuberculosis Class, under the direction of a physician, with the aim of treating consumptive patients both physically and "morally," that is, by giving them encouragement and hope. Pleased with the success of this campaign, Worcester then extended his efforts to "the nervously and morally diseased."[19]

Reverend Worcester had no medical credentials of his own—though a coauthor of *Religion and Medicine* was Isador H. Coriat, M.D.—but Worcester had studied psychology with some of Europe's masters and held a Ph.D. from the University of Leipzig. This presumably is what authorized him to practice a type of clinical psychology. He embraced a theory of the subconscious mind, believed that hypnosis helped the therapist gain access to it, and claimed that Charcot had failed to see the full extent of the benefits that hypnosis could provide. The functional-organic distinction was absolutely fundamental to his view of nervous diseases, and he was convinced that therapy of the sort that he practiced, based as it was in Christian principles, must be confined to functional cases.

The Emmanuel Movement initially attracted little attention outside Boston, but readers in other parts of the country didn't have to wait for the appearance of *Religion and Medicine* in order to hear about it. Starting at the very beginning of 1908, the *New York Times* and popular periodicals began to carry stories about the movement, and readers came to learn about the functional-organic distinction, the therapeutic value of hypnosis, the psychology of the subconscious (or unconscious), and the miraculous ability of that psychology to cure a host of mental and moral ills.[20] Skeptical references appeared in the press over the next few months, but by the end of the year, the Emmanuel Movement, its methods, and similar methods practiced by professionals not directly associated with it were the talk of the town. It would have been difficult for any American who read any newspapers and magazines above a very modest level of sophistication to avoid encountering the new view of mind, or "New Psychology," as it was often called.

By far the most thoughtful and extensive treatment of the Emmanuel Movement in the popular press was an article published at the very end of 1908 in the *American*. It was by Ray Stannard Baker, and it was called "The Spiritual Unrest" (part of a series later published as a book under the same title). Baker, together with Lincoln Steffens and Ida Tarbell, had been a staff member at *McClure's*, the era's great muckraking magazine, and had left with those two writers in 1906 to help found the more staid and moderate *American*. At this moment, he seems to have been taken as much with the overarching phenomenon of religious revival as with the details of the Emmanuel Movement's psychological theories. Baker was exultant: "The world is just now being swept with a great wave of idealistic philosophy. It is a rebound from the years of materialism and materialistic philosophy which swayed the intellectual and spiritual life of men during a large part of the last century. . . . The new idealism lays its emphasis upon the power of mind over matter, the supremacy of spirit."[21] "Idealism" to Baker clearly meant something like "the opposite of materialism" (not what it meant to Helmholtz). Above all, in keeping with the tenor of the current age, the new faiths were optimistic, just as the now-outmoded materialism was deterministic and therefore pessimistic. "'I do not' and 'I cannot' are superseded by 'I do,' 'I know,' 'I will,'" he wrote.[22]

Then, just as suddenly as it had appeared on the scene, the Emmanuel Movement dropped out of sight. Newspapers and popular magazines ran dozens of articles per year on the movement from early 1908 through the end of 1911. By 1912, there was hardly a mention anywhere, and after that the name came up only in connection with, say, the funeral of someone who had been associated with it in its heyday.

But if we're speaking about a view of the human mind, as something relatively independent of the brain and nervous system, it hardly mattered. That view was intact, with or without a religious movement yoked to it, and it was receiving powerful support from a European intellectual who, like the representatives of the New Psychology, offered a captivating view of a mind divided in two.

The Independent Mind, Part II. A French Philosopher Seduces Some Americans into Giving Up Science—Partly

If you had gone to hear Henri Bergson lecture at Columbia University in February of 1913, you might not have been surprised at the size of the crowd that turned out. The press had looked ahead to the visit for a year. The previous August, *The Independent* reported that if Bergson's upcoming lectures at Columbia proved to be as well attended as the ones he was giving in Paris, the university would have to hire Carnegie Hall to accommodate the crowds. It didn't, but for all we know it might have. As Edwin E. Slosson, one of Bergson's American admirers, put it, the lecture rooms at Columbia were "packed to the doors."[23] We read that over two thousand applied for tickets to the lectures—a little short of the roughly 3,500 needed to fill Carnegie Hall but considerably more than the 319 that the lecture room in Havemeyer could accommodate.[24]

If we look back today at the Bergson fad in America, we're likely to be stunned at both the strength it achieved and, given that strength, how quickly it came and went. It was an utter flash-in-the-pan sensation. Bergson's name began to appear in print in the very last days of 1910. As the Columbia lectures approached and for a short time afterwards, it was all over the place. With the start of the Great War, Bergson, as a public figure with views on the international conflict, still appeared in American newspapers, but as a philosopher he essentially vanished. The chronology has a great deal to do with the publication history of his works translated into English, but what generated this publication history was certainly the spirit of the times and the accompanying expectation that the works would find a hugely favorable reception. They did.

There were three that mattered most: *Time and Free Will*, *Matter and Memory*, and *Creative Evolution*. The first of these bore an ungainly original title whose English equivalent would be "Essay on the immediate data of consciousness." The translator understandably used that phrase as the subtitle and chose something more salable for the main title. The publication date of the original French edition was 1889. *Matter and Memory* and *Creative Evolution* (both titles accurately translate the French) were originally published, respectively, in 1896 and 1907. But all three English translations came out during a roughly six-month period between 1910 and 1911, so that a reviewer for the *New York Times*, in August 1911, could plausibly report "the simultaneous appearance of these three volumes," as if a single publisher had decided that the moment had arrived to introduce the English-speaking world to the luminous mind of France's greatest living philosopher.[25] The first two, in fact, were published by Macmillan, the third by Henry Holt. So the editors at Macmillan were betting that one book published twenty-one years earlier and another published fifteen years earlier were now going to sell in the United States. The editors at Holt were making the same bet about a book published only three years earlier. All were right, for a time, but especially Holt: *Creative Evolution*, by the time the last ad for it appeared in the *New York Times*, in April of 1913, was in its ninth printing.

A fussy academic might want to draw a fairly sharp distinction between what Henri Bergson *really* said in his books and what the popular press reported about what he said. And of course, no matter how responsible, intelligent, and conscientious a popular writer might be on the subject, short accounts in magazines and newspapers (for that matter, short accounts even in full-blown academic journals) will always leave out whole swaths of what Bergson said in his books.

If you wanted to set out an extremely short *logical*, as opposed to truly *chronological*, sequence of Bergson's thoughts, from *Time and Free Will* through *Creative Evolution*, it might look something like this:

Everything begins with a set of reflections on time. Time as we experience it in the modern, industrialized world, with our clocks, watches, and train schedules, is an artificial invention. It serves a practical purpose, but it does not correspond to our real experience. That experience Bergson called "real duration," and by it he meant the way we feel the flow of life separate from all measurement and all social and practical conventions (such as the need to meet a friend at a commonly accepted "noon" or to arrive at the Gare Saint-Lazare no later than a nationally agreed-upon 12:33 p.m., for the scheduled departure of a train). Real duration follows laws that are peculiar to *me*, an individual set apart from everyone else. Duration ebbs and flows according to my personality, my past, and the circumstances in which I find myself. It cannot be reduced to a linear, spatially conceived chain of discrete, equal temporal units. In fact, states of consciousness not only stretch and contract; they *overlap*, in ways that would baffle a timekeeper with a stopwatch. The distinction that truly matters in connection with the mind corresponds to the one between real duration and time as measured scientifically: it's the distinction between the *deep self* (*moi profond* in French, rendered "deep self" by the English translator) and the *superficial self.* The deep self is *me*, an independent being with his own internal laws and characteristics. The social self lives in a world of established convention, with standardized measurements that allow a large community of individuals to function efficiently.

And so Bergson set up a long list of pairs of terms, one term in each pair correlated with the deep self and real duration, the other with the superficial self and measured time: intensity vs. extensity, quality vs. quantity, continuity vs. discontinuity (of mental states), internal vs. external, private vs. practical, and, perhaps most important, freedom vs. unfreedom. For the deep self is the inner core of the person and is therefore a realm of freedom. If Bergson placed one aim above all others, it was to rescue the individual—together with the individual's prized freedom of will—from the spirit-destroying ravages of nineteenth-century scientific materialism and determinism.

That's the gist of *Time and Free Will*. In *Matter and Memory*, Bergson took on the neurophysiologists. Think about the date: 1896. As I mentioned earlier, by that year science had made a set of colossal strides and, with its understanding of the brain and nervous system, was threatening to reduce all human mental life to physiology—and even the public knew it. Bergson, ever the diligent and careful student, did his homework. Let no one suspect that the philosopher of real duration and the deep self was merely ranting. He had read and understood the work of the major brain scientists precisely so that he could defeat them all the more decisively. Even a pre-psychoanalytic Freud (without first name) is mentioned in *Matter and Memory* as the author of a thoroughly neurophysiological, brain-centered, therefore blinkered work on aphasia.[26]

"Memory" really means "mind"—well, mind in the sense of the most essential inner sphere in which our thoughts and experiences live. Bergson used "memory" in the title, instead of "mind," because he believed our memory preserves *everything* in our past and is therefore the core of our nonphysical self. But the main point was to stake a claim for mind over brain. Anyone who bought the book and looked no farther than the table of contents could see in the titles of chapters 2 and 3 what Bergson was getting at: "Of the Recognition of Images. Memory and Brain" (chapter 2) and "Of the Survival of Images. Memory and Mind" (*l'esprit* in French) (chapter 3). Never denying that the brain plays a role in our experience of the world, Bergson was intent once again on retaining a sacred province of the self that is independent of it. So he offered not only the distinction between brain and mind but an additional distinction as well: between what the English translators rendered as "intellect" (*entendement* in French, more accurately rendered as "understanding") and "intuition." Intellect is responsible for making sharp distinctions between things, decomposing and recomposing the data of experience according to its own artificial habits and laws. Intuition, on the other hand, gives us pure experience as the "undivided continuity" that it really is.[27]

And then there was *Creative Evolution*, which I spoke about in chapter 2, "The Biological Self." The intellect vs. intuition distinction played a major role in that book as did one of the phrases for which Bergson became most famous: *élan vital* in French, "vital impulse" in the published English translation. Bergson sought to show in his revisionist evolutionary work that evolution was neither a form of chaos happily resulting in what looks to us like order nor the result of a purposeful intelligent design. The actual results are enough to show how absurd the second idea is. Instead, there is "a force which is evolving throughout the organized world." It is "a limited force which is always seeking to transcend itself and always remains inadequate to the work it would fain produce." So do we get to think of the evolutionary force as a kind of intelligence or not? It's hard to say, but it's just as hard to resist the power of Bergson's words, especially when rendered into the seductively high-style English that his translator used: "Life in general is mobility itself; particular manifestations of life accept this mobility reluctantly, and constantly lag behind. It is always going ahead; they want to mark time. Evolution in general would fain go on in a straight line; each special evolution is a kind of circle. Like eddies of dust raised by the wind as it passes, the living turn upon themselves, borne up by the great blast of life."[28]

Guess why American publishers and commentators thought their readers would devour all this. First, even if you never actually read any of these books but just read *about* them and their author, you'd realize that Bergson possessed a mesmerizing writing and speaking style. Words such as "limpid," "lucid," and "incisive" became mandatory for characterizing the philosopher's prose. Again and again you'd read descriptions of the lectures he was giving in Paris, where members of the public would throng the hall at the Collège de France, pushing and shoving for seats, and Professor Bergson would transfix them with his "intense and burning" eyes.[29] James Gibbons Huneker, that great American importer and translator of European culture—*all* culture, from dance to music to visual art to literature to philosophy—attended Bergson's lectures in Paris and offered his countrymen a portrait of the spellbinding speaker—a portrait that was entirely typical for the era:

> He is bald, with a beaver-like brow, the brow of a builder born; his nose is slightly predaceous, his features cameo-like, his deep-set eyes are dark, the eyes of an oracle, though there is nothing of the pontifical in his attitude toward his audience. . . . And as Bergson's closely linked argument flowed on, the image of his rushing river of apperception arose in my mind. What a wealth of examples! And what a picture-maker! What magic there is in these phrases.[30]

But of course the content was what sold. Given the popularity of the New Psychology and what apparently lay at the root of that popularity, it's no big surprise that Bergsonism caught on so spectacularly. The writer who reviewed the three translations for the *New York Times* in August 1911 managed to capture most of the ideas that Americans would find so appealing. We read there about freedom, hope, promise, the creative nature of evolution, intuition over intellect, the failure of science to explain things spiritual.[31] The author of the big spread in the Sunday Magazine that appeared the following week added to the list Bergson's "vital impetus," his opposition to materialism, and the possible future conquest of death as suggested in *Creative Evolution.*

The Columbia University lectures gave Bergson a living forum in the United States to display his oratorical skills and propagate his ideas. Because only a small number of people were privileged to find seats in the auditorium, it would be wrong to say that the lectures themselves had a great impact, unless we had a way of measuring how many additional people the lucky audience members spoke to afterwards about what they'd heard. But we do have an idea of what Professor Bergson said on some of those evenings, and we have quite a few published reports. By a great stroke of good fortune, Bergson left behind seven pages of notes he made for his presentations. They are kept in the Columbia University Archives. In his neat, highly legible handwriting, he set down an outline for six lectures in English and six in French. His English, of course, was perfect.

The titles of the two series themselves were tailor-made to disseminate the new view of mind. The English series was called "The Method of Philosophy," but it was subtitled (in Bergson's notes) "Outline of a Theory of Knowledge." The French series was titled "Spiritualité et Liberté (Spirituality and Freedom). If the lectures even roughly followed what Bergson wrote down, then members of the audience on those evenings got to hear about lots of fairly technical philosophical issues. But they also heard about (at least some of) these topics: "Need to return to intuition, but to expand it." "Real duration." "Capital importance of the problem of *mind*." "Relation of this problem to that of *freedom*." "The relation of mind to body." "To what extent does a mental act depend on a cerebral act?"[32] "The brain is not a material substrate upon which mind depends for its existence," Bergson is reported to have said during one of the English lectures.[33] The *Times* kept up with the series: scarcely a day went by during the three-week visit when the newspaper did not run at least a brief article or an ad. "Bergson Stands by Will," New Yorkers read on February 5. "Believes in Intuition," they read the following day. "Human Will Makes Energy," they read on February 11.[34]

What about the human mind specifically? What Bergson had to say was really quite different from what you'd find in the New Psychology or Freud. Bergson's "deep" self is no netherworld of buried drives, guilty passions, and harmful memories. It's the essence of *me*, the sanctuary where the self follows its own unique laws in accordance with the precious gift of freedom. Commentator after commentator was drawn to the conquest-of-death passage in *Creative Evolution*, not only because of the optimistic promise of immortality but because the passage distilled Bergson's philosophy for the lay reader down to its core ideas about the mind: intellect vs. intuition, life vs. sterile science.

To appreciate just how very opposite Bergson's view was to that of Helmholtz and other neurophysiologists, consider that both featured a self that was in some way self-contained and closed off to the outside world: Helmholtz's nerve-apparatus and Bergson's deep self. The crucial difference is that Helmholtz's self boasts a foundation in science, operates according to laws that are presumably universal, and above all is *networked*. Bergson's inner self resists scientific explanation, operates according to laws that are entirely its own, and is autonomous. As we'll see in the next chapter, there *is* a network in Bergson's worldview, one with a scientific foundation, but it's one that links the self with the outside world, with the result that the opposition to the neurophysiologists is complete: their self is networked internally but not externally; Bergson's is networked externally but not internally.

So here was the counterforce: Bergson, waging his valiant struggle. And yet . . . to speak structurally, there was a similarity between Bergson's views and those of the New Psychologists that must have been sufficiently striking that the American public just might have overlooked the differences—for a short time. As it was revealed to the American reading public, Bergsonism, just like the New Psychology and just like the theories of "Dr. Sigmund Freud, of Vienna," was there to overthrow nerve-and-brain physiology as a form of pessimistic, deterministic, soul- and spirit-denying materialism, in favor of the lusty assertion of mind, spirit, intuition, the inner self, the unconscious, and other qualities unsusceptible of physical localization in the brain. Who cared if the lower part of the mind in Bergson's formulation was the land of real duration and not the land of repressed sexual drives, as long as there *was* a lower part and an upper part and as long as "lower" and "upper" had purely metaphorical, not spatial meanings? But soon Freud offered something much more appealing in the nether realm that *he* envisioned—at least, as that realm was interpreted for the general public.

The Independent Mind, Part III. A Viennese Doctor Seduces Some Americans into Rejecting Brains and Nerves for Sex, Unconscious Drives, and the Externally Networked Self

In 1927, a relatively young E. E. Cummings (or e. e. cummings), already known as a poet, wrote a play, titled *Him*. The following year it ran in New York for twenty-seven performances, to full houses. Reaction from critics was mixed, to put it kindly. Even today, after more than a century's worth of weird, "experimental" plays like this one, it's hard to describe what *Him* is. For now, it's enough to say that it presents a more-than-three-hour, often bewildering hodge-podge of scenes, spun from the imagination of the central character (Him, a playwright) and often drawn from the world of burlesque and urban street life. In one ("*Fifth Avenue—midnight*"), an Englishman enters the stage bearing on his back a large trunk marked FRAGILE. Confronting him is a plainclothesman, who speaks in the dialect of lower-class, ethnic New York (Irish, no doubt). The plainclothesman wants to know what's in the trunk. The Englishman has no idea what the plainclothesman is talking about. The audience then hears this dialogue:

> PLAINCLOTHESMAN: (*Menacingly*): Dat ain uh trunk?
>
> ENGLISHMAN: I should say not. Dear, dear no. The very idea—ha-ha-ha.
>
> PLAINCLOTHESMAN: Wal if dat ain uh trunk, will youse kinely tell me wut dat is?
>
> ENGLISHMAN: (*To himself*):—A Trunk! That's really not half bad, you know. (*To the* PLAINCLOTHESMAN) But since you ask me, I don't mind telling you.
>
> PLAINCLOTHESMAN: Wal, wut is it?
>
> ENGLISHMAN: Why, that's my unconscious.
>
> PLAINCLOTHESMAN (*Hand at ear*): Yuh wut?
>
> ENGLISHMAN: My unconscious, old egg. Don't pretend you haven't heard of them in America.—Why, my dear boy, I was given to understand that a large percentage of them originated in the States: if I'm not mistaken, the one I've got is made hereabouts, in Detroit or some where like that.
>
> PLAINCLOTHESMAN: Nevuh mine ware it wus made; wuts in it?
>
> ENGLISHMAN: In it? (*He utters a profound sigh*) Ah—if I only knew.

The plainclothesman orders the Englishman to drop the trunk. There's a noise from inside it, as of shattering glass. The plainclothesman opens it, looks inside, recoils in horror, and falls down dead. A policeman rushes in to see what the commotion is all about. He too looks inside the trunk and falls lifeless to the ground.[35]

Very, very funny. Brooks Atkinson, the *Times* theatre critic (signing himself in those days as "J. Brooks Atkinson"), didn't like *Him*. He was on to Cummings's jokes: "In the printed text as well as in the performance the irony and satire are more mannered than apposite—rather hackneyed in their omniscient flings at spinsters, medicine men, victims of Freudianism, capitalists and the public, rather mannered in the facetious glibness of the mad dialogue."[36] So it seems that by 1928 references to "victims of Freudianism" were hackneyed.

No surprise. Despite anemic sales of his books in English translation before 1920, Freud acquired a serious reputation in the United States shortly after Bergson began to acquire his.[37] Of course, Freud's name never went away; Bergson's did. And yet the fates of Freud and Bergson in this country were yoked together. In August of 1913, J. B. (John Barrett) Kerfoot wrote an article for his recurring column "The Latest Books" in *Life* magazine (in this instance and a few others jocularly presented as "Ye Latest Books"). Here's how Kerfoot began:

> Once in a blue moon (as when Bergson's "Creative Evolution" came out in English two years ago) a book written for the specialist or addressed to the expert catches the attention of a fortuitously waiting public and blazes into a sort of esoteric popularity. These books invariably turn out to have appeared at a "psychological moment"—to have happened along just in time either to focus the floating curiosities or to crystallize the suspended judgments of the popular mind. And while psychological moments are unpredictable affairs, one can not but imagine on looking up at the end of the new English version of Professor Sigmund Freud's "The Interpretation of Dreams" (Macmillan. $4.00) that a bluish tinge is once more discernible on the lunar disk. It seems quite on the cards that before snow flies "The Interpretation of Dreams" may be found at the head of weekly lists of non-fiction demands in such scattered literary centres as Montclair, New Jersey; and Montezuma, New Mexico.[38]

This was quite an extravagant prediction, anticipating the perspective of the classic Saul Steinberg *New Yorker* cover from 1976. New Mexico had entered the union only a little over a year before Kerfoot's article appeared, so if they were going to be reading Freud *there* of all places, then Freud's reputation would surely be secure all over the country.

August 1913 seems to have been some sort of marker for the emergence of Dr. Freud into the public imagination. At least you'd think so, to judge from what newspapers and magazine editors were offering their readers that month. It's the month that Arthur B. Reeve's "The Dream Doctor" came out in *Cosmopolitan*. I mentioned the story in "Sex O'Clock in America" (chapter 3) because of the fictional Professor Kennedy's reference to sex as "one of the strongest of human impulses." In the same scene, Kennedy also outlined for his listeners Freud's theory of dreams, using passages that Reeve stole from *New York Times* articles. Those articles quoted a book by Columbia University's A. A. Brill (whose translation of *The Interpretation of Dreams* had recently appeared). But despite all his literary thievery, Reeve did a skillful job of concisely capturing the essence of Freudian psychology—at least the psychology of dreams—for a popular audience. Immediately after the sentence (plagiarized from Brill, via the *New York Times*) about the dream as something other than "an absurd and senseless jumble," Professor Kennedy says this: "It is as though we had two streams of thought, one of which we allow to flow freely, the other of which we are constantly repressing, pushing back into the subconscious, or unconscious. . . . But the resistances, the psychic censors of our ideas, are always active, except in sleep. Then the repressed material comes to the surface. But the resistances never entirely lose their power, and the dream shows the material distorted. Seldom does one recognize his own repressed thoughts or unattained wishes. The dream really is the guardian of sleep to satisfy the activity of the unconscious and repressed mental processes that would otherwise disturb sleep by keeping the censor busy."[39]

Anyone who has seriously studied Freud, even someone resolutely hostile to his ideas, knows that there's a great deal more to those ideas than this. Not that there's any sound reason to reproach the Reeves and the Kerfoots—they never pretended to be doing anything more than popularizing in the first place. But by 1913, it seems clear that, of all the ideas a thorough American student might find in the works of Freud published in English translation to that date, a very few had shaken out, thanks to the popular press, to constitute "Freudism" (as it was usually called in those days) in the eyes of ordinary people. Here they are: (1) we have a conscious life and a hidden, unconscious one; (2) the unconscious one harbors primitive impulses (Brill, to his credit, used "impulse," rather than the unfortunate and highly misleading "instinct" adopted by subsequent translators) in addition to memories that get buried, or "repressed"; (3) the contents of the unconscious reveal themselves indirectly via dreams, mistakes, and neuroses; (4) impulses buried in the unconscious tend overwhelmingly to be sexual in nature; (5) the sex impulse is born in us in infancy and remains all-powerful throughout our lives; (6) underlying everything else is the belief that none of these features can be localized in the brain or nervous system and that the mind is an independent entity. Reduced to its utmost simplicity, as in Professor Kennedy's presentation, "Freudism" is this: (1) our minds are split into a conscious realm and an unconscious realm, and (2) sex is hugely important.

The popular understanding could conceivably have turned out differently—that is, it could have been closer to what Freud himself had actually been saying. Let's go back a few years. Before 1909, if you were not a professional academic specialist and didn't read German, there's almost no chance you'd ever even heard of Freud. In the initial months after the Clark University conference, in September of 1909, you'd probably have encountered Freud's name only if you were such a specialist.

In April of 1910, the *American Journal of Psychology* published the lectures Freud had given at Clark. At the conference, Freud spoke in German, reportedly without notes, so it was impossible for a reader of the journal to know precisely what he said. But you could read in a footnote that the lectures were translated by Harry W. Chase, a Clark University fellow in psychology, and revised by Freud himself. Whether or not Freud said exactly what you read in the journal, this was just about your only source of his ideas, unless you had attended the conference. According to Chase, Freud had told the story of how psychoanalysis emerged from the discoveries he had made with Josef Breuer in the 1880s and early 1890s. He spoke of resistance, repression, wishes, sublimation, wit (as in *Wit and Its Relation to the Unconscious*, as the book would first be translated into English in 1916), dreams, and sex—especially the theory of childhood sexuality.[40]

Freud certainly referred to the distinction between consciousness and the unconscious, but he did so almost in passing, by way of explaining his techniques for retrieving disturbing memories from his patients. Nowhere did he think to state that this distinction was a cornerstone of the entire edifice of psychoanalysis. Maybe he thought it was obvious to his audience. After all, *The Interpretation of Dreams* (first published in German in 1899, though bearing the date 1900) and *Three Contributions to the Sexual Theory* (first published in German in 1905 and translated into English under this title in 1910) were both shot through with the distinction, even though neither work contained an explicit statement that it was a fundamental principle.

Writers in the popular press soon began to take up the topic of Freud and psychoanalysis, and they quickly settled on a short list of his positions and a greatly simplified view of his system. In April 1911, the same Harry W. Chase, now on the faculty at the University of North Carolina, decided to present Freud's ideas to the public in an article he wrote for *Popular Science Monthly*, titled "Freud's Theories of the Unconscious." Chase didn't mention a single work by Freud, so it's difficult to say exactly what he was using as the basis for his remarks on the theories (plural) of the unconscious. In fact, he wrote oddly about two layers *of the unconscious* in Freud's theory: a lower layer and one that serves as a "vestibule to consciousness." The lower one he termed the "lowest dark chamber of the soul"; it's where all the nastiest thoughts and impulses from childhood live, hidden from ordinary view. He spoke of dreams and of the "censor" (this term appears dozens of times in *The Interpretation of Dreams*) that stands guard at the threshold of consciousness, admitting only those thoughts and impulses that have been transformed into sufficiently innocuous substitutes for themselves. He wrote of the sex lives of children. And, in a twist that sets him apart from many other commentators, Chase offered the reflection that in Freud's theories we can define the true relation between the unconscious and consciousness by saying that the *unconscious*, not consciousness, is "the most real part of ourselves," that "it is in the depths below consciousness that true reality is found."[41]

It's unlikely that many people read this article. But a month after it appeared, *Current Literature* brought out a summary of it, rich with quotations from the original, under the dramatic title "Freud's Discovery of the Lowest Chamber of the Soul." There readers learned about the existence of an unconscious, about the division of that unconscious into two layers, and about sex, repression, and dreams.[42] What they almost certainly did not catch, however, was a distinct shift in emphasis away from Chase's initial report of the Clark conference as well as from what Freud himself had actually written in his own books. Anyone familiar with Freud's theories would know that the contents of the unconscious fall into two broad categories: (1) primitive drives ("instincts," as later English translators rendered it) that are present from birth and (2) experiential material that's driven into the unconscious because of the threat it presents to conscious life. Repression can refer to either (1) the process of driving threatening experiential material into the unconscious or (2) the process of holding existing primitive drives in check. At the conference, as Chase reported, Freud had spoken at some length about repression, but he used the term almost exclusively to refer to *experiential* material. In fact, Freud's discussion of primitive drives was confined almost entirely to his lecture on sexual life.

But to read Chase's account as presented in the popular press, you'd think that the unconscious was exclusively a realm of primitive desire, above all *sexual* desire. You'd think that repression was a force designed only to hold such desire in abeyance. The two-tiered unconscious—something Chase appears to have invented—serves the purpose of containing what's inside, not driving in something from outside. Here's how *Current Literature*'s writer summarized Chase's own summary of Freud:

> All the unethical acts and unsocial ways of thought of the child, repugnant to us to-day, still exist in the lowest dark chamber of the soul, not strong enough

> to break out into action, but alive. It is the penalty which we pay for our civilization that it imposes standards of thought which are foreign to the deepest tendencies in us, modes of life of the cave man and of the ages before civilization which have left their marks upon the soul forever. For all of us there has been some strain in adjusting to its requirements, resulting in an abandonment after a struggle of the old racial ways and the substitution of newer and more ethical modes of action. But a part of our personality still lives in the troglodyte stage. We may not allow this part expression. We may not even be conscious that it still exists. Yet it lives and works below the threshold, just as the remembrance of the death of her mother affects a girl although consciously it has lapsed.[43]

So, by 1913, two years later, editors clearly felt safe betting that their readers knew about Freud and that the catchwords were "unconscious" and "sex." August was the month when Reeve's "Dream Doctor" came out in *Cosmopolitan* and Kerfoot's article came out in *Life*. It's also the month when *Current Opinion*, renamed in that year from *Current Literature*, published "Sex O'Clock in America." That article contained no reference to Freud, but the magazine's writers must have believed that the founder of psychoanalysis either had played some role in thrusting sex into the spotlight or simply was one important manifestation of the obsession.

No one would ever dispute that sexual drives play a hugely important role in Freud's theories, nor would anyone dispute the centrality of the conscious-unconscious distinction. The question is why popular writers continually emphasized primitive drives and rarely mentioned the repression of experiences from post-infantile life. After all, you don't need to read very far in Freud's most basic works to discover his belief in the effect that repressed memories can have on behavior and conscious life. In fact, when Freud speaks of actual patients he treated, especially those that he allegedly cured, he is virtually always speaking of traumatic life experiences whose memory has been repressed and that, through analysis, need to be uncovered. Yet little of this was mentioned in the popular press during the early days of Freud's notoriety in the United States.

It's impossible to know what was on the minds of those who wrote about Freud for the popular press, and it seems unlikely that any of them deliberately decided to conceal a crucial dimension of his thought. Whatever they were thinking, it seems very much as though they were responding to trends that were already present among members of the reading public. In an era already obsessed with sex, writers and editors were aware that "sex sells" and that readers were likely to buy magazines and newspapers that contained articles on the subject.

In addition, respected researchers had demonstrated the existence of a set of impulses that were primitive and common to all mankind. Chase's "struggle of the old racial ways" is especially revealing, because (as we'll see in chapter 8) "racial" suggested *hereditary* (even if the reference was not to a specific race), so that "old racial" (together with "troglodyte stage") suggested a biologically explicable, evolutionary heritage common to all humankind. Here was yet another force, brought to light by the latest science, that binds us to our fellows, creating a universal network. Primitivity meant two things: (1) I'm connected to my own childhood and therefore to all childhood, and (2) if I regard myself as a member of an "advanced" race, I'm connected to *all* individuals of *all* races, even those that then-contemporary science has shown to be "primitive," genetically inferior to me. (I'll speak of this in chapter 8.)

In June 1914, just weeks before the world's attention would be sharply diverted by events of an entirely different order, *Current Opinion* ran an article called "How Psycho-Analysis has Obsessed the World with Sex." It was a report on a reaction against Freudianism from the camp of the neurophysiologists. The *British Medical Journal* had just published an assault on Freud's exaggerated emphasis on sex. As *Current Opinion* reported it, the argument against Freud was based on the physiology of the nervous system and what appeared to be just plain common sense. Curiously, the actual article in the *British Medical Journal* (unsigned) took aim precisely at the two cornerstone concepts of Freudianism as presented to the ordinary reading public in the popular press: (1) conscious vs. unconscious and (2) sex. The central complaint was that Freud and his followers really had no solid proof of much of anything. The author appeared to believe that claims about behavior and the mind needed to be based on the physiology of the nervous system. Freud and his followers had proposed theories based on almost nothing substantial, and ordinary, empirical observation would yield the conclusion that life is something more than "one long sexual pursuit," as Freud is alleged to have claimed.[44] The article in *Current Opinion* focused exclusively on the topic of sex. No doubt the editors, having appealed to their readers' salacious imaginations a year earlier with "Sex O'Clock," felt they could attract readers by reducing Freudianism to the assertion that "life is one long sex-pursuit."[45]

And yet, possibly without knowing it, the editors were pointing to a divide in the field of psychology that turns out to be highly characteristic of the era both inside and outside that field. Neurophysiology gave us the internally networked psychological self, a self solidly grounded in the internally networked biological self. Naturally the field needed to investigate the self as it existed in a world of external forces, and not every investigator was moved to indulge in idealist philosophical speculations of the sort we find in Helmholtz. But the Helmholtz–Ramón y Cajal–Sherrington model was essentially a self-contained one. Stimuli (real or not) triggered responses, to be sure, but investigators studied responses and other activity *within* the network. Functional psychology in general and psychoanalysis in particular, as presented to the public, gave us the *externally* networked self. With a flagging interest in both brain localization and the physiology of the nervous system, practitioners of the New Psychology could focus on an immaterial mind that bore immaterial qualities connecting every individual with that individual's past, with all other individuals, and with the archaic past of the entire species, no matter how vaguely this past was described. Before long, Carl Jung would introduce the notions of primitive archetypes and a collective unconscious. Talk about a network!

Henri Bergson fits into this picture only insofar as he focused attention on a division between an outer and an inner self. The inner self he envisioned is not an externally networked one. But, perhaps despite himself, he built one of the most powerful cases in the era for a self that, like it or not (and Bergson didn't like it) is completely trapped in a virtually all-encompassing external network. That's the subject of the next chapter.

PART II: THE NEW PHYSICAL WORLD

5 The Network of Spatialized Time

IF YOU WERE an educated American in the 1880s and 1890s, it's very unlikely you made it your business to follow the latest publications in French academic philosophy. On the extremely slim chance that you did, however, you would have noticed something remarkable that required you to consult an encyclopedia or, if you'd had a good classical education, to reach back into the memory nooks of your boarding school or university years. Especially between the mid-1880s and the mid-1890s, there was an explosion of books and articles about "Zénon d'Élée," or Zeno of Elea.[1]

Who was Zeno of Elea? (Elea is today known as Velia, in the Campania region of southern Italy.) It's a good question, because there appears to be no solid proof this man even existed. We know about Zeno because he appears as a character in Plato's *Parmenides* and because Aristotle discussed him at some length in the *Physics*. On the basis of what Plato reports in the *Parmenides*, we can infer that if there was a Zeno he was probably born sometime early in the fifth century BCE. Whoever Zeno of Elea really was, whatever he really wrote, and whether or not he ever existed, he's come down to us as someone who loved to think contradictory thoughts, and primarily as the author of four famous paradoxes, often called Zeno's Paradoxes of Motion. It's been customary over the years to dress up the paradoxes slightly in language that conforms to the state of knowledge in the period in which they're being presented. At one point, they even received titles.

Here, in my own language, is a short version of the first three paradoxes. The fourth one is discussed less often than these, so I won't present it here.

1. "The Dichotomy": You can never reach any destination, because you always have to cover half the distance between where you are right now and the destination, then half of the half that remains, then half of *that* half, and so on. No matter how many halves you cross, there will always be an infinite number of halves left to cross.

2. "Achilles": This is the most famous, because it comes as a nice story. Fleet-footed Achilles and a tortoise agree to compete in a footrace. Since Achilles is a much faster runner than the tortoise, he gives the tortoise a head start. Say Achilles runs exactly ten times as fast as the tortoise (note that this is not the way Aristotle, or presumably Zeno himself, told the story), and say the racecourse is anachronistically measured out in meters. Achilles gives the tortoise a 100-meter lead. By the time Achilles reaches the 100-meter mark, the tortoise has plodded ten meters ahead. By the time Achilles reaches that 110-meter mark, the tortoise has made it another meter beyond *that*, and so on. Achilles will never catch up with the tortoise.

3. "Arrow": An arrow, shot from a bow, will never go anywhere. That's because, if you mentally capture its position at any moment during its flight, it will be at rest in that position. If it's at rest, it can't move to the next position. Therefore it never moves. Therefore neither does anything else.

Countless philosophers and mathematicians have grappled with these thought-puzzles over the centuries. The terms of the discussion expanded, to include continuity, divisibility, limits, infinite summation, and much else. But no one ever lost sight of the basic concepts: time, space, and change—specifically change in the form of motion. It was largely a matter of emphasis and method. By the 1880s, mathematics had long since developed the concepts of limits and infinite summations, both of which would be required for an explanation of, if not a "solution" to, the Paradoxes of Motion. Almost all the commentaries from the era focus on continuity and divisibility. After all, in order for the paradox of Achilles to make sense on the face of it, we need to accept that the space the two competitors traverse may be subdivided into tenths an infinite number of times (regardless of how we answer the question whether Achilles actually catches up with the tortoise). If space is infinitely divisible, how can it also be continuous? The Dichotomy, the Achilles, and the Arrow all challenge, or at least raise, the notion of continuity in space—nothing new in this, since continuity and divisibility were primary topics for Aristotle in the section of the *Physics* that includes the references to Zeno. But because the central topic of the paradoxes is motion, commentators in the late nineteenth century, like Aristotle before them, knew that the concepts of continuity and divisibility had to do not only with space but with time as well. The big question was whether the two were in some way equivalent or parallel. French philosopher Charles Dunan addressed the equivalency issue at the end of *The Arguments of Zeno of Elea Against Movement* (1884): "In a given, finite time, the tortoise will have traversed a certain space; that Achilles in the same time will have been able to traverse the same space and, in addition, the space that separated him from the tortoise at the starting point—this is what, according to Aristotle, we are wrong to contest, provided that we admit, on the one hand, that motion can take place, in no matter what fashion, and, on the other hand, that time, like space, is indefinitely divisible."[2] Over the next couple of decades there were plenty of opinions about the parallelism of time and space and about how to interpret the paradoxes in light of that parallelism, but the issue was constantly present.

All this discussion would properly remain entombed in rows of bound journals in academic libraries were it not for a singularly dramatic event that forms part of the story—a part that managed to break free into the light, where the contemporary generation and future generations could see it. A very young Henri Bergson, having finished his studies at the École Normale Supérieure, was teaching at the Lycée Blaise Pascal in Clermont Ferrand (Auvergne region), while fishing around for a doctoral thesis topic. As he later told the story, he was standing at the chalkboard one day, presenting Zeno's paradoxes (or "sophisms," as he referred to them) to his young students, when he was struck by an insight that would essentially define his philosophical outlook for the remainder of his career. Up to this time, Bergson had been a faithful devotee of the mechanistic and deterministic science that was, as he put it, "the order of the day"—including what I've called the neurophysiological self.[3] His thoughts as he explained Zeno to his students brought him into the conversation that was just beginning in the French academic journals. What Bergson came up with was not a *solution* to the paradoxes in the conventional sense, but rather a sort of escape from them. He was convinced that the paradoxes were founded on an untenable assumption, namely that time and space are equivalent or "coextensive." He had no problem with the conception of *space* that implicitly underlies the paradoxes—that is, as something divisible into discrete, measurable units. The problem was the corresponding conception of *time*, because if time is divisible in the same way that space is, then *motion* becomes impossible. That's because time, when spatialized, breaks down into a sequence of mutually discrete moments that are necessarily stationary. If they're stationary, they're not continuous, and if they're not continuous, there can be no such thing as motion.

Bergson had found his thesis topic. He wrote up the core ideas from 1884 to 1886 and published the finished product in 1889. Its title was *Essay on the Immediate Data of Consciousness* (published in English translation as *Time and Free Will*), which I mentioned in chapter 4. Since this started out as a doctoral thesis, not as a popular book, Bergson spoke the language of academic philosophers—in part. His aim was to show that time cannot be thought of as space, that motion is something indivisible and continuous. Here's how he put it:

> On the one hand, in fact, we attribute to motion the very divisibility of the space that it traverses, forgetting that one can very well divide a thing but not an act, and, on the other hand, we accustom ourselves to projecting this act itself onto space, applying it to the entire line that the moving object traverses, in a word, solidifying it. . . . It is from this confusion of motion with the space traversed by the moving object, in our opinion, that the sophisms of the Eleatic [Zeno's] school are born, for the interval that separates the two points is infinitely divisible, and if motion were composed of parts like those of the interval itself, the interval would never be crossed. But the truth is that each of Achilles' steps is a simple, indivisible act, and, after a given number of these acts, Achilles will have passed the tortoise.[4]

So, time must be construed as continuous and indivisible, and therefore so must motion. Each step that Achilles takes must be seen as a simple, continuous arc unto itself, not as something that can be broken down into discrete, measurable units. When we break down time and motion into such units, we are treating them as if they were the same thing as space. They're not.

Whether or not you agree with these claims and whether or not you think they somehow resolve the difficulties that sneaky Zeno and his "Eleatic school" invented, they were Bergson's contribution to the scholarly debate about space, time, and motion. And from these claims the humble *lycée* instructor would elaborate the philosophy that eventually brought him such widespread renown in France and abroad. I'll return to that philosophy shortly.

Railroads and Standard Time

I can't think of a single work of scholarship that treats Bergson's moment of revelation and the subsequent emergence of his philosophy as anything but an event in a history, long or short, of thoughts and ideas. It's as if the story went something like this: Zeno's paradoxes had been around for over two thousand years; the field of mathematics had brought new methods and concepts to aid our understanding of those paradoxes; recent figures, major and minor, had continued to write about them; and so, in the intellectual climate that existed in France in the early 1880s, thanks in part to what was currently being taught at the École Normale Supérieure, Henri Bergson, reflecting on Zeno, came up with his own peculiar approach to the problems of space, time, and motion. Sure, he would never have come up with these ideas in complete isolation from the era and the circumstances in which he lived, but the era and the circumstances provided him exclusively with *ideas*. In this story, everything that happens in the world happens in books and universities.

But let's have a look at something that was going on at exactly the same time that Bergson had his revelation and wrote the *Essay*. Peter Galison told much of *this* story in *Einstein's Clocks, Poincaré's Maps: Empires of Time* (2003), an account of how two modern conceptions of time (Henri Poincaré's and Einstein's) developed in the late nineteenth and early twentieth centuries. A key episode in the story preceding the work of Poincaré and Einstein has to do with clocks and railroads. In fact, you can get a vivid sense of the story, as it unfolded in France, by looking at two articles (both mentioned by Galison) that serve as bookends to Bergson's own story. There's almost no chance that Bergson himself read either of them; in fact, in all likelihood very few members of the public read them, since they were published in industry trade journals.

The first was titled "Unification of Time in Major Cities by means of Electricity," and it was written by Antoine Breguet. A contemporary reader would have recognized the surname, as will many readers today. It's the name of a French watch company, founded in 1775 by Abraham-Louis Breguet. Breguet watches, affordable only by the very wealthy, were legendary in the nineteenth century. The pampered hero of Alexander Pushkin's *Eugene Onegin* (written 1823–31), for example, relies on his pocket Breguet, equipped with an alarm (almost unheard-of in the era), to keep track of his many social engagements. Antoine Breguet, who is not identified in the trade journal other than by name, was the great-grandson of Abraham-Louis. His father, Louis-François-Clément Breguet, ran the Breguet company for many years but was also a physicist with a number of patents for electrical inventions to his name—quite a few relating to the measurement of time. In the article, Antoine Breguet addresses the problem of synchronizing clocks in a major city, such as Paris. The discussion is highly technical, and, as his subtitle indicates, he believed electricity, with its ability to send signals that take an immeasurably (at least in 1881) short time to reach their destination, offered the solution.

What led this scion of the great chronometer manufacturing firm to weigh in on the issue of standard time? The probable answer is buried in the middle of his article: rivalry with Great Britain. Breguet mentioned that the British had devised a system for communicating time, measured at the Greenwich Observatory, as early as 1833, by means of a "time ball," which, visible from a great distance, would drop every day at an established time. In 1852, they had introduced an electrical mechanism to regulate the descent of the time ball. What Breguet did not mention, and what almost certainly was driving the concern in France over the issue of standardization, was that Great Britain had instituted uniform time for the entire country, major cities and urban areas, in 1848. It was the first country in the world to do so, and it used the time at the Greenwich Observatory as its standard.[5]

The second article, titled "The Unification of Time," was published in the French railroad trade journal in 1888. The author, M. W. de Nordling, gave a summary of the progress that had been made in recent years toward the goal of unification. He wrote that the spread of railroads had created the need. He mentioned that a kind of standard had existed in France since the previous year. The railroad system had adopted Paris mean time as its standard, though it remained true that cities other than Paris continued to reckon time in their own way. Railroad stations outside of Paris thus displayed at least two different times: Paris mean time and the local time, which could differ fairly substantially. De Nordling gave a brief history of "unification" and described the current state of affairs worldwide. Once again, Great Britain received credit for taking the lead in 1848, and de Nordling emphasized that that nation had adopted standard time not only for its railroads and its telegraph system but "for all public and private life."

In more recent history, however, it was the United States that had been in the news. There too the issue was dominated by railroads. De Nordling wrote that the country had adopted Standard Railroad Time in 1883 and then had hosted an international conference in October 1884, in Washington, D.C. The purpose of the conference was to encourage participating nations to adopt a single meridian as standard. The assembled nations, by a majority vote, had chosen Greenwich. De Nordling finished his article by describing what he called "the American system." It bore two components: (1) the use of a twenty-four hour clock for reckoning time and (2) the division of the world into twenty-four time zones.

Tucked away innocently in the middle of de Nordling's article are some details about the vote taken at the Washington conference. Three countries, he reported, voted against the choice of Greenwich. One of them was France.[6] In fact, the conference in Washington, called the Prime Meridian Conference, was the stage for considerable international brouhaha, precisely because of France. The intentions of the conveners were perfectly noble and commendable. Because of advances in transportation and communication, they thought, the moment had arrived to standardize time not just in individual nations but throughout the world. The Greenwich meridian seemed a good one to adopt as a standard since it had already informally served as one in the modern world for over a generation. But France would have none of it. The French delegates bickered endlessly over the issue of the meridian and, in the end, refused to support Greenwich. As Galison shows, the behavior of the French representatives amounted to little more than obstructionism, and France ended up looking backward and foolish. The campaign to unify time in the capital was a failure during the 1880s, and France held out till 1911, a full twenty-seven years, before joining the international community in recognizing the Greenwich Prime Meridian.[7]

I have no evidence that Henri Bergson was conscientiously following the story of time unification in Paris and the Prime Meridian Conference in Washington, D.C. But the entire affair shows that, for the ordinary French citizen, time had necessarily achieved a significance different from what it had had a few generations earlier. De Nordling put it beautifully and succinctly in his article for the railroad trade journal. He wrote about the impact of railroads: "But as the lines radiating out from Paris grew longer, they chased away before them the different local times, and today, over the entire extent of continental France, all the clocks in the railroad stations, large and small, show only Paris time."[8] With the possibility and the practical necessity of electronically synchronizing clocks hundreds of kilometers away from one another came a conception of time that was ineluctably tied to space—and in two senses: (1) standardized, synchronized time was measured out over great distances, and (2) time itself needed to be conceived as a linear medium, measurable, like space, in discrete units. And the basis of the *need* for this conception was the railroad *network*.

This conception is what Bergson had in mind when he wrote the *Essay on the Immediate Data of Consciousness*, and it appears to be what struck him that day when he was teaching his high school students about Zeno. The idea was to find a sanctuary from this spatialized conception of time and to give that sanctuary a more essential status than its alternative. And so "deep self" and "superficial self," "real duration" and spatialized time are bound together by an irresistible logic. Bergson uses the word "homogeneous" to describe spatialized time, because it rests on the assumption that time is a single substance that can be divided into equal units. It corresponds to the superficial self, the one that is obliged to live in the outside world, in conformity with the social conventions that rule the community. The inner self, by contrast, lives in conformity with its own laws, and the time in which it lives, "real duration," consists of states that overlap and interpenetrate. "In a word," he wrote (and since for the moment I'm interested more in what he wrote than in what Americans read when the book was later translated into English, I'm using my own translations here):

> our self touches the external world at its surface; our successive sensations, though they melt into one another, retain something of the reciprocal externality that objectively characterizes their causes [for example, a series of distinct noises that we hear]; and that is why our superficial psychological life unfolds in a homogeneous medium without this mode of representation's costing us any great effort. But the [purely] symbolic character of this representation becomes more and more striking as we penetrate more and more into the depths of consciousness: the internal self, the one that feels and grows passionate, the one that deliberates and decides, is a force whose states and modifications penetrate one another intimately and undergo a profound change as soon as we separate them one from another in order to unfold them in space. But since this deeper self forms one and the same person with the superficial self, the two necessarily appear to exist in the same duration.[9]

This is the new and bold element in Bergson's philosophy—what he stands for and urges. But more revealing is his description of the time and the self that he relegates to a lower status. They appear, innocently enough, to arise of necessity, simply as a function of our existence as social beings. In fact, the natural and necessary tendency to live at least partly outside, in a spatial world, is precisely what allows us to enjoy a social life in the first place. Bergson goes on at some length about this, and it's worth paying attention to the language he uses.

> But in addition, note well, the intuition of a homogeneous space is already a step in the direction of social life. Unlike us, animals no doubt do not

> represent [to themselves], apart from their sensations, an external world quite distinct from them that is the common property of all conscious beings. The tendency by virtue of which we imagine clearly this externality of things and this homogeneity of the medium in which these things exist is the same one that leads us to live in common with others and to speak. . . . Thus is formed a second self, which overlays the first one, a self whose existence possesses distinct moments, whose states detach themselves from one another and express themselves easily by means of words.[10]

It makes perfect sense to say, more or less literally, that social beings like us have two "selves," one of which lives as a member of a community while the other one lives privately, inside. An Elizabethan could very well speak of "the sessions of sweet silent thought" where he summoned up "remembrance of things past," referring to a vaguely understood inner world of thoughts, memories, and feelings. But would the Elizabethan have contrasted that sanctuary with a social world characterized by the "externality of things" and the "homogeneity of the medium in which these things exist?" To a culture that reckoned time always locally and almost exclusively by means of the sun and the chiming of the village church bells, the words that Bergson uses—characterizing a universal condition of human beings, in all eras, as the archetypal social animals—would have been incomprehensible. How could the word "homogeneity" in this context possibly mean anything except to significantly large numbers of people, dispersed over a large area, who are connected by a network (railroads, not to mention telegraphs) and who absolutely must manage their lives according to precisely synchronized timepieces—timepieces that of necessity measure time spatially?

So it took *railroad culture* to bring about the internal-self/external-self dichotomy in exactly the form that Bergson conceptualized it. The stakes are high in this culture: commerce suffers when important people miss trains; people die when two trains collide because the watch of the engineer on one train, as it roars around a blind curve, is several minutes behind the watch of the engineer on the other; a marriage founders because a hapless young man who couldn't afford the precision and reliability of a Breguet misses his return trip from an illicit, out-of-town assignation and arrives home hours late, without a plausible explanation for his wife. Sure, *real duration* and the *deep self* seduced thousands of French and American readers between 1889 and 1914. But let's be honest. Bergson's true contribution was to identify the hallmarks of the modern experience of time: its spatially conceived homogeneity as a medium and the synchronization of the means of measuring that medium.

Train Wrecks, Time Balls, and Mass-Produced Watches

Very few Americans would know about Bergson until more than a quarter-century after the ghost of Zeno paid him a visit at the chalkboard. By 1911, quite a few Americans, innocent pragmatists that they were, had long since discovered and internalized the conception of time that Bergson found so repellent—and without the siege mentality he fostered in confronting that conception. The story has a certain compelling logic to it: a need arises, technology steps in to fill the need, then official policies and popular attitudes follow. Naturally, you can't reduce the story to simple causal relations, since technologies develop out of more than just a single, immediate need, and popular attitudes are hard to measure. But at the very least there's an unmistakable cluster of need, technology, and attitudes whose story unfolds from the middle of the nineteenth century to the first decade or so of the twentieth. Key events in the story are the emergence and adoption of standard time, together with time zones, and the rise of widely available and affordable timepieces. The result is the temporally networked individual.

If you wanted to find an event that would at least symbolically serve as the reason for the eventual adoption of standard time in the United States, you could do worse than choose the horrific train collision that occurred on August 12, 1853, between the small towns of Valley Falls and Pawtucket, Rhode Island. Here is what apparently happened. A passenger train on the Providence & Worcester Railroad was traveling north, from Providence, Rhode Island, to Worcester, Massachusetts. Another P & W train was traveling south on the same track from Uxbridge, Massachusetts, to Providence. At Valley Falls and at Pawtucket there were turnouts, where a train would be switched off the main track to allow an oncoming train to pass. The southbound train, slightly behind schedule, was to remain on the Valley Falls turnout, while the Worcester-bound train passed the "Boston switch" between the two small towns. Instead, the conductor on the southbound train pressed the engineer to make for the Boston switch before the northbound train passed. The southbound train, traveling at a brisk pace (forty miles per hour by some estimates), didn't get there in time. The northbound train, traveling slowly on a blind curve, had already passed the Pawtucket turnout. The two trains collided on that curve, with gruesome consequences. Fourteen passengers were killed (fifteen by some accounts) and dozens injured. To add to the human drama, the "down" (southbound) train bore an excursion party of factory operatives from the town of Whitinsville,

Massachusetts, on their way to Providence, where they would have boarded a steamer to Newport, to watch a sailing regatta. Many of the dead and injured were from this group.

A coroner's inquest, complete with a jury, was held immediately after the crash. The chief culprit was determined to be the conductor of the down train, not only because he urged the engineer to make up time by racing to the Boston switch, but because his watch was wrong. And yet the jury also held company managers responsible "for not ascertaining that every conductor was provided with a suitable and correct watch to run their trains by."[11] So, clearly part of the problem was the down train conductor's irresponsible decision to flout company regulations in an attempt to gain time, apparently so the excursion party wouldn't miss its steamer in Providence. But had the conductor's watch been set correctly, then presumably he would have seen that beating the up train to the switch was not just risky but completely impossible. In addition, true time here meant Providence & Worcester Railroad time, as set in Providence. Since both trains were P & W, this should not have presented a problem; the issue was simply the inaccuracy of the timepieces controlled by the company and the failure to synchronize those timepieces. But it cannot have been lost on the public that, with roadbeds shared by companies setting their clocks to different standards, the risk of collision was always present.

The P & W wreck represented a crisis moment in American railroading. A quick glance at newspapers from the era when it occurred will show that collisions weighed heavily on the public's mind. If you read the account of the coroner's inquest for the P & W collision in the *New York Observer and Chronicle* on August 25, 1853, all you had to do was move your eyes to the right of the story, and in the neighboring column you'd see the small title "Railroad Slaughters." The entry listed the number of accidents nationwide, including numbers killed and wounded, for every month of that year up to the present. Totals by August: 65 accidents, 176 killed, 333 wounded.[12] If you were measuring casualties (the sum of deaths and injuries), the trend even for that year was definitely up, from 65 in January to 105 in August. It was the peak year for railroad accidents in the United States. The *Maine Farmer* titled its first article on the disaster "Another Terrible Railroad Collision." The editorial in the *New York Times* on the tragedy was titled "More Slaughter by Railroad."[13] "Another Railroad Accident/Collision/Disaster/Catastrophe/Tragedy" was used twelve times as an article title in the *New York Times* in 1853, and of course that's just under *that* title format. There were far more than twelve reports of railroad accidents that year.

Immediate remedies were imperative. The Rhode Island Railroad Commissioners and the state legislature saw to it that two types were implemented within a couple of months of the P & W crash, at least in Rhode Island. The late Ian R. Bartky told this story in an absorbing book about timekeeping in nineteenth-century America. The first remedy, Bartky explained, was an extensive revision of regulations governing the operating schedules of railroads. Time was the big issue here, but not the *measurement* of time. In fact, the idea was to take into account the difficulty of precise measurement and synchronization. Railroad companies would now be required to adjust their schedules so as to allow for such errors in timekeeping as had taken place in the August crash.

The second remedy *was* about the measurement of time, and it was simple. Conductors would now be required to carry accurate and reliable timepieces. An immediate result of the twin measures was the establishment of "standard time," not on the Providence & Worcester line but on the Boston & Providence Railroad. In a list of rules published by the superintendent of the Boston & Providence at the end of August 1853, just weeks after the P & W calamity, standard time was defined as "two minutes later than Bond & Son's clock, no. 17 Congress Street, Boston" (Wm. Bond & Son was a famous Boston chronometer firm), conductors would be required to check their watches against standard time according to a schedule, and they would further be required to submit their watches to Bond & Son for inspection. Bond & Son would be in charge of repairing and regulating the watches.[14]

As gruesome as it was, the P & W crash was only one incident in the intertwined history of American railroading and timekeeping and should not be construed as the cause of everything that followed. But it can be conveniently seen as a starting point for subsequent developments. It crystallized public fear of time-related railroad disasters, it directly led to a decline in such disasters, and it's easy to see how two subsequent episodes in the story emerge from (or simply after) it: (1) the move toward, first, standard national railroad time and, then, universal standard time and (2) the dramatic development of the watch business in the United States.

In the decades following the P & W crash, a host of new ideas and technical innovations made possible the adoption of Railroad Standard Time in 1883. This story has been told over and over, and its smaller details are not important here. Before any sort of reliable standard time could be instituted and widely accepted, there needed to be (1) an accurate means for measuring time, (2) a means for transmitting the accurately measured time, as close to instantaneously as possible, to numerous locations across the country, (3) general willingness to recognize the standard, and (4) division of the country into time zones, together with general acceptance of those time zones. What was needed was a network that was physical (wires for transmitting signals) and social (common recognition of the standard).

By the middle of the nineteenth century, it was clear that the most accurate measurement of time must come from observatories staffed with professional astronomers. There were a great many observatories in the United States capable of offering precision time measurement. The ones that rose to prominence were those that developed the ability to transmit time signals. The telegraph, introduced in 1844, was the obvious means for doing so, since it possessed the ability to send signals almost instantaneously. The first telegraphic distribution of time took place in Boston in 1851, when Bond & Son began providing signals, received from the Harvard College observatory, to any interested parties—primarily the railroads of New England. Starting in 1879, Samuel P. Langley, director of the Allegheny Observatory in Pittsburgh, began selling telegraphic time signals from his institution to such clients as jewelers in Pittsburgh and the Pennsylvania Railroad.

The best-known collaboration of the era was the one between Western Union and the U.S. Naval Observatory in Washington, D.C. In 1877, a time ball was built atop the telegraph company's New York office building, located in lower Manhattan, at the corner of Broadway and Dey Street. The "ball" was actually not a ball at all, though from a distance it looked like one. It was constructed of vertical, semicircular sheets of copper arranged around a central axis. Starting in January of 1878, the ball would drop at exactly noon six days a week (modern science still bowed to the Christian Sabbath, observing a day of rest on Sundays). Because the Western Union headquarters building was tall (for its era), because the ball was large, and because it was located near the harbor, it could be seen for many miles—by passengers and crew aboard ships entering the harbor, for example. When the ball dropped, you knew it was noon, because, after being hoisted (five minutes before noon) to the top of the twenty-three-foot pole on which it was mounted, it was released by an electronic signal sent from the Naval Observatory in Washington on the stroke of noon. (Technically, this meant that noon corresponded not to the moment when the ball hit its base, but to the *start* of its fall.) So people who saw the ball drop could set their watches by it and be assured that they were in possession of the most accurate noon—a noon bearing the scientific authority of the Naval Observatory and delayed only by the amount of time an electrical signal takes to course through a couple hundred miles of cable and the almost infinitesimal amount of time it takes for light to travel from the ball to the retinas of the eyeballs of the citizen or ship's captain.

Well, actually people were not always in possession of the most accurate noon. For one thing, before Railroad Standard Time came along in 1883, there was still no agreement in New York on what the correct time *was*, even among railroad companies. For another, the time ball was not always accurate, as New Yorkers knew if they happened to consult page eight of the *New York Times*. There, from October 30, 1877, until December 30, 1884, the reader could see the feature "Western Union Time Ball," which told whether or not, on the previous day (except when the previous day was a Sunday), the ball had dropped correctly. If it hadn't, the article reported by exactly how much it was slow or fast (to within a tenth of a second). The time ball survived a fire in the Western Union Building in 1890 and continued to drop, as the *Times* reported in 1910, even after the view of it was eclipsed by the many skyscrapers that had lately started to crowd around nearby.[15] It dropped for the last time in June of 1914, when Western Union moved to its new building a mile north, on Walker Street.

Luckily for New Yorkers, Macy's department store in Herald Square was ready to step into the breach. The Macy Time Star, positioned above the clock (still there today) over the store's Broadway entrance ("Manhattan has grown northward, until today the modern city's centre is Herald Square and the modern city's store—Macy's"), would now drop every day at noon, on a signal from the Naval Observatory, giving city passersby the opportunity to set their watches to the exact time.[16] The store entrance was not exactly visible for miles, as the ball on the Western Union Building had been; in fact it was visible at best from the front of the *New York Herald*'s headquarters across the street, on the other side of Broadway. But presumably by 1914, anyone desiring the precise time had options for finding it other than by traveling to Herald Square.

Railroad Standard Time introduced time zones to the United States. In 1883, William F. Allen, former train engineer and secretary of the General Time Convention (the association of American railways), proposed a division of North America into five time zones (including an Intercolonial one for eastern Canada), each one being cut through by a meridian based on the Greenwich

mean and each one having its boundaries determined by a combination of geographic, political, and commercial factors. A version of these zones was adopted as part of Railroad Standard Time. Borders of the zones changed over the years (for example, Michigan, Indiana, Ohio, and Georgia, now in the Eastern Standard Time Zone, were Central Time Zone states in Allen's plans), but the basic conception has remained unchanged to the present day.

The Prime Meridian Conference in 1884 included plenty of discussion of time zones, and it was closely followed and widely reported in American newspapers. The question is whether the public really took any notice. That's hard to say, though it makes sense that Americans would have taken far more notice of the adoption of Railroad Standard Time the year before. The Prime Meridian Conference had almost no practical effect on the United States, since its resolutions merely confirmed what the railroad companies had already done in November of 1883. There's some disagreement among historians about the impact of both Railroad Standard and the Prime Meridian Conference on the public. Michael O'Malley, in his history of American timekeeping, writes of the opposition that Railroad Standard Time provoked in certain states durin[illegible] the years after its enactment, but he notes that most states adopted the r[illegible] time willingly and without much fuss.[17] At the end of his book on ninete[illegible] century timekeeping, Ian Bartky claims that the adoption of stand[illegible] "passed almost unnoticed."[18]

That may be true, though the *traveling* public couldn't h[illegible] from the day Railroad Standard Time took effect, that waitin[illegible] stations now displayed only a single clock where earlier th[illegible] many. (The four faces of the famous clock in the waitin[illegible] Central Terminal all showed the same time, of course[illegible] members of the public didn't register their acknow[illegible] in conspicuous ways, it was because they simply— internalized its impact. Historians tell us, rig[illegible] written into federal law till 1918. What to m[illegible] long (thirty-five year) delay from the inf[illegible] railroads to the formally, legally impos[illegible] was caused by all that opposition fr[illegible]

Have a look at what happen[illegible] signed into law by President Wo[illegible] Time Act." You'd have to look [illegible] this name in the era. In fact, you'd h[illegible]

find evidence that the bill had anything to do with standard time at all. It was universally called the "Daylight Saving Bill (or Act)," for the simple reason that it also instituted daylight saving time. All the newspapers reported its progress, its enactment by Congress, and Wilson's signing it into law. And yet the only newspaper I've come across that mentioned anything about standard time was the *Washington Post*, and that's because it printed the text of the bill. That bill was indeed called "An act to save daylight and to provide standard time for the United States." It named Greenwich as the location of the Prime Meridian (without using this exact phrase) and identified and named this country's five time zones (including one for Alaska). But the article in which the text appeared was titled "Daylight Bill Sent to President."[19] To my mind, the only inference to be drawn here is that, by 1918, standard time was so ingrained in the popular mind that no one noticed or cared that a federal law had officially sanctioned it.

But not everyone lived near Macy's, a time ball, a railroad station, or an observatory. So how were ordinary people finally and completely pulled into the network of standardized time? The answer, of course, is personal timepieces. In order for standardization to work for everyone, timepieces needed to be (1) affordable, (2) widely available, and (3) reasonably accurate. The United States, in the second half of the nineteenth century, is where they came to be all three.

The story is dazzling in its own right, and no one has told it better than David S. Landes, the master historian who, late in his career, turned his attention to the history of clocks and watches. In the middle of the nineteenth century, say, at the time of the P & W crash, Switzerland dominated the world
market. In fact, it never ceased to dominate the *world* market. What changed in
he second half of the nineteenth century was that the American industry grew
ponentially and, within the United States, American-made watches overtook
ss imports as a share of the *national* market. While Switzerland continued
xport healthy numbers of watches to the United States, more Americans
buying watches than in the first half of the century, and after a certain
ore Americans were buying *American* watches than were buying Swiss
. It's because you could buy an American watch that, for all practical
, was as dependable as a Swiss one—but for far less money.
ade this possible was that the Americans figured out how to mass-
tches by means of a mechanized process. The key was *interchangeable*
mid-nineteenth century, this was a distinctly American concept
tly speaking, it did not originate in the United States). It had
ly been applied to musket manufacturing and had spread from

there to locks, clocks, and other goods. Watchmaking presented a particularly daunting challenge, because the parts that needed to be interchangeable were tiny and delicate, while at the same time, given the need for high levels of accuracy in the finished product, the "margin of tolerance" for error (a slightly defective gear-tooth can set back the entire mechanism by a train-crash-causing ten minutes per day) in individual parts was extremely narrow.[20]

Credit goes to Aaron Lufkin Dennison, a watchmaker from Brunswick, Maine, who had been inspired by the methods that the United States Armory used in the manufacture of guns. He decided to produce his watches using interchangeable parts made by machines. In 1850, together with another watchmaker and an investor, he founded the company that later came to be called the Waltham Watch Company. There were technical problems from the outset, and the company went bankrupt in 1857. The details of the problems are not important, but it was not till 1859 that the company actually started producing watches from its factory on the Charles River in Waltham, Massachusetts, just outside Boston. Two years later the Civil War started and briefly threatened to shut down operations. But the war turned out to be a tremendous boon to the company, which produced its "Ellery" model, the "soldier's watch." Production and profits soared. Between 1862 and 1865, the company's output went from 12,000 pieces per year to 72,000, while sales went from roughly $61,000, with earnings in the red, to over $838,000, with earnings at close to a half-million dollars. Output continued to grow, shrank back during the recession years of the 1890s, regained its former levels in 1901, reached a peak in 1907–8, and then, with hard financial times and management scandals in the 1920s, fell back again.[21]

The success of the company from the middle of the Civil War through World War I was staggering. In June of 1867, the *New York Times* brought out a lengthy celebratory article about the Waltham-based company, then known as the American Watch Company (it went through numerous name changes between 1850 and 1925). "What is the time?" the reporter began. "American, decidedly. Ten years ago it was Swiss, or English, or French. Now, ask your nearest live, progressive, patriotic neighbor. The watch he pulls out in reply is labeled, not 'Geneva,' nor 'Liverpool,' nor 'Versailles,' but 'Waltham, Massachusetts.'" The inspiration for the success of the Waltham plant was Eli Whitney and his reliance on "absolute uniformity in each detail," which, the reporter wrote, "has proved the *characteristic, distinctive American principle in manufactures.* We apply it to everything; comparatively, foreigners apply it to nothing." As a consequence, American watches were cheap and easy to repair. Each pivot, wrote the reporter, "is not only carefully fitted and adjusted in its place, but accurately *measured* by those miraculous machines, and a record made of its dimensions. So, when, in any part of the world, a pinion or jewel breaks, by sending the number of your watch to the manufacturers you receive through return mail a new wheel to replace the old, with absolute certainty that it will fit. And thus with any piece." And Waltham-produced watches were *accurate*, as evidenced by the circumstance that the Pennsylvania Central, New York Central, and "other leading railways" had adopted them as their standard.[22]

To the best of my knowledge, there are no statistics showing the percentage of the population that owned watches in the era after they became widely available. The United States continued to import plenty of watches from Europe. Some sixty American companies turned out watches from the mid-nineteenth to the mid-twentieth century. By one set of estimates (the one that Landes gives), the total American production for that period was between 300 and 400 million watches.[23] Establishing a number for per capita ownership would be difficult: the total production figure is only a crude estimate; if we wanted to know how many new timepieces appeared, we'd need to add to the American production in this period the number of watches imported (and deduct the number of American watches *exported*); we'd need to factor in watches already in existence at the beginning of the period we're examining; determining the number of watches *in circulation* at any given moment would require data on discarded watches; given that some two-thirds of the 300–400 million were cheap "dollar watches," the number of discards is probably quite high; and finally, we don't know how watches were *distributed* among members of the population (how many people owned more than one watch).

Still, the numbers are so high, it seems safe to infer that a very significant percentage of the population—certainly the adult population—owned personal timepieces. Here's an eloquent statistic from the middle of our period. In the Sears, Roebuck catalogue for 1897, fully twenty-one pages were devoted to watches (twenty-four, if you count the introductory, explanatory material), in a section titled "Watches Almost Given Away." That's more pages than for any other single item offered for sale that year. The runner-up was guns, at seventeen pages. Even such broad *categories* of goods as men's clothing (ten pages) received less space than watches. For all intents and purposes, *everyone* owned a watch.

The Temporally Networked Individual

So imagine yourself at the Bergson lecture in Havemeyer Hall on Thursday, February 6, 1913. If you're a gentleman, perhaps you're wearing a 14-karat, solid-gold Waltham, with a seven-jeweled movement and a sunk second dial (that is, a dial showing seconds, sunk beneath the surface of the main dial to allow the hour hand and minute hand to pass over it). If you value accuracy and punctuality, you regularly stop in at your jeweler's to have your watch set, or you pass by your jeweler's and set your own watch by the chronometer in his window. The jeweler owns a chronometer connected to the Naval Observatory in Washington, D.C. Since the Waltham is reputed to be highly accurate, then, between visits to the jeweler, you have every confidence you're "on time." If you're catching a train at the new Grand Central Terminal, then thanks to your Waltham you know how long it will take you to get there from home, and, on entering the colossal new waiting room, you can expect to find that the four-faced station clock (made by the Self-Winding Clock Co., Inc., New York, and connected to the Naval Observatory, of course), and your watch are off by no more than a few seconds—if at all.

In fact, here's an odd confluence in history. The Grand Central Terminal Building opened its doors officially at, not 12:00 midnight, not 12:02 a.m., but precisely 12:01 a.m. on February 2, 1913, to great fanfare. A display ad in the *New York Times* on that day showed the façade of the magnificent building. Over the central portal, you could clearly see a clock, surrounded by statues of Mercury, Hercules, and Minerva. In reality, however, there was neither clock nor statues. The image in the display ad was an artist's creation, not a photograph. This monument to "Progress, Mental and Physical Force"—but really to Time—was, amusingly, behind schedule, and the sculptural grouping would not be finished till the following year.[24] The irony could not be more complete: the tardy clock, atop an edifice representing the industry responsible for the very standard that made it possible to speak of a precise 12:01 a.m. opening, was being built in Paris by a French sculptor—two years after the sculptor's native land finally, grudgingly, adopted the internationally recognized meridian in Greenwich.

On the same day that the Grand Central Terminal opened, the *New York Times* moved its printing operations into a new annex building, a wonder of modern, lightning-fast communication technology (displaying "Speed, Efficiency, and Modernity"), on 43rd Street. The next day Henri Bergson gave his first lecture at Columbia. The February 3, 1913, edition of the *Times* was the first to be printed in the new facility. In the first five pages, it included a story about its own new building, a story about the newly opened railroad terminal (minus the French-made clock), and an announcement for a lecture that evening by France's great enemy of clock time.

That lecture was given in French. If you read the *Times* on Wednesday, February 5 (the day before the lecture you're attending), you saw that Bergson had spoken before a "record-breaking audience" on Monday and Tuesday.[25] So, there you are on Thursday evening for the first in the English series. Owing to that gold disk in your vest pocket, you're a walking network hub. The pocket watch links you through your jeweler, through the synchronized clocks in your place of business, through the clock above the Broadway entrance to Macy's (though not yet to the Time Star), to the Naval Observatory in Washington and from there to . . . what? A year earlier, prominent reformer and Presbyterian minister Charles H. Parkhurst, in an essay on the perennial conflict between standards and man's unregulated feelings, reported a conversation he had had with his jeweler. "Who is it at the Washington Observatory that makes it? Where does the Washington Observatory get it?" he asked. The answer: "Gets it from the sun; telephoned down from God; [the jeweler's chronometer] ticks then, indeed, not by fancy but by inspiration."[26]

God or no God, *it* came from a central, authoritative source, and it spoke through the millions of Walthams, Elgins, Hamiltons, and other makes, linking the individual owners of these devices with one another. And each mass-produced watch, with its fully interchangeable parts—with its own interchangeability, for that matter—is a network hub in its own right. The moment a pinion or jewel breaks, you have only to write to that factory on the Charles River. A replacement for the defective part will arrive in the mail, you'll leave the broken watch and the part with your jeweler in the morning, and by the time you come home from work, the Waltham will be waiting for you, wound and set, just like new.

Bergson's lectures at Havemeyer Hall are scheduled for 4:30—*everyone's* 4:30, not your or the professor's private 4:30. The Waltham allows you to establish typical times for your daily itinerary, and it also allows you to gauge your arrival at Columbia so there's ample time to find a seat by a universally recognized 4:30. In the English series, Bergson draws a sharp distinction between a common-sense, intuitive approach to experience and a scientific one. He speaks of the difference between time, spatially conceived, and duration, experienced personally. As Professor Wendell T. Bush, in his summary for the *Columbia Alumni News*, will report a few months later, Bergson "makes time a central feature of reality," but time understood, of course, as duration. In Bergson's view, Bush writes, "intuition concentrated upon immediate experience empirically, not theoretically, discovers that duration, novelty, and freedom are its characteristic marks."[27] Bergson speaks at Columbia of how both philosophy and common sense often confuse things that ought to be kept separate. "One must distinguish," he says, "between time and duration, between space and extension, among the diverse forms of the causal relation."[28]

And there we have it. Alone with your thoughts as you listen to the spellbinding words of Henri Bergson, finding the late afternoon lecture by turns more and less stimulating, feeling the passage of time by turns to be slow and quick, mingling memories and stray thoughts, overlappingly, with the present impressions you receive from the philosopher's ideas (Bergson actually speaks of this: "a force essentially free and essentially memory, a force whose very character is to pile up the past on the past like a rolling snowball, and at every instant of duration to organize, with this past, something new which is a real creation"), living in a private world with laws of its own, you are an autonomous inward realm. But you are networked to the outside, like the biological self and the neurophysiological self. As your mind wanders, you look up to the left of the speaker, high over the door, at the clock (made by the Self-Winding Clock Co., Inc., New York, just like the four-faced one in Grand Central Terminal). Inside your vest pocket is that little ticking machine. It has its own internally networked system. But then so does the machine in the handbag and pocket of every lady and gentleman sitting in Havemayer Hall with you this late February afternoon.

And what might that be ticking away—its delicate needles traversing a meticulously measured number of millimeters (or fractions of millimeters) along the circumference of a tiny, recessed circle every second, every minute—in the vest pocket of the man at the front of the hall? Perhaps an invisible Zeno has come back to haunt his doubting disciple in *this* classroom three decades after his previous visit, cocking an ear toward that pocket, mischievously reaching in to see what's inside, pulling out the strange contraption, inspecting it, figuring it out. What would he say? The needles *move*. They *get there*. There *is* motion. Over space. Embodying time. For everyone.

6 The Networked House and Home

IN THE EARLY 1900S, Section 7 of the Sunday *New York Times* was called "Resorts, Drama—Fashions." It was designed primarily for women readers. On a typical Sunday, you'd see scarcely a single image of a man in the ten pages or so that made up the section. The final three pages were explicitly addressed to women, covering fashion ("What the Well-Dressed Woman Is Wearing") and general topics ("Matters of Interest to Women"). On July 6, 1913, there was an article titled "The Woman Who Invented Scientific Housekeeping." The subject is Mrs. Christine Frederick, who, as the subtitle runs, "applied 'efficiency' methods to the everyday round of work in the home and showed that it could be systematized quite like work in an office or factory." According to the article, Mrs. Frederick, inspired by a conversation between her husband and a business associate, both of them efficiency experts, and a separate conversation between that business associate and herself, decided to apply the principles used in manufacturing to housekeeping. By standardizing household tasks, the homemaker could accomplish more and cause herself less strain than by using conventional approaches. The article's author speaks of a "changed attitude coming." "Economic necessity" has forced many women into the business world, where they are obliged to learn the efficiency methods of the modern workplace. The application of those methods to the domestic arena will allow homemaking "to take its honored place among occupations for women."

The photos accompanying the article showed Mrs. Frederick in her "Efficiency Kitchen," a kind of laboratory in which she perfected her time- and labor-saving techniques. One photo bore the caption, "A Kitchen Where Things Are 'Handy.'" If you looked closely, you saw that Mrs. Frederick had lined up her icebox, food preparation cabinet, stove, and serving table in that order, so that, in the preparation of a meal, the cook could move from the first to the last step with little retracing of steps. The serving table stood next to the door leading into the dining room. Another photo showed Mrs. Frederick at the sink, washing dishes. The sink had two faucets, obviously for hot and cold running water. In the photo that showed her at the serving table, Mrs. Frederick was standing, presumably because she was about to carry a dish into the dining room. In all other photos, she was sitting.[1]

A book by Mrs. Frederick, called *The New Housekeeping*, was due out in 1913, according to the article. In fact, the book, consisting of an expanded series of articles published in *Ladies' Home Journal*, came out in 1912. Mrs. Frederick chronicled the momentous changes that the American house and home had undergone over the past couple of generations. To begin with, there was a change that was primarily economic and secondarily social. It was fairly simple to describe. Mrs. Frederick began chapter 14 of *The New Housekeeping*, "The Homemaker's Relation to Business and Economics," like this:

> To-day, in Podunk, Mich., or Flagstaff, Ariz., the young men are wearing the same styles of collar and tie that are seen on Fifth Avenue, New York City. As some one has put it, "the country is now metropolitan from edge to edge." Due to this great fact (made possible largely by national periodicals serving as advertising mediums) we find the same kinds of goods being sold all over the country at the same time.
>
> Woman, as the "new homemaker," needs to understand this highly complex machinery of distribution which makes it possible for the Podunk youth and the New York youth to be wearing the same style collar on the same day; or for the woman in Tallahassee to be using the same peanut-butter, neckwear, and flatirons that are the last word in the metropolis.[2]

The following year, in an article published in *The American Review of Reviews*, Frederick captured the essence of the change and its impact on the American household: "The old home, which manufactured for all its needs within its own walls, demanded chiefly labor and manual skill. The modern home demands much less manual skill, but vastly more mental and spiritual qualities. The old-fashioned woman—no matter how attractive in romance—cannot compete with the requirements of to-day. She is only a housekeeper and her housekeeping is far below modern standards!"[3] The demand for mental and spiritual qualities arose because all the manufacturing activity was now happening outside the home, and it was up to the homemaker to find her way through the dizzying array of products and services that now came into the house.

Christine Frederick (1883–1970) was not the only one to notice the big change that the modern world of manufacturing had brought about, nor was she the first to notice the effect of that change specifically on the lives of women. Nowadays, to someone raised in the era of Betty Friedan and Gloria Steinem, it might come as a surprise to learn that many educated women at the time Frederick first appeared on the scene believed that their sex (as they called it then) had already undergone a tumultuous and irreversible transformation in the direction of equality with men. Writing in 1909 in *Harper's Bazaar*, Helen Louise Johnson, an author of cookbooks and a commentator on domestic issues, described the transformation as though it were established fact and common knowledge:

> Previous to the Civil War woman's place was in the home and in the main she could stay there. Whatever avenues of livelihood were open to her pertained to the home and, for the main part, were performed there. When that great struggle was over, leaving many of the wage-earners on the battlefield, women were forced into the industrial arena with little or no business training and less desire to cope with its difficulties. The practical knowledge of household administration, which had been the pride of the housewives of an earlier period, could not be passed on from mother to child because in many cases either mother or daughter was working elsewhere.

Mrs. Johnson stated too, as if it were a universally accepted truth, that the nineteenth century had brought "the great gift of equal educational opportunity to both men and women."[4] So, women had already won a colossal victory almost two generations earlier, questionable though the true value of that victory might have been. Christine Frederick reflected the ambivalence that some women of her era felt, when she wrote toward the end of her book that good housekeeping "is a fine antidote against the unnatural craving for 'careers.'"[5]

The unnamed author of the *New York Times* article about Christine Frederick mentioned a "changed attitude." The reference clearly was to the hope that American society would begin once again to respect what the new position of women had caused to fall into disrepute—namely housekeeping. But if we speak more broadly about attitude, it makes sense to say that a change was taking place about the very nature of a house (or other domicile) and about the meaning of home.

The Tentacular, Networked House

To get a sense of the tremendous changes occurring in the American residence, think of the Riverside Park neighborhood I described in the Preface, and imagine it, in 1913, transformed into an animated cartoon world and following the physical laws that apply in such a world. The enormous hand of a giant reaches down, grabs the top of, say, the classic Aqua Vista apartment building (completed in 1909 by the Paterno Brothers architectural firm and located on Riverside Drive just south of 119th Street) and starts to yank it out of the ground, as if it were a wine cork. The next shot shows the scene from the viewpoint of the giant in the sky. As he slowly uproots the building, we look at the surrounding landscape (we're way up high, of course, so we can see for miles) and notice that a number of features and structures are being moved—or swallowed into the earth beneath them. If we look about twenty-nine miles to the north, in Westchester County, the dam at the edge of the Croton Reservoir collapses, as the aqueduct that carries water to New York City is pulled southward by the force of the water pipes attached to the bottom of the Aqua Vista. Six miles to the north, in the Bronx, water rushes through the Jerome Park Reservoir, a way station between Croton and New York, as the aqueduct pulls away from the southern edge of the water. Less than a mile to the west, beyond the tracks of the New York Central & Hudson River Railroad, a swirling eddy forms in the Hudson, as the dislodged building's drainage pipes, which normally carry their contents into the river, pull back their effluent from beneath the city streets and hoist it skyward. If we turn our gaze a mile and a half southward, to West 89th Street, we see that a stately stone building is being sucked into the ground. It's the Riverside Exchange, housing the switchboards that service telephone subscribers in northern Manhattan. The carefully engineered paper-wound cables running under the streets and up into the apartments of the Aqua Vista are pulling the consoles, where dozens of "telephone girls" sit and manage the crackling flow of conversation, through the floors. The same fate awaits the electrical substation a half-mile northeast on 121st Street and the two massive, smokestack-topped Waterside Stations of the New York Edison Company (supplying roughly half of Manhattan's electricity), a little under five miles to the southeast, on First Avenue between 38th and 40th Streets. The buildings are pulled into the ground by huge cables that snake through a network of subterranean ducts (named "subways" before the underground trains were introduced in 1904).[6]

But the giant isn't through. He means to put the building in his pocket and head off to his next city, so once he's pulled the Aqua Vista out of the ground, he has to get rid of its roots. Holding the structure with his left hand, he wraps his right hand around the pipes and wires hanging from the underside and gives a firm tug. Another shot in our cartoon world: now we're inside an apartment in the Aqua Vista, bouncing off the walls and ceiling as the giant jerks the building this way and that. We watch in terror as the kitchen sink, the gas stove, the bathroom sink, bathtub, and toilet crash through the floor. The light fixtures, switches, outlets, and appliances plugged into the outlets smash through the walls and ceilings and disappear, as does the candlestick telephone with the RI (for Riverside) number.

If you were middle-aged in 1913, you might have remembered a book called *Women, Plumbers and Doctors*, by Mrs. H. M. (Harriette Merrick) Plunkett. It was first published in 1885 and reprinted six times by the turn of the century. Mrs. Plunkett was the rare woman in the 1880s who had cultivated a sufficient level of expertise in sanitary science that she could write about it with authority, as she did in this book. She expressed the aim of the book with admirable clarity in the subtitle: "Showing that, if women and plumbers do their whole sanitary duty, there will be comparatively little occasion for the services of the doctors." So, it's a book on household sanitation. But if you took a look at the frontispiece, you saw that *Women, Plumbers and Doctors* was much more than this. It was both a witness to a change that had already begun to take place as far back as the early 1880s and implicitly a glimpse into the future.

The frontispiece presents two lithographed images, the first bearing the caption "Then!" and the second "Now!" In the first image ("Then!"), you see a house set in rolling hills. The nearest (and only other visible) dwelling structure, what appears to be a farmhouse, is at least a half-mile in the distance. The featured house closer to us has a chimney, from which smoke rises. At the far left is an outdoor privy. To the right of it is a well, serviced by a sweep (lever) mounted on a tall, forked pole, for lifting buckets of water. Next to the well is the woman of the house. She's scrubbing clothes in a wooden basin. Two pigs stand in the open air, without a pen to enclose them.

In the second image ("Now!"), you're inside a house, in the kitchen. Three objects initially command your attention: a sink equipped with two taps; a storage tank for hot water, with a cut-out view for your benefit; and a cast-iron kitchen range, also with a cut-out view, featuring six stove lids on the hotplate (cooking surface) and two ovens at eye level. The real point of the image, however, is not the fixtures; it's the pipes that connect the fixtures to one another and to two unseen worlds: one above the ceiling and the other beneath the floor. Two pipes rise from the floor, one leading into the range, the other branching in three directions: to the sink, into the boiler, and then through the ceiling. The cut-out of the range shows the reservoir, where the water is heated and sent into a pipe leading back into the storage tank. From the top of the storage tank a pipe emerges to carry hot water in two directions: to the kitchen sink and then through the ceiling. You can guess from the diagram that directly above the kitchen is a bathroom with at least a tub and sink. What lies beneath the floor? In 1885, water would be supplied to the house either from a city waterworks or from a tank inside the house. Tanks were usually placed on the upper floors, so that the force of gravity would give the water the pressure necessary to carry it through the plumbing system. Since the pipes in the image rise from the basement, the house is probably supplied from a city waterworks.[7]

In 1885, the image titled "Now!" was a bit of an exaggeration—more of a prophecy than a reality. Close to 80 percent of the urban population at the time was supplied with water (where "urban" referred to any town with 2,500 inhabitants or more).[8] In that year, rural houses were still likely to look like the one depicted in the picture titled "Then!" But having a city water supply is not the same thing as having hot and cold running water throughout the house, let alone having a fully equipped bathroom with a toilet (assuming the "Now!" house has one). Those conveniences were not commonplace till the 1920s.[9] The great majority of American households at the end of the nineteenth century still had outdoor privies, like the "Then!" house in Mrs. Plunkett's book.

Still, even though the picture in Mrs. Plunkett's book was not broadly representative in all of its details, it was certainly representative in one basic respect: the American residence showed an increasing tendency to reach down into the earth and connect with vital products and services. The house in the "Now!" picture has its intake plumbing on the ground floor. What isn't visible is the outflow plumbing—in all probability because such plumbing was more common and thus less amazing in 1885 than plumbing that brought city water into the house. Even houses serviced by pumps or wells in that era frequently were plumbed for sewerage. In fact, the aim of *Women, Plumbers and Doctors* was not to celebrate the wonders of the modern networked house but to teach readers about sanitary science. Mrs. Plunkett wrote during that transitional phase in the Public Health Movement between the sanitarian and the bacteriological phases, and, even though she gave her readers a remarkably solid, up-to-date, brief course in the germ theory, she still believed in the dangers of sewer gas as a source of infection. So, despite the frontispiece image, she devoted far more space to outflow plumbing in the book than to intake plumbing. But it's safe to infer that her readers, for the fifteen-odd years when her book was selling copies briskly, were accustomed to the idea of a house that was networked with the outside world, no matter how modestly.

In the last decades of the nineteenth century, American houses and apartment buildings increasingly began to grow a circulatory system within their walls for gas—generally the sort extracted from coal (not natural methane gas, which became common only several decades into the twentieth century) and, at first, usually for lighting only. Gas had been used for urban street lighting starting in the early nineteenth century, but it was decades later before it made its way into most private residences. When electricity began to edge out gas as a source of energy for interior lighting, gas increasingly came to be used for cooking and eventually heating. You can find isolated references to gas ranges (even gas water heaters) in newspapers and magazines around 1890.[10] The first ad I've seen for a gas range appeared in 1893 ("Reliable Gas Ranges," made by The Schneider & Trenkamp Co., Cleveland).[11] By the end of the 1890s, when Detroit Stove Works was producing its "Detroit Jewel" line of gas ranges, you could find dozens of ads for these modern kitchen appliances. In fact, Detroit Stove Works was probably the source of the colloquial expression "Cooking with gas," which appeared as the title of an instructional manual/advertising pamphlet published by the company in the early twentieth century. By 1913, newspapers and magazines were filled with ads for gas ranges and recipes that included special instructions for cooking with gas.

By that year, if you had modern lighting of any sort, you probably had electricity. Gas and electricity had begun a fierce competition for home lighting in the early 1890s, and over the next few decades electricity clearly won out. These were the years when most modern kitchen and household appliances first made their appearance.

Take vacuum cleaners, for example. Starting around the second decade of the twentieth century, the wealthy could have the ultimate *internally* networked house, thanks to (among others) the Spencer Turbine Cleaner Company of Hartford, Connecticut (which also introduced electric blowers—essentially "vacuum cleaners in reverse"—for church organs).[12] Large vacuum motors were installed in the cellars of private residences, with pipes in the walls and baseboard-mounted brass inlets throughout the house for the vacuum hoses. You plugged in the hose, pushed a button to start the motor downstairs, and then vacuumed the floor, furniture, the coats of visitors—anything with dust and dirt that needed to be removed. The companies that manufactured these large systems predictably sought to raise fears proper to the sanitarian movement (now a generation out of date, of course), with dust in its role as the Prince of Darkness. "The Doom of Dust," proclaimed an early ad for vacuum cleaners. The new machines, it said, do not simply *transfer*, but *eradicate* "the multitudes of invisible germ-infected dust particles."[13]

The hugely expensive "stationary systems," as they were called, never caught on with the general public and, by the teens, began to make increasingly rare appearances in magazine ads. That makes sense: companies sold them in an era when "portable" vacuum cleaners were still so heavy as to be hardly portable. Once the newer machines became lighter and easier to handle, closer to the 1920s, almost no one remained interested in plumbing a house for dust, in addition to water and waste. Nonetheless, anyone reading popular newspapers and magazines in this era was likely to encounter at least the image of the private residence internally networked for the finest in modern sanitation.

What was true of vacuum cleaners was true of the many other electrical appliances that hit the market in the first two decades of the twentieth century (irons, washing machines, refrigerators, dishwashers, toasters, waffle irons, mixers, percolators): they existed but did not become commonplace until the 1920s or even 1930s.[14] In fact, the two rooms in the house that most clearly reveal the state of its technological modernity, the kitchen and the bathroom, did not assume their modern shape in substantial numbers of residences in the United States until those decades. As for electrical power, in 1912 only 15.9 percent of American residences had it. Even in 1920 only 34.7 percent did. It was not until about 1925 that the figure passed the 50 percent mark and not until mid-century that it hit 90 percent (though in all those years the figures were much higher for urban residents).[15] Still, whether or not the vast majority of the population actually had electrical service or owned any of the new labor-saving devices run by electricity, the image of the house that was networked externally to electrical service and mechanized internally by it was everywhere to be seen.

Nothing networked the American residence to the outside world so much as the telephone. Service had been around since 1876. By 1913, roughly one in four households in the United States had a telephone.[16] This was far from a majority, but the device had already brought about its own enormous social, cultural, and commercial transformation by that year. In 1910, business and science writer Herbert N. Casson published *The History of the Telephone.* Though the technology was by then in its third decade, Casson could not resist celebrating its wonders on almost every page of his book. No detail was too trivial, from the design of the underground wires, to life inside a telephone exchange, to the activities of the "wire chiefs," who laid, strung, and repaired telephone lines. They were "a corps of human spiders, endlessly spinning threads under streets and above green fields, on the beds of rivers and the slopes of mountains, massing them in cities and fluffing them out among farms and villages."[17]

A man of his times, fully in tune with the details of the biological self, Casson drew a comparison between the ultimate network, the human body, and the network that was the telephone system: "It is an interlocking unit, a living, conscious being, half human and half machine; and an injury in any one place may cause a pain or sickness to its whole vast body." This being renews itself, he said, like a cellular organism:

> And just as the particles of a human body change every six or seven years, without disturbing the body, so the particles of our telephone systems have changed repeatedly without any interruption of traffic. The constant flood of new inventions has necessitated several complete rebuildings. Little or nothing has ever been allowed to wear out. The New York system was rebuilt three times in sixteen years; and many a costly switchboard has gone to the scrapheap at three or four years of age.[18]

In the days before the rotary dial became commonplace (dial phones first came into use in 1892, in Indiana, and Bell Telephone began making them in 1919), the telephone connected you not only with your friends and business associates but also with the entirely new, carefully planned social world of the telephone exchange, populated by rigorously trained "telephone girls."[19] Casson told the story of this world and how it evolved. Originally switchboard operators were "boys" (young men, no doubt). But owing to the characteristic behavioral traits of the male sex, these operators proved to be a disaster. The decision to hire women instead of men brought about a revolution. "If ever the rush of women into the business world was an unmixed blessing," Casson explained, "it was when the boys of the telephone exchanges were superseded by girls. Here at its best was shown the influence of the feminine touch. The quiet voice, pitched high, the deft fingers, the patient courtesy and attentiveness—these qualities were precisely what the gentle telephone required in its attendants."[20] Telephone girls, carefully trained at a highly selective school founded in 1902 by the New York Telephone Company, transformed the very nature of social interaction in a sphere that, while in its own peculiar way as public as could be, was completely invisible.

> The truth about the American telephone girl is that she has become so highly efficient that we now expect her to be a paragon of perfection. To give the young lady her due, we must acknowledge that she has done more than any other person to introduce courtesy into the business world. She has done most to abolish the old-time roughness and vulgarity. She has made big business to run more smoothly than little business did, half a century ago. She has shown us how to take the friction out of conversation, and taught us refinements of politeness which were rare even among the Beau Brummels of pre-telephonic days. Who, for instance, until the arrival of the telephone girl, appreciated the difference between "Who are you?" and "Who is this?" Or who else has so impressed upon us the value of the rising inflection, as a gentler habit of speech? This propaganda of politeness has gone so far that to-day the man who is profane or abusive at the telephone, is cut off from the use of it. He is cast out as unfit for a telephone-using community.[21]

Not only the businessman but also the residents of a private home—at least those who were "subscribers"—had become networked into a community that operated according to the rules of a universally accepted and strictly enforced etiquette manual.

Of all the tentacles reaching out from the new, turn-of-the-century residence, the telephone wire was simply the one with the most obvious connection to the world of business outside. But all the other tentacles—water supply pipes, sewerage pipes, gas lines, electrical lines—necessarily put residents of the new domicile into direct contact with the often high-stakes drama of Big Business, with all its pitfalls and all the headaches it caused the ordinary customer. Where the residents of the "Then!" house were at the mercy of ground supplies when they needed water, residents of a "Now!" dwelling in, say, New

York City were at the mercy of the municipal politics that led to the construction, first, of the Croton Aqueduct and, subsequently, of the New Croton Aqueduct, which went into service in 1890. Before additional aqueducts were built, there was no reasonable alternative for obtaining water in one's residence. Where inhabitants of the "Then!" house probably relied on candles for light, inhabitants of the "Now!" house may well have had a range of choices for illuminating the books and magazines they read in the evening: not only gas or electricity but, for many years, several different providers of each. This was not to say that the existence of choices set gas and electric consumption radically apart from water consumption. As gas and electric companies competed, consolidated, went bankrupt, and formed monopolies, the ordinary consumer of these utilities was sucked into an existing commercial state of affairs (change though it might from year to year or month to month) just as ineluctably as the water consumer.

The same was true of telephone service. The story of the technology from the 1890s to the end of World War I is the story of the gradual emergence of AT&T as the universal provider of service. Standardization was the name of the game, as Theodore N. Vail, president of AT&T, promoted a policy designed to give the company exclusive control of the telephone network.[22] Media historian Tim Wu has recounted the fascinating twists and turns of the story in *The Master Switch: The Rise and Fall of Information Empires.* Vail's vision of a private monopoly serving the public good was expressed in the grandest terms, Wu shows. As Vail put it (in a passage that Wu quotes), the telephone system he envisioned would transmit not merely speech, but "intelligence." Without actually using the word "network" (he used "system" instead), Vail captured the essence of the concept succinctly and perfectly. The system would one day spread its commodity (intelligence) by operating "from every one in every place to every one in every other place, [so that it would be] a system as universal and as extensive as the highway system of the country which extends from every man's door to every other man's door."[23] Starting in 1908 and through 1925, Americans would read hundreds of ads broadcasting the slogan "One Policy—One System, Universal Service." Ordinary subscribers did not necessarily devote a great deal of thought to the details of the process that led AT&T to dominate the market, but they were unavoidably players in that process every time they picked up a candlestick phone or dial phone to place a call.

The Networked, Rational, Standardized Home

That Christine Frederick was "The Woman Who Invented Scientific Housekeeping," as the *Times* put it in 1912, was a wildly erroneous claim. She was not even close to being the inventor of scientific housekeeping. A number of candidates might present their credentials for this position, all of them active before Mrs. Frederick was even born. One might be William A. Alcott (uncle of Louisa May), a medical doctor who published *The Young Housekeeper, or Thoughts on Food and Cookery* in 1838. Dr. Alcott aimed to convince his readers that housekeeping could be based not just on tradition but on *principles.*[24] Another candidate is Catherine Beecher, author of *A Treatise on Domestic Economy for the Use of Young Ladies at Home and at School*, published in 1841. Though the *Treatise* concerned the education of women in the broadest possible sense, much of it focused specifically on such practical domestic matters as food preparation, cleanliness, proper attire, "economy of time," house construction, and cleaning.[25] Next would be the team of Catherine Beecher and her sister, Harriet Beecher Stowe (author of *Uncle Tom's Cabin*), who published the classic manual *The American Woman's Home: or, Principles of Domestic Science* in 1869. The new book was in many ways an updated version of Beecher's *Treatise*, but it also emphasized science more than its predecessor.[26]

Still, in 1869 two essential elements were missing, in addition to the appliances and other modern conveniences that Christine Frederick and later domestic science experts had at their disposal: modern sanitary science and a scientific approach to time and motion. *The American Woman's Home*, like Catherine Beecher's *Treatise*, includes an entire chapter on "Economy of Time and Expenses," but the subject in both books is approached, weirdly, from a Biblical standpoint (complete with an excursus on "Laws appointed by God for the Jews"). In 1885, Plunkett knew about bacteria, but in a fairly rudimentary way. Only in 1881 did Frederick Winslow Taylor, the great apostle of efficiency in industry, first began elaborating the principles of scientific management that Christine Frederick drew on, and he didn't fully develop them until the early 1890s.

In fact, there *was* a predecessor to Frederick, one of truly Titanic stature, who possessed a professional mastery of sanitary science, bacteriology, chemistry, hygiene, and dietetics. All that was missing was the laws of scientific management (those would have to wait for Christine Frederick herself). This predecessor helped found an entire movement, complete with a national organization and brand-new academic departments in scores of American colleges and universities—all this years before Mrs. Frederick had the epiphany about rearranging her kitchen.

She was Ellen Henrietta Swallow (1842–1911), and she was one of the most extraordinary American women of her generation—or any generation, for that matter. Much of what she did was unprecedented for women in the late nineteenth century. Having taken an A.B. (Bachelor of Arts) degree at the newly opened Vassar College in 1870, she was accepted as a "special student" at MIT, where she earned an S.B. (Bachelor of Science) degree in 1873. She was the first woman to be admitted to the institute and the only one until ten years later. She helped open a special laboratory for women several years after she received her degree. For years, she was a "resident graduate" at MIT, finally receiving a faculty position in 1884. She married MIT professor Robert Hallowell Richards in 1875 and was known thereafter as Ellen H. Richards. Apart from the specialized work in chemistry she carried out as an academic scientist and as a consultant to the insurance industry, she had three missions in life: promoting women's education generally; building the movement to bring the methods and achievements of modern science into the home—"home" being broadly construed as both the physical structure and the living space of a small community (most commonly a family); and establishing a science of the environment.

The three missions were intimately linked, and the logic was wonderfully simple: education arouses "a spirit of investigation" in girls and women; armed with such a spirit, they will approach the problems of everyday household life scientifically; women will then bring about reform of a sort that will affect not only their individual households but also the collectivity of households, which is to say the environment. As early as 1879, Richards showed the path her thinking would always take. She was addressing a group of three hundred women in Poughkeepsie, New York, home to Vassar College. Her woodenly academic title, "Chemistry in Relation to Household Economy," did not do justice to the speech. Applying chemistry to the maintenance of a household was merely one example of what a woman could do with a good education.

The true core of the speech was the promise of what would happen, broadly speaking, once women became properly educated and once properly educated women began to apply their new knowledge. "We must awaken a spirit of investigation in our girls," she said, "as it is often awakened in our boys, but always, I think, *in spite of* the school training. We must show to the girls who are studying science in our schools that it has a very close relation to our every-day life."[27] That's the first step: becoming educated and seeing the possibility of applying one's knowledge. Next comes the actual application: "The housekeeper is the one person who visits all parts of the house daily. She alone is in a position to detect the first trace of the escape of sewer gas, to notice the neglected corner of the cellar, to test the cream of tartar if the biscuits come to the table yellow and alkaline, and she should know enough of science to do all this and more."[28] Then the movement spreads to a larger community: "Perhaps the day will come when an association of housekeepers will be formed in each large town or city, with one of their number as a chemist. Some similar arrangement would be far more effective in checking adulteration than a dozen acts passed by Congress."[29] After all, she said, "men do not often think about these things, and it is for women to institute reforms."[30]

The part that had to do with the environment became what Richards subsequently named "oekology" and then "euthenics." Neither name stuck (though oekology came back into common use with a less forbidding spelling, "ecology"), but the philosophy and methods lie at the origins of the modern environmental movement. I'll have more to say about that in the next chapter. The part that had to do with the home became "home economics." Ellen H. Richards, not Christine Frederick, was the true guiding force behind scientific housekeeping in the form that it took in the twentieth century.

Richards had worked on food preparation and nutrition problems back in the 1880s. Almost every scientific project she ever undertook included a social and moral component. In 1886, she published *Food Materials and Their Adulterations*, a manual for schools and the home. Richards, as she explained in her preface, drew on a wide array of technical sources in order to offer ordinary readers the knowledge they would need to understand the basics of nutrition. The moral thrust of the project was absolutely primary, and she opened the first chapter with it. What could be simpler than this? "The prosperity of a nation depends upon the health and the morals of its citizens," she wrote, "and the health and the morals of a people depend mainly upon the food they eat, and the homes they live in."[31] Modern life had made a reasoned, scientific approach to housekeeping in general and food preparation in particular a matter not of choice but of necessity. Her thinking was that housekeeping should also be a source of pride for those women who chose to devote themselves to it. "This is an age of progress," she wrote. "Our girls must be taught to recognize the profession of housekeeping as one of the highest, although not necessarily the only one; but whatever art or accomplishment they may acquire besides, let them consider that the management of a household is not to be neglected."[32]

In 1890, Richards helped found the New England Kitchen of Boston, an establishment whose purpose was to feed poor people while convincing them of the benefits of inexpensive and nutritious food. For the World's Columbian Exposition (Chicago World's Fair) in 1893, twenty years before Christine Frederick's "Efficiency Kitchen," Richards set up the "Rumford Kitchen." It was housed in a small, Cape Cod–style structure, and, in addition to presenting an array of charts and books, it offered fairgoers luncheons prepared in accordance with the latest scientific principles. Since the Rumford Kitchen was primarily an educational exhibit, the menu cards included dietary information about the "ration" of ingredients that each item contained.[33] In 1894, Richards spear-headed a campaign to improve the quality of the lunches served in Boston public schools.

Home economics, under that name and as a formal educational discipline, was born in Lake Placid, New York, at the vacation resort of Melvil Dewey (founder of the decimal system). Together with a number of other luminaries of the scientific approach to household management, Richards put together the conceptual structure of a movement and groundwork for a national organization to promote that movement. A decade later she explained the rationale for the name the founding members chose. A number of names were already in existence, and "home economics" was among them (others were "domestic science," "domestic economy," "household economy," and "household economics"). A household manual published in 1880 had used the phrase as part of its title, *Home and Health and Home Economics*, although the authors of this "cyclopedia" used home economics to cover a list of instructions for doing certain household chores, not to denote a reasoned field of inquiry and practice.[34] In 1898, Maria Parloa, one of the Lake Placid participants, had published a book under the title *Home Economics: A Practical Guide in Every Branch of Housekeeping*. This book provided a systematic approach to matters of household management, from the selection and design of a house, to housework, to table service, marketing, and polishing wood floors.

For Richards at the Lake Placid meeting, the idea was to combine "the economic and ethical." So the group chose, from the existing possibilities, "home economics." Richards later explained it like this: "*home* meaning the place for the shelter and nurture of children or for the development of self-sacrificing qualities and of strength to meet the world; *economics* meaning the management of this home on economic lines as to time and energy as well as to money."[35] The emphasis on home was essential to Richards. As her biographer explained in 1912, Richards was deeply ambivalent about organizations that devoted their efforts exclusively to women as a separate group, because even as early as the 1880s, she believed American women had already made enormous strides toward equality in education and professional life. Yet her belief in the primacy of the home was so powerful that she threw her support behind a movement designed to bring to that institution all the benefits of modern science. "Tomorrow, if not today," she wrote, "the woman who is to be really mistress of her house must be an engineer, so far as to be able to understand the use of machines."[36]

Ellen Richards died in March of 1911. By that time, the Lake Placid Conference on Home Economics had met ten times, both at Lake Placid and elsewhere. There was a national organization, called the American Home Economics Association, and a journal, called the *Journal of Home Economics.* Home economics or domestic science was being taught in public schools as a practical course and in numerous colleges and universities as an academic discipline.

One of the first colleges to offer home economics as an academic discipline was Simmons in Boston. The Department of Household Economics (as it was called there at first) evolved directly from one of Ellen Richards's projects. It started out as the Boston School of Housekeeping, an institution founded in 1897 by the Women's Educational and Industrial Union, to address the shortage of household servants at that time. The idea was to lure immigrant women away from other jobs and back into household service. The experiment failed, and Richards stepped in to turn the institution into a professional training ground for women interested in the newly conceived field of home economics.[37] In 1902, the year it opened, Simmons College purchased the School of Housekeeping, leasing its buildings on St. Botolph Street in Boston's Back Bay district and including its courses in the new Department of Household Economics. Ellen Richards taught as a special lecturer at Simmons during the first year of the college's existence.[38] It was an easy trip for her: MIT at the time was only about a half-mile away, between Clarendon and Berkeley Streets.

The "Preliminary Announcement of Simmons College" set out the mission of the Household Economics Department. Even at the relatively early date of this statement (just three years after the first Lake Placid Conference), you can see the nexus of ideas that had emerged as the guiding principles of not only housekeeping but also the professional, scientific study of it. Reflecting the fundamental beliefs of Ellen Richards as well as the spirit of the college-to-be, the announcement also included references to the social dimension of the field. The statement began:

> In this department it is proposed to give courses in all subjects that are of advantage to a woman who has charge of an institution, a social settlement, or a private home, or who wishes to prepare for teaching the household arts or for nursing. These will include the construction of a house and its appropriate architecture, the plumbing, heating, lighting, and ventilation of a building, the artistic principles of house furnishing and decoration, the materials used in furnishing, their preservation and care; the laws of sanitation and health, the principles of cookery, the planning of meals and dietaries for people of different ages and conditions, food-values, and the proper economy of food; the care of accounts, the supervision of domestic servants, and the general sociological questions that are involved in the relations of employer and house assistants.[39]

If you followed Simmons College in the news for a decade or so after it opened, you would have read primarily of the professional training it gave its graduates. "College for Women Workers" was the title of the article in the *New York Times* that announced the opening of Simmons in October of 1902. The *Times* repeatedly returned to the women's college over the years, stressing the careers for which its students were being prepared. Simmons was known, too, as an institution that prepared women for housekeeping, but where housekeeping was now a scientifically conceived enterprise. In 1907, Boston social historian and columnist Mary Caroline Crawford wrote an article for *Ladies' Home Journal* on Simmons. Crawford devoted most of the article to the professional training that Simmons offered, but she wrote also that most of its students studied housekeeping, which Simmons taught in such as way as "to combine the scientific and the spiritual." Crawford also claimed, amusingly, that support for young women to attend Simmons came from their fathers more than from their mothers. Was it because so many fathers in 1907 supported professional careers for their daughters? Not exactly, to judge from the example Crawford gave. She quotes from a letter that a "prosperous physician" had recently sent to the dean: "I have three daughters, two of whom have already been graduated from college. Neither of them, however, is fitted for self-maintenance, nor can either look properly after my home. I'm going to send my third girl to Simmons for the Household Economics Course! When she gets through she shall be my housekeeper until she marries, and if she does not marry and is thrown upon her own resources—as she very likely may be after my death—she'll be able to turn her education into money."[40]

So when Christine Frederick came along in 1912 with her *Ladies' Home Journal* articles, promoting efficiency and standardization in homemaking, a solid foundation for her approach was already well in place. Ellen Richards had already spoken of standards (though not standardization) and efficiency in her address to the tenth annual Lake Placid Conference, in 1908. She mentioned "standards of living in the conduct of the home and in relation to sanitary science" and "*efficiency* as the key note of the 20th century."[41] What Christine Frederick contributed was the specific focus on first the management of time, motion, and effort, with the application of the principles of Taylor, and second, the business dimension of homemaking. The sitting position in which we see Mrs. Frederick in the *Times* article was part of the first focus: sitting spares your body the unnecessary strain that standing causes.[42] The second focus increasingly occupied Frederick's attention after she published "Putting the American Woman and Her Home on a Business Basis" in *The American Review of Reviews* in 1914, receiving extensive attention in her 1920 book *Household Engineering: Scientific Management in the Home* and exclusive attention in her 1929 *Selling Mrs. Consumer.*[43]

Of course, only a handful of American women in the early twentieth century were alumnae of Simmons College or any other institution of higher learning that offered advanced courses in home economics. And it wouldn't be accurate to say that the changes to houses as physical structures were universal or even widespread until the 1920s—or even later. But what unquestionably emerges in the first two decades of the twentieth century is at least a model version of the new house and home and the wide visibility of the model, even to those who themselves didn't enjoy its features in their own lives. The result was a complicated and paradoxical set of attitudes toward house and home that in many ways reflect the peculiar consciousness that emerged at the dawn of the twentieth century. If there was a logical (but not necessarily chronological) order to the process that led to these attitudes, I think it would look something like this:

(1) The "servant problem" forced the middle-class housewife back into the

kitchen. The School of Housekeeping that Ellen Richards took over came into being in response to a curious phenomenon that set the United States apart from the rest of the affluent Western world. By the 1870s, plenty of middle- to upper-middle-income families in this country could afford household help. Over the next couple of decades, the number of households employing domestic servants decreased by about half, from roughly one in eight (1870) to roughly one in fifteen (1900). According to social historian Ellen M. Plante's fascinating history of the American kitchen (and life in and around it), two related factors were responsible for the drop: the number of women willing to work as servants decreased because of a rise in other, more attractive employment opportunities for them, and, as the wages of servants rose in response to competition from those other opportunities, the number of families that could afford servants dropped.

And so, as Plante puts it in a chapter subtitle, "Madam Returns to Her Kitchen." The challenge, from the 1890s forward, was for women at income levels that earlier had supported the employment of household help to maintain respectable households resembling those of families who still could afford such help (those families now being only the comparatively wealthy)—but to do so *without* help.[44] Seen in this context, the campaign to bring efficiency and scientific management into the home looks less like a brilliant idea that happened along thanks purely to new thinking and new technology, and more like a predictable and almost desperate response to a social crisis (one with economic consequences, of course) that at first affected only a privileged few; it's just that the response created standards that eventually came to be accepted both by those privileged few and by a much larger share of the population. The truth was, if you wanted a decent home (decent by standards of the previous generation or by standards of the wealthy of the current generation), you had to do all the work yourself. The trick was to fit all that work into your waking hours and still have a few minutes left over for pursuits besides housekeeping. Such pursuits, after all, were the prerogative of the modern housewife, because of another social development.

(2) The New Woman took her bow. Helen Louise Johnson was not the only one in the era who believed that women had already gone quite some distance toward closing the educational and professional gap between men and themselves. When Ellen Richards was invited to join the Board of Lady Managers of the World's Columbian Exposition in 1893, she refused. She offered this explanation:

> Massachusetts usually leads and she has left behind her the period of woman's laboratories and woman's exhibitions. Our own Tech [MIT] has known no sex [distinction] since 1884 and no profession or occupation is now closed to a perfectly qualified woman. Hence it is appropriate that the space should be left vacant. You might have a large banner, "Massachusetts points to her women, their works do follow them." . . . I do not wish to be identified with a body, the very existence of which seems to me out of keeping with the spirit of the times. Twenty years ago I was glad to work on Woman's Boards for the education of women. The time is some years past when it seemed to me wise to work that way. Women have now more rights and duties than they are fitted to perform. They need to measure themselves with men on the same terms and in the same work in order to learn their own needs.[45]

The New Woman was much written about (not to mention much ridiculed and vilified) in the press. Commenting for *Outlook* in 1895, Lillian W. Betts, the future muckraking author of *The Leaven in a Great City* (1902, about the slums of New York), described the process that led to the emergence of the New Woman like this:

> Every year the giants of science and invention have been taking out of her control the industries that had been the objects of her effort, the subjects of her control. As they were lost, the unemployed activity found for itself some new field. Before woman realized the change, she found herself in a world that needed the cultivation of new powers, and she met the demand. Her education grew broader, her range of interest larger, her field of opportunity greater, and, without intending it, the woman of to-day finds herself a different being from her grandmother. Her standards of life have changed.[46]

The gospel of the phenomenon was *The New Womanhood* (1904) by Winifred Harper Cooley. Having described at great length and with great passion the struggle of women over the centuries, Cooley distills the achievements of the New Woman—and she considers them *actual* achievements, not goals still to be met in some distant future—down to three: "(1) education—lower, higher, professional; (2) employment—industrial, commercial, (with financial returns for labor); and (3) recognition—legal and civil."[47]

One sign of the newly won independence of the newly educated women was the rise of clubs, something possible only for women with leisure time. But club life and the home were inseparable, as it turned out: "Not only have women leisure and capability," Cooley wrote, "but the machinery with which to labor. A few years ago, clubs were regarded as an unsexing innovation; now they are accepted as a normal feature of modern life. Women have plunged into them, taken them seriously, delightedly seized upon household economics and child-study, until every home is an experimental laboratory, from which are expected good results."[48] If the home became an experimental laboratory, even for the woman who was not employed outside of it, it was no doubt because so many women *were* employed outside the home and the character of work, for women as well as for men, had changed. In his classic *Paths to the Present*, Arthur M. Schlesinger long ago observed that, at least in the lives of urban women, this era freed up time both for activities outside the home and for cooking in the home—but cooking regarded as an activity carried out by choice, for pleasure.[49]

(3) The New Work took *its* bow. This was the era that saw the birth of scientific management. In 1911, Frederick Winslow Taylor, who invented the field with his famous stopwatch studies, published *The Principles of Scientific Management*. That same year the husband-and-wife team of Frank and Lillian Gilbreth published *Motion Study*, in which they presented their meticulous analysis of motion in labor. In the new science, standardization was an overarching idea for any kind of work—at home or in the factory: standardizing the physical working environment, the tools, the motions performed by workers.

No one better captured the essence of that movement or expressed it in simpler terms than Christine Frederick, in a conversation she reported having with her husband's business associate, an efficiency expert (like her husband). Nor, of course, did anyone better grasp its implications for the home. That, rather than inventing domestic science or home economics, was Frederick's great contribution to American society. If by 1912, as Frederick learned in her conversation, there was already such a thing as "efficiency engineers," who studied time and motion in order to promote maximum output for any given effort, then the very character of work outside the home had undergone a profound transformation. If you wanted to reduce it to its simplest terms, it would be *the application of principles*. The words "principle" and "principles" occur over a dozen times just in the short chapter in which Frederick describes her conversation. Before leaving the house, her husband's associate sums it up, saying, "Now you understand clearly what efficiency means—not expensive equipment or impractical theories, but simple principles of work which enable you and every homemaker to do her household tasks in the best way, with least effort and greatest success."[50]

In the industrial and domestic spheres, standardization was inseparable from efficiency. If the standardization of tasks in the workplace leads to greater industrial output, as Mr. Frederick's associate explained to Mrs. Frederick, then the standardization of kitchen operations will certainly lead to greater domestic output (Frederick actually applied this term to household work). Efficiency and standardization led to enormous changes in the world of products and services.

(4) Commerce became "metropolitan." When Christine Frederick wrote about the "metropolitan" nature of the country (I think "cosmopolitan" might have been a better word), she was referring to the standardization of products and services. Her description of business practices in the years leading up to 1912 could almost have been written today. She celebrated the brilliance of the "one-price idea," that is, the idea of charging all customers, no matter who they were and where they lived, the same price for the same article (not counting shipping costs, of course). The department store magnates John Wanamaker and Marshall Field were largely responsible for developing the idea, which reflected the increasing tendency of department stores not only to sell goods from their physical locations (Philadelphia, Chicago) but also to ship by mail order to virtually any location in the country. The one-price plan was its own version of standardization, since it implied "standards of value." For a given item offered at Wanamaker's, presumably, not only the price but the quality would be the same regardless of who purchased it. The more important result of the one-price idea, however, was the possibility of "standardized branded articles."[51] If companies were making such standardized articles and shipping them to either Podunk or Flagstaff, then products generally speaking had increasingly become standardized.

As Frederick observed, it wasn't just collars and ties; it was household articles as well, including food (the peanut butter being purchased in Tallahassee as well as in the metropolis). She was right. When she turned her scientific eye to housekeeping, the larder of the typical middle-class home had been transformed beyond recognition from what it had been in the days of her grandmothers. Ellen Plante tells the story of how mass-produced packaged goods took over in the final decades of the nineteenth century. At the turn of the century, she writes, "the housekeeper was no longer the primary producer of food and clothing; she'd advanced to the position of consumer, bringing home a variety of store-bought foodstuffs that slowly began to reduce the amount of time spent cooking."[52] The prepackaged industry attracted its customers, naturally, by advertising, with the result that, a decade into the twentieth century, when the middle class homemaker stocked her pantry (which, for reasons of efficiency, increasingly took the form of a free-standing cabinet inside the kitchen), for a great many items she had at her disposal a selection of standardized products limited by the number of national companies that produced them. If you wanted to serve pork and beans in 1912 or 1913, you were unlikely to make them from scratch, so your choices pretty much came down to Van Camp's, Snider, and Heinz. Tomato soup? Campbell's or Heinz. Catsup/ketchup? Blue Label, Snider, Beech-Nut, or Heinz. The peanut butter that Christine Frederick mentions? Beech-Nut or, once again, Heinz. Toasted Corn Flakes? Kellogg's (Sanitas from 1906 to mid-1907). There were other brands, of course, including regional ones, but where the pantry of 1860 was likely to be filled with paraffin-topped jars (containing preserves and vegetables made at home), the pantry of 1912 was probably filled with factory-sealed, brand-name-labeled cans, vacuum jars, and boxes, while the icebox was likely to be stocked, in part, with dairy products produced elsewhere and delivered to the house.

(5) The new housekeeping/homemaking appeared, reflecting all these trends. If we trust the image—or at least *an* image—that comes through, as we've seen, in the popular press and in the home economics literature of the era (around 1912 or 1913), then we can say that housekeeping (the narrower term, meaning the practical activities of running a household) and homemaking (the broader term, where home is a social unit and not just the physical structure plus its business dimension) became (a) more socially respectable; (b) more "professionally" respectable, as if reflecting the new perceived status of educated women who worked outside the home; (c) more scientific, rational, and efficient; and (d) more standardized.

(6) As a result, the American home acquired a paradoxical combination of autonomy and networked connection with the outside. Once again, Christine Frederick put her finger on it. When she wrote that the modern home demanded "mental and spiritual qualities," she was referring to the obligation of the 1912 housewife to make her way through the thicket of products and services that came from outside. Her grandmother produced what her home needed and did so *within* that home. That would lead one to think the grandmother's home was the more autonomous one, especially if she lived in a "Then!" house, physically cut off from its surroundings. But the grandmother, especially if she was middle class and urban, certainly did not pro-

duce everything inside her home, and even for what she did produce she relied on a network of social and commercial associations: women friends, girls and women in her own household, the baker, the butcher, the dairy man, and others. But that network was primarily local, not national (or "metropolitan," as Frederick called it), personal, and non-physical (no pipes and wires). So, at least as Frederick and others expressed it, the idea was that, as hard as the work might have been and as physically isolated from her neighbors as an individual homemaker might have been in Grandma's day (especially if she was rural), how to do the work was not much of a mystery, and it required little in the way of education and brain power. If Grandma had servants, there was even less mystery and need of brain power. The local social and commercial network provided tradition and community, making the "Then!" homemaker relatively *less* autonomous *within her household.*

In Christine Frederick's era, the physical house, especially an urban one, was often networked internally and externally. The internal networking, coupled with such modern labor-saving devices as a homemaker might have possessed in 1912 or 1913, gave that homemaker considerable autonomy within her household. Deprived of servants and increasingly lacking assistance from female family members living in the home, she made her own decisions and relied on the physical conveniences that her modern house afforded her. At least, that was the image the home economists served up for their readers, and it was the image that came through in the popular press. When Ellen Richards said that the mistress of the house "must be an engineer," she certainly didn't mean literally that every housewife needed an advanced degree in engineering, but she did envision the modern homemaker as a lone, trained figure, using her education to run the intricately networked machine that was a modern house and home.

But when it came to external networking, both the physical tentacles (pipes and wires) that attached the house to products and services outside and the figurative tentacles that connected the household to an increasingly national and international array of branded, standardized products and services forced the homemaker into a position of dependence unlike what her grandmother experienced. And here was an additional paradox. The necessity of such external networking, with the presumed convenience and time saving it brought, together with a loss of autonomy, came along for some women because of the "servant problem" but for others because of expectations associated with the new status of women. A woman who jealously guarded her

time, in order that she might have the freedom to carry out personal activities other than housework, considering such activities now an entitlement rather than a luxury, was of course asserting her autonomy, her right to make choices about her own life and destiny that were independent of the obligations of running a household. If we take Christine Frederick at her word, then wholesomely used leisure time was a worthy goal of the modern woman and an expected product of her new efficiency. Efficiency must never create simply an "increased slavish devotion to work." Work and efficiency must never be ends in themselves:

> I do not call that woman efficient who thinks it a sacrilege to change her schedule of work, leave dishes unwashed and house upset to take advantage of a pleasant afternoon for a jaunt in the woods with the children. Neither do I call that woman efficient who complains that her schedule of work leaves her no time to read a good book or attend an afternoon musical or club meeting. Efficiency would be a sorry thing if it simply meant a prisonlike, compulsory routine of duties. *But it doesn't, please believe me.* Its very purpose is more liberty, more leisure, a shrewder sense of values, and the elimination of wasted energy.[53]

(7) The result was progress and grounds for optimism. Seen in this light, the American home was a microcosm of the American individual of the era, as a number of commentators, including Ellen Richards herself, observed. The new individual was conceived as one end of a polar system whose other end was a community of some sort: a neighborhood, a city, one's race, the nation (as we'll see in coming chapters). It goes without saying that the two poles were in constant tension—nothing new about that. But the relationship as defined in this era was characterized as much by the continuity as by the tension between the two poles. The individual was irretrievably bound to the larger community, not only because the individual, by moral obligation, *ought* to be so bound (at least, that's what progressive reformers said) but because modern circumstances had made the connection inescapable. As Richards saw it, the tension and continuity were the source of *progress.* "Progress is a series of zigzags: now the individual goes ahead of the community; now the community outstrips the individual," Richards wrote in 1910. "The community cannot rise much above the level of the individual home, and the home rises only by the pull of the community regulations, or by the initiative of a few especially farsighted individuals."[54]

This dynamic operated at all levels. The biological self, seen as a cellular

system, was networked internally. But the biological self, seen as caught in a web of pathogens, was networked to external systems or communities. So it was with the house and home. The house was networked internally by its system of pipes and wires, the home by the homemaker's scientific management. But the house was networked externally by the same pipes and wires, the home by the social and commercial web to which both physical and non-physical pipes and wires connected it. The "health" of the internally networked house and home and the health of the larger social and commercial network were inextricably interlocked. The optimistic perception at the time was that the interlocking was the secret to progress.

The commercial products and services I've been speaking of are those directly related to the physical management and upkeep of a household (and its tenants). Of course, the web of products and services in this era was much wider than that—not only in the sense that there were many categories of goods besides those comprising household necessities (for instance, in the world of culture and entertainment) but also in the sense that there were goods that either physically came from increasingly distant shores or bore a significant connection with distant locales. And these goods were available to increasingly large numbers of ordinary people. That's the subject of the next chapter.

7 The Globalized Consumer Network

From Pineapples to Turkey Red Cigarettes to the Bunny Hug

ON FEBRUARY 14, 1895, Mr. Byron Sherman of Morristown, New Jersey, purchased a model X Steinway upright piano, serial number 81169. The piano had been built the previous year. An amateur player, Mr. Sherman must have been struck by the stunning beauty of the physical materials from which the instrument was constructed and the craftsmanship that shone through in its every component part, including elaborately carved pilasters supporting the keyboard console and intricate fretwork on the instrument's front panels—elements that would become so costly that, in the following generation, featureless solid wood would increasingly become the norm on uprights. He must have been struck, too, by the rich sound and weighty action, which mimicked those of a grand piano.

Did Mr. Sherman know the provenance of the materials that made up his new possession? Did he know that, if he took out the family globe and located all the parts of the world that supplied raw materials for his instrument, putting a thumb on one place and a pinky on another in various combinations with both hands, he'd have found himself clutching the sphere like a basketball? The distances and the spread would be palpable.

Mr. Sherman might have known that Steinway manufactured almost everything in its own pianos. He surely didn't know in detail where the various raw materials had originated. If he'd given the matter any thought he would just as surely have guessed, correctly, that those materials came from virtually all over the world (though the company purchased some of them

from American suppliers and importers). Here is where the materials actually came from (or in some cases *probably* came from):

Ivory: Steinway purchased from two companies in Ivoryton and Deep River, Connecticut, but most of the elephant tusks themselves came originally from Zanzibar, the remainder from Congo. *Spruce*, used for the soundboard, the white keys (onto which the ivory coverings were glued), and the bracings on the back of the upright: the source was domestic, specifically the Adirondack mountains north of Albany. *Ebony*, for the black keys: from American suppliers, who probably imported it from southern India, Ceylon, and Madagascar (the sources of the finest ebony at that time). *Wool*, for the felt in the hammers and dampers: from merino sheep in Australia. The felt itself was made by one of two American firms or by the German manufacturer Weickert. *Mahogany* and *rosewood*, for the case: probably Nicaragua or somewhere in South or Central America. *Iron ore* for the cast steel strings, tuning pins, and plates: Sweden, England, and the United States. *Maple* for the wrest planks (which hold the tuning pins): from the United States and Canada.[1]

And if this in itself was a source of wonder, another simple fact would be equally astonishing at the end of the nineteenth century. Of course, trade between places separated by great distances had been around for all of recorded history. Think of the "navy of Tharshish" that brought King Solomon "gold and silver, ivory, and apes, and peacocks" (1 Kings 10:22). Wherever or whatever Tharshish was, it could not possibly have been a place as far from King Solomon as Zanzibar was from Morristown, New Jersey. And the recipient of these exotic goods was a *king*. The great European imperial powers of earlier centuries had snatched up articles of all sorts from their conquered territories, but few of these articles ever found their way into the abodes of ordinary people. Yet in Morristown in 1895, Mr. Sherman was the proud owner of an object whose parts, a few hundred years earlier, only a tiny number of the very richest Europeans could have acquired. In late-nineteenth-century America, that object was well within the reach of a middle-class family.

Not everyone owned a Steinway piano, grand or upright, though a higher percentage of the population owned some sort of piano in the decades leading up to 1920 than in any other period in American history. And even cheaper pianos bore on their white keys the remains of elephants slaughtered thousands of miles away in Africa. As Alfred Dolge, a manufacturer of piano parts and historian of pianos put it in 1911, "All inhabited parts of the globe contribute, more or less, the raw material for a piano."[2] But, starting in the last few decades of the nineteenth century, you didn't need to own a piano at all to be connected, through ordinary household objects, to distant parts of the globe. And above all, you didn't need to be rich.

The word "globalization" wasn't around in this era. It first came into prominent use in the 1970s, when the late economist Ronald E. Muller famously began writing about multinational corporations, as in his bestselling *Global Reach* (1974, with coauthor Richard J. Barnet). Starting in the mid-1980s the term came to embrace an increasingly wide set of meanings but referred, at the most general level, to an interlocking, international economy. Before long, historians began to use "globalization" in connection with an earlier era, to describe a process that began in the second half of the nineteenth century. Some have referred to this as "first-wave globalization."

An especially good study of this process is a book called *Globalization and the American Century*, by historians Alfred E. Eckes Jr., who served as a member of the U.S. International Trade Commission in the 1980s (chairing the organization from 1982 to 1984), and Thomas W. Zeiler. The "American Century" (the phrase coined in 1941 by magazine magnate Henry Luce), of course, is the twentieth century, by the beginning of which the United States had become the top industrial power in the world. But as Eckes and Zeiler point out, being the top industrial power in this period meant more than producing a greater quantity of domestic goods and boasting a higher income per capita than other nations. It meant a position of international dominance in an increasingly interconnected world. In part, this was a matter of raw military power. With a powerful, modern navy, the United States was able to achieve victory in the war with Spain, occupy the Philippines, and annex Hawaii, all between 1898 and 1902. Military victory led to an expansion of overseas trade, as American corporations grew ever more powerful and international. And even though the United States did not trade nearly as avidly as the great European powers, by 1913 trade (defined as imports plus exports as a fraction of national product) in the country's own history reached a pinnacle before the Great War.[3] As to exports, as Eckes and Zeiler show so compellingly, they were not only commercial but cultural as well. In addition to the consumer goods that the American industrial colossus was cranking out, there were religious missions, Wild West shows (like Buffalo Bill's), and, for upper-class Europeans in search of an income to match their social standing (Winston Churchill's father is a good example), wealthy American heiresses for the plucking.[4]

It's unlikely that most Americans in this era were busy studying import and export statistics, though, during the McKinley and Roosevelt presidencies, they could hardly have avoided being aware of their country's new position in the world. And this position necessarily translated into a feeling of connectedness with distant climes at the level of the individual citizen and the private household. As we saw in chapter 6, households by the early twentieth century were networked commercially with the rest of the United States. But now, for the first time in history, ordinary Americans with modest or even very low incomes ate, drank, played, smoked, listened to, danced, and gawked at the exotic every day. And, courtesy of clever advertising, they knew it—and celebrated it. Everyday life swept them into a network whose sheer geographic reach would have stupefied their grandparents. Here are just a few examples.

The Tropics Come to Your Table . . .

In the 1820s, when Alexander Pushkin wanted to show how rich and pampered his young hero, Eugene Onegin, was, he had his narrator describe the typical fare served up at Talon, the French restaurant that the young dandy frequents in St. Petersburg. On the menu is French champagne, "rost-beef" (spelled just like this, in Roman letters, to imitate the French, as the French imitated the English), truffles, and Strasbourg goose-liver pie, served between courses of Limburger cheese (from Limburg, at that time a province of the Netherlands) and "golden pineapple." In fact, everything about the 18-year-old Onegin that is distinctive and enviable is distinctive and enviable precisely because it comes from somewhere else. From his hat à la Simón Bolívar, to his Breguet alarm watch, to his amber-tipped Turkish smoking pipes, to the dozens of English and French personal toiletry items that fill his dressing room, to the luxurious bill of fare *chez* Talon, everything has been transported arduously and at great expense from a faraway place (or at least faraway in an era without railroads and largely without steamships).

And the "golden pineapple"? When you first read *Eugene Onegin*, having been duly impressed by the origins of the hero's possessions, you find yourself wondering how in heaven's name this fruit managed to survive a voyage from the central Pacific, around the tip of Tierra del Fuego, to northern Europe, and then overland to Russia, without rotting. It didn't. Pineapples originally came to Europe from South America and the West Indies. In the eighteenth century, wealthy Englishmen began to build special hothouses, or "pineries," on their country estates for the cultivation of this tropical fruit. If eating pineapple in that society bespoke exalted social status, it was not because the squire could afford the price of a rare import; better yet, it was because he could afford the price of a dedicated building and an elaborate horticultural technology (not to mention the personnel to attend it) that could create a carefully controlled tropical climate in the cold, damp English countryside. Eugene's dessert in all likelihood had traveled the same route ("through the Baltic waves") as his haberdashery items.

During the nineteenth century and into the very first years of the twentieth, the fruit followed a rather peculiar path. With the rise of railroads and steamship transportation, the United States began to import pineapples from the West Indies. California then began to cultivate them in the 1850s, Florida in the 1880s. With several domestic sources and other sources relatively close to home, the price appears to have remained relatively stable throughout the century: twenty cents in season and fifty cents out of season.[5] At those prices, pineapples were not the rare luxury they had been when almost all of them came from private greenhouses, but they were not exactly working-class fare either. The big change came with the advent of canning. In the second half of the century, Baltimore was the food canning capital of the United States, and by the 1890s, with the invention of a coring and peeling machine, that city was producing the bulk of the nation's canned pineapple. So far, the progress of this "king of fruits," as it entered the age of mechanization and increasingly efficient transportation, was roughly what you might expect. Pineapples were imported relatively quickly from nearby, then processed domestically and shipped by rail all over the country.[6]

All this changed in the opening years of the new century. Pineapples had apparently been cultivated in Hawaii since the beginning of the nineteenth century and exported to California as early as mid-century. But transportation of the fresh fruit over such a distance was difficult and inefficient. By the 1890s, a cannery was opened in Hawaii, but it was short-lived. Then, in 1899, the year after the United States annexed the islands, James Drummond Dole, the son of a progressive Unitarian minister from Boston (whom we'll meet in chapter 8) arrived. Within a year, he had set up a pineapple plantation on the island of Oahu, and within two more he had opened his first cannery, calling it the Hawaiian Pineapple Company (it wasn't renamed Dole Corp. till 1961). According to one account, from 1903 to 1907, the company's annual output of canned pineapple went from 1,893 cases to some 125,000.[7]

This staggering four-year burst of industrial productivity in Hawaii led to the next phase of America's romance with the pineapple. Two principal features characterized the period. First, pineapples, now sold in cans, became far more plentiful than ever before, and though they were not cheap, they were affordable for ordinary households—as treats, perhaps, more than as everyday items. Second, their exotic origin became an inseparable part of their appeal. The two features were inextricably connected. In order to corner the market, Hawaiian producers launched an aggressive advertising campaign at the very end of 1908 that sought to join the word "Hawaiian" to the word "pineapple" in the public mind.[8] In January of 1909, if you took *Harper's Bazaar* or *McClure's*, you could read these messages, courtesy of the Hawaiian Pineapple Growers' Association: "No, You Have Never Tasted Pineapple." "Hawaiian Pineapple is so different." "The flesh is tender without a trace of woody fibre." "Hawaiian Pineapple. Better than any fresh pineapple. Better than the housekeeper can put up. Better than ordinary canned pineapple." "Hawaiian Pineapple. Picked Ripe—Canned Right. Cuts with a spoon like a peach." For the price of the postage, you could receive the association's free recipe book, *How to Serve Pineapples*.[9]

The campaign was a huge success, both in boosting sales of canned pineapple and in firmly establishing the idea that the best—in fact, the only good—pineapple came not from California or Florida but from tropical islands thousands of miles away in the Pacific Ocean. You can easily trace the American appetite for pineapple as well as the incorporation of "Hawaiian" and "canned" into that appetite by looking at some of the most popular cookbooks over the half-century from the mid-1860s to the 1910s. To be sure, the recipes in individual cookbooks are never an absolute indication of what readers actually eat, but a trend clearly emerges in this series. Pineapples were well established in American cookery by the 1860s, at least in principle. The widely known columnist Jane Cunningham Croly (mother of Herbert Croly, whose book *The Promise of American Life* we'll encounter in chapter 10) published *Jennie June's American Cookery Book* in 1866 (Jennie June was her pen name), including in it five recipes that called for pineapple.[10] By the 1880s, most all-purpose cookbooks contained numerous recipes for pineapple, and the number of recipes increased over the next few decades.[11]

By 1910, the word "Hawaiian" had made its appearance in connection with pineapple, and virtually all recipes called for the canned version. Marion Harland (pen name of Mary Virginia Terhune, 1830–1922), a prolific author of novels, cookbooks, and other nonfiction, illustrates the emergence of the new way of thinking. *The Cottage Kitchen: A Collection of Practical and Inexpensive Receipts*, published in 1883, contained no mention of pineapple at all.[12] Her *365 Desserts: A Dessert for Every Day in the Year*, published in 1900, included five pineapple recipes, with canned pineapple optional in two and mandatory in one.[13] By 1912, when Harland and her daughter, Christine Terhune Herrick, published the *Helping Hand Cook Book*, Dole and his competitors in the islands had had their way. The word "pineapple" occurs twenty-nine times in the book. In almost every instance where it appears as a menu item or recipe ingredient (rather than as part of a phrase such as "pineapple ice cream"), it is qualified with "Hawaiian," "canned," or both. When you serve it as the fruit component of breakfast, it is either "Hawaiian pineapple" or "canned Hawaiian pineapple." When you make pineapple salad, you use a slice of canned Hawaiian pineapple. When you make banana and pineapple ice cream, you use shredded Hawaiian pineapple.[14]

Then in 1914, the Hawaiian Pineapple Packers' Association, a marketing consortium, published a little pamphlet titled *How We Serve Hawaiian Canned Pineapple*. Here, after you read the four-page introduction, in which the product was always referred to as "Hawaiian Canned Pineapple" (complete with upper-case initials, never simply "pineapple"), you found recipes by America's most renowned cookbook authors, including Fannie Farmer, Marion Harland and two of her daughters, and Maria Parloa. In the recipes, with only a few exceptions, the fruit is qualified with the word "Hawaiian." And just to set the mood, lest the public had come to regard the pineapple as a humdrum commonplace on the American table, the association's writers set the scene on the inside front cover: "Hawaii is a land of perpetual wonder, where some strange and beautiful scene, unknown before, confronts you at every turn. Among the most beautiful sights of the Islands are the immense pineapple fields which are full of fascinating subtleties of tint and form. . . . The perfume of a fully ripened pineapple cut in the field is of exquisite quality, unapproached by any other fruit odor." And in case you were tempted to run out and look for non-Hawaiian, fresh pineapples: "To preserve this fragrance intact it must be imprisoned at once, so the great canneries of Hawaiian Pineapple are located as nearly as possible to the plantations."[15]

After Hawaiian Canned Pineapple had been around for a decade or so and the growers had mounted their drive to convince the public that this fruit was strange enough to be fascinating but not too strange to be purchased frequently, it became the ultimate affordable delicacy. Yes, *delicacy.* Pineapples were never meant to be seen as socially common. They were a bit of a splurge, but a splurge for ordinary people: maybe you weren't in a position to buy an expensive automobile, but surely you could manage tropical fruit on your breakfast or dessert plate. What made pineapples worth it was that you never lost a sense of their exotic aura. Dole and company wouldn't let you. The globalized network of consumer goods was palpable—or gustable.

Bananas might have followed a similar path. In fact, from the perspective of the 1860s, they had a better reason than pineapples to remain exotic: they couldn't be reliably cultivated in this country. Instead, having started out, like pineapples, as a strange imported delicacy, they quickly became the very symbol of plebeian food: cheap, plentiful, sold from pushcarts in teeming immigrant neighborhoods, and consumed in public by society's humblest elements.

Before the mid-1870s, almost no one in the United States had ever even heard of a banana. *Jennie June's American Cookery Book* (1866) makes no mention of the fruit. Bananas first started to make an appearance in the late 1870s, and by the end of the century, cookbooks were filled with recipes featuring bananas or including them as ingredients. Fannie Farmer's *Boston Cooking-School Cook Book* boasted nine recipes expressly for bananas (fritters, ice cream, custard, cake, and more) and many others that included bananas as an ingredient. In 1912, bananas were such a staple of the American diet that Marion Harland and her daughters included some forty references to them in the *Helping Hand Cook Book*, not only in their own recipes (banana soufflé pudding, the ever-popular banana fritters) but as something to be included on the table routinely for breakfast, luncheon, and dinner.

What had happened between the 1870s and the turn of the century? Believe it or not, there are quite a few book-length histories of bananas and the banana business. This, in simplified form, is the story they tell:

Bananas had been cultivated in the Caribbean as well as South and Central America for centuries before the United States began to import them in large quantities. A pivotal event appears to have been the Philadelphia Centennial Exposition in 1876, where a banana plant on display in the Horticultural Hall attracted a great deal of attention from the public. At the same time, bananas wrapped in tinfoil were being sold as delicacies in Philadelphia.[16]

The next phase in the story was the emergence of the large corporations that would expand the banana business beyond anyone's wildest dreams, while also coming to dominate the economy and politics of Central America and parts of the Caribbean. The story is long and complicated, but the upshot was the emergence of the United Fruit Company in March of 1899 (to become United Brands in 1970 and Chiquita Brands International in 1984). The company arose from the merger of several earlier companies, and it quickly snapped up seven smaller subsidiary fruit companies.[17] United Fruit became known as the Banana Trust. It and two other companies would dominate the banana market in the United States for decades to come.[18]

Whereas the pineapple business by the turn of the century had changed by coming under the domination of a single locale, if not a single company, the banana business changed by a convoluted process of consolidation and acquisition, with two important results: first, there were more bananas around, at absurdly low prices, than Americans knew what to do with, and second, bananas did not carry with them quite so explicit a reference to their place of origin. You didn't read ads urging you to buy Costa Rican bananas—or Jamaican, or Honduran, or Cuban—as the *only* suitable fruit for your table and your palate. Even if you took notice of the brand name, there was no way of knowing whether the banana you were eating had been plucked from a plant in the jungles of Costa Rica or whether it had sailed across the Caribbean from Jamaica; nor did anyone encourage you to take notice.

By the late nineteenth century, no one even bothered to maintain the idea that the banana was a delicacy, as the Hawaiian growers and canners did with pineapple. There were at least two reasons. One was the sheer quantity and low price, which led to the fruit's decline in social status. Bananas quickly became associated with society's lower classes. Banana peels on the street were allegedly a health hazard, because people could slip on them and injure themselves. The peels came to be on the street in the first place because they were eaten by the sort of people who eat in public (at a time when proper citizens never did). People who eat in public do so because they are poor and because they lack refinement—*immigrants*, in other words. As one historian of the banana shows, banana peels became a target of the great sanitation campaigns that were waged in American cities at the end of the nineteenth and beginning of the twentieth centuries, and, as we saw in chapter 2, immigrants were frequently blamed for public health hazards.[19]

The other reason for the banana's image also had to do with public health. The peel that became such a peril once its contents had been consumed was also the reason that its contents earned such a good reputation as a wholesome food. Unlike the natural coverings of other fruits, the banana peel, as even medical authorities believed in those days, created a sterile seal for the fruit inside. As long as the peel of the banana you purchased was unbroken, you could rest assured that the fruit would not sicken you.[20] Foods that were this cheap, sensible, and salubrious simply could not qualify for the appellation "delicacy."

And yet it was never lost on the public that, whether bananas came from Central America or the Caribbean, those places were relatively exotic. Attempts to grow them on American soil, even in Florida, were abandoned early. Everyone was quite certain that the cargo holds on banana boats were positively crawling with tarantulas, centipedes, scorpions, lethally poisonous snakes, and other life-threatening creatures native to distant jungle climates.[21] A semblance of the glamour of exotic locations remained tied to the banana business in the Boston Fruit Company's (and then United Fruit Company's) Great White Fleet of steamships. It carried not only bananas but also passengers, offering them luxurious cruises to the Caribbean and Central America. "À la Carte to Panama," ran an ad for the line in 1913. "Managed and operated by an American company—understanding American demands—the principle of 'Nothing too good for Americans' has been our guiding thought." The fleet's three vessels even bore intriguing Spanish names.[22]

The Near East Comes to Your Lips . . .

"Camel Cigarettes Are Here! To cigarette smokers of America. Here are Camels. A better flavor, a better fragrance, secured by an expert blend of the choicest Turkish and choicest Domestic tobaccos. This blend of finest tobaccos makes a smoke far superior to either Turkish or Domestic tobacco smoked straight. You will like the difference immediately. Camels leave no cigaretty after-taste." Ads announcing the arrival of Camels began to appear in 1914, after a series of teaser ads the year before promised readers that the new cigarettes were on their way. The ad copy might strike us today as crude and unsophisticated. Modern advertising was in its infancy at this time, and in fact was being raised and nurtured precisely by the tobacco industry. But it doesn't take much thought to figure out the message in the description of the tobacco blend. What? Straight Turkish tobacco wouldn't taste so good? But by the time you've finished that sentence, you've read the word "Turkish" twice, and Turkish tobacco was listed ahead of "Domestic" in the previous sentence. And you've probably already guessed that the actual proportion of Turkish leaf in Camel cigarettes was minimal—a "seasoning," as one historian of cigarettes put it.[23] In reality, a Camel cigarette contained the two domestic tobaccos that had been standard in American cigarettes, precisely because of their mildness: Bright (flue-cured) and Burley (air-cured), both lightly sweetened with molasses. If you bought Camels for their taste, it was Bright and Burley that produced that taste, not Turkish.

But, as everyone knows, the inducement to purchase and continue purchasing *this* brand of cigarettes instead of *that* one stems from factors other than how the product functions—how good the smoke tastes and feels, how good it makes you feel. In fact, the more you learn about the cigarette business in the United States, the more convinced you become that once a certain standard of taste was established—mild and sweet, by comparison with what smokers in France and the Near East enjoyed—there were at most minor differences in taste from one brand to the next, and a preference for a particular brand was aroused almost entirely by images that clever advertising was able to link with those brands. The industry became so enormously successful only after it began selling its products in packages that bore carefully planned visual and verbal messages. A camel (actually a dromedary). One pyramid on the right and another one in the back left. Three palm trees (an oasis). Turkish tobacco. Well, maybe "Turkish" in 1913 connoted, broadly, "Ottoman Empire," in various parts or former parts of which you might have found camels, pyramids, and oases. But what in the name of heaven did these things have to do with the intoxicating experience you enjoyed once you shook a cigarette from the package, put one end between your lips, struck a cardboard match from a matchbook (invented in 1892 expressly for smokers), lit the other end, and pulled the first mouthful of smoke deep into your lungs?[24]

What's odd about the cigarette market in the United States, if we compare it with, say, the banana or the pineapple market, is the state of tension that always existed between the image of the exotic on one side and the comforting image of domestic provenance on the other. No one ever tried to convince the American public that bananas or pineapples were somehow down-home, old-fashioned American products—partly for the good and simple reason that they weren't. But by the time Camels came along, cigarette manufacturers had correctly bet that Americans would buy if they felt they were getting a slice of the exotic tempered with the local and familiar.

That so many Americans were smoking cigarettes at all by the beginning of the twentieth century was the result of two key developments. The first was the invention of a reliable machine that could produce cigarettes faster than human beings could hand-roll them. Cigarette and tobacco historians have told the story over and over again (in fact, a remarkable number of books have been published on the tobacco and cigarette industries that tell essentially the same story, using the same evidence, even the same anecdotes, but often without citing their sources). A young man by the name of James Albert Bonsack patented a rolling machine in 1880. The invention made its real impact on the business four years later, when James Buchanan ("Buck") Duke, who had been manufacturing cigarettes in Durham, North Carolina, purchased two machines, tinkered with them to improve their speed and efficiency, and was soon cranking out 120,000 cigarettes in a single ten-hour work shift.[25] Other companies followed Duke's lead, and within two years, according to one historian, annual production of cigarettes rose by more than a factor of six, from some nine million to sixty million.[26] In 1889, Duke persuaded his largest competitors to join with him, and the American Tobacco Company was incorporated in January of the following year. Like other enormous concerns of the era, it eventually fell victim to the Sherman Antitrust Commission and was broken up into four companies in 1911. Needless to say, the split did nothing to slow the growth of the cigarette industry in the United States (nor was that its purpose).

The second key development was advertising. At first, Americans, coming late to the game, needed to be convinced that smoking cigarettes was an acceptable thing to do. The paper-wrapped tobacco product had begun life in the humblest of circumstances, as a smoking vehicle assembled by paupers from cigar remnants and scrap paper (cigars, of course, being wrapped not in paper but in actual tobacco leaves). The commercial production of cigarettes grew up in Spain and Cuba, then Portugal, Italy, and Russia. The big moment appears to have been the Crimean War, in the mid-1850s, when British soldiers discovered the cigarettes that their Russian enemies were smoking. By the end of that decade, two British firms, one of them Philip Morris, were producing cigarettes. Buck Duke met with such success a generation later because the industry had rallied to convince men first that cigarettes were for them. Women would come later. And so the advertising began. This is the same era when pineapples and bananas began to make their increasingly frequent appearance in the American diet, which means their increasingly frequent appearance in advertisements. But nothing the fruit companies did came close in scope and cost to the efforts that the cigarette manufacturers unleashed.

It must have been in the air, for here too the minds in charge of selling the product soon hit upon the idea of exoticism. Before the era of machine-produced cigarettes, the most prestigious brands, such as Philip Morris in London, contained Turkish and Egyptian tobaccos. Since automated production began in the United States and since the original idea was speed and efficiency, American manufacturers using the machines initially put home-grown leaf in their cigarettes, especially the familiar Bright variety from Virginia.[27] But cigarette companies big and small found that the Near East, as a pictorial theme on the package and as a geographic source of tobacco (no matter how small its actual proportion in the blend), had the power to attract customers. Americans of a certain age in the early twenty-first century will remember that Jack Webb, star of the *Dragnet* radio series, did ads on air and in print for Fatima cigarettes, the show's sponsor. Fatimas started out in 1887 as a Turkish blend product of the small Richmond, Virginia, firm Cameron & Cameron, later acquired by Liggett & Myers. The brand's package featured a dark-haired woman, veiled up to her eyes (replaced with more neutral images by the time Webb was doing print ads for Fatimas in the 1950s).

With the success of Fatimas, there came a steady succession of brands that sported the Near East theme. S. Anargyros & Co., which would be acquired by Duke's American Tobacco Company in 1900 but continue to operate under its own name, was a formidable presence in the manufacture of cigarette products with Near East themes and Turkish or Egyptian tobacco. It produced Mecca Cigarettes starting in 1891, Mogul Egyptian Cigarettes in 1892, Murad Cigarettes, and Turkey Red Cigarettes, both in 1905. Anargyros wasn't the only company. A few years later, we find Hassan, Omar (both from American Tobacco Company), Nebo, Zira, and Zubelda (all three from P. Lorillard Co.) brands on the market. In the years leading up to the introduction of Camels, which would then flood the market, Turkish cigarettes came to account for one-third of all the American Tobacco Company's sales, and there were numerous Turkish cigarette companies independent from American firms. By 1910, there were some 2.6 billion Turkish cigarettes produced annually in the United States, by American Tobacco Company and independent companies.[28]

Predictably, packaging was everything.[29] Turkey Red Cigarettes, for example, allured male customers with the image of a woman, from the shoulders up, dressed in what are apparently meant to be a "Near Eastern" robe and

a tiny, absurd, fez-like hat. Attire aside, she's all Western, with lips slightly parted in a provocatively sensual smile. She holds in her hand a package of the product whose package she adorns—which includes a picture of herself with the same package (and so on, in theory, ad infinitum)—except that, unlike the package that you, Mr. Male Customer, are holding in *your* hand, the pictured package bears the intoxicatingly arousing invitation (including the obscene slang connotation, already in use at the time), "Come to Stay."[30] You're in the dark of night, and the woman is bathed in red light. What section of town does that call to mind, sir? Light up a Turkey Red and you can go there, at least in your imagination. What with Prince Morrow and his lieutenants marauding about, exposing the Social Evil, this is probably the safer course anyway.

The ultimate in crafty advertising was developed for a brand designed to appeal not only to the American public's taste for the exotic but also to its reliable, time-tested yen for social class status of the sort that only European aristocracies and royal families possess. By the turn of the century, if you were a smoker, you were already being enticed by ads for "The Best Cigarette," a cigarette "specially recommended to gentlemen who are accustomed to smoking the finest blends of choice Turkish tobacco," the cigarette "For the Connoisseur." This was Pall Mall, the "London Cigarette," introduced in 1899. After Queen Victoria, an outspoken opponent of tobacco use, died in 1901, her son, the newly crowned king Edward VII, smoked unabashedly in public. Butler-Butler, the manufacturers of Pall Malls, began to run ads shamelessly bearing the British royal coat of arms and a "Proclamation" stating that the cigarettes would now be produced in a longer version: "H.I.M. [His Imperial Majesty] the KING'S SIZE." Smoked in any size, Pall Malls boasted "the same delicious blend from the same carefully selected oriental tobaccos as are furnished to the courts of Europe."

How much more appealing could a cigarette be? The Pall Mall featured Near Eastern provenance in addition to its connection—nonexistent, of course, but heavily hinted at—with Western European royalty. Mind you, no ad ever claimed that H.I.M. actually *smoked* Pall Malls; as it happened, Edward was known to favor cigars. But that detail was easy to overlook in an ad densely filled with iconic and typographical symbols of monarchy and empire. "Oriental," "Turkish"—what did it matter that the first was meaninglessly vague and that the second referred to one of the odd territories outside Europe *not* ruled by Great Britain? The thicket of associations was pure

genius. And when the American Tobacco Company snapped up Butler-Butler and its Pall Mall brand in 1907, Duke's men cleverly pared the ads down to the bare essentials: "Famous Cigarettes for Connoisseurs," "A Shilling in London, A Quarter Here" (in other words, not cheap), and "the highest quality Turkish cigarettes." Like the pineapple, this cigarette was the ultimate exotic, yet affordable luxury.

After Camels came along, the entire cigarette industry changed. Within a few years, three brands rose to the top: Camels (R. J. Reynolds), Lucky Strikes (American Tobacco), and Chesterfields (Liggett & Myers). According to one source, the three brands accounted for 82 percent of the entire market in 1925.[31] The Great War bore a large share of responsibility for the change. For one thing, given the role the Ottoman Empire played in the war as an ally of the Central Powers, "Turkish" was no longer the selling point it had been. Brands that used the Near East as their primary attraction went into decline. For another, once the United States entered the war, the War Department, in order to support morale, sent huge numbers of cigarettes overseas in the soldiers' rations, buying them from companies in proportion to the companies' market share. Camels and Lucky Strikes headed the list. Still, the theme and the tobacco were there in two of the three best-selling brands. Camel never dropped either the images or the "Turkish & Domestic Blend" on the package. When Liggett & Myers introduced Chesterfields in 1917, it was to a country that apparently still liked the idea of "foreign" but wasn't so sure about "Turkish" any more. So the cigarettes were made "of IMPORTED and DOMESTIC tobaccos—Blended." And yet if you looked closely at the package, behind the staid and conventional typography used for the brand name and the word "cigarettes," you could just barely descry the outlines of a vintage Near Eastern scene, complete with minarets, domes (as on mosques), and, of course, a dhow floating lazily in an unidentifiable body of water.

Most cigarettes would change their personalities over the ensuing decades. Marlboros started out as primarily a women's brand in the mid-1920s, adopting the cowboy image only in the 1960s. Camels took off at the beginning because they were mild, by comparison with the fully Turkish and Egyptian brands still on the market. Once Americans, after World War II, began to take seriously what they were hearing about the health risks that cigarettes posed, traditional, unfiltered Camels, like Lucky Strikes (also a mild brand in the beginning) became the symbol of hard-core tobacco machismo. By that time, the brands with the "Oriental" themes had ceased to promote the associations

that their package imagery had promoted in the early days. Besides, in the 1960s, how much exotic enticement could a camel and a couple of pyramids exert on the average American smoker?

But in the mid 1910s, after several decades of exposure to the link between cigarette smoking and various vaguely imagined (or cleverly designed) Near Eastern locales, ordinary Americans who wanted to spend only a dime on a package of cigarettes, like housewives who served banana and pineapple salad for lunch, had the satisfaction of knowing that even their modest budget could connect them to the mysteries of places they could never afford to visit and social classes to which they would never belong. And by the middle of the next decade, *everyone*, it seemed, was smoking, including women. They were in the network—for keeps.

And Africa Comes to Your Fingertips

A little more than a hundred miles north and east of New York City, roughly halfway to Boston, the Connecticut River ends its course in a generous bay. In fact, the river remains so wide so far upstream that you'd almost be inclined to characterize the bay as extending ten miles inland. At the mouth of the river, two narrow spits of land curve inward, like pincers, partially sheltering the waters of the bay from the turbulence of the open water outside. Even better, that open water is not the ocean but the Long Island Sound, itself protected by the eastern end of the land mass for which it's named, just eight nautical miles south. From the early eighteenth century to the mid-nineteenth, the construction of sailing ships was the dominant business in the small inlets at the mouth of the Connecticut. Once steamships replaced the older vessels, the shipbuilding business collapsed, but it was soon replaced by a new one whose time, for two important reasons, had come. The new business was the importation of ivory and the manufacture of ivory objects. The two reasons were the popularity of pianos in the United States and the newly plentiful availability of ivory from Africa, thanks to the imperial conquest of Congo. From the factories in the Connecticut Valley came ivory combs, toothpicks, billiard balls, and other luxury items. But far and away the chief product was coverings for piano keys.

Not all ivory came from Congo. In fact, as it happened, the quality of the ivory, meaning its suitability for being made into billiard balls, combs, and piano keys, rose in proportion as the location of its animal source moved from

west to east in Africa. The very best ivory was to be found on the east coast of the continent and the nearby inland mountains. Congo ivory was generally (but not always) a notch or two below this, and ivory from Sierra Leone, in the west, was the least desirable. Nonetheless, the opening of Congo brought so much new ivory to the world market, at a time when African elephants were thought to be on the verge of extinction, that prices were kept stable for more than a generation.[32]

What did ordinary people know about the ivories they were tickling (as was beginning to be said in this era)?

Congo was at the center of it. The bare facts of this long, sordid story, forgotten almost completely by the Western world between the second and last decades of the twentieth century, can be set out fairly simply. In 1884, German chancellor Otto von Bismarck convened a meeting in Berlin, inviting heads of state and representatives of the United States and various European nations. The aim (not stated explicitly, of course) was to divide up the African continent—or the huge portion of it not already under European control. A swath of land surrounding the Congo River was given to Belgium, ruled at that time by King Leopold II. For the most part, the Berlin Conference, which lasted from November of 1884 to February of 1885, did not simply hand over territories to eagerly waiting European nations. Some areas were to be established as "protectorates," and some were to be ruled more or less directly from Europe. What set the Congo territory apart from others was that, at first unofficially, then legally and officially, it was given personally to King Leopold to dispose of as he saw fit.

He saw fit to dispose of it sumptuously—for himself. At the time of the conference, he knew the land was rich in ivory. A few years later he discovered it was even richer in rubber, a raw material much in demand in an international civilization increasingly fond of automobiles, bicycles, and insulated electrical wiring. Having hoodwinked the entire world into regarding Belgian involvement in Africa as a civilizing mission, Leopold established a brutal reign of terror in his colony, sending Belgian troops and conscripting native Africans to enforce his policies. Those policies were simple: extract as much ivory and rubber as possible by relying on the forced labor of the native population; kill and mutilate those who failed to obey or who fell short of the quotas demanded of them.

In chapter 8, we'll see that, early in the twentieth century, the public began to hear about the atrocities being committed in Congo. Before that, there was

almost nothing in the press to suggest that Europeans were guilty of much of anything. Belgium was frequently celebrated for the great humanitarian work it was carrying out on "the Dark Continent." Henry Morton Stanley, the explorer who had been commissioned by King Leopold to negotiate "treaties" with African tribes before the Berlin Conference but who had left a grisly trail of carnage during his adventures, was portrayed as a hero and defender of Christian virtues. Not till a certain British shipping clerk (more about him in the next chapter) and others began to expose King Leopold for what he really was did the public learn the sinister character of Belgian rule in Congo. Still, when it came to ivory, the only thing that changed after 1900 in the eyes of the public was the identity of the culprits. Before that, there was plenty of culpability to report, and it was reported extensively. It's just that the villains in the story were Arabs instead of Europeans. Anyone who followed the ivory trade, even before the Berlin Conference, had learned that wicked Arab adventurers were busy enslaving thousands upon thousands of native Africans (or "savages," as they were often called in the press), plundering vast stretches of territory, burning down villages, murdering at will, and leading long trains of captives, who bore on their backs the precious cargo of elephant's teeth, through seemingly impassable terrain, to market on the east coast or on the island of Zanzibar, many of them perishing before reaching their destination.

In these stories, Europeans such as Stanley were the heroes, even when they themselves were gathering ivory. In 1887, Stanley led an expedition to "rescue" the governor of an Egyptian province in the upper Nile, bordering on Congo. The governor bore the exotic-sounding name Emin Pasha (*emin* meaning "faithful" in Arabic, *pasha* being the Turkish honorific title for powerful officials in the Ottoman Empire). In reality, Emin Pasha was a German-born Jew named Eduard Schnitzer. How Schnitzer came to be the governor of an Egyptian province is a long story, but in the early 1880s he found himself under attack by a group of Muslim fundamentalists, and in 1886 he appealed to European leaders for help. Stanley was the lucky man who got the assignment. The expedition lasted three years and took a great toll in human lives, both among Stanley's men and among members of the native populations in his path.

Stanley got a best-selling book out of his adventures and, as was widely reported in the press at the time, an enormous haul of ivory—six thousand tusks by some estimates, two and a half thousand or thirty-one tons by another—to sell in Antwerp. In the book, titled *In Darkest Africa, or the Quest, Rescue, and Retreat of Emin Governor of Equatoria*, Stanley amusingly added his voice to the chorus of those who were shocked at the enormous loss of life that the ivory trade had brought about. Every pound of ivory, he claimed, came at the cost of one human life. At that rate, sixty thousand men, women, and children would have perished on the ivory-gathering portion of the Emin Pasha mission alone. But only Arabs caused casualties in Africa, Stanley seemed to be saying, and newspapers in the United States reported the great explorer's ivory acquisition purely factually, generally offering no comment on the human lives that were lost during the rescue expedition. These did not run into the tens of thousands, but they certainly ran into the hundreds—and that's counting only Stanley's own men.[33]

In 1895, when Mr. Sherman of Morristown purchased his Steinway model X from the factory, what could he have known about the beautiful, off-white key coverings, with their delicate swirling grain patterns and a surface texture seemingly designed by the gods to resist gently, and yet surrender to, the skin on human fingertips as they seek to coax from the finely tooled inner workings of the instrument the most dulcet tones that compacted merino wool can yield when it strikes tightly stretched steel wire? The milky, semi-opaque surfaces emerged perfectly cut from the factories in the Connecticut River basin, but they were born in a riot of blood and mayhem. Elephants slaughtered, villages burned to the ground, trains of shackled African slaves being marched to the coast, death, disease, carnage, and larceny—this was the nursery in which those key coverings had passed their tender infancy. Five years before Mr. Sherman's piano was delivered to his home in New Jersey, the entire English-speaking world came to know *In Darkest Africa*, if only through notices and reviews. Stanley got off scot-free, but what did it really matter whether the rogues were Arab slave-traders or swashbuckling European adventurers? Either way, when Mr. Sherman (or Anton Rubinstein, or Ignace Paderewski, or some other illustrious Steinway concert artist of the day) sat down to play the piano, he laid his fingertips on the splendor and savagery of a distant, exotic, dangerous land.

Blue Notes, Broken Rhythms, and the Bunny Hug, or "the music that gets to the toes and finger-tips of the average American"

Between the last decade of the nineteenth century and the third decade of the twentieth, three types of popular music, all Negro in origin, captured the attention of ordinary Americans. Ask any knowledgeable music historian to tell you where each type came from and when it first emerged, and you'll probably get a very murky answer indeed. Most likely you'll hear that ragtime first appeared sometime in the 1890s. As for jazz, the answer will include a discussion of the word itself, the mystery of its origins, and when it first occurred in print. Then it will move on to the difficulty of establishing boundaries around what it denotes. But when it comes to the blues, the answer in most cases will founder completely. You'll hear that it undoubtedly had its precursors among slave populations in southern plantations. You might hear that it actually existed in some form long before white America took notice of it. You'll probably hear that its rhythmic, harmonic, and melodic characteristics were born in Africa, "Africa" being mentioned as if it were a small nation with an ethnically and culturally homogeneous population (do we mean Gold Coast? Egypt? Abyssinia? Congo? Madagascar?).

Most of this is not the historian's fault, of course. If, in the nineteenth century, or even in the eighteenth century, there was some musical form very much like what came to be called the blues, we can't really know much about it, since the population that produced it neither read nor wrote music, since no one who did write music made any transcriptions, and since mechanical recording didn't exist. So whether something like the blues existed for a long time, whether the blues emerged from a musical culture that gave us Negro spirituals (which *were* written down, widely listened to, and commented on, especially once the Fisk Jubilee Singers began touring the world in 1871), or whether the form grew out of some other tradition, we will probably never know for sure. All we can be reasonably certain of is that the blues has a longer history than either ragtime or jazz.

But here we run into a problem of definition. Ask a jazz musician or historian anytime after the middle of the twentieth century to define or describe blues and ragtime, and you'll probably get a fairly precise answer. Ask for a definition or description of jazz, and you'll get a jumble of speculation, qualification, and ambiguity.

The standard modern history of the three types of music places them, by origin, in this chronological order: (1) blues, (2) ragtime, (3) jazz. But this is not the way the three types emerged into the public spotlight at the end of the nineteenth century and beginning of the twentieth. If we're looking only at the words and the dates by which they began to appear with frequency, then the order is (1) ragtime (for almost an entire generation), (2) blues, (3) jazz. To complicate matters, all three words in their early years were far less precise in denotation than they are today. This is because (a) many individual popular musical compositions escaped the boundaries of the definitions and descriptions that we use today, (b) "ragtime" in that era was applied to a much wider variety of compositions than today, and (c) once all three terms were in common use, each of them for over a decade was used to denote both of the other types of music, even when these two other types recognizably did conform to the more precise definitions and descriptions that we use today.

But on one count there seemed to be fairly widespread agreement. Whatever obviously perceptible differences there might have been between, say, a rag composed by Scott Joplin, a blues composition in blues form composed by W. C. Handy, and a tune classified as jazz that sounded like neither of the other two, all of this music had an origin that was paradoxically local and exotic. That's because, virtually all commentators agreed, it was created by Negroes, which meant to ordinary Americans (Negro or non-Negro) that it was ultimately African.

No one seems to know exactly where ragtime came from or when it was born. The word ragtime itself didn't come along till about 1896. Before that, it's largely a question of which music—if any—gets to count as ragtime. But two things are certain. First, despite what subsequent historians have insisted, early ragtime was not exclusively or even primarily a musical form restricted to solo piano. In the early days, if you heard a ragtime composition (or heard music that would later be called ragtime), it was more likely than not a song (that is, it was sung). Second, whatever the true origins of ragtime might be, in the mind of the public, especially in the early years, it was almost always associated with Negroes and the "African" culture they were thought to carry about with them (even if they were an untold number of generations removed from the ancestors who crossed the Atlantic).

Modern ragtime historian Edward A. Berlin shows that, in its early days, ragtime music formed part of a larger musical culture that included music and dance styles closely identified with Negroes and their perceived African heritage—even when the creators were white. The sheet music for "coon songs," for example, with lyrics and melodies written by white composers in parodied imitation of Negro speech mannerisms and music, featured caricatured images of Negroes either dressed in tattered clothing or done up, with intended comical effect, in formal evening attire. The formal garb suggested the cakewalk, a dance traditionally connected with a contest in which prizes were awarded for style and grace. (The winning couple would "take the cake," hence, apparently, the name.) As Berlin sees it, ragtime music shed the association with Negro culture shortly after the turn of the century, when it became increasingly instrumental and when more of it was being written by white composers. "Ragtime as an exoticism, as a quaint music from the fringes of society," he writes, "was replaced by ragtime the white American popular music."[34]

It may be true that ragtime ended up being appropriated by white America after the turn of the century. Berlin produces statistics to prove his case, showing that "ethnic depictions" in ragtime publications declined sharply starting in 1903.[35] White composers began to write their own ragtime tunes or tunes that were designed to suggest ragtime music, the most famous among these being *Alexander's Ragtime Band* (1911), by Irving Berlin. In addition, shortly after 1910, a series of dances closely associated with ragtime took the nation by storm. Most were named for animals: the bunny hug, the grizzly bear, the turkey trot, and a bit later, the fox-trot. You can well imagine why the new steps struck terror into the hearts of genteel Americans and why priggish, stuffed-shirt Woodrow Wilson canceled his inaugural ball in 1913 for fear that his guests would indulge in the scandalous ragtime dances.[36] Not only did the names evoke impulses too primitive for respectable society, but the dances truly were highly suggestive—more than suggestive, in fact, for in some cases they involved very close contact between the dancers. This is also likely why they became so hugely popular. You can bet your bottom dollar that, after reading enough news accounts of municipal bans, arrests, and scolding lectures from finishing-school mistresses, white Americans, from youth through middle age, signed up en masse to learn the forbidden moves. Their highly visible models were Irene and Vernon Castle, the husband-and-wife dancing sensation who, in the second decade of the twentieth century, became the public arbiters of popular terpsichorean taste. With a dance studio in New York (the Castle House), a nightclub on Long Island, and a highly visible career in vaudeville, on Broadway, and in Paris (before the outbreak of the Great War), the Castles were well positioned to call the moves.

But if we're interested in what ordinary Americans of all races heard about the music itself, then it's important to take note of a continuing conversation that was carried on from the end of the nineteenth century till after ragtime's ultimate fall from popularity, around 1920. It's not just that ragtime became the music of white Americans; it's that Americans, white and Negro, not to mention Europeans, increasingly came to regard this syncopated, popular style as a foundation for a new, distinctly American musical idiom.

Shortly before there was any talk of ragtime under that name, ordinary Americans received advice—welcome to some, unwelcome to others—from Antonín Dvořák, who was in New York from 1892 to 1895 as president of the National Conservatory of Music. A member of a minority population (Czech) from the multi-ethnic Habsburg state, the composer was deeply interested in the idea of a national music. The United States, long looked down upon by musical Europeans as a philistine musical backwater, presented him with a true challenge. When it came to "serious" music, Americans generally seemed content to borrow from abroad, presenting in the pitifully small number of concert halls and opera houses they possessed the standard fare of European masters. In two famous articles, Dvořák proclaimed that he saw hope for a future national music in the United States where others had never looked before: in Negro melodies, by which he meant primarily "plantation melodies" and "slave songs." He acknowledged that some of the melodies he had in mind were not actually the creations of American Negroes on plantations. Some were written by white men, such as Stephen Foster, but others, he claimed, "were imported from Africa." "In the Negro melodies of America," he said, "I discover all that is needed for a great and noble school of music. They are pathetic, tender, passionate, melancholy, solemn, religious, bold, merry, gay, or what you will. It is music that suits itself to any mood or purpose. There is nothing in the whole range of composition that cannot be supplied with themes from this source."[37]

If there was any ragtime music around at this time, Dvořák doesn't appear to have known about it. But his articles set the tone for the reception of ragtime and other popular Negro forms over the subsequent quarter-century.[38] In February 1906, in fact, no less a personage than President Theodore Roosevelt created a minor stir by essentially repeating what Dvořák had said over a decade earlier, though attributing the judgment to an unnamed "great French literary man." The occasion was a gathering, at the White House, of students from the Manassas Industrial School for Colored Youth. The students, introduced by Booker T. Washington, sang some songs for the president, who told them that the future of American music depended on Negroes and "the vanishing Indian folk."[39] Later in the month *New York Times* music critic Richard Aldrich wrote glowingly of Roosevelt's comments, remarking that Negro songs certainly bore African characteristics and that "they are easily intelligible and highly sympathetic to the white race." Witness, he said, the ragtime craze.[40]

A great champion of Negro music in the era was Natalie Curtis, the renowned musicologist who published a four-volume collection of Negro folksongs in 1918 and 1919. In an article for *Craftsman* magazine in 1913, she wrote of the Negro's contribution to American music. Ragtime was the very first type of music she mentioned. Since she wrote the article before the research that led to her pathbreaking anthology, much of the historical discussion was by her own admission speculative, but she was confident that ragtime originated in Negro songs and that Negro music was a dominant influence on American music of the day. If there was a common element in Negro music generally speaking, both ragtime and folk music from plantation life, it was syncopation, and if there was a common origin for all Negro music, it was "the voice of the African."

Curtis was interested in more than just acknowledging the debt that American music owed to Negro music and forecasting a bright future for American music because of that debt. She was a socially conscious observer and passionately supported the quest of American Negroes for dignity and equality in all realms of life—not just the realm of music. But music was what she knew best, and she was convinced that through music talented Negroes could establish themselves in positions of prestige, earning recognition that was so slow to come to other members of "the race." Two years earlier, with violinist David Mannes and others, Curtis had helped establish the Music School Settlement for Colored People, inspired by the settlement movement and designed to give Negroes in New York City formal musical training that was otherwise hard to come by. In May of 1912, the Clef Club Orchestra, under the direction of the most famous Negro conductor of the age, James Reese Europe, put on a concert in Carnegie Hall for the benefit of the settlement. Curtis described the event as "an epoch in the musical life of the Negro and also in the development of Negro music." It also marked a moment in race relations: "An unexpected force for better understanding between whites and blacks has been liberated in this conscious admission of the Negro into our musical life," she wrote. Negro music "appeals to the listener with that elemental truth of feeling in which race has no part and humanity is one." And yet the essence of the Negro's contribution, as Curtis saw it, was precisely the set of musical elements that were peculiar to the Negro race, and those elements were primitive and exotic.[41]

Ragtime had many prominent boosters during the 1910s. The theme remained essentially the same: it was there to save the soul of American music, it was Negro in origin, it therefore was connected with Africa, its most significant feature was syncopation, and thus it was archetypally *American*. Theatre and music critic-at-large Hiram K. Moderwell, one of the era's most exuberant advocates of ragtime, ended an article on the musical form in the *New Republic* in 1915 like this:

> As you walk up and down the streets of an American city you feel in its jerk and rattle a personality different from that of any European capital. This is American. It is in our lives, and it helps to form our characters and condition our mode of action. It should have expression in art, simply because any people must express itself if it is to know itself. No European music can or possibly could express this American personality. Ragtime I believe does express it. It is today the one true American music.[42]

In May of 1912, when James Reese Europe lifted his baton in Carnegie Hall and began to conduct William H. Tyers's *Panama: A Characteristic Novelty*—a ragtime composition if ever there was one—something remarkable happened. As Lester A. Walton, a journalist and critic (and later U.S. ambassador to Liberia), wrote for *The New York Age*, "White men and women then looked at each other and smiled, while one lady seated in a prominent box began to beat time industriously with her right hand, which was covered with many gems. It was then," Walton continued, "that after a brief mental soliloquy I was forced to conclude that despite the adverse criticism of many who are unable to play it syncopation is truly a native product—a style of music of which the Negro is originator, but which is generally popular with all Americans."[43] But something had already changed in the world of Negro music, though the fashionable, bejeweled white lady in her Carnegie Hall box seat couldn't have known about it yet. In 1919, after Europe was murdered by one of his own band members, a writer for *Outlook* paid the fallen conductor what he must have considered the ultimate tribute, crediting him with helping to establish ragtime as a reputable contribution to American music. The true American musicians of the day, he wrote, are "the men who in the Broadway shows and in the cabarets are supplying the music that gets to the toes and finger-tips of the average American."[44]

And the blues. Peter C. Muir tells this story in *Long Lost Blues*, his history of this musical form in America. In January of 1912, a New York publishing company brought out a piece of sheet music titled simply "The Blues." It sounded almost nothing like what musicians today would label "blues." The term today usually denotes a fairly specific formal structure, generally twelve bars long, built on a modified scale (a major scale, with the third and seventh notes often flattened), and with certain harmonic changes occurring in specific places (above all, the IV-chord, that is, the chord built on the fourth note in the scale, in the fifth and six bars). In fact, "The Blues" sounded a lot like a ragtime composition, though the words ("I've got the blues, but I'm too blamed mean to cry") conform to the spirit of typical blues lyrics. Three more songs bearing the word "blues" in their titles would be published that year: "Baby Seals Blues," by H. Franklin Seals; "Dallas Blues," by Hart A. Wand; and "The Memphis Blues," by W. C. Handy, who would become the best-known composer of blues in this early era. All three of these songs contained at least one section that was written in the standard twelve-bar blues form. As Muir shows, the number of compositions published annually with the word "blues" in the title ("titular blues," as they are called) grew by a factor of thirty over the next eight years.[45]

Alone among historians, Muir has come up with a plausible account of how and when the twelve-bar blues form emerged and has even identified some of its immediate sources (though like other historians, he concedes that the ultimate sources are probably not discoverable). A precursor in twelve-bar form was the "blues ballad" genre, whose most familiar representative is "Frankie and Johnnie." Blues ballads were common around the turn of the century. From the point of view of harmony, the blues ballad differs from the twelve-bar blues in what might seem the most insignificant of details: its IV-chord lasts three bars (bars 5 through 7) instead of two. But, as Muir has brilliantly explained, the difference is essential. True blues songs rely on a call-and-response pattern in the lyrics: the singer sings for two bars (call) and the instrumental accompaniment plays for two bars (response). The two bars of IV-chord correspond to the sung portion of the middle four bars, and the remaining two bars (of I-chord) correspond to the instrumental response. Blues ballads did not use call-and-response, and if genuine blues songs did, this was one of the clearest signs of the form's Negro heritage, Muir speculates. Though we can't know for sure what the precursors to this tradition were on southern plantations or, for that matter, in parts of Africa from which slaves were transported, we can be reasonably sure that call-and-response formed part of plantation culture in some part of the

South. In any case, the true twelve-bar form emerged during the couple of years after 1910.[46]

In the next decade, a number of tunes were published that would become standard in the repertoire. At the top of the list no doubt would be those by W. C. Handy (1873–1958), often (though not quite accurately) referred to as the "Father of the Blues" (as in the title of his autobiography, published in 1941). Handy wrote, in addition to "Memphis Blues," "St. Louis Blues" (1914), "Yellow Dog Blues" (first published 1914 as "Yellow Dog Rag"), "Hesitating Blues" (1915), "Beale Street Blues" (1916), "Aunt Hagar's Blues" (1920), and many others. Blues songs, as we've come to know them since immediately after this era, are single-strain compositions; that is, they consist of just one twelve-bar sequence that is repeated (usually with improvisation) one or more times. In Handy's era, however, popular songs almost always had more than one strain—usually three. All of Handy's compositions that I just mentioned consist of at least two strains. "Memphis Blues" opens with a standard blues strain, moves into a ragtime-style strain, and finishes off with a second blues. Handy's most famous composition, "St. Louis Blues," is similarly divided into three strains. Once again, the first and third are in standard twelve-bar blues form, rather different in spirit, the first being slow and languorous, the third more energetic. The middle section is, of all things, a tango, because the Latin dance was enjoying a short period of intense popularity in the United States at the time Handy wrote his famous tune.

What did ordinary Americans understand when they heard the word "blues" in this era? One part of the difficulty of answering this question lies in the music itself. Published compositions that bore the word "blues" in their titles were often (by later, stricter definitions) hybrids, including strains that fully qualify as blues along with others that were drawn from a number of popular music styles, including ragtime. Some "titular blues" were not blues at all, such as the classic 1926 Dixieland tune by Spencer Williams, "Basin Street Blues." Not only does this composition not follow the twelve-bar format of standard blues, it contains almost no blue (flattened) notes in its harmonies.

The other part of the difficulty stems from the circumstance that scarcely had the blues attracted popular attention when the word "jazz" began to be heard. As early as 1915, the confusion between the two terms and the music to which they referred began to be solidified for the public. Readers of the *Chicago Daily Tribune* might have seen a tidbit in July of 1915 by Gordon Seagrove (later, incidentally, the ad-man who invented the Listerine slogan "always a bridesmaid and never a bride"), called "Blues is Jazz and Jazz is Blues." It was a short story, actually, about a woman and her husband, "the Worm," who refuses to dance the fox-trot with her at a restaurant. She threatens to sue for divorce. Then suddenly the music takes over. "The Worm had turned—turned to fox trotting. And the 'blues' had done it. The 'jazz' had put pep into the legs that had scrambled too long for the 5:15 [commuter train]." The key, as for ragtime, was syncopation: "That is what 'blue' music is doing for everybody—taking away what its name implies, the blues," Seagrove wrote. "In a few months it has become the predominant motif in cabaret offerings; its wailing syncopation is heard in every gin mill where dancing holds sway." Not to mention the blue notes, as the pianist in the restaurant explains: "A blue note is a sour note . . . It's a discord—a harmonic discord. The blues are never written into music, but are interpolated by the piano player or other players. They aren't new. They are just reborn into popularity. They started in the south half a century ago and are the interpolations of darkies originally. The trade name for them is 'jazz.'"[47] The article featured two cartoon drawings: one depicting the quarreling couple and the other depicting a caricatured Negro (black face, white lips) playing the blues on a saxophone.

Given the date, it's remarkable that Seagrove insisted not only on equating blues and jazz but also on associating jazz with the fox-trot. The fox-trot had been introduced to the public one year earlier by the Castles. There are several versions of the story that tells the origin of the fox-trot, but most agree that W. C. Handy's "Memphis Blues" was, if not the actual inspiration, at least the first musical accompaniment for the Castles (who may or may not have invented the dance). But then the Castles were way ahead of their time in quite a few ways. In the mid-1910s, Irene was already bobbing her hair and dancing in skirts that were above the ankle (though not as short as skirts would be in the 1920s). Two decades before the famously integrated jazz ensemble that included Benny Goodman and Teddy Wilson in the 1930s, the Castles were performing with James Reese Europe's all-Negro "Society Orchestra." It was merely a matter of time before the word "jazz" would come into common use to describe not only the music that people were dancing to but the entire spirit of an era.

That began to happen around 1917. Partly because of the residual popularity of ragtime, partly because of the shakiness already present in the definition of blues, and partly because of the very short time that separated the early blues craze from the early jazz craze (that is, where the words "blues" and "jazz" themselves were used in connection with these crazes), from the last few years of the 1910s through the 1920s the three words as well as the music they denoted formed at times a slurry of indistinct ingredients. A major reason for the sudden prominence of the word" jazz" in the American vocabulary starting in 1917 was that the Original Dixieland Jazz Band ("Jass Band" in the beginning), an all-white group led by Dominic "Nick" LaRocca, burst on the scene in the early months of the year with the first recordings ever billed as jazz. Their first 78 RPM disc already showed how slippery the concept of jazz was. On one side was "Livery Stable Blues," a tune in twelve-bar blues form but with a sprightly, cheerful beat utterly foreign to the spirit of conventional blues. On the other side was "Dixie Jass Band One-Step," a classic, up-tempo Dixieland composition reminiscent of ragtime. There was syncopation all over the place, and there were plenty of blue notes and trombone glides, but the music was neither strictly ragtime nor strictly blues. Jazz had stepped in to fill the vacuum.

It wasn't long before jazz had become the loose, generic term, referring broadly to styles of music, dance steps, an entire way of life. Ragtime and blues were often used to suggest certain specific features in music, primarily syncopated rhythm for ragtime, wailing melody and harmonic "discord" for the blues.

The association with Negro culture and hence with "Africa" was omnipresent. A very young F. Scott Fitzgerald caught it and placed it front and center in one of his earliest short stories, "The Offshore Pirate" (published in May of 1920 in the *Saturday Evening Post*). The heroine is Fitzgerald's customary 19-year-old, rich, tart-tongued flapper. Ardita finds herself on her uncle's yacht, pining for a man that her family finds unsuitable. Her uncle, Mr. Farnam, has in mind for her another young man, Toby Moreland. Farnam heads for shore, leaving his niece on board alone with the crew. Before you know it, the yacht is commandeered by the most unlikely of pirates, a callow young white man and six Negroes. Curtis Carlyle, or so he calls himself, says he's pulled off a heist and intends to use his ill-gotten gains to set himself up eventually as a rajah in India, then Afghanistan, then England. As if this in itself were not enough of an attraction for the spoiled debutante, Carlyle, before becoming a bank robber, had been a ragtime musician—and all because he grew up around Negroes. As a child, he had learned to play the piano from "a colored woman named Belle Pope Calhoun," and, with the ragtime craze, he found his six "darkies" (his current accomplices) and took them on tour.

Of course Ardita falls for Curtis. As the two enjoy their forbidden escape to an uninhabited island, there is jazz and rhythm all the time. How could there not be? "The Negroes had brought ashore their musical instruments, and the sound of weird ragtime was drifting softly over on the warm breath of the night," we read. If this music inspires romance, or lust, it's naturally because of its African origins: "And from trombone and saxophone ceaselessly whined a blended melody, sometimes riotous and jubilant, sometimes haunting and plaintive as a death-dance from the Congo's heart." It's the perfect set-up: "'Let's dance!' cried Ardita. 'I can't sit still with that perfect jazz going on.'" The narrator goes on to speak of cannibals and the "unconquerable African craving for sleep."[48]

Young Fitzgerald had a big surprise in store for his readers. As it turns out, wouldn't you know, the whole thing is a ruse. Curtis is Toby Moreland! He, his father, and Mr. Farnam hired the six Negro musicians and staged the abduction. It's testimony to the power of jazz that the trick worked. Far from being furious at the deception, Ardita, as Negroes sing in the background, accepts her suitor with open arms. Fitzgerald is said to have invented the expression "Jazz Age." Even if he didn't, he could hardly have paid it a more heartfelt tribute than by composing this silly story.

But with or without Fitzgerald's help, jazz and blues by the early 1920s were being expressly marketed for their connection with Negro and "African" culture. The phrase "race record" seems to have first appeared in 1922. Before long, it was all over the place. It referred to recordings of Negro music performed by Negro artists. Most of the music featured on these recordings was blues or dance music. Many of the big recording companies got in on the action. Paramount Records pushed the blues singing career of Alberta Hunter, "The Pride of the Race," and blues hits by other "race stars." Vocalion Red Records had its inventory of race records, as did Columbia ("The finest talent among colored artists records for the Columbia Graphophone Company"), and Victor.[49] But the greatest force in the business was Okeh Records. The company was producing race records before the phrase was invented, making history in 1920 with the release of the world's first blues recording, Perry Bradford's "Crazy Blues," sung by Mamie Smith. Starting in 1923, Okeh pioneered a practice that other labels would soon follow and that gave Negro music a whole new dimension—whatever the race of its consumers. It was called "remote recording," "location recording," or "field recording." At first, Okeh engineers traveled to other cities, such as Chicago, to record resident musicians, instead of having the musicians come to New York. Before long, however, recording engineers were taking their portable equipment to rural areas in the United States and recording local music. Much of what they captured was Negro music.[50]

Cultural historian Karl Hagstrom Miller tells how the practice developed. During the first decade and a half of the twentieth century, record companies saw the value of marketing locally and domestically to immigrant communities, whose members were eager to listen to music that represented their own culture. During the Great War, the practice became yet more vigorous. Savvy businessmen saw nationalist sentiment aroused by the war in immigrant populations as a source of interest in ethnic music. Meeting the demands of such a market meant importing recordings from abroad, which in turn meant a type of globalization. But once the idea of "race records" emerged (even before the phrase), the idea also emerged that such records were analogous to the ones imported for the foreign-born. Okeh Records and other companies were seeking out the music of an exotic population, recording it, and selling the recordings in a domestic market. It's just that, in the case of race music, the exotic population in question lived here, in the United States. It was a form of globalization in miniature.[51] Not all race records were recorded remotely; in fact, the best-selling ones were recorded in large cities. But the remote recordings contributed to the sense that race records in general presented something exotic.

In the conventional version of globalization, we think of an individual nation as it trades with other nations. In *this* version of globalization, what corresponds by analogy to the individual nation is a market—mostly urban but within the same nation—that is physically or culturally distant from the source of the desired goods. A remotely recorded blues record necessarily carried a true exoticism with it, but even blues records produced in the city were marketed to appear as something foreign. "Crazy Blues" may have been recorded in New York City, but the idea was that, listening to it, even New Yorkers had the sense that they were enjoying an exciting import. And the beauty of it was that it came right into your parlor or living room. All you needed were some records and a Victrola. You didn't need to go anywhere.

At the top of the white socio-cultural hierarchy, jazz appears to have been received as an exotic import—from within the United States. Nowhere is this clearer than in a signal event of the mid-1920s: the world premiere of George Gershwin's "Rhapsody in Blue" on the afternoon of Lincoln's Birthday, 1924, in Aeolian Hall (right across Forty-Second Street from the New York Public Library). Gershwin wrote the work at the invitation of the hugely successful Paul Whiteman, whose all-white Palais Royal Orchestra had been making the rounds playing "jazz" and what was already being called "pops" (as in Boston Pops, founded in 1885 and so named in 1900). It's not entirely clear what Whiteman understood by "jazz," as he himself admitted in an attention-grabbing defense of it that he wrote three years later for the *New York Times*. "With battles over jazz raging again I can only repeat that after playing jazz for twelve years I don't know what it is," he wrote. In the article, he never once mentioned Negro culture. The Lincoln's Birthday concert, grandly called "An Experiment in Modern Music," was all about white people. Some of the classical music world's top luminaries, including Serge Rachmaninoff, Jascha Heifetz, and Walter Damrosch, were in attendance. The opening selection was "Livery Stable Blues," by Nick LaRocca. Much of the program was given over to standard pops fare: hits by Irving Berlin, Edward MacDowell, Rudolf Friml, Victor Herbert, and Edward Elgar.[52]

But then there was "Rhapsody in Blue," composed and performed by the young George Gershwin (1898–1937), who was best known at this time for "Swanee." What to make of the new composition? Its title was clearly designed to be suggestive, not denotative. It wasn't called "The [Something-or-Other] Blues," and it wasn't written in twelve-bar blues form. But the sound of the blues was completely unmistakable from the opening bars and for the first few minutes of the piece. At the start, the clarinetist ripped upward through a two-and-a-half-octave scale passage, playing most of it glissando-style, landed on a screaming, high b-flat, and then played a lazy, uncounted melody in which three notes of the major scale were flattened and everything seemed to be accented off the beat. When the orchestra came in, it too syncopated and stuck to the blues scale. To almost anyone hearing it for the first time, the "Rhapsody" appears to have a rather loose structure (though some modern musicologists have found it to be quite tightly organized), and large expanses of it sound less "bluesy" than the opening. There are strains of popular song, lots of music designed to mimic the sounds of the city, even, some listeners have thought, sounds reminiscent of the Jewish shtetl. But there can be no doubt that the message of this remarkable piece was that jazz—and by extension the blues—had now been officially brought to the classical concert stage, complete with gentleman musicians dressed in formal evening garb, sporting starched, white shirtfronts and bowties.

In an essay on jazz published in *The New Negro*, James A. Rogers, a music critic associated with the Harlem Renaissance, captured the essential tension in the new music between the local (in this case racial) and the universal or cosmopolitan. "Jazz is a marvel of paradox," he wrote, "too fundamentally human, at least as modern humanity goes, to be typically racial, too international to be characteristically national, too much abroad in the world to have a special home. And yet jazz in spite of it all is one part American and three parts American Negro, and was originally the nobody's child of the levee and the city slum."[53] The paradox is the common theme of the era. Negro music was the product of an exotic home-grown culture, the product of African culture, and a product that dwelt in an international community simply because of its universal appeal (not to mention its dizzy popularity in parts of Europe). Any way you looked at this music, it was filled with the enticing mystery of exoticism, enjoying the same status as the dietary fare that found its way to American tables and the smoking materials that found their way to American lips. In some ways, a cigarette, a banana, and a single Okeh record are like a lonely railroad siding: each one may be here, right now, but it can also connect you with a spot thousands of miles away.

PART III: THE SECULAR, ECUMENICAL COLLECTIVE

8 Race Goes Scientific, Then Transnational

PROBABLY VERY FEW AMERICANS noticed the scholarly gathering that took place in Philadelphia on April 12 and 13, 1901. It was the annual meeting of the American Academy of Political and Social Science. The topic was "America's Race Problems." Anyone who followed the issue in the press might have recognized at least one prominent name on the list of speakers: Booker T. Washington. There was also a certain Dr. W. E. Burghardt Du Bois of Atlanta University (whose *Souls of Black Folk* would not be published for another two years). And then there was Edward A. Ross, Ph.D., University of Nebraska.

Only a few months earlier Professor Ross had been the subject of a minor scandal when the administration of Stanford University, where he was chairman of the economics department, forced him to resign. The request came from none other than Leland Stanford's widow, and the issue was Chinese immigration. Ross was for restricting it; the Stanford family, having greatly profited from the labor of Chinese immigrants in the railroad industry, was for permitting it. At stake, of course, was academic freedom, and even liberal publications rushed to Ross's defense. The question remained, however, what to make of his views.

Professor Ross gave the Annual Address at the Philadelphia meeting, and his topic was "The Causes of Race Superiority." The address was printed in the academy's *Annals* that July. Assuming that the printed version roughly matched the spoken one, we can safely say that Ross's audience found the very opening of his remarks to be sane, balanced, and remarkably progressive. The importance of race had been grossly exaggerated in recent times, he seemed to say. At the same time, race must not be completely discounted; a middle ground was necessary. "There is the equality fallacy inherited from the earlier thought of the last century," he said, "which belittles race differences and has a robust faith in the power of intercourse and school instruction to lift up a backward fold to the level of the best. Then there is the counter fallacy, grown up since Darwin, which exaggerates the race factor and regards the actual differences of peoples as hereditary and fixed." The second error, he said, was "the more besetting" at the time he was speaking.[1]

But astonishingly, the moment Ross had finished his brief introduction, he launched into a lengthy discussion of all the factors that *do* make one race superior to another. Throughout he maintained complete fidelity to the classic racial stereotypes of the day, and even contradicted himself within this portion of the speech in order to reaffirm repeatedly the dominance of what he finally referred to as "the Superior Race"—by which he appeared to mean Americans, minus the Negro population. Ross listed his causes of superiority: (1) climatic adaptability, (2) energy, (3) self-reliance, (4) foresight, (5) the value sense, (6) stability of character, (7) pride of blood, and (8) strong sense of superiority. The first two traits, he conceded, clearly give the upper hand to nonwhite races. In fact, Ross even stated explicitly that "lack of adaptability" is "a handicap which the white man must ever bear in competing with black, yellow, or brown men," commenting that the white man's sciences and inventions are only a "temporary advantage."[2] For in the last analysis, he said, "it is solely on its persistent physiological and psychological qualities that the ultimate destinies of a race depend."[3]

But curiously, as he made his way through the list he increasingly saw causes that were advantages for the white races, especially the dominant one in the United States. From "self-reliance" through a "strong sense of superiority," Ross made his point by drawing unfavorable comparisons between "the Anglo-Saxon race" and others, specifically named and described. When it came to "foresight," for example, Ross made such statements as these: "In British Honduras the natives are happy-go-lucky negroes who rarely save and who spend their earnings on festivals and extravagances, rather than on comforts and decencies. In Venezuela the laborers live for to-day and all their week's earnings are gone by Monday morning."[4]

In the end, Ross raised the specter of "race suicide." Though he avoided explicitly Darwinian language, the approach clearly stemmed from two generations' worth of evolutionary theory. Race suicide for him appeared to have nothing to do with intermarriage; instead, it would arise if another race (he had in mind specifically the "Asiatic" one) were to gain an advantage through raw numbers (by multiplying faster than "we") or through successful competition in the workplace—arising, of course, from the economic prowess innate in members of the Asiatic race. Still, on the whole Ross saw signs of great hope for the American people. Here's how he expressed it:

> It is true that our average of energy and character is lowered by the presence in the South of several millions of an inferior race. It is true that the last twenty years have diluted us with masses of fecund but beaten humanity from the hovels of far Lombardy and Galicia. . . . Yet, while there are here problems that only high statesmanship can solve, I believe there is at the present moment no people in the world that is, man for man, equal to the Americans in capacity and efficiency.[5]

Ross's address did not cause a huge stir in the press; nor is it likely that many ordinary Americans troubled to consult the *Annals of the American Academy of Political and Social Science* for the printed version. Its value for history is the pivotal moment it represents in American attitudes toward race. To later generations, Ross has been known for the concept of "social control," developed in his book of that title published the same year as his address on race superiority. I'll have more to say about that concept in chapter 10. But if he was known for anything in the years leading up to this speech, it was his criticism of big business, his defense of the common laborer, and his outspoken rejection of laissez-faire capitalism. Not that racial animosities are necessarily inconsistent with these positions; Ross's hostility toward Chinese immigrants, after all, arose in part from his anger at what he regarded as the unfair competition such immigrants created for native-born American workers. But on some level, Ross clearly regarded a rejection of "the race factor," especially when that factor pretended to scientific validity because it claimed to be based in Darwinism, as consistent with—even necessary to—the outlook of the progressive he considered himself to be. And yet the very race factor he thought he was rejecting was so utterly ingrained in his thinking that he never for a moment stopped to consider the purely logical absurdities—let alone the moral offenses, for someone of his views—in the speech he gave in Philadelphia. And this was an academic, a social scientist with the loftiest credentials.

And so it appeared to be for almost everyone in this era. By the turn of the century, race as a classificatory category had become absolutely fundamental to the American's view of the social world. More than a century later, we need to stop and think what this meant and what it did *not* mean. What it did not mean was that the category was used exclusively for malign purposes. The word "racism," denoting the employment of racial categories with hostile intent, did not come into use until the 1930s, when it served an increasingly terrified public in Europe and the United States as a label for the evolving policies of Hitler's Germany. Of course there *was* plenty of what could accurately be described as racism in the United States, before the term was invented. Clustered around the year 1900, for example, was a whole collection of books that took aim at "the Negro," characterizing him as "a beast" and "a menace to American Civilization." But the *category* of race was far more fundamental than its extensive and frequent manifestations as hatred. It was used not only unfavorably but also favorably, and for that matter, neutrally.[6]

The classic study of the subject of race in America remains Thomas F. Gossett's *Race: The History of an Idea in America.* It was published at the very end of 1963, a couple of weeks after the assassination of John F. Kennedy, a couple of months after the Birmingham, Alabama, church bombing, and several years before the catastrophic racial disturbances in Los Angeles, Detroit, and other American cities. Gossett struck a note of optimism at the end of his book, seeing much recent progress in race relations and grounds for hope that things would continue to improve in the future. Anyone reading the book by the end of the 1960s is likely to consider this a serious flaw. But Gossett may have had his reasons for being hopeful, and of course he had no way of predicting that four years later, to take just one example, the remarkably integrated city of Detroit would go up in flames and never recover. The real flaw—and it's a minor one—is Gossett's tendency to conflate racial thinking with racism, a term he uses innumerable times. While it's no doubt true that in a huge number of cases racial thinking shows up as malevolent prejudice (especially from the perspective of later generations), the real question has to do with the concept of race itself, how it arose and developed, how it attached itself inseparably to Americans' views of their fellow human beings.

In fact, Gossett does go a long way toward answering this question. The concept arose in the middle of the eighteenth century, but Darwinian evolutionary theory gave it a scientific foundation, or the semblance of one, which altered it dramatically by the end of the nineteenth century. Social Darwinism, or what Gossett calls "Social Darwinist individualism," a collection of theories that assign the struggle for existence a central place in human experience, easily included racial traits among the factors that promote or hinder survival.[7] The same may be said for eugenics, created and developed in England during the 1860s and 1870s by Francis Galton and imported into the United States in the late 1870s. The title of the book by Galton that introduced eugenics to the world conveys the message and the prospect of its application to race: *Hereditary Genius* (1869). Here's one sample of what Galton had to say about the "negro race": "The number among the negroes of those whom we should call half-witted men, is very large. Every book alluding to negro servants in America is full of instances. I was myself much impressed by this fact during my travels in Africa. The mistakes the negroes made in their own matters, were so childish, stupid, and simpleton-like, as frequently to make me ashamed of my own species."[8] If intellectual gifts are inherited and certain races possess more of them than others do, it's easy to see how members of those races will produce offspring that will continue to be superior to the offspring of the less-favored races. Race will thus carry with it a destiny, as it always had done, but one whose explanation apparently possesses a firm foundation in scientific investigation.[9]

I'm not going to tell the story of the eugenics movement. What's worth knowing is how uncritically the public appears to have embraced it and its founder, though Galton himself was hardly in the news every day. Gossett tells the story of how other academics adopted and adapted Galton's theories. What he left out is what was served up to ordinary Americans. When Galton died, in early 1911, eugenics had been around for over forty years and had received a powerful impulse from the rediscovery of Mendel and the rise of genetics. Here's what the *New York Times* printed, by way of an obituary, about Galton and his mysteriously inadequate fame:

> Just why the fame of Francis Galton should have been confined to circles so much narrower than those of the other men in the little group to which he belonged is not easy to see. That he stood near, if not close, beside the leaders who made the second half of the nineteenth century more important in the history of science than all the preceding centuries put together is doubted by none who knows the extent and the originality of his researches, his accuracy as an observer, and the practical value of his many achievements.

The writer speculated that, among evolutionists, Galton managed to escape controversy. "Among scientists, however," the article continued, "his fame is safe as well as bright, in spite of the fact that most of them nowadays are inclined to ascribe something more of weight to environment and less to heredity than he did."[10]

One of Galton's pupils built his own small corner of modest fame by taking the master's principles in what might seem today a surprising direction. He was Joseph Jacobs, Australian-born literary critic, folklorist, and Judaic scholar. In the early 1880s, having settled in London during the previous decade, he undertook to examine the question whether the Jews properly constitute a race and, if so, what their purely racial characteristics are. There was a compelling reason for undertaking this research. Anti-Semitism, under that name, was born in Germany in 1879, with the foundation of the League of Anti-Semites by former anarchist Wilhelm Marr. The very choice of a name showed a particularly "modern" approach to anti-Jewish sentiment. Why not call the organization the League of Anti-Jews, since Jews alone, among "Semitic" peoples, were targeted? The reason was that, at a time of post-Darwinian pseudo-biology, "Semite" carried the suggestion of tribalism, therefore race, therefore hereditary character. In 1881, German socialist Eugen Dühring published the book whose title aimed the debate in the direction it would take for generations: *The Jewish Question as a Race, Custom and Culture Question*. Dühring gave the answer to the "question" in the opening pages of the book: Jews were a race, not merely a group of people voluntarily following the same set of religious beliefs and practices.[11] If they were a race, then their habits and conduct were predictable and irremediable, which meant that members of that race were to be regarded with the profoundest suspicion and fear. Some four decades later, Adolf Hitler devoted an entire section of the chapter "People and Race" ("Volk und Rasse") in *Mein Kampf* to reasserting this point about the Jews.

So Jacobs set out to determine if Jews were, in fact, a race. His approach seemed eminently rational and scientific. He took a long list of characteristics frequently attributed to Jews as distinguishing them from other groups and submitted each characteristic to scrutiny. The vast majority he chalked up to social and environmental conditions rather than to heredity. What was left? Purely physical features: height and girth; craniometry; hair, eyes, and complexion; color-blindness; noses; lips; facial expression. As to this last feature, Jacobs enlisted the help of Galton, who, it turned out, had the skills (whatever else you might think of him, he was a multiply talented man) necessary to create composite photographic images of a set of "typical" Jewish faces. Jacobs's evidence ended up showing that there *were* such faces and that even the classic Jewish nose, the one that showed up in so many hundreds of anti-Semitic cartoons, had a basis in reality. Jacobs published his results first in an article titled "The Racial Characteristics of Modern Jews" (1885) and then in a short book, *Studies in Jewish Statistics* (1891) (which included the article as an appendix). Galton's name appeared some two dozen times in the book.[12]

Jacobs's conclusion was crystal clear: "I am inclined to support the long-standing belief in the substantial purity of the Jewish race, and to hold that the vast majority of contemporary Jews are the lineal descendants of the Diaspora of the Roman Empire."[13] Race might not explain behavioral characteristics commonly attributed to Jews or, for that matter, such physical characteristics as their alleged tendency to live long lives, but in the end Jews were a race in the modern, scientific meaning of the term. Jacobs's assertion bore out what Dühring had said a few years earlier; it's just that the intent behind that assertion was different. Jacobs was claiming to offer a purely empirical observation whose moral force was neutral.

Jacobs's work did not have any significant, direct impact on life in the United States. References to him in the press were relatively rare, many of them having to do with his work as a folklorist. Still, if he was representative of the age, it should come as no surprise that American Jews themselves and other Americans who harbored no ill will toward the Jews unquestioningly considered Jews to be a race. In this era, the Jewish-owned *New York Times* regularly used or reported the phrase "Jewish race" in a purely neutral or even favorable sense. By a crude estimate, occurrences of the phrase in the first decade of the twentieth century were double what they had been in the previous decade and continued to rise (peaking later, in the 1930s, dropping off sharply after World War II, and dwindling to almost nothing by the end of the twentieth century).[14]

If you comb through Gossett's book for references to specific races in the United States, you'll quickly find that three command the lion's share of attention: Indians, Negroes, and Jews. After the turn of the century, it was Negroes and Jews that dominated conversations about race—that is, when race itself was the topic. Why? There was certainly plenty of talk about various immigrant groups and their characteristics. Think of *How the Other Half Lives*, for example, published in 1890. Jacob Riis, as he described the inhabitants of New

York City's various tenement neighborhoods, had occasion to speak of Greek, Italian, Chinese, Bohemian, German (as distinct from Bohemian), and Polish races in that book, in addition to the Negro race and the Jewish race. But these other groups in the United States, even if they were often regarded as races, also carried an identification with nations. Through the late nineteenth century, Indians were regarded as an impediment to nationhood for the superior Anglo-Saxon race. You have only to read the young Theodore Roosevelt on the subject to get a sense of the status this group enjoyed in the eyes of many progressive, educated, white Americans. Roosevelt was more than willing to examine the social and political structures of various tribes, but he did not consider Indians to be Americans by the same right as people such as himself (even with his potentially questionable Dutch heritage). Nor did he regard them as forming nations in any meaningful sense before white Europeans came to confront them.

A few sentences from an appendix to the first volume of *The Winning of the West* (1889) tell the whole story about race and claims to territory. Roosevelt has just acknowledged that the white man has sometimes been terribly unjust to the Indian. But, he says:

> It was wholly impossible to avoid conflicts with the weaker race, unless we were willing to see the American continent fall into the hands of some other strong power; and even had we adopted such a ludicrous policy, the Indians themselves would have made war upon us. . . . To recognize the Indian ownership of the limitless prairies and forests of this continent—that is, to consider the dozen squalid savages who hunted at long intervals over a territory of a thousand square miles as owning it outright—necessarily implies a similar recognition of the claims of every white hunter, squatter, horse-thief, or wandering cattle-man.[15]

By the beginning of the twentieth century, with territorial issues safely settled in favor of the white majority, Indians no longer commanded the same attention in discussions of race as did Negroes and Jews, who also failed to conform to any conventional sense of nationality—Negroes in their forced diaspora and Jews in their sometimes voluntary diaspora. Whether or not some Negroes and Jews in the United States enjoyed the same civil status as white Americans of non-Jewish, European descent, they certainly bore no perceived "organic" association with a nation either then or in the recent past. In the eyes of their compatriots, they were neither *of* one nation nor *of* many different nations. They were therefore neither national nor international in status. Rather they were what we might call transnational (though the word was not used in the era), in the sense that they transcended the existing system of nations.

If the concept of race in the early decades of the twentieth century tended to come up especially frequently in connection with these two transnational groups, then two closely related inferences may be drawn. First, since the concept of race applied to groups lacking a nationality, then it must have been a very powerful concept indeed, given the continuing strength of European nationalism throughout our period. As we've seen, the race concept rested on a "scientific" foundation, something perceived as apparently more solid than the circumstance of having resided (or having descended from those who resided) within the borders of a recognized nation. Second, with the emphasis on transnational groups, the concept of race in the public mind began to be decoupled from the concept of nation, and a tendency arose to regard members of the most discussed races as existing in a condition that transcended nationality.

This tendency was given particular force by the moral dimension of the race question in a number of high-visibility international rights cases. But at least for the two transnational groups, race provided a binding social network. According to the conception of race prevalent at the time, if you were an individual Negro or Jew, your very essence was connected to and defined by the aggregate of all other Negroes and Jews. Biological science said so, and no one doubted it.

As It Turns Out, The Race Question Has a Moral Dimension

It would be quite some time before anyone began seriously challenging the concept of race itself—the existence, that is, of a taxonomic principle that distinguishes among groups according to physical attributes handed down from generation to generation. The anthropologist and popular science writer Ashley Montagu attempted to do just this in 1942, with his *Man's Most Dangerous Myth: The Fallacy of Race*. But in that year there were compelling reasons for a British Jew to attack the validity of the race concept. Before that, it had remained rock-solid for decades. The only questions in the era were whether race has a determinative influence on behavior, customs, and intelligence and what attitude people should adopt toward members of a race different from their own. If race had a scientific basis and if, as a consequence, there truly were groups that showed at least significant *physical*, if not behavioral, cultural, and intellectual differences, then nature itself had created a means for dividing society in such a way that the individual's primary attachment was to one of these groups and not to something larger. The problem would seem particularly pressing in the United States at that time, given the presence of so many competing racial groups.

But around the turn of the twentieth century, something began to happen that paradoxically produced a reaffirmation of the concept itself together with a shift in attitude toward race and a means of transcending it. It involved the two transnational groups, Negroes and Jews, but not only those in the United States. In this setting, "Jew" referred to a Jewish person living anywhere in the world, and "Negro" referred to a black African, whether he or she resided in Africa or as a slave and immigrant (including descendants thereof) in other lands. Black Africans increasingly came to the attention of the West both as examples of modern-day "primitive man" and as victims of exploitation and brutality at the hands of Western Europeans. At the turn of the century and in the early years of the twentieth, a series of international events focused American attention on the destructive human consequences of the attitude of superiority that one race adopts toward another. Let's have a look at just two examples.

Congo

In chapter 7, speaking of the ivory trade, I told part of the story of King Leopold's adventure in Congo. What eventually went wrong with that adventure was that Leopold bumped up against modern communications technology and a fledgling attitude toward race, especially in Great Britain and the United States. In the 1890s, Edmund Morel, a British-born clerk for a shipping firm that provided service between Belgium and the Congo Free State (as, with grim irony, it came to be called), observed that what was being presented to the outside world as "trade" between the European imperial power and her colony was not trade at all. Inbound ships groaned under the weight of goods taken from the African territory, but outbound ships were laden with military troops, arms, and ammunition. Morel began to investigate and then to report, beginning in 1900. Over the next decade or so, he would publish dozens of articles and numerous books on King Leopold's colony and the atrocities being committed there. In 1904, he helped found the Congo Reform Association, an organization that shortly attracted international support and membership. In the 1890s, European and American missionaries began to visit Congo and document abuses there. What lent credibility to their descriptions was a new tool: the "Kodak." Thanks to missionaries and reporters who gathered extensive photographic evidence, Morel was able to show the public gruesome images, for example, of Congolese children with their hands severed (as punishment for failing to bring in a sufficient quantity of rubber) and of the various instruments of torture used to enforce colonial rule. And at the beginning of the nineteenth century, once Morel had images and information in hand, it was easy to broadcast them around the world almost instantaneously (though they invariably took some time to get from Africa to Europe).

In 1908, King Leopold sold the colony to his own country for a tidy sum. The following year he died. The story resurfaced in 1998 thanks to Adam Hochschild, an American journalist who wrote *King Leopold's Ghost: A Story of Greed, Terror, and Heroism in Colonial Africa*. Hochschild estimated that some ten million Africans died as a direct result of Leopold's policies.[16] Given the enormity of what happened, one of the most striking features of the story is that it passed into oblivion. The evidence was all there in the era when the events were occurring, and the public was exposed to it repeatedly and frequently. So it's probably safe to assume that many Americans received an extended lesson in the real consequences of hostile racial attitudes.

When did they receive it? Newspapers printed accounts of atrocities, as reported by missionaries, as early as the 1890s, but these accounts tended to assign guilt to either Arab slave traders or native African conscripts, while simply raising the question of Belgian responsibility. George Washington Williams, a Negro U.S. Army colonel and veteran of the Civil War, traveled in Africa, visiting Congo, in 1890. From there, he wrote an "open letter" to King Leopold, detailing the abuses and atrocities he'd witnessed and assigning responsibility to both the king and famed explorer Henry Morton Stanley, whom Leopold had commissioned to negotiate "treaties" with African tribes before the Berlin Conference. The document was published in pamphlet form and reported in the press in 1891. But the public was clearly not ready for the news that the open letter contained. The *New York Times* printed a couple of stories about Williams that April, one of which featured Stanley's characterization of the pamphlet's allegations as "blackmail," while the other represented Williams as essentially a notorious con man.[17]

Reporting in the press that laid responsibility squarely at the feet of King Leopold's government, or King Leopold himself, first appeared in earnest at the turn of the century, even before Morel's writings began to circulate. Once those writings came to the public's attention, the press provided almost continuous grounds for public outrage at policies and practices in the Congo Free State. At issue were not only the greed and cruelty of the Belgian king but also the crimes he had been committing since the beginning of the occupation. Of course, crime must be understood not in a strictly legal sense, since the issue was not whether the king was running afoul of his own nation's laws (he apparently wasn't). But this is precisely the point. The crimes in question were not civil or national. They were international, and their victims were construed as either the Negro race or, simply, humanity.

This sense of the crime arose again and again in the press, as did the question of race—though not in the way we might expect today. In April of 1900, the *New York Times* reported that a Belgian socialist member of the Chamber of Deputies had mounted an attack on King Leopold and his regime for atrocities committed in the Congo. For the first few years of the new century, especially after Morel's writings began to appear, the leadership of the *Times* joined in the attacks on Belgian colonial rule. As early as 1902, the paper ran an editorial under the title "The Unfortunate Congo Free State," lamenting King Leopold's failure to abide by a promise to build "a powerful negro kingdom" and supporting Edmund Morel's hope that the Congo State be "called to account for its crime against civilization, for its outrages upon humanity." For the next several years, the editors of the *Times* joined in the chorus of condemnation that arose in the United States and abroad. The year 1906 seemed to mark a high point in the international expression of protest. British journalist (Edward) Harold Spender (father of poet Stephen Spender) gave a lengthy account of the imperial occupation's crimes, citing the arguments the regime used in its own defense and decrying the duplicity and hypocrisy of that regime. The arguments, he wrote, "seem a horrible parody of much that we have heard in recent years within our own Parliament. Glorifications of what is quaintly called 'civilization' mingle grotesquely with appeals to racial and religious prejudice."[18]

When it came to capturing public attention, probably no newspaper or magazine articles were as effective as the international pantheon of high-visibility figures that Morel's rights movement attracted: Mark Twain, Lyman Abbott (Congregationalist minister, writer, social reformer, author of *The Rights of Man*, 1901, and editor of the progressive magazine *Outlook*), Henry Van Dyke (poet, professor of English literature at Princeton, and reformed opponent of abolitionism), Booker T. Washington, and John Wanamaker (founder of the Philadelphia department store) were all officers of the American branch of the Congo Reform Association. In Europe there was the Archbishop of Canterbury, Sir Arthur Conan Doyle, and Anatole France, to name just a few. Booker T. Washington wrote (or at least signed—there's been some question about authorship) an article for *Outlook* in 1904 titled "Cruelty in the Congo Country." Race was central: "My interest in the race to which I belong," the writer began, "and in the advancement of the cause of humanity regardless of race, is my excuse for discussing a subject which I have not hitherto called attention to in public print." The issue was international: "The oppression of the colored race in any one part of the world means, sooner or later, the oppression of the same race elsewhere."[19]

Probably the most conspicuous celebrity product in the movement was the pamphlet *King Leopold's Soliloquy* (1905), by Mark Twain. Clearly choosing to shun subtlety, Twain represented Leopold as a shameless, scheming, unscrupulous monster, self-pityingly licking his wounds as his designs were revealed to the world. The pamphlet included classic photos of children with severed hands. Among the acerbically funniest lines in the king's speech to himself:

> Then all of a sudden came the crash! That is to say, the incorruptible *kodak*—and all the harmony went to hell! The only witness I have encountered in my long experience that I couldn't bribe. Every Yankee missionary and every interrupted trader sent home and got one; and now—oh, well, the pictures get sneaked around everywhere, in spite of all we can do to ferret them out and suppress them. Ten thousand pulpits and ten thousand presses are saying the good word for me all the time and placidly and convincingly denying the mutilations. Then that trivial little kodak, that a child can carry in its pocket, gets up, uttering never a word, and knocks them dumb!"[20]

King Leopold's Soliloquy sold for twenty-five cents, all proceeds being donated to relief for the people of Congo. Still, don't think for a moment that everyone who defended the people of Congo against the murderous Belgian king did so on the grounds that black people were the equals of white people. Consider Lyman Abbott, whose *Outlook* openly supported the cause of the Congo Reform Association. In the spring of 1903, there were two large meetings, one in New York, the other in Richmond, Virginia, devoted partially or wholly to the topic of Negro education. Abbott spoke at both. Grover Cleveland and Booker T. Washington spoke at the first. Abbott and the former president agreed on one important point: suffrage is *not* a natural right for Negroes; it must be earned. Abbott and Washington both spoke again at the end of the month, at the thirty-fifth anniversary of Hampton Normal and Agricultural Institute, the Negro school at which Washington had studied before attending seminary. While Washington spoke of the "mutual regard and esteem and affection existing between the white man and the colored man of the South," Abbott staked out his position with this ungenerous slogan: "Manhood first and suffrage afterward." For weeks, Abbott and Cleveland were in the news for their opposition to Negro suffrage. At the end of April, the *Congregationalist and Christian World*, considerably to the left of the Congregationalist *Outlook*, condemned both men in an editorial titled "The Negro—a Vassal or a Citizen," and in May, Reverend Newell Dwight Hillis, who had succeeded Abbott as pastor of the famously progressive Plymouth Church in Brooklyn, denounced them from his pulpit, saying that "not even an ex-President or a religious editor can revise or enlarge or improve God's word, that says: 'All ye are brethren.'"[21]

And from the academy, there was G. Stanley Hall, who had just published his monumental two-volume *Adolescence* and who in a few years would invite Freud to Clark University. Hall was deeply involved in the Congo reform movement, publicly denounced the crimes of the King Leopold's Belgian regime on many occasions, and served as president of the International Congo League when it was formed in 1908. At issue was the human toll of those crimes, and yet Hall firmly believed in a hierarchy of races. An entire chapter of *Adolescence* is devoted to "ethnic psychology" and is shot through with references to "adolescent races," "lower races," "primitive people," "savagery," and their opposites.[22] At the Thirteenth Universal Peace Congress, held in Boston in February of 1905, and devoted to "the mutual relations of races" in connection with the Congo question, Hall spoke passionately about the "selfish greed of man" and about how "the lower races of mankind are being destroyed by the so-called higher," not only in Congo but in colonies and dependencies all over the world. He introduced a note of what we would call today cultural relativism, acknowledging that our (Western) civilization was not necessarily "the last and best thing in history" and that "some of the primitive races still had their future before them." He appeared not even to agree with the presiding member, Reverend Charles F. Dole (Unitarian minister and father of the man who founded the pineapple empire), who proclaimed (as reported) "that men are our brothers whatever the color of their skin."[23] Dole's statement suggested a currently existing equality. Hall's statements didn't.

But the point seemed to be precisely that what was being violated in Congo and elsewhere was *not* the principle that all men (to use the language of the era) of all races, currently, at that time, were equal with respect to intelligence, civilized development, or civil rights within their own countries, but rather the principle that no man deserved to be enslaved, unduly exploited, tortured, or murdered *because of his race*. Race was still there. It remained a fundamental organizing concept; and the judgment that certain races were superior to others was not even close to disappearing. Instead, the principle that emerged among the vast majority of those active in the Congo reform movement was an essential concept of human dignity: the right not to be persecuted on the basis of race.

This was immensely significant. This right was a human right, not a civil one belonging to a specific nation. And as much as we might be inclined today to condemn the racial assumptions that underlay the good deeds of so many reformers in that era, there's an oddly happy paradox that appears: because of exactly those assumptions, a more broadly construed conception of rights began to emerge. It was all because of the "even" that was implicit in this conception: *even* members of "lower races" have the right not to be mistreated. The topic of rights thus gave the American public a means for transcending the category of race. The group in question was one whose legal and national status, in Western terms, was ambiguous almost wherever its members dwelt. Native-born Africans in Congo, whether or not under Belgian occupation, were not citizens of a recognized nation and thus lacked the civil status that such citizens would enjoy. American Negroes were historically excluded from the legal protections that most white Americans enjoyed. Thus any rights that might be claimed for black Africans in Africa or people of African descent in other parts of the world needed to be claimed in an arena that transcended both race and nation. Such rights needed to be transnational and needed to be conceived as stemming from the fact of being not a member of a race or a citizen of a nation but simply human. Negroes, understood transnationally, were a perfect group for which to claim transnational rights. In the paradoxical thinking of the era, they were inextricably networked to their race, with all of its biologically determining forces, while at the same time they were networked through their race to what would later be officially named the "human family." Jews were the other perfect group.

The Dreyfus Affair and Jews in America

Again, the bare facts can be stated simply and quickly, though the drama lasted for twelve long, tumultuous years. In 1894, Alfred Dreyfus, a French army captain of Alsatian Jewish origin, was arrested on suspicion of forwarding secret military documents to the German embassy. A court martial promptly tried and convicted him. He was exiled to Devil's Island, off the coast of French Guiana. Within two years, evidence surfaced that the handwritten memorandum incriminating Dreyfus had been written by army Major Ferdinand Walsin Esterhazy, and that Dreyfus was thus innocent. A secret military tribunal tried Esterhazy for treason but acquitted him. In the meantime, another officer, Colonel Hubert-Joseph Henry, forged additional documents in order further to incriminate Dreyfus. In January of 1898, Émile Zola published his famous open letter "J'accuse!" in the newspaper *l'Aurore*. In August, Colonel Henry confessed to his forgeries. He was sent to prison, where he committed suicide. The case was reopened, and Dreyfus was granted a new trial in 1899. He was again found guilty by a court martial, but French president Émile Loubet pardoned him. Nonetheless, Dreyfus had to wait almost seven years, till July of 1906, before a civilian court officially overturned this second guilty verdict and restored him to his rank.

This episode could have been seen merely as an egregious miscarriage of justice and a sign that France's political institutions had fallen apart. But it very quickly developed a life of its own as something only marginally related to the legal morass it created. By 1896 it had captured the public's attention, as it became a referendum not on Captain Dreyfus's actual guilt or innocence but rather on France's Jews—in fact, on the "Jewish race" as a whole. And, especially after Zola's courageous and highly inflammatory letter, it overwhelmed French society, dividing it as no other issue had done for decades. It became, simply, *l'Affaire*. There were *antidreyfusards* and *dreyfusards*. The former were not those who, on sober reflection, had concluded that Dreyfus was guilty; they were simply enemies of the Jews. And of course the latter were not those who, on sober reflection, had concluded that Dreyfus was innocent; they were defenders of the Jews.

Contemporaries might have seen something of this nature coming. Modern anti-Semitism, as introduced by Wilhelm Marr in 1879, made its way to France not long before the arrest of Alfred Dreyfus. In 1889, journalist Édouard Drumont formed the Anti-Semitic League of France. Four years earlier he had published a lengthy, ostensibly scholarly work titled *La France juive* (Jewish France), in which he sought to demonstrate the long-standing malign influence of the Jews on the French nation. Everything in the book was about race. The term appeared close to a hundred times, both to explain the character of the Jews and to draw a contrast between them and other groups. Like Eugen Dühring in Germany before him, Drumont found it in his interest to repudiate any religious explanations of his enemies' deplorable nature, insisting instead on racial explanations. For example, there were such gems as this: "At first, [the Jews] celebrated their rites among themselves, and then, little by little, maintaining the instincts of their race, they lost whatever is good in any religion; they were overcome by that sort of frightful despondency that seizes the man who no longer believes in anything."[24] In 1892, Drumont founded a newspaper, *La Libre Parole* (Free speech), which boldly dispensed with any pretense of intellectual substance and simply spewed anti-Semitic venom.

It would be difficult to overstate how pervasive the view was in France that Dreyfus's "race" was adequate grounds for finding him guilty. Today an exceedingly broadminded person might be tempted to conclude that millions of French people, sharing a visceral and reprehensible antipathy to the "Jewish race," uncritically believed in Dreyfus's guilt. But how could a French person with any sense or education consciously and deliberately formulate this syllogism: (I) all Jews are treacherous; (II) Dreyfus is a Jew; (III) ergo he committed treason (yes, this particular act of treason)? Yet it did happen in almost exactly this way. Consider Maurice Barrès, one of France's most esteemed writers and intellectuals. In 1902, after both of Dreyfus's trials, Barrès published *Scènes et doctrines du nationalisme* (Scenes and doctrines of nationalism), much of it devoted to the Dreyfus Affair. With all the exculpatory evidence that had long since surfaced by that year, Barrès remained a passionate *antidreyfusard*, because for him Dreyfus's Jewishness and his guilt were one and the same thing. "I do not need anyone to tell me why Dreyfus committed treason," he wrote. "In psychology, it is enough for me to know that he is capable of committing treason, and it is enough for me to know that he has committed treason. The interval is filled. That Dreyfus is capable of treason I conclude from his race." To be fair to Barrès, we must not omit the next sentence: "That he committed treason I know because I have read the pages of Mercier and Roget [two of Dreyfus's accusers], which are magnificent pieces of work."[25] But this was almost an afterthought. For Barrès, the preponderant evidence in the case was Dreyfus's race. The innate, biologically determined capacity to commit treason obliterated any doubt raised by the published facts or by the glaring irregularities in the proceedings against the Jewish officer. Individuals are determined by their ancestors. They are *net-*

worked to their biological past. That's why Frenchmen behave in accordance with the dictates of honor, and it's why Jews commit treason.

The American press began to take serious notice of the Dreyfus Affair starting in 1897. Articles proliferated with Zola's letter in 1898, after Dreyfus's second conviction in 1899, and after his final rehabilitation in 1906. From the very beginning, there appeared to be complete unanimity on what was happening in France: Dreyfus was being condemned, sentenced, and vilified for no reason other than that he was a Jew. In June of 1897, *Forum*, a moderately progressive political commentary magazine, published an article by a writer mysteriously signing himself "Vindex" (Latin for "protector" or "avenger"). Vindex remarkably laid out the whole story, as a knowledgeable and properly skeptical observer could have done at that date. The bulk of his piece was devoted to a meticulous dissection of the case against Dreyfus and a refutation of all the charges he had faced. But, most important, Vindex cut to the core of the affair as it stood at that relatively early date. What possible explanation, he asked, could there be for the hatred that this officer, a man of impeccable personal and professional character, had aroused in the French population? "Have I not said that Capt. Dreyfus belonged to a class of pariahs?" Vindex wrote. "He was a soldier; but he was also a Jew: and it is on this account that he has been thus prosecuted. That is why his trial is a story of passion. On account of it his cause becomes not merely a national affair, but one which concerns humanity. It creates an interest in one who was the victim of prejudice, not only among his compatriots, but among all men,—who are his brothers, since they are human beings." Vindex excoriated the "anti-Semitic mob," which he held responsible for the persecution of this most loyal of French citizens. Race was at the bottom of the animus the public bore against the Jewish officer. In the anti-Semitic papers, "the most furious diatribes were hurled against the Jews,—the hated race to which Dreyfus belonged. The term Israelite was a synonym for traitor," Vindex wrote.[26]

He was right. Whoever Vindex was, he provided the departure point for the entire American reception of the Dreyfus Affair. When the *New York Times* ran an editorial on the latest developments in October, the writer cited the *Forum* article and clearly used it as the authoritative source for all the factual claims he presented, as well as for his opinions. France needed a scapegoat, the editor wrote. "Dreyfus was chosen for that function, because he was a Jew, and because the anti-Semitic part of the army and of the press and of the public would find evidence conclusive against him, which it would dismiss as flimsy and worthless if offered against an officer of another nationality."[27]

The press in the United States closed ranks around Dreyfus and against the French until the case was finally settled, and even afterwards. Race prejudice, in the form of anti-Semitism, was the charge leveled against Dreyfus's homeland, and this appeared to be unacceptable to practically everyone, including those who harbored no particular love for the Jews. A month after the publication of Zola's "J'accuse!," an editor for the *New York Observer* expressed what might well be the essence of non-Jewish America's response to the crisis. Having reviewed the indignities to which "the race" had recently been subjected in lands other than France, he wrote this uncannily prescient comment:

> And the worst feature of it all is that there is absolutely no reason for this condition of things save the old one, that the Jew is a Jew. Centuries of repression and of confinement in Ghettos have developed in him some unlovable characteristics, as they would in other people. But they are not, as a whole, greatly different from those of other men. Yet, intellectually at the top of the human race, the Jews are nowhere in Europe given an equal chance with Christians, and in most countries suffer under compulsory limitations which prevent their rising at all. . . . The growth of this anti-Semitism can have only one ending, and that is catastrophe. The Jewish problem is, therefore, one of vital concern to every nation, and one that cannot be shelved, if our civilization is not one day to be disgraced by massacre.[28]

When it was all over, in July of 1906, the *Outlook* offered a sobering set of reflections on what had happened. The author, possibly Lyman Abbott himself, having briefly reviewed the entire affair, did not mince words: "In the history of fiction there is nothing bolder in invention or more dramatically striking in incident than this famous trial. Captain Dreyfus came to stand as the protagonist of a race and the victim of a people." Dreyfus was "a man of fortune and of unusual promise, publicly degraded as the result of one of the vilest plots in the history of jurisprudence, surrounded by scoundrels who heaped lie upon lie and forgery upon forgery, condemned to spend two years of solitary confinement on a lonely island in another hemisphere from that in which he was convicted."[29]

Mind you, almost no one was calling for the wholesale amalgamation of the "Jewish race" with the majority race (whatever *that* was construed to be). And no one I can think of, Jew or non-Jew, anti-Semite or champion of the Jews, was trying to claim that the race concept was either inapplicable in this case or invalid altogether. No, the Jews were considered a race, and, as such, to bear certain characteristics. And they continued to have their detractors, even among the intellectual elite of the country. E. A. Ross, for example, as late as 1914, wrote a ghastly article for *Century* magazine titled "The Hebrews of Eastern Europe in America" and in that same year included it as a chapter in his nativist book *The Old World in the New: The Significance of Past and Present Immigration to the American People*, in which he took aim at a number of immigrant groups (while praising one or two). True to his long-standing populist, anti-immigrant stance, when he spoke about American Jews he trotted out the entire standard litany of scurrilous charges against them, all based on the supposition of the determining force of race.[30]

Jews had their passionate non-Jewish defenders, too. But above all, they had their non-Jewish *observers*. It's in these two categories, often difficult to distinguish from one another, that we see the transformation that was taking place in the period when the Dreyfus Affair was in the news.

In the summer of 1898, Mark Twain wrote what has become a famous or, to some, notorious essay called "Concerning the Jews." "I am quite sure," he declared at the beginning, "that (bar one) I have no race prejudices, and I think I have no color prejudices nor caste prejudices nor creed prejudices." The "bar one" (I'm fairly certain) referred to the French—and precisely because of the Dreyfus Affair. Jews have been accused of all sorts of things but have never been able to present their side, Twain says. "To my mind, this is irregular. It is un-English; it is un-American; it is French. Without this precedent Dreyfus could not have been condemned." Later on, when he reproached Jews for not standing up for themselves, he again turned on the French: "Among the Twelve Sane Men of France who have stepped forward with great Zola at their head to fight (and win, I hope and believe) the battle for the most infamously misused Jew of modern times, do you find a great or rich or illustrious Jew helping?" There was a long list of characteristics that Jews possessed because of their race. That suggested, in accordance with contemporary thinking, that Jews can't always help what they do. At the same time, Twain believed, hatred of Jews stemmed not from religious motives but from "race prejudice." But, in a wry, jocular comment toward the end of his essay, he typified a growing consensus developing among self-styled unprejudiced observers of Jews. Speaking of Theodor Herzl's Zionist movement, one year old that summer, he wrote, "I am not the Sultan, but if that concentration of the cunningest brains in the world was going to be made in a free country (bar Scotland), I think it would be politic to stop it. It will not be well to let that race find out its strength."[31]

To my mind, among the era's most informative documents on attitudes toward the "Jewish race" is a pair of articles that Burton J. Hendrick published in *McClure's Magazine*, one in 1907, the second in 1913, on "the Jewish invasion." We met Hendrick in chapter 2, as the author of an article on Alexis Carrel. At the time the first "Jewish invasion" article came out, Hendrick was making a name for himself as a kind of gadfly advocate-for-the-common-man/enemy-of-big-business. In January of 1907, he had just finished for *McClure's* what became a widely discussed exposé series on the insurance industry (shortly afterwards published as a book) and was just about to begin a similar exposé series on Americans who made fortunes in the financing of street-railways. "The Great Jewish Invasion" came out that month. "The Jewish Invasion of America" came out in March of 1913, two months after his piece on Alexis Carrel.

It's tricky to speak about these articles today. In both, Hendrick appeared to be using the word "invasion," in "Jewish invasion," in roughly the same sense it had in the 1960s phrase "British invasion." You weren't necessarily objecting to the music of the Beatles in 1963; the phrase was simply a comment on their having musically taken the country by storm. Hendrick was offering a similar comment about the Jews in his era. The 1907 article lists a long series of triumphs for American Jews, especially for those in the most recent wave of immigration. Hendrick did not shy away from racial characterization, but virtually every quality he mentioned was presented as an object of admiration or envy. The Jew, he said, is "a remorseless pace-maker," allowing himself "no rest or recreation." In addition, he is an individualist. It's thanks to these two qualities that Jews have been so dazzlingly successful. It's how they came to dominate, for example, the clothing industry and "the former homes of the Knickerbocker aristocracy" on Fifth Avenue, between Fourteenth Street and Twenty-Third Street.[32]

Hendrick then asked about the Jew, "But is he assimilable? Has he in himself the stuff of which Americans are made?" He never answered the question yes or no, but he offered evidence to support the idea that Jews could look and act like white, non-Jewish Americans: they change their names to American-sounding names, they change their homes to look like American homes, they generally adopt American customs. So yes, if assimilate meant this, then "the Jew" was assimilable. There was no talk of assimilation by intermarriage, however, and, even though Hendrick never explicitly said this, he appeared to think that Jews would stake their claim to a share of American life but that they would remain, for better or for worse, a race apart with their own characteristics. To take Hendrick at his word, however, they deserved our admiration and respect and certainly did *not* deserve the treatment they had suffered in other countries as well as in their earlier days in North America *because of their race*. As he put it in the 1913 article, "The Jews study hard and long, and their examination papers are so immeasurably superior to the average offered by representatives of other races that they invariably secure preferred places in the eligible lists."[33]

Some historians have found Hendrick to be an out-and-out anti-Semite.[34] I don't agree, but the point is not to defend or attack everything Hendrick said. Here's what I think these articles show us: (1) the extent to which the concept of race had taken possession of and continued to hold sway over American thinking; (2) a growing recognition in the American public of the power and success of this particular "race"; and (3) a willingness to declare a *human* (not a civil or national) right to dignity for all races—*even* (as in the case of Negroes) the Jews. This willingness was not always expressed in the affirmative. Much safer in this era was the rejection of a negative example: you could lambaste France for her barbaric, medieval persecution of Jewish citizens/subjects, without flatly saying, "I embrace members of the Jewish race and believe they are entitled to all the same rights and the same status as Americans of Anglo-Saxon descent" (though quite a few commentators did express sentiments something like this).

One should be cautious about pushing the analogy between Jews and Negroes too far. No one needs to be reminded that American Negroes suffered far more legal and social persecution than did American Jews and that the negative images of the two groups were of an entirely different nature. The cruelest popular iconography portrayed the Negro as a creature of an altogether lower biological order, while it portrayed the Jew as a greedy, cunning, therefore potentially successful opportunist. Even in the eyes of "enlightened" observers such as Lyman Abbott, Negroes needed to be excluded from the franchise because, at least for the time being, they were unworthy to vote. Similarly "enlightened" observers of the Jews were more likely to worry about a massive takeover of American business than a contamination of the voting pool.

But from the perspective of non-Jewish white Americans, Jews shared an essential characteristic with Negroes: they were a race apart, they lived not only in America but in numerous other locations around the world too, and they did not fit into any conventional national category here or anywhere else. If, as a non-Jewish white American, you wanted to champion their rights, as opposed to the worthiness of their American representatives to share space at a country club with you, matriculate as a student at your Ivy League alma mater, or work as a senior partner in your law firm, then you had to resort to the same arguments that King Leopold's enemies used: rights can ultimately stem from being human, rather than from enjoying citizenship in a political state that graciously grants those rights. Once again, the individual member is networked first to the race and then to the collectivity of human beings.

Did such thinking produce any practical effect, such as a diminution in racial strife in the United States? By one very crude measure, such strife, at least between Negroes and whites, had fallen off in the first two decades of the twentieth century: the number of lynchings per year declined from over a hundred at the turn of the century to around fifty by 1920. As to the Jews, if Hendrick's articles are any indication, there was at the very least a grudging acceptance of their presence in American life, as well as the acknowledgment that many of the immigrants from Russia and Eastern Europe, as well as their sons and daughters, had achieved considerable financial and social success in the United States. But in 1913 and even, for that matter, during the United States' involvement in the Great War, few could have expected that racial strife would shortly grow significantly *worse*, and yet that's exactly what happened. Once again the two transnational groups were front and center. This time, however, they stepped into the breach.

Race Returns with a Vengeance

It may come as a surprise today that racial prejudice at its nastiest came roaring back in the 1920s to haunt the nation. The summer of 1919, named "Red Summer" by James Weldon Johnson, and the summer of 1921 brought violent race riots to over thirty American cities.[35] The disturbances were spread out over the country, roughly half taking place in the South, several in large northeastern cities, and others in such unlikely places as Bisbee, Arizona, and Omaha, Nebraska. Precipitating causes varied so widely and in some cases appeared so inconsequential that historians have had to reach for explanations stemming from a context broader than, say, a verbal insult allegedly hurled by a Negro at a military policeman in a tiny Arizona backwater.[36] Historians speak of the influx of Negro workers into northern and midwestern cities during World War I, the demobilization and return of American troops to a depressed economy, and the resulting competition between whites and Negroes. These factors certainly served as contributing causes. Whatever the explanation, there is no doubt that an intensely poisoned atmosphere prevailed among whites and blacks in the United States during the terrible summer of 1919 and well into the 1920s. If we're speaking of the raw magnitude of violence and destruction in a race riot of this period, the record goes to Tulsa, Oklahoma, in the spring of 1921. Over a period of three days in that city, starting on Memorial Day, up to several hundred people (estimates vary widely) were killed, close to a thousand were injured, and several dozen city blocks were destroyed by fire. The cause: an alleged assault by a Negro shoe-shine man on a white female elevator operator in a downtown building.

Race was back as a divisive force in the world of books, magazines, and newspapers. Slick, Harvard-educated Lothrop Stoddard raised a nationwide alarm in 1920 with the publication of *The Rising Tide of Color Against White World-Supremacy.* Given the obvious meaning of "color" here, the title does an excellent job of conveying the message of Stoddard's book. If you read only the opening few pages carefully, you discovered not only that the author was going to assert the superiority of the white races over the yellow, brown, black, and red (as you saw in the table of contents) and the danger of the white races' being overrun by the inferior ones, but also that he had a fundamentally compelling reason for raising the problem in the first place: "the truth that the basic factor in human affairs is not politics, but race."[37] Race transcends politics. Think about that: this comment came two years after the end of the most destructive war in human history to that point, a war fought among what Stoddard regarded as members of *the same race.*

Commentators on race from a generation or two earlier had often attempted (or pretended) to rely on what, in their own era, counted for solid science. To us today, that science might appear more than a little naïve, not to mention that, when it came to race, in the end even the most scientifically inclined almost always gave way to their own ingrained views. Stoddard appears to have abandoned science altogether, though he was fond of throwing around the words "biology," "biological," and "evolution" in a loose, popular sense. When it was time to make his case about the "lower races," he offered not a shred of substantiating evidence:

> From the first glance we see that, in the negro, we are in the presence of a being differing profoundly not merely from the white man but also from those human types which we discovered in our surveys of the brown and yellow worlds. The black man is, indeed, sharply differentiated from the other branches of mankind. His outstanding quality is superabundant animal

vitality. In this he easily surpasses all other races. . . . The negro's political ineptitude, never rising above the tribal concept, kept black Africa a mosaic of peoples, warring savagely among themselves and widely addicted to cannibalism.[38]

Believe it or not, this book was taken seriously, even by many who were moderately skeptical of some of its claims. The staid *New York Times* ran a review in which the writer expressed some doubt about the level of danger, as *The Rising Tide of Color* presented it, but he found the presentation "sane and measured" and felt that people would give the book "respectful consideration." After all, as Stoddard and the reviewer ominously reminded us, we had Bolshevism to think about too: its most ruinous effect would be to foment revolution within the white world, because it "seeks to enlist the colored races in its grand assault on civilization."[39] While it's very easy to believe that lots of Americans and Western Europeans in 1920 were frightened by the Bolshevik Revolution, it's very difficult to figure out how anyone could seriously think that drawing on the rabid energies of the world's colored races in order to subjugate the white race was the central goal of those who brought about that event. And yet Lothrop Stoddard had a Ph.D. in history from Harvard and was a member of several learned societies! If F. Scott Fitzgerald saw fit to sneak Stoddard into the conversation of a blatantly philistine character in his best-known work of fiction, then you know *The Rising Tide of Color*, which went through five printings in its first year of publication alone, had had a major impact by the mid-1920s. Tom Buchanan, in *The Great Gatsby*, holds forth loudly and stupidly on a book called *The Rise of the Colored Empires* by "Goddard"—a transparent reference to Lothrop Stoddard.

These are the years when the Ku Klux Klan rose from the dead to emerge in its second, doubly brutish incarnation—or rather when an entirely new Klan emerged. Inspired in large part by the exalted image that D. W. Griffith presented of the original Reconstruction-era Klan in the epic 1915 feature *Birth of a Nation*, a group of white Southerners formed an organization driven primarily by hatred of three groups: Catholics, Jews, and Negroes. Growing up in a later generation, you might think the new Klan and its lethal brand of mischief had been a phenomenon exclusively of the deep South. Think again. This group spread out, especially in the Midwest. In 1924, Michigan by one estimate had more than 70,000 members, half of them in Detroit.[40] The mayor of Highland Park (a small city located within the city of Detroit) and the police chief of Royal Oak (a suburb of Detroit) were Klansmen. The Detroit mayoral election of 1924 was a squeaker—won on a highly questionable technicality by a progressive Catholic candidate over a Klansman.[41]

But then Detroit was a focal point for all sorts of racial antagonism, and because it conveniently serves as a model for what was going on in so many other parts of the country, let's turn there for a moment.

"Our Friend" the Anti-Semite

If you've ever visited Detroit, you've probably noticed that "Our Friend" Henry Ford left a number of highly visible marks on the Motor City, in addition to the automobile company he founded. Greenfield Village, the great theme-park monument to Americana, was founded by Ford in 1929. Numerous institutions in the city bear the name of the titanic industrialist of the early twentieth century. What almost everyone, including many a native Detroiter, has somehow forgotten is an extracurricular project to which Ford devoted a major amount of time, money, and energy. In 1918 he purchased *The Dearborn Independent*, a local newspaper that had been around since 1901 (the city of Dearborn, adjoining Detroit, was the site of the Ford Motor Company). From 1919 to 1927 the *Independent* was Ford's personal journalistic enterprise.

By the late teens, for reasons that no biographer or acquaintance has been able fully to divine, Ford had conceived a virulent antipathy to the Jews, those both in the United States and everywhere else. The *Dearborn Independent* was the forum he chose for expressing this antipathy. He assembled a team of managers and writers, and for a couple of years they disgorged a steady torrent of verbal hatred. Then the mercurial factory owner ordered the discontinuation of anti-Semitic writing in the *Dearborn Independent*, though bits of it appeared from time to time before the paper was finally shut down in 1927. Not everything in the *Dearborn Independent* for the first few years under Ford's ownership was about Jews; there were other topics covered too, of course. Ford intended it to be a respectable newspaper. But just in case there were readers whose primary interest *was* the Jews, he was thoughtful enough to bring out four book-length anthologies of articles, under the general title *The International Jew: The World's Foremost Problem*. Here, if you found general news about Detroit and the world boring, you could feast yourself on a steady diet of unadulterated anti-Semitism.

You learned, on page after page, that the Jews constituted a race, not a religion, that no one had anything against the Jews merely on account of their

religion, that (as an implicit or explicitly stated corollary) being a member of a race directly causes you to behave in certain ways—a staple of modern anti-Semitism going back to Eugen Dühring. The second volume of *The International Jew* contained an article devoted exclusively to this question, using the testimony of prominent Jews themselves to prove that Jews are defined not by their religion but by their status as a race. The article, titled "Jewish Testimony on 'Are Jews a Nation?'," purposefully conflated the terms "race" and "nation," as was common in the era, since the idea was to show that Jewish racial unity, necessarily suggesting something similar to national unity, threatened the various *nations* in which the Jews dwelled. In other words, they constituted a kind of nation within a nation. To dispel any confusion, the writer stated early on that the point was separate status, not religion. Race and nation were essentially interchangeable. "It should also be observed during the reading of the following testimony that sometimes the term 'race' is used, sometimes the term 'nation.' In every case, it is recognized that the Jew is a member of a separate people, quite aside from the consideration of his religion."[42]

By the mid-1920s, Ford's defiant and courageous stance against the evil in his own country had attracted the attention of an embittered Austrian veteran of the Great War who had just spent the better part of a year in a Bavarian prison on treason charges and was working on a book. Before his prison term, the veteran had kept an abridged copy, in German translation, of *The International Jew* on display in the waiting room of his office in Munich, as well as a portrait of Henry Ford in the office itself.[43] "Our Friend" earned himself a favorable mention in the first edition of that book, *Mein Kampf*, where he was described as the "only great man" in America who "is standing up independently" against this "controlling master [the Jews] of the workforce."[44] On Ford's seventy-fifth birthday, consular officials of the German regime, now headed by that former veteran, conferred upon the American industrialist its highest honor, the Order of the German Eagle, adorned with four swastikas, at a ceremony in Detroit.[45]

Above all, in the *Dearborn Independent*, you learned that the Jews were organized and poised to take over—everything. Ford did his readers a big favor by publishing, in the regular issues of the paper, excerpts from the *Protocols of the Learned Elders of Zion*. The story of this slanderous pamphlet is all too well known. Published first in Russia, in 1903, and subsequently translated into numerous other languages, it allegedly presented the machina-

tions of a conspiracy of powerful Jews whose aim was world domination. In his desire to bring the alarming news to his fellow American citizens, Ford received the assistance of Boris Brasol, a refugee from the Russian Revolution who was devoting his life at this time to exposing the two primary evils facing the modern world: Bolsheviks and Jews. According to E. G. Pipp, the man who briefly served as editor of the *Dearborn Independent* before resigning in protest over its anti-Semitism, Brasol was a key figure in swaying Ford toward anti-Semitism in the first place.[46] He may also have been the person who made Ford aware of the *Protocols*. He anonymously published his own translation in 1920, and even though this was not the one that the *Dearborn Independent* writers used, the one they *did* use, published the same year, was one with which Brasol had been personally involved.[47]

In 1921, between the time the two translations came out and Ford's order to cut back on the anti-Semitic writing in the *Dearborn Independent*, the *Protocols* were definitively exposed as a fraud, by two different experts: Philip Graves, a reporter for the *London Times*, and Herman Bernstein, an American who wrote a book on the subject. The *New York Times* ran a full-page story about the exposure, under a banner headline, in September of 1921.[48] Nonetheless, the *Dearborn Independent* kept on writing about the *Protocols* as if nothing had happened.

The details of Brasol's relationship with Ford are unfortunately not known. There's one idea, however, that shows up in the section of his book that Brasol himself wrote as well as in articles in the *Dearborn Independent*. It shows up in the mainstream press too, so Brasol was certainly not the first person in the United States to come up with it. But it has a curious possible history that's worth pondering for a moment. The idea was that Jews either sought or already constituted a "state within a state" (I already mentioned the idea of a nation within a nation)—that is, their own autonomous, racially homogeneous political unit within a larger political unit foreign to them. Brasol quoted E. J. Dillon, a former Russian correspondent for the London *Daily Telegraph* who reported on the Paris Peace Conference in his widely read *Inside Story of the Peace Conference* (1920). At one point, Dillon wrote about the participation of Jews from various countries, describing how, after Poland, Rumania, and Russia had enfranchised their Jews, the "Western Jews" (including American Jews) had sought further protection for "their Eastern brothers." As Dillon put it, the Western Jews "proceeded to demand a further concession which many of their own co-religionists hastened to dis-

claim as dangerous—a kind of autonomy which Rumanian, Polish, and Russian statesmen, as well as many of their Jewish fellow-subjects, regarded as tantamount to the creation of a state within the state."[49]

What Brasol took from a passage unequivocally sympathetic to Jewish interests was the author's purported singling out of Western, specifically American, Jews and their "demands for special national privileges."[50] The phrase that clearly scared him was the final one in the excerpt: "state within a state." And in case his readers failed to detect the ominous warning, he returned to it, with a perverse, gratuitous leap of logic in the final sentence of the book. American Jews, he said, should condemn the nefarious plot for world domination outlined in the *Protocols*. "Aside from their position on these matters," he then darkly concluded, "there is no likelihood of any change in the favorable situation of the Jews in this country unless by their own conduct they convince the American people that they are hostile to our institutions or to our system of government, or that they desire to constitute within the borders of the United States a race apart,—to be treated as members of a foreign nation, enjoying special rights, privileges, or immunities."[51]

Ford's writer in the *Dearborn Independent* feared the same thing—or at least sought to inspire his readers to fear it. In the "Seventeenth Protocol," the scheming Jews speak of the *kahal* (the governing body of a Jewish community in the Diaspora). Since, as everyone knew, the recent Bolshevik Revolution was part of the Jewish plan for domination, the writer regarded the new institution of the *Soviet* as a thinly disguised *kahal*.

> In spite of all assertions to the contrary, the Jews have never ceased to be "a people"; that is, a consciously united racial group, different from all others, and with purposes and ideals which are strictly of the Jews, by the Jews and for the Jews in distinction from the rest of the world. That they constitute a *nation within the nations*, the most responsible Jewish thinkers not only declare but insist upon. And this is wholly in accord with the facts as observed. The Jew not only desires to live apart from other people, but he works with his own people as against others, and he desires as much as possible to live under his own laws. In the city of New York today, the Jews have succeeded in establishing their own court for the settlement of their own questions according to their own laws. And that is precisely the principle of the Soviet-Kahal.[52]

The Jews of New York, he wrote in a later article, have established "a government within a government in the midst of America's largest city." Given the continual conflation of "nation" and "race" in the pages of the *Dearborn*

Independent, the message could not have been clearer. It was still all about race.[53]

I don't know if Ford's writer was inspired on this point by Brasol, but the idea of the state within a state either as a goal of the Jews or as the reality of their existence in certain lands was something that Brasol was undoubtedly familiar with. One of Brasol's favorite authors, Dostoevsky, in several of the many ugly moments when he felt a powerful aversion to the Jews of his own motherland, referred to what he perceived as the customary condition of Russian Jews—their voluntary existence apart from the rest of the population—using the Latin phrase *status in statu* (state within a state). His comments appeared in *Diary of a Writer*, the single-author journal that Dostoevsky published in the last eight years of his life (he died in January of 1881). The man who translated the full run of that diary into English in 1949, having then established himself as an émigré scholar of Russian literature, was none other than Boris Brasol.[54]

Henry Ford saw to it that as many of his fellow citizens as possible would read the alarming news in the *Dearborn Independent* or, if not in the *Dearborn Independent* then in *The International Jew*. The price was kept low; *The International Jew* was not copyrighted, so that it could be freely reprinted; and Ford dealers across the country were required to purchase subscriptions to the newspaper for themselves and their friends.[55] The publications did not go unnoticed. There was a huge reaction in the press, and not only in such relatively progressive papers as the *New York Times*. American Jewish leaders responded with massive force. Two prominent Jews who had been the target of *Independent* vilification, Herman Bernstein, the author of the book that exposed the *Protocols*, and Aaron Sapiro, a Jewish businessman involved in the farming co-operative industry, filed libel lawsuits against Ford. Finally, in 1927, defending himself in court and watching the fortunes of his automobile company sag, Ford issued a public apology (written by lawyer and Jewish leader Louis Marshall and possibly never even read by Ford himself) to American Jews and shut down the *Dearborn Independent*.[56] All of this received extensive coverage in the press. The *New York Times* covered every detail of the Sapiro libel trial and the apology, sometimes running more than one article on it in a single day. Other major American newspapers did likewise.

Ford's motives seem destined to remain a mystery. To any moderately skeptical observer it appears plain that the anti-Jewish sentiments were genuine, that they did not abruptly disappear in 1927, and that the blatantly disin-

genuous apology stemmed not from any actual contrition but from a desire to rescue the automobile business. We can leave this issue to Ford's biographers. Many saw a sharp drop-off in American anti-Semitism after the apology and the closure of the *Dearborn Independent*. That may very well be, but that too belongs to another story. There's a short episode in the saga of the *Dearborn Independent* itself that's worth examining both because it's oddly emblematic of the era and because, in my view, it's been completely misunderstood and misrepresented.

It has to do, once again, with Burton J. Hendrick. Here's a ticklish matter for the historian. Nine years after his second article on American Jews, Hendrick came back with a four-part series on the same topic, published in *The World's Work* (1922–23) and then again in book form (1923). The title of the series and the book was *The Jews in America*. The almost universal view of the series is that it is anti-Semitic, and it's easy to see why. If you skipped the entire first part of the series and the first few paragraphs of the second, you'd find yourself reading, without context, a description of the "Jewish race" that includes a set of startling claims. Because of their "intense individualism," Jews show, as "a deep-lying racial trait," an "inability to cooperate for the achievement of a unified purpose." Contrary to popular opinion, he wrote, the Jewish mind is *not* superior to the non-Jewish European mind. If you thought Jews excelled in the arts, you're mistaken; they don't. The Jew "has made no astonishing economic progress in this country." "The story of Jewish monopoly in the clothing trades is not a pleasant one; it is a story of exploitation, commonly of an exceedingly cruel kind, and exploitation of Jews by Jews." In the fourth and final installment, Hendrick lambasted the "Polish Jews" of New York for being socialists. In their number he included Abraham Cahan, editor of the *Jewish Daily Forward* and thus quite possibly the most powerful Jewish figure in the United States (at least among immigrant Jews).[57]

Putting aside for a moment any gut response to these apparently denigrating comments, you can't help noticing that every one of them, with the possible exception of the first, directly contradicts a claim Hendrick had made in his earlier articles. There he had praised the Jews for their superior intellect, for their accomplishments in the arts (above all, in theatre), and for their dazzling success in business. Their domination of the clothing trades was evidence of their fitness for survival, not part of a nefarious plot. There was nothing about the exploitation of Jews by other Jews. He had named Abraham Cahan as an example of "a distinguished Jew."

What was going on? The answer lies in the opening of the first and second parts of the series. Let's take Hendrick at his word for just a moment. He began the series by sounding an alarm in three impassioned, italicized paragraphs. "The wave of anti-Semitism, which has been sweeping over the world since the ending of the World War, has apparently reached the United States," he wrote.

> An antagonism which Americans had believed was peculiarly European, is gaining a disquieting foothold in this country. The one prejudice which would seem to have no decent cause for existence in the free air of America is one that is based upon race and religion. Yet the most conservative American universities are openly setting up bars against the unlimited admittance of Jewish students; the most desirable clubs are becoming more rigid in their inhospitable attitude towards Jewish members; a weekly newspaper, financed by one of the richest men in America, has filled its pages for three years with a virulent campaign against this element in our population.

He issued a call for "facts" in answer to the questions that he said were being posed: "Is it true that they dominate American finance. . . . Are they the brains of the Nation in the professions, in education, in journalism, in literature, in music, in the drama. . . . Above all, is it true, as is so commonly charged, that the Jews constitute an utterly unassimilable element in our population?" In the opening of the second piece, he took aim with towering contempt at the *Protocols* and at anyone who was gullible enough to believe in their authenticity. "That Henry Ford should base his anti-Jewish campaign upon these 'Protocols,'" he wrote disdainfully, "is perhaps not surprising; but that such organs of public opinion as the London *Morning Post* and the London *Spectator* should take them seriously is much more significant" (Hendrick's concern over anti-Semitism extended to the *other* Anglo-Saxon nation).[58]

If what Hendrick did next had not led to the publication of dozens upon dozens of statements that reek of anti-Jewish poison, the result would be almost funny. It was all a response to the *Dearborn Independent* and a few other anti-Semitic publications: were Ford's writers claiming that the Jews were organizing themselves in order to take over the country and eventually the world? In fact, he said, the Jews are the most disorganized, scattered race of individualists in the world. Was the *Dearborn Independent* protesting that Jews controlled Wall Street? Hendrick filled the article with photographs of powerful non-Jewish American businessmen to show that *they*, not Jews, were at the center of American industry. Were anti-Semites complaining that Jews had come to dominate the professions, the schools, and the universities? That couldn't be true, he insisted, because Jews aren't really any smarter than the rest of us. Were cranks in the press charging that Jews are disproportionately represented in the arts? Well they're not, period.

Hendrick's comments on the clothing trades would appear to put him on the same side as Ford and his newspaper. But look closely at what Hendrick was saying, nasty as it sounded: the Jews are fighting among themselves. As Hendrick apparently saw it, the overarching fear that the *Dearborn Independent* in particular and the anti-Semitic press in general sought to arouse was the fear of *Jewish unity.* And what Hendrick did in response was to return to the fundamental concept of race in order to destroy the basis for that fear. The Jews will never take over the world, he assured his readers, because in order to do so they would need to achieve unification within their own numbers. Fear not: the biologically determining features of their race make such unification entirely impossible.

And yet there remained an odd contradiction. Hendrick needed to say whether the Jews could be assimilated. He had posed the question in his 1907 article and had at least appeared to answer in the affirmative. He devoted the entire third article of the new series to this question, giving a clear, negative answer at the conclusion, at least as regards immigrants of the latest wave, who he now said were racially distinct from German and Spanish Jews of earlier waves. Amusingly, he now referred to these Jews as "Polish Jews," where earlier he had called them "Russian Jews." Perhaps this was an expression of an instinctive need to defend the Jews from another anti-Semitic charge that, because they were Russian, they were Bolsheviks. In any case, Hendrick reviewed all the businesses in which the "Polish Jews" had been successful and decided that the way they managed their affairs kept them separate from the rest of the population. "Any race fifty per cent. of whose people live in one city," he wrote, "and the remaining fifty per cent. in other large American cities, can hardly be regarded as having become flesh of the flesh of the American body. Perhaps, in the course of a century or so, a wider distribution and a wider range of energies may be accomplished, but the task of incorporating the 3,000,000 and more already here will monopolize the Nation's digestive powers for a long time to come." Hendrick declared himself fully in support of the immigration restrictions then being considered in Congress.[59]

If Jews weren't unified, as *true* anti-Semites such as Henry Ford and his collaborators were charging, then what was to keep them from being assimilated? As Hendrick saw it, what the Jews lacked was organization, the ability to cooperate. But the explanation for their failure in this respect was their race, and so in fact they *were* unified as a group by the biologically determining factors of genetic heritage. It's just that one such unifying factor was the trait that prevented the group from, well, being unified.

So here we have another paradox. In his effort to defend the Jews against the charges of "anti-Semites" (in whose ranks he clearly did not wish to count himself), Hendrick had to argue both for and against Jewish unity: voluntary, organized unity they lacked; unity as a group sharing racial characteristics they had. Perhaps they didn't form a political state within a state (because they never organize themselves), but they certainly formed a nation within a nation, provided that "nation" was construed loosely, in such a way that it overlapped with race. Hendrick wasn't challenging the right of Jews—at least those already here—to formal citizenship in the United States, but he was identifying them with the customs and habits of their origins, suggesting that they had merely transplanted those customs and habits from one geographic location to another. Wherever the Jews lived, he hinted, they remained the nation they had been for centuries, enjoying (at least in theory) the same formal civil rights that other Americans enjoyed, but forming a national group apart.

Wasn't this what Ford and his cohorts were saying, with some of the terms changed and, of course, with a different emotional thrust? The *Dearborn Independent* writers characterized American Jews as organized in a colossal conspiracy to take over the financial, political, and cultural spheres of the country. But they saw the Jews as unified by "race," a term that the writers blurred with "nation," especially when they described the "nation within the nations" that the Jews allegedly constituted. The idea, as with Hendrick, was that Jews, because of their race, led an existence apart, no matter what nation they resided in and no matter what their civil status in that nation might be.

At first glance, the *Dearborn Independent* episode might appear to be nothing more than a depressing return to barbarism and intolerance. To my mind, it did nothing to unseat race as a concept or the belief that Jews were a race. At the same time, it provoked a stunningly effective response from members of that "race," which demonstrated that unity, whether racial in origin or not, produced results. Jews *in their unity* were a force to be reckoned with, and no American, anti-Semitic or not, could realistically deny it.

Dr. Sweet, Defender of Property and Second Amendment Rights

Ossian (pronounced "ŏshen") Sweet was born in Florida, in 1895, to parents who were both children of slaves. When he was 13, his parents sent him to Wilberforce University, in Ohio, where he attended the college preparatory division before enrolling as an undergraduate. In 1917, after a total of eight years, he received his degree. He went on to Howard University Medical School, the elite training ground for Negro physicians in the era, and received his M.D. in 1921. He moved to Detroit that summer as Dr. Ossian Sweet.

As a young boy Sweet either heard about or directly witnessed a ghastly lynching in his hometown in Florida. The victim was a 16-year-old boy accused of raping and murdering a white woman. And in 1919, when he was studying at Howard, he was on hand for the Red Summer as it struck Washington, D.C. By the time he arrived in Detroit's Black Bottom neighborhood, he was no stranger to racial violence. During his first four years in Detroit, Dr. Sweet built up his medical practice and got married. Then, in September of 1925, he and his wife Gladys purchased a small house in East Detroit. The house was simple and attractive, in the Craftsman style. A single, wide dormer protruded from the front roof, with three windows in one frame. The roof hung low over a cozy front porch. The ground floor was built with brick, the second with painted timber.

The Sweets knew well in advance that the move would not be easy. The area was all white, and there was no reason to expect a welcoming response from their new neighbors. There was every reason to expect the contrary, and the contrary is exactly what happened, starting on the evening of September 8. The Sweets had a pretty good idea of what might lie in store for them in their new surroundings, so when they moved in, they were armed to the teeth. On that night, they filled the house with friends and family members, having decided that they were prepared to assert the age-old right—at least the one that white men appeared to enjoy—to defend your family and property with deadly force if circumstances led you to consider such force necessary. On that evening there was a tense stand-off with a very large crowd that gathered in the street in front of the house. The men in the house had locked and loaded and were ready to shoot if they had to. The police were out in force. Nothing happened.

But on the following night, September 9, all hell broke loose. The crowd returned, armed with rocks, and after an interval filled with sickening apprehension, they let loose a hailstorm, smashing windows and littering the entire property. This time the threat was palpable. Dr. Sweet's younger brother Henry, armed with a Winchester rifle, fired into the crowd from the second-story window, hitting two white men. One was injured in the leg. The other, shot through the back, was killed.

Mrs. Sweet and all ten men who had been inside the house that night were arrested. There were two trials, both presided over, fortunately for the defendants, by Frank Murphy, a liberal judge who would later go on to become mayor of Detroit, governor of Michigan, U.S. attorney general, and, finally, an associate justice on the Supreme Court. James Weldon Johnson, at the time executive secretary of the NAACP, saw in the Sweet trial an extraordinary opportunity for his organization and for Negro America. His greatest coup in the case was to nab Clarence Darrow, fresh from the trenches in Tennessee, where the most famous defense attorney in America had fought the dark forces of medieval obscurantism in the famous Scopes trial (losing the trial, of course, but gaining national recognition for reducing to ashes his fundamentalist opponents, including, above all, William Jennings Bryan). The first go-round ended in a mistrial, in December of 1925. In the second, the following year, Henry Sweet as the gunman was put on trial alone for murder, with the understanding that if he was acquitted charges against the other defendants would be dropped. In the end, the jury voted to acquit Dr. Sweet's younger brother, and, in mid-May, the trial was over.

Kevin Boyle, in his gripping account of the Sweet story, tells how the years immediately following the trial astonishingly brought a relaxation of tension between the races in Detroit, as well as a marked downturn in the fortunes of the Ku Klux Klan.[60] Lawyer David E. Lilienthal (later chairman of the Tennessee Valley Authority) wrote for *The Nation* in the immediate wake of the inconclusive first trial. Despite the jury's failure to acquit, he was sanguine. The answer to the question in his title, "Has the Negro the Right of Self-Defense?," was clearly yes. Though he had some doubts about whether white people had made any progress, Lilienthal was confident that Negroes had. "But that the black man is making headway is clear beyond doubt," he wrote.

> Of this, the young defendants themselves are striking evidence. Most of them are either graduates or students of colleges or professional schools; their grandparents were slaves who could neither read nor write! At the press table

sat two colored newspaper men the match of any correspondent there. The factories seen from the courtroom windows are employing more and more Negroes every week. And there is encouragement, too, in the fact that Negroes can command so fair a trial in a land where most trials of Negroes have been mob-dominated travesties. For the trial was probably the fairest ever accorded a Negro in this country."[61]

In January, right after the mistrial was declared, Dr. and Mrs. Sweet traveled to Harlem, where they attended the annual meeting of the NAACP. The crowd on hand for the occasion was estimated at 1,500 and was racially mixed. Arthur Garfield Hays, the attorney who had served as Clarence Darrow's co-counsel in the first Sweet trial, spoke passionately about segregation, characterizing it as "a street of intolerance, a street of bigotry, a street of hate, and a main street of death." Dr. Sweet himself gave a short speech, in which he predicted that the second trial would "determine whether or not mobs shall tell colored people where or where not to live."[62] Two days later Dr. Sweet spoke at a dinner meeting of the North Harlem Medical Society, an association of Negro physicians, reportedly describing at great length the suffering he and his codefendants had endured while imprisoned during their trial.[63]

The story of Sweet's life after the trial was hardly a happy one. His wife and daughter contracted tuberculosis, and within two years both were dead. Though Sweet enjoyed a few years of professional success, a curse appears to have descended on him, as if in a grim, hubris-driven tragedy. Personal relationships, including two marriages, failed, as eventually did Sweet's finances. The good doctor committed suicide in 1960, at the age of 64. The house still stands, at the corner of Garland and Charlevoix in East Detroit. A sign in the front yard tells you that it's listed on the National Register of Historic Places. The surrounding neighborhood, like so many others in that sad city, has seen better days.

Racial Pride, the Transnational National, and a New Conception of Rights

There's something oddly poignant about the appearance of Ossian Sweet, a victim of mob justice, his future completely uncertain, in Harlem during the first week of 1926. Not a month earlier, a pivotal event in black America had taken place: the release of *The New Negro*, in book form, by the publishing house of Albert and Charles Boni in New York. The anthology, edited by

Howard University philosophy professor Alain Locke and published earlier in the year, in slightly different form, in *Survey Graphic* magazine, is traditionally described as the "bible" or "gospel" of the Harlem Renaissance. It presented fiction, poetry, visual art, criticism, and cultural-philosophical commentary by men and women, Negro and white.

This is not the place to retell the history of the Harlem Renaissance. That *The New Negro* was a monument to Negro pride and was itself a formidable cultural object in its own right hardly needs to be stated. That the pride its contributors expressed was conceived explicitly as *racial* is evident from a perusal of almost any random selection of pages. Locke's opening essay, also titled "The New Negro," drove the point home again and again. Race as a concept was alive and well, it was the unifying force among New Negroes, and Harlem could now be regarded as a "race capital." A "deep feeling of race" was "the mainspring of Negro life," Locke proclaimed.[64] The words "race" and "racial" occur almost two hundred times in the volume, in connection with virtually every topic covered.

But something else was going on in *The New Negro* that's worth calling attention to. We find an inkling of it in Locke's opening essay. Locke mentioned African peoples outside the United States, and he wrote of "rehabilitating the race in world esteem." Harlem, he said, has become "the home of the Negro's 'Zionism.'" The race problem has thus become a "world problem," and the Negro mind "has linked up with the growing group consciousness of the dark-peoples and is gradually learning their common interests." He spoke of Marcus Garvey's flamboyant pan-Africanism and related movements. But here's the key thought: "As with the Jew, persecution is making the Negro international."[65]

The supreme statement of the idea came in a masterful essay that appeared at the end of *The New Negro*. It was titled "The Negro Mind Reaches Out," and it was written by W. E. B. Du Bois. The essay was somewhat loosely organized, ranging widely over a host of international political questions and including accounts of the author's personal travels and experiences. But if there was a central idea, it was Africa and Pan-Africanism. In the final pages of the essay, Du Bois let loose on imperialism and the militarism that supports it, singling out for particular blame the widespread practice, among imperial powers, of taking members of the populations that dwell in their colonies and conscripting them into the military forces that hold those very colonies in subjection. Then he wrote this:

> Above all this rises the shadow of two international groups—the Jews and the modern Negroes. The Jews are, in blood, Spanish, German, French, Arabian and American. Their ancient unity of religious faith is crumbling, but out of it all has come a spiritual unity born of suffering, prejudice and industrial power which can be used and is being used to spread an international consciousness. Where this spirit encounters a rampant new nationalism as in Poland or bitter memories of national loss as in Germany, or racial bigotry as in America, it stirs an Anti-Semitism as cruel as it is indefinite and armed in fact not against an abused race but against any spirit that works or seems to work for the union of human kind.
>
> And toward this same great end a new group of groups is setting its face. Pan-Africanism as a living movement, a tangible accomplishment, is a little and negligible thing. But there are twenty-three millions of Negroes in British West Africa, eighteen millions in French Africa, eleven millions and more in the United States; between eight and nine millions each in the Belgian Congo and Portuguese Africa; and a dozen other lands in Africa and America have groups ranging from two to five millions. This hundred and fifty millions of people are gaining slowly an intelligent thoughtful leadership. The main seat of their leadership is to-day the United States.[66]

Jews and Negroes: two racial/ethnic groups that cruelty and prejudice have prevented from fulfilling the (purely ideal) requirement of traditional nationalism, namely that the physical boundaries defining a nation shall enclose only and all members of the racial/ethnic group dwelling therein.[67] As for the Negroes and the Jews, one can speak of life in diaspora, and one can focus on the hardships that members of the two "races" have endured in the various nations that have hosted or enslaved them. Locke spoke of Zionism, in the figurative sense for Negroes and, by implication, in the literal sense for Jews. But Zionism suggests an actual realization of the nationalist aspiration: Jews, as a race or ethnic group, will come to occupy a land that is almost entirely of and for themselves. The comparison is not entirely appropriate, even in Locke's own essay. What he and Du Bois had in mind was something other than identifying one piece of territory where (again in the purely ideal sense) all or only Jews will reside and another where all or only Negroes will reside. What really set the two groups apart from others was their then-current status: rather than living within (or aspiring to live within) national boundaries, members of these groups *transcended* those boundaries. And this was something good, progressive, and modern (a word that Du Bois used repeatedly in his essay).

Admittedly the language gets a little murky in Locke and Du Bois when it comes to the question of race and internationalism, but as best I can tell both were seeking to describe a peculiar new status for the individual of the future. I think it goes something like this: As always, race is fundamental; there is no effort whatsoever to contest its existence. But the category now stands in tension with an opposite pole. Whereas, for groups other than Jews and Negroes, race in a traditional nationalist setting had theoretically/ideally formed a coherent whole with nation—nation referring to a political state—so that the individual was (again, theoretically/ideally) rooted in one as in the other, in the conception for the future, the one that Jews and Negroes already exemplified, the individual retained his or her roots in a race while at the same time enjoying a connection to a larger community ("the union of human kind," as Du Bois put it). Locke and Du Bois used the term "international" for this larger community, but, as with Burton Hendrick's description of the Polish Jews, the idea appears to be not so much that Negroes and Jews partake of the features of many existing nationalities (in the political sense) as that they transcend such nationalities. They are transnational, rather than international, but—this is the essence of the new individual—*they are rooted in their own race at the same time.*

So, the race networks its individual members, and a transnational humanity networks races and the individual members of those races. That sounds like a relatively harmonious state of affairs, if race is going to stay around as a category. We already saw, in the case of the victims of Belgian imperialism in the Congo, the idea of relocating the individual outside the political and civil system of a particular nation. Outrage over the treatment of Congo natives stemmed from a sense that certain rights had been violated, and since those rights clearly did not stem from any civil system in the Congo itself, they had to be construed as transnational (though this word was not used). But in that era, the notion of *transnational status* (not called that, of course) appeared to arise only in connection with international rights cases. Du Bois was claiming the status independently of cases where rights are violated. Still, at the time that Du Bois was writing, transnational status existed (as he saw it) only for the two groups. As a global condition, it could be only a dream for the future.

This brings us back to the conception of the individual. In the United States at the end of the nineteenth century and the beginning of the twentieth, your core identity, your *self*, was inextricably tied to your race. That was your first, immediate network. Almost no one questioned this assertion, nor was there much talk of racial mingling, except as a danger to be avoided. The presence in this country of "foreign" races made the notion of racial classification seem all the more inviolable. So did the presence of two transnational races—Negroes and Jews—that formed their own peculiar identity outside the then-current system of existing nations. But race as a concept tended to attract huge amounts of attention when members of those two races found themselves under attack. Because the two races were not exclusively or even primarily confined to existing, territorially construed political states, injuries against them took on a transnational character. So, say you were a member of one of these races and you became a victim of prejudice, persecution, or brutal violence. That would have been unjust. Why? Because, even though on one side, when it came to core identity, to your sense of self, your place was in a racial or national community, on the other, when it came to *rights*, your place was in the *human* community. That community was transnational. And *that* was your second, overarching network.

9 Religion Goes Worldly, Ecumenical, and Collective

On the evening of October 24, 1910, the Ethical Culture Society is holding a public dedication ceremony for its new building on Central Park West in New York City. On the roster for the evening are Dr. Felix Adler, the head and founder of the Ethical Culture movement; such Jewish luminaries as industrialist Isaac N. Seligman, NAACP co-founder Henry Moskowitz, and Free Synagogue founder rabbi Stephen S. Wise; and the most famous man in the room, Lyman Abbott. You're struck by Dr. Abbott's appearance. In this modern age, when so many men appear in public with neatly trimmed hair and smooth-shaven faces, this man is disheveled (except where he's bald), with a disorderly long white beard. He could almost pass for one of the Chasidim that you might see on the Lower East Side and whose appearance the progressive, impeccably groomed Jewish leaders in attendance studiously shun.

Abbott speaks about "The Religion of Service." He begins by describing himself as a disciple of Jesus of Nazareth. He spends the next few minutes of his speech telling the story of Jesus as a Jew, a man apart from creeds, rituals, and established organizations, a man who expressed his views "by deeds of service." Abbott has come "to give the right hand of fellowship to Felix Adler." He addresses the congregation: "It is true that your faith does not express all that I believe, does not express some beliefs which I cherish as very sacred." But, he says, Christians "reverence" Jesus "by doing all that we can to make this world a happier world because a better one, and this life a life better worth living." He turns to Dr. Adler. "And no man in this city," Abbott says, "has, in my judgment, devoted himself to this service, this upbuilding of character, this message of life, this making of the world happier by making it better, more faithfully than has Felix Adler. I do not know any one who has more consistently and with greater self-devotion given himself to carrying glad tidings to the poor, release to the captives, education to the ignorant, liberty to them that are bruised."[1]

These events would have been impossible a century earlier. Ethical Culture? What in the name of heaven (or its absence) might that be? Certainly not a religion in any conventional sense of the word, although you might have noticed that this godless organization is listed alphabetically in the *New York Times* each Saturday under "Church Services To-Morrow," right after "Disciples of Christ (Christian)." You might have heard that Felix Adler is Jewish and was originally destined for a career in the rabbinate. And then there's the Congregationalist minister, who finds common cause not only with Dr. Adler but also with the other Jews present. That minister even refers to Ethical Culture as a "faith," and when he uses the word "religion," it is to couple it with the notion of "service." What Ethical Culture and Christianity share, Abbott says this evening, is an insistence on rendering to one's fellow man *in this world* "the highest, the best, and the most enduring service."

Certainly much has changed, not only over the past century but even in a couple of generations. In fact, to some it might seem that religious life has been shaken to its very foundations.

The "Higher Criticism" Knocks Scripture off Its Throne

In 1883, the Reverend Francis A. Henry, an Episcopal minister in Morristown, New Jersey, wrote for the *Princeton Review* on "The Critical Study of the Scriptures." "Most people," he began,

> will agree that probably no quarter of a century since Bacon's day has witnessed such a rapid "advancement of learning" as the one lying immediately behind us, which opened, roughly speaking, with the publication of the *Origin of Species* (1859); and there are some who are disposed to think that during this period no one field of research has yielded more fruit to the scholar's labor than that of Biblical Science. A new school of historical critics has arisen—if we may so class independent writers of all countries, united only by

> holding the same general principles and applying the same general method; and the work has been to open a new era in Scriptural study, an era as completely new as that which the work of Darwin and his compeers opened in Natural Science.[2]

Rev. Henry went on to explain what he meant. Under the old theory, "Moses was the author of the Pentateuch, and the Levitical Law in its entirety was given to the Israelites before they entered Canaan."[3] But, Henry reported, a careful study of the texts revealed that there are actually three different systems of law, each corresponding to a discrete period in the history of the ancient Israelites. He then set out the three systems and the three periods. Most Biblical scholars nowadays, in light of more recent evidence and scholarship, would disagree with certain details of Henry's account. But what's important is not whether Henry was correct; it's the underlying premise of his argument: that a reasoned examination of Scriptures will reveal not the unmediated Word of God but instead intelligence about the human beings for whom those Scriptures were a living reality. Since the human beings in question were numerous, since they lived over a period of centuries, and since the society in which they lived changed during that time, as all societies do, the Scriptures need to be regarded as a kind of organic being that grew and developed or, to use a word suggested in Henry's first sentence, evolved. None of this is meant to destroy religious faith or deny the existence of God. At the end of the article, Henry speaks about the living God of Israel. "A scientific criticism establishes this result," he wrote. "It shows God in Israel's history not in occasional supernaturalism, but in the continuity of the nation's actual experience; not here and there in fleeting glimpses, but everywhere in broad sunlight, the source and life of the whole."[4] God is *here* in this nation, and as this nation evolves, so presumably does God.

In the world of scholarship, Henry's general approach was not new in 1883, though some of the specifics were. In 1835 and 1836, German theologian David Friedrich Strauss shocked the world of the faithful with the publication of *Das Leben Jesu, kritisch bearbeitet* (The life of Jesus, critically examined). His method was fairly simple: Strauss took various stories from the Gospels, submitted them to "critical" examination, and in almost all cases concluded that they could not be accepted as literally true—because they included supernatural events (which reason tells us cannot have occurred), because they contained internal contradictions, or because the account of an event in one Gospel is completely different from the account in another. He concludes that the stories are *myths*; that is, they are not true, but they bore a certain value for the population that believed in them.

Strauss had lots to say that modern scholars would take issue with, but once again it's the method that counts. That method consisted in (1) standing outside the community of believers in order to approach the problem from a position of scholarly skepticism, (2) denying the reality of all supernatural elements, (3) identifying a natural, *human* trait, namely the tendency to believe in myths, as the motive force behind the stories in the Gospels, and (4) finding explanatory evidence, as in literary and historical studies of any sort, in *documents*—the Gospels themselves, other portions of the Scriptures, or such outside documents as the works of Roman Jewish historian Josephus. Strauss's title pretty much told the story: a book title that begins with "a life of" is almost invariably a biography, which means the life story of an actual human being. To believers, this means reducing the Son of God to just another naturally born man. And "critically examined" is another shot across the bow of traditional Christian belief: one doesn't critically examine writing that is divinely inspired. The English-speaking world came to know Strauss's work beginning in 1846, when George Eliot (the pseudonym of Mary Ann Evans, author of *Adam Bede*, *The Mill on the Floss*, and *Middlemarch*) published her translation, *The Life of Jesus: Critically Examined*. The translation, running to well over a thousand pages in its original three-volume edition, was still sufficiently widely read in 1893 to warrant a reissue in a one-volume, small-print edition.

Strauss was not the first to characterize miraculous events in Scripture as myths, nor was he the first to use the title "Life of Jesus."[5] He wasn't the last, either. French historian Ernest Renan published a *Vie de Jésus* in 1863. Renan followed essentially the same path as his German predecessor, reducing the Gospel narratives to the status of legends that tell us more about the people who created them than they do about Jesus of Nazareth. When it came to method, Renan had a leg up on Strauss, for the Frenchman had actually visited the Holy Land and conducted archeological research there. This pushed the "critical" method a step farther, adding artifacts to a collection of evidence that formerly had consisted almost exclusively of written texts. Renan's book was translated into English the same year it was published in French. It was a sensation in both languages, selling many thousands of copies in several printings, and making the author a fortune. A sign of the book's renown is the brief appearance it made, fifty years after publication, in D. H. Lawrence's

Sons and Lovers (1913). In one scene roughly halfway through the novel, Paul Morel and Miriam have been increasingly questioning their own religious faith, and Paul is "setting full sail towards Agnosticism." "They were at the Renan 'Vie de Jésus' stage," the narrator explains. He offers not a word of further comment, obviously assuming that everyone would know exactly what he was referring to.[6]

In the 1870s and early 1880s, from Germany, came the pathbreaking works that constituted the foundation for what was dubbed the "higher criticism." Chief among them was the book that provided Rev. Henry with his account of the periods in ancient Jewish history and the textual divisions of the Pentateuch (Torah) that correspond to those periods. This was *Geschichte Israels* (History of Israel), published in 1878 by Julius Wellhausen (and republished in 1883 as *Prolegomena zur Geschichte Israels* [Prolegomena to the history of Israel]). Wellhausen presented an account of the Pentateuch that divided the text among four authors, each writing in a different period, plus three redactors. His approach was called the "documentary hypothesis" because it was based on an analysis and dating of the documents; and even though he did not invent the method and even though "documentary hypothesis" had been applied to the work of scholars before him, he came to be most closely associated with the phrase and the method. In fact, for those members of the public who cared about the mysterious band of German scholars who lay behind what everyone was simply calling the "higher criticism," Wellhausen loomed larger than just about anyone else.

The method, the phrase "higher criticism," and its implications began to seep into the popular consciousness in the 1880s, though it's important to bear in mind that, through an acquaintance with Strauss and Renan, many Americans at that point were already well on their way to absorbing a skeptical, secular, "scientific" approach to the Jewish and Christian Scriptures (whether or not they accepted the approach and the conclusions to which it led). But starting in the 1890s, the higher criticism was truly big news, and the public read and heard about it frequently. This was thanks in large part to two men.

The first was Presbyterian minister Charles A. Briggs (1841–1913). (Biblical scholars will recognize his name as the third in what is informally referred to simply as "Brown-Driver-Briggs," meaning the authoritative *Hebrew and English Lexicon of the Old Testament.*) When the trouble began, Briggs was a professor of Hebrew and Cognate Languages at the Union Theological Seminary in New York. Early in 1891, his inaugural address for that position unleashed a scandal that made news for the next two and a half years. The issue was scriptural authority. Here, according to the "authorized syllabus" of the address are some of the statements Dr. Briggs made in the section concerning "Barriers to the Bible." First, on divine authority: "There is nothing divine in the text, in its letters, words or clauses. The divine authority is not in the style or in the words, but in the concept." On the authenticity of the Scriptures: "The great mass of the Old Testament was written by authors whose names or connection with their writings are lost in oblivion. If this is destroying the Bible the Bible is destroyed already. But who tells us that these traditional names were the authors of the Bible? The Bible itself? The creeds of the Church? Any reliable testimony? None of these! Pure conjectural tradition! Nothing more!" On the notion of inerrancy: "There are errors in the Scriptures which no one has been able to explain away, and the theory that they were not in the original text is sheer assumption upon which no mind can rest with certainty." On miracles ("violations of the laws of nature"): "The miracles of the Bible are miracles of redemption" (I take Briggs here to be cagily avoiding the outright claim that the miracles recounted in the Scriptures never took place).[7]

These statements did not sit well with certain authorities in the Presbyterian Church. The governance structure of that church allows for members to be charged with heresy and put on trial. After a series of proceedings, Briggs was suspended from the Presbyterian ministry in June of 1893. But the directors of the Union Theological Seminary stood by him, voted unanimously to retain him in his academic position, and thus effectively severed themselves from the direct control of the Presbyterian Church. Through the entire ordeal, Dr. Briggs never wavered in his views. In 1899, he was ordained a priest in the Episcopal Church, but he remained a professor at the Union Theological Seminary for the rest of his life.

The niceties of the arguments and the judicial proceedings associated with this case make for very dull reading today, and I doubt that very many Americans even in the early 1890s immersed themselves in them. But the affair was a sensation, and Briggs retained his notoriety long after it was settled. As *The Independent* put it years later, in Briggs's obituary, "Dr. Briggs's particular heresy was his higher criticism." The higher criticism was also his big claim to fame, and, to judge from contemporary accounts, the attention he brought to it and to the views that accompanied it left a mark on the American public—at the very least on the church-going public. The obituary writer for *The Independent* added this: "During the twenty years that have since elapsed the feeling in the Presbyterian and other Churches has so far been modified that such a trial could hardly be repeated."[8] Every major newspaper in the country covered the trial extensively, and many ran articles on Briggs regularly for years. By the end of Briggs's life, the popular view seemed to be not that he had attacked Christian religious faith but that, having freed that faith from superstition and arid scholasticism, he had invigorated it, provided it with a sounder basis.

The Briggs affair by itself probably did more to acquaint the American public with a modern, scientifically-based mistrust for the previously unquestioned authority of tradition than it did to enlighten them about just what the higher criticism was and what its implications were for belief. That's where Lyman Abbott came in.

In an era before radio and television, Abbott was quite possibly the most widely known clergyman in the United States. From 1876 until he died in 1922, he was the editor of *Christian Union*, renamed *Outlook* in 1893. He wrote popular books and lectured extensively. He was the pastor of Plymouth Congregational Church in Brooklyn from 1887 till 1898. This was the famous church, founded in 1847, whose pastors and members had always been devoted to the socially progressive strain within their denomination of Protestantism. It's where Henry Ward Beecher had preached his fiery abolitionist sermons in the years leading up to the Civil War. From the late 1880s to the end of his life, Abbott was a constant object of public attention. In some years, the *New York Times* ran over a hundred articles on him—rarely fewer than forty.

When Rev. Abbott gave three series of lectures at Plymouth Church in the 1890s, on the broad theme of "The Bible as Literature," he was in the news all the time, not only in New York, but all over the country. He turned two of the series into books and all three into parallel series of articles in *Outlook*, so his ideas were widely dispersed. The first series was devoted almost entirely to the Hebrew Bible. The second series was devoted to St. Paul and the third to the Hebrew prophets. The higher criticism was a constant refrain in all three series—not only the phrase itself but everything associated with it. Here's how Abbott explained it in the introduction to the book version of the first series:

> This new method goes by the infelicitous title of the "Higher Criticism." I call it infelicitous because, while to scholars its meaning is perfectly clear, to many people it is not, for the simple reason that it is a technical term, and in it the words are used in a technical and non-popular sense. . . . To the scientific stu-

> dent the word "criticism" applied to the Bible means "inquiry into the origin, history, authenticity, character, etc., of the literary documents" of which it is composed. . . . Higher criticism means inquiry into the documents as a whole, their integrity, authenticity, credibility, authorship, circumstances of their composition, and the like, and is equivalent to literary criticism.[9]

The noteworthy statements he made in his lectures (and repeated in the articles and books), those that grabbed the attention of the press and also provoked the strongest opposition, flowed from this description of the higher criticism. "The Bible is a human book," he declared in the first series.[10] Expanding on the idea in the last lecture of the third series, he said, "I have treated these old Hebrew books as literature—that is, as the unveiling of human experience. I believe they are that, and exactly that. I believe that God's revelation is not something different from experience, but something in human experience, and that we are coming to learn not that God inspired a book, but that He inspires men."[11] The sacred texts are not infallible, Abbott repeatedly stated in the written versions of his lectures, nor are any of their authors, he explicitly said of Paul in the first of his lectures on the Apostle. In fact, the very notion of authority in the Scriptures is a problem, since they were written by human beings, with all the flaws and failings such creatures possess.[12] The reporter covering the last series for the *New York Times* was unequivocal in assessing the importance of what Abbott had done: "No series of lectures or sermons in late years," he insisted, "has attracted more widespread attention than Dr. Abbott's effort to popularize the results of higher criticism."[13]

Needless to say, not everyone jumped to embrace the higher criticism; but predictably controversy simply attracted more attention. Nor were Protestant pastors the only ones to enter the fray. In 1904, a conflict developed within Judaism when an association of orthodox rabbis censured the Jewish Theological Seminary for introducing the higher criticism into its curriculum. The personal target of the attack was Solomon Schechter, president of the Seminary and, nine years later, founder of the official Conservative Jewish movement. A spokesman for the association identified Schechter as "an apostle of the higher criticism of the Bible," saying that such criticism "has no place in orthodox Jewish teaching."[14]

And of course the new school of criticism did not escape the notice of the Catholic Church. In July of 1907, Pope Pius X issued a Papal Syllabus that included a lengthy list of propositions to be "reproved and proscribed," explicitly associating the propositions with the higher criticism. Among the reprehensible propositions were these: "The authorities of the Church cannot determine by dogmatic definitions the proper sense of the Holy Scriptures." "Those who believe that God is in truth the author of the Holy Scriptures show too great a simplicity or ignorance." "Divine inspiration does not extend itself over all the Holy Scriptures in such a manner as to guarantee all and every part thereof from all error." In all, there were sixty-five propositions to be reproved.[15]

There's no way to know how many Americans both absorbed the impact of the higher criticism and accepted its findings and implications. But if we're speaking of an encounter with the new ideas, rather than the actual conversion of the public to a new way of thinking, it's safe to say that the blow had struck. And plenty of observers were convinced that the higher criticism *had* triumphed. With all the dissension in the ranks of rabbis over the new methods, in 1910 Joseph Jacobs declared victory for those methods, saying that they had become "the orthodoxy of the present day."[16] In 1923, Stephen Wise felt secure in announcing to the world that "the Bible is not God's book, but man's book. The Bible," he said, "was made for man, not man for the Bible. The higher criticism restores the Bible to the hand of its rightful owner, man."[17]

The Kingdom of God Is Not at Hand; It's Right Here

"Go, and do thou likewise." This instruction to "a certain lawyer" in the Gospel According to St. Luke finishes the episode in which Jesus tells the parable of the Good Samaritan. The parable itself answers the question, "And who is my neighbor" (if I am to love him as myself)? As the lawyer correctly guesses, the neighbor is the non-Jewish Samaritan, "He that shewed mercy on him" (the Jewish victim). Owing to the casual character of the verb "to do," English probably does not adequately convey the force of Jesus' command. We don't know exactly what the original Aramaic words would have been, but the Greek translation, which is as close as we get, has Jesus say *poiei*: do/make/act. The idea is *active doing*: go out into the world and *act* as the Samaritan acted.

Charles Monroe Sheldon surely had this parable in mind in 1896, when he wrote *In His Steps: What Would Jesus Do?* (originally serialized, then published as a book in 1897). Sheldon was a Congregationalist minister in Topeka, Kansas, with only a local following before *In His Steps* came out. He then quickly became a nationally and internationally recognized figure. The book sold 100,000 copies within months of its release and, by one estimate, eight million copies worldwide over the next fifty years. It was a work of fiction, entirely mediocre by any standard of literary taste, but Sheldon's readers were not looking for grand style. The story line was simplicity itself: a small-town minister, like the author himself, is awakened from the routine of his life by a tramp, who shows up in church one Sunday, rises from his pew to chide the parishioners for overlooking the plight of people like himself, and then dies a few days later in the minister's house. Conscience-stricken, Rev. Maxwell gathers a group of prominent congregants and proposes to them that they spend the next year leading their lives by asking themselves, before every significant undertaking, "What would Jesus do?" So, for example, the editor of the town newspaper stops publishing advertisements for whiskey and tobacco, because if Jesus were running a newspaper, that's what he would do. By the end of the story, townspeople have fought back against local saloons, worked to improve the lives of workingmen, and established a settlement house, all because these are things that Jesus would do.

What's odd about Sheldon's book, as one critic noticed years ago, is that there's very little mention of Christianity as such in it.[18] Sheldon makes a single reference to a Gospel text by name (Matthew), and that only by way of telling us the theme of a sermon. He refers to the Bible only when the physical book is part of a scene, saying little about its contents. For it's clear from the way Rev. Maxwell approaches the project he's conceived for his fellow townspeople that the finer points of Biblical interpretation are not essential. At the initial meeting, Rachel Winslow, who sings in Maxwell's church, asks the obvious question: what to do if one parishioner's idea of what Jesus would do in a particular case differs from another's? "How am I going to tell what he would do?" she asks. Maxwell answers: "There is no way that I know of . . . except as we study Jesus through the medium of the Holy Spirit." A little later he adds, "If Jesus' example is the example for the world, it certainly must be feasible to follow it."[19] This hardly sounds like a "higher criticism" method for answering questions about Jesus. Maxwell offers no historical analysis of documents to advance a claim about what Jesus would do in the face of, say, the saloon problem in his town. And yet two features of his approach unquestionably fly in the face of some older, traditional methods. First, he does not look to the text of Scriptures for an inerrant meaning that can be applied to real life. Instead, he acknowledges that different congregants will likely have different views on particulars. And second, he treats Jesus above all as a man who *acted* and who thereby serves as an example. That's why the wording of the question that Sheldon had Maxwell repeatedly ask, the one that served as a subtitle for *In His Steps* and that experienced a powerful revival among young American evangelical Christians in the 1990s, is so crucial. Not "What Would Jesus Think?" or "How Would Jesus Judge Me?" but "What Would Jesus *Do*?"

When *In His Steps* came out, the idea of doing good for society in the name of religion—Christian or otherwise—was certainly not new. Sheldon's book both captured the public's mood and then helped propel that mood to the lofty heights it would attain in the next couple of decades. It was the basis for an entire movement in American Protestantism, though of course the movement was not centrally organized and many of its leading figures would have resisted the idea that they were operating in concert under a single banner.

By sometime in the first decade of the twentieth century, people were calling it the Social Gospel Movement. By the end of that decade, books began to appear with those words either in the title or as the title. There are many histories of the movement, and there's some disagreement about who should be included on a list of its noteworthy figures. Congregationalist minister Washington Gladden (1836–1918), who preached in Massachusetts and then Columbus, Ohio, is often identified as one of the movement's founders. Lyman Abbott would qualify, as would Shailer Mathews, whom we encountered in chapter 2 as dean of the University of Chicago Divinity School, editor of *Biblical World*. He was also author of *The Social Gospel* (1910).

But the man who truly gave the movement its most sophisticated and also most popularly accessible intellectual foundation was Walter Rauschenbusch (1861–1918). Rauschenbusch was born in the United States but came from a long line of German Lutheran ministers. His father, after immigrating to this country, joined the Baptist Church. Rauschenbusch was educated partly in Germany and partly in the United States. In 1886, he became minister of the Second German Baptist Church in the notorious Hell's Kitchen neighborhood of New York. He remained there till 1897, when he accepted a faculty position at Rochester Theological Seminary, the institution where he had received his education and where his father had taught. As he later told the story, his encounter with the squalor of the neighborhood on the West Side transformed his religious convictions.

The book that made a name for Rauschenbusch, while giving shape to the Social Gospel Movement, was *Christianity and the Social Crisis*. If you were a member of one of the conventional American Protestant sects when the book came out in 1907, having developed your religious views before the 1870s, two closely related facts would have struck you from the beginning. First, there was almost no sign that the author was a "believer" in any of the common senses of the word. There are almost no references to the fundamental features of almost all Christian theology—Jesus as the Son of God, the Virgin Birth, the Resurrection. When Rauschenbusch did refer to the Resurrection (which he spelled with a lower-case *r*), it was to redefine the term figuratively, as something taking place *now* (meaning in history, after Jesus) or as something having to do with *us*—giving the human race "potential immortality" (whatever that might mean).[20] Second, Rauschenbusch was everywhere secular, scientific, historical. He read Scriptures for historical content, and he treated them from an historical perspective, citing Wellhausen and others associated with the higher criticism. Like many scholars of his era, Rauschenbusch regarded the era of Jewish history in which Jesus lived as one characterized by priestly emphasis on the purely ritualistic components of the religion, and he regarded Jesus himself as heir to the earlier tradition of the prophets, a tradition that, for Rauschenbusch and others, expressed the true core of Judaism. The way Rauschenbusch saw it, for Jesus the prophet, morality was a public matter, not a private and individual matter, as it was for the priests. And so it was but a single step from this view to the view of Jesus the social reformer—not, mind you, exactly of the sort you see in the early twentieth century, but one whose aims were peculiar to his era. Since the kingdom of Israel had long since vanished, the idea now for someone who sought to liberate the religion from its focus on ritual and on individual purity was to make that religion international, ethical, and focused on the interests of all humanity. These terms might strike us as anachronistic, but they are the terms that Rauschenbusch used in his historical account of Judaism.[21]

But Rauschenbusch's work was shot through with anachronisms—or at least modernisms. This brings us to the central concept: the kingdom of God. For Rauschenbusch, this kingdom was a theocratic ideal, and so it necessarily had something to do with God. And yet almost every feature he listed in connection with it was purely earthly. It was a "national and collective idea." "It involved that social justice, prosperity, and happiness for which the Law and the prophets called, and for which the common people always long." It was not to be brought about by bloodshed and violence or by a "divine catastrophe." Instead, Rauschenbusch thought, Jesus saw the kingdom of God as already growing organically among the people.[22] And, even though he sought to represent Jesus as a man tied inextricably to his own era, Rauschenbusch described the Christian ideal by employing concepts that did not even exist until shortly before his own birth. In fact, like so many of his contemporaries, when he needed an image to describe the social order, he resorted to the human organism, envisioned as a network (though he didn't employ that word):

> Because Jesus believed in the organic growth of the new society, he patiently fostered its growth, cell by cell. Every human life brought under control of the new spirit which he himself embodied and revealed was an advance of the kingdom of God. . . . It is just as when human tissues have been broken down by disease or external force, and new tissue is silently forming under the old and weaving a new web of life. . . . By living with men and thinking and feeling in their presence, he reproduced his own life in others and they gained faith to risk this new way of living. This process of assimilation went on by the natural capacities inherent in the social organism, just as fresh blood will flow along the established arteries and capillaries. When a nucleus of like-minded men was gathered about him, the assimilating power was greatly reinforced. . . . Thus Jesus worked on individuals and through individuals, but his real end was not individualistic, but social, and in his method he employed strong social forces.[23]

Throughout his mature life, Rauschenbusch consistently defined the kingdom of God in relation to human society. This runs like a thread through *Christianity and the Social Crisis* and other works as well. "The Kingdom of God," he wrote in one place, "is humanity organized according to the will of God . . . the Kingdom of God, at every stage of human development, tends toward a social order which will best guarantee to all personalities their freest and highest development. This involves the redemption of social life from the cramping influence of religious bigotry, from the repression of self-assertion in the relation of upper and lower classes, and from all forms of slavery in which human beings are treated as mere means to serve the ends of others."[24]

Nothing could be more characteristically modern than these ideas. "Stage of human development," as well as "freest and highest development," takes us back to sociological theories inspired by Darwin. "Treated as mere means" takes us back to Immanuel Kant's categorical imperative, one of whose formulations is, "Act in such a way that you treat humanity, both in your own person and in the person of everyone else, never merely as a means to an end but always, at the same time, as an end." Rauschenbusch knew his Kant, which means he knew that for the author of *The Critique of Practical Reason* (1788), the ethical imperative to treat one's fellow man as an end in himself was closely linked to the idea of the kingdom of God. That's because both represented for Kant the "highest good."[25] But "kingdom of God" for Kant was hardly a conventional Christian concept. In *The Critique of Practical Reason*, it essentially stands as an equivalent to "the highest good," either in the figurative sense or, hypothetically, for those who actually profess a Christian faith. Kant's system of ethics, despite whatever religious language he used to describe it, was human to the core. And the talk of bigotry, social classes, and slavery comes from Rauschenbusch's own era.

Rauschenbusch was not the only Social Gospelist to speak of the kingdom of God in these terms. Shailer Mathews, in *The Social Teaching of Jesus*, published in 1897, described it as "a concrete reality rather than an idea," adding that "this reality was not to be left as an unattainable ideal, but was to be progressively realized, perhaps evolved." He then supplied the definition of the phrase that he thought Jesus himself would have given: "By the kingdom of God Jesus meant *an ideal* (though progressively approximated) *social order in which the relation of men to God is that of sons, and* (therefore) *to each other, that of brothers*."[26] The following year he conducted a "symposium" on the topic for *Biblical World*, like the symposium he later conducted (as I described in chapter 2) on the theory of evolution. Invited participants were all scholars and authorities on Christian theology. Mathews received a variety of responses on the meaning of "kingdom of God," many of them at odds with the views he had expressed in his book of the previous year.[27] But he himself never wavered from his insistence that the expression referred to something that, while divine in origin as well as perhaps in spirit, (a) is realized in this world and (b) is inextricably connected with the social order. In *A Dictionary of Religion and Ethics*, he defined kingdom of God succinctly at the beginning of his entry on the phrase: "The reign of God over an ideal social order conceived of both temporally and transcendentally."[28]

Whether or not you prominently employed the expression "kingdom of God," if you were a clergyman who embraced the modern view of religion, you emphasized *action in this world*, carried out for the benefit of your fellow human beings, both individually and collectively. This was the era in which many of the religious organizations committed to social action were formed in the United States. The Young Men's Christian Association (YMCA) had existed in this country since 1851, the Salvation Army since 1880. In 1908, an interdenominational group of Protestant religious leaders, including Washington Gladden, Walter Rauschenbusch, and Shailer Mathews, joined to form the Federal Council of Churches. One of the first acts of the council was to issue a declaration of principles, under the title "The Social Creed of the Churches." It's a remarkable document, because it's devoted exclusively to human problems associated with industrial capitalism. The council announced that it stood "For equal rights and complete justice for all men in all stations of life; For the abolition of child-labor; For such regulation of the conditions of toil for women as shall safeguard the physical and moral health of the community; For the suppression of the 'Sweating System,'" and so on. There was no mention of God or Christ; in fact, if you didn't read the name of the organization at the top of the document, you'd have no idea that there was anything religious about the program at all. A slightly revised version promulgated in 1912 included a reference to "Christian principles."[29] But apart from this, the Social Creed was indistinguishable from the list of demands that a moderately socialist union leader might issue. The council unabashedly took on a political role, initially promoting progressive reform and eventually acting as a lobbyist for its political positions.[30]

One of the era's most amazing manifestations of Christian social activism was the Men and Religion Forward Movement. It was in large part the brainchild of a lay YMCA officer named Frederick D. Smith, who possessed the genius to surmise that Christians could accomplish their goals not only by relying on a wide array of religious leaders but also by enlisting the talents (and money) of businessmen. In fact, the complete list of these latter was far too long for Smith to add to the article he wrote for the *New York Times* introducing the movement, but it included J. P. Morgan, John Wanamaker, and John D. Rockefeller.[31]

The goals? At the outset the movement sounded like a colossal missionary movement, pure and simple. Several months before it got started, Smith wrote that the central aim was "to make real the Christian ideal from the individual clear out into the last recesses of society." The idea seemed to be to recruit as many men (yes, men, because women already effectively ran the churches) into "the churches" (remember, it was an interdenominational movement). The movement was short-lived, by design. It was conceived of as a sort of seed effort, so it lasted only from October of 1911 to April of 1912, when it was disbanded, with the understanding that subsequent work would be carried out by local churches, the YMCA, and Sunday School Associations.[32] During that time, according to figures reported after the movement ended, the organization held over 7,000 meetings in 60 cities and some 1,500 towns, attracted 1.5 million people to those meetings, recruited over 7,000 men into the church, and induced 26,000 existing church members to work for its various causes.[33]

But Men and Religion Forward was much more than a proselytizing campaign. It operated on six fronts: (Social Service, Bible Study, Boys' Work, Missions, Evangelism, and Community Extension). After the movement concluded its work, its leaders, under the auspices of the YMCA, brought out a book titled *Making Religion Efficient*, which told the history of the movement and provided details about each of the six component campaigns, in addition to a seven-volume series called *Messages of the Men and Religion Movement*, which contained essays and speeches about the campaigns. We've seen so far how Protestant religious leaders came to mingle generally in the world and more especially in the social life of their communities and the entire nation. What was particularly striking about the Men and Religion Forward Movement, however, was how unabashedly its leaders focused on economic questions. Given the strong presence of businessmen in the movement, this is hardly surprising, but it's important to remember that, whatever the sequence of events might have been that led up to the founding of the movement (that is, whether the initial idea came from a layman or from a clergyman), the idea as the movement presented it was that economic life was an essential concern for all Christians.

Nowhere was the point more clearly made than in the "Report of the Social Service Commission," published in *Messages of the Men and Religion Movement* (volume 2, *Social Service*). The second chapter of that report was titled "The Kingdom of God and the Economic Life." The unnamed author came across as someone who had read, but did not wish to mention, Karl Marx. He wrote:

> Whatever else the Kingdom of God involves it certainly demands a righteous and brotherly social order on earth. But a just and fraternal social life cannot be built on an unjust and unfraternal economic life, for the economic life is the rough foundation of all higher social relations and determines their character. If that foundation is out of plumb, every wall will become a threat and need the iron clamping of force to keep it together. If great classes are submerged in poverty, political liberty collapses. If men are economically unfree, they cannot be free intellectually. If inequality of possession thrusts

> men apart in antagonistic social classes, even religion cannot permanently create a real sense of their brotherhood, and the church finds itself forced into the position of a class organization.[34]

Let's say you were a moderately observant Christian, for some reason you had never heard of the Men and Religion Forward Movement, and you picked up a copy of *Making Religion Efficient* soon after its publication in 1912. You'd probably have been surprised by the title. The concept of efficiency was at the pinnacle of its popularity, having been covered by such figures as Christine Frederick, whose *New Housekeeping: Efficiency Studies in Home Management* came out that same year, and Frederick Winslow Taylor, whose *Principles of Scientific Management* was published the year before. Efficiency was a concept associated with management, whether of household or of business. What could it possibly have to do with religion? Baptist minister Allyn K. Foster explained in the introductory chapter, as he described the Men and Religion Forward Movement:

> Itself the child of previous influences at work, it became the climax of that adaptation of the spirit of the times to the Christian enterprise, which has been so noticeable in secular institutions. The keynote of commercial, political, educational, and social effort in this generation has been "efficiency." All the expedients proposed and adopted have grown out of this idea. It was high time that the principle should be applied to religion in general and to the Christian Church in particular. The Men and Religion Movement was the composite of those forces which have produced cooperation in business and in philanthropy, progressivism in politics, and efficiency in all administration. It borrowed its cooperation from big business, its progressivism from University Extension, its efficiency from the Young Men's Christian Association and Laymen's Missionary Movement.[35]

The book presented a chapter on each of the movement's six campaigns. Given the unapologetic embrace of methods from the world of commerce, politics, and education, perhaps it would not then have surprised you to see, in the chapter "Social Service," how very much Men and Religion Forward immersed itself in the national life of the era. Under the headings "municipal," "industrial," "immigration," "education," "social agencies," "field surveys," "cooperation with other agencies," and "Christian publicity," there was a list of virtually every social concern that attracted public attention in the Progressive Era. Here are a few of the many things that movement leaders were for: the enforcement of pure food regulations, closing down saloons, checking the spread of the social evil, collective bargaining for workers, factory inspections, federal and state protection for the unemployed, education for immigrants, educating the public on sanitation and health, instruction in sex hygiene for young and old, physical education, and industrial and vocational training.

What counted in the end was the practical impact the movement had on the lives of Americans. Teams of leaders and religious workers fanned out across the country during the six months of the movement's active existence. A typical visit to a major city would last eight days, and then there were visits to surrounding towns. Residents of a given city were usually treated to a series of speeches on the six campaigns, they almost invariably heard a harangue about the evils of saloons (including the claim that there were more saloons than churches in their town), and of course they were exhorted to join a church, if they did not already belong to one. In Washington, D.C., people heard about the thirty-three evils of slum life and learned that inadequate wages were the chief cause of poverty in the nation's cities.[36] In Los Angeles, people heard about the sufferings of casual laborers and the strain caused by the corporate control of capital.[37] In Chicago, movement leaders made a plan to place successful businessmen and professional men in settlement houses for a couple of months so that, in the interest of social reform, they could study the lives of immigrants.[38]

"What shall I do to inherit eternal life?" the ruler had asked Jesus (Luke 18:18). To followers of socially progressive Christian movements, the answer seemed obvious. It was not necessarily selling all your belongings and giving to the poor. *Doing* was the key. For others. Here and now.

God (or Something like Him) Wants You to Cooperate

When the Federal Council of Churches was first established, its founding members decided the organization needed a section devoted to social service, so they formed the Commission on the Church and Social Service. As the movement's historian put it years later, "The positive idea on which all could agree was that Christianity meant, in broadest terms, cooperation and service."[39] A couple of years later, the council needed a leader for the group, so they recruited a middle-aged Congregationalist pastor from South Norwalk, Connecticut, named Charles S. Macfarland (1866–1956). In 1912, Macfarland would become the general secretary of the entire council. He was already one of the guiding spirits of Christian social service in America. In that same year, he published *Spiritual Culture and Social Service.* Nowhere have I found a more forceful statement of the sentiment that cooperation, or "mutual service" as he called it in that book, constituted the very core of Jesus' teaching, that in fact it underlay all God's creation. Jesus, Macfarland wrote, "gave utterance here to the twofold law of life. Man is both to be served and to serve. Jesus saw the two aspects of religion; and taught that the ultimate expression of religion was in this law of service." The entire universe is pervaded with "interdependence and interrelation." God has made "an altruistic natural order." "This law pervades the universe, natural and spiritual," he continued. "We are in each other's hands. We are absolutely dependent upon each other. The comfort of all is impaired when any cease to do their service. Let the strike come in the mines, and men shiver in their cold houses. It is all mutual; we cannot live without each other's service."[40]

Macfarland had behind him not just the words of the Gospel but modern science (theistic science, to be sure). His authorities were John Fiske and Henry Drummond. Fiske (1842–1901), a popular lecturer and writer, was one of America's early religious champions of evolutionary theory. He was best known as the author of the forbiddingly titled *Outlines of Cosmic Philosophy,* a four-volume work in which he sought to combine the findings of Darwin and Herbert Spencer into a coherent worldview. Macfarland had read the more recent *Through Nature to God* (1899), in which Fiske presented a shortened version of a view dear to him, representing a modification of classic Darwinism, namely that altruism (self-sacrifice, cooperation) was a natural product of evolutionary development. As Fiske saw it, altruism evolved in the human species when *sociality* replaced egoism as a dominant force. The source from which altruism sprang is *maternity,* a relatively recent development in the earth's history because, as Fiske explained, "God's highest work is never perfected save in the fulness of time."[41] (As we'll see in the next chapter, nontheistically inclined biologists in this era agreed that evolutionary theory provided an explanation for the rise of altruism and cooperation.) Macfarland was especially attracted by Fiske's concept of "the cosmic roots of love and self-sacrifice" (the title of the second part of *Through Nature to God*).[42]

Drummond (1851–97) was a Scottish naturalist, explorer, professor, and theologian who made a name for himself in the United States by publishing a number of articles in *McClure's Magazine* in the last years of his life and by giving a series of lectures in 1893 at the Lowell Institute in Boston on the evolution of man. He revised and published the lectures the following year as *The Lowell Lectures on the Ascent of Man.* Here he presented himself as the great apostle of altruism and co-operation (as it was commonly spelled back then), locating the altruistic/cooperative spirit in the very core of the Cosmos itself. "Everything, indeed, came into being because of something else," he wrote "and continues to be because of its relations to something else. The matter of the earth is built up of co-operating atoms; it owes its existence, its motion, and its stability to co-operating stars. Plants and animals are made of co-operating cells, nations of co-operating men. Nature makes no move, Society achieves no end, the Cosmos advances not one step, that is not dependent on Co-operation; and while the discords of the world disappear with growing knowledge, Science only reveals with increasing clearness the universality of its reciprocities."[43]

The titles of two consecutive chapters tell the story of Drummond's allegiance to, and revision of, Darwinian theory: "The Struggle for Life" and "The Struggle for the Life of Others." "Altruism," "altruistic," "co-operation," and "co-operative" occur over fifty times in the book. For Drummond, the idea is far more fundamental and goes much farther back in evolutionary history than for Fiske. In fact, the "Co-operative Principle" appears at the moment of transition from unicellular to multicellular organisms. In his fanciful account:

> Every life at first was a single cell. Co-operation was unknown. Each cell was self-contained and self-sufficient, and as new cells budded from the parent they moved away and set up life for themselves. This self-sufficiency leads to nothing in Evolution. . . . But soon we find the co-operative principle beginning its mysterious integrating work. Two, three, four, eight, ten cells club together and form a small mat, or cylinder, or ribbon—the humblest forms of corporate plant-life—in which each individual cell divides the responsibilities and the gains of living with the rest.[44]

Drummond pictures nature as a vast web in which the actor who has played the greatest part is "self-sacrifice."[45] As we'll see in the next chapter, there were others of the same era who saw cooperation and altruism in various species as the result of evolutionary processes.

Macfarland was not one of the giant religious intellects of his age, nor did he pretend to be. There's nothing strikingly original or thought-provoking in his writing. His contribution was, through the service he carried out and through his writings, to strengthen in the public's mind the connection between such service and religious faith. But that connection had been there for quite a while by the time Macfarland came along. From the 1890s on, ordinary Americans heard frequently about the concept of cooperation in connection with religion, especially when the religion was some form of Protestantism. Not everyone used the word "cooperation." A host of other words and phrases meant the same thing or roughly the same thing. And not everyone saw cooperation as the underlying idea of the Cosmos, the fundamental principle in Christianity, the key to salvation and the kingdom of heaven.

Protestants were not the only ones who were crusading for cooperation and making of it a sacred or semi-sacred human virtue. Ethical Culture was founded on principles that led irresistibly to the idea of cooperation, and, to the extent that Ethical Culture was a religion, cooperation took on a kind of sacrosanct status for its leaders. Felix Adler (1851–1933) created Ethical Culture in 1876, and even though the society he founded was never centrally controlled, and individual leaders were given considerable freedom to express views that differed from Adler's, Adler remained the guiding spirit of the organization for his entire life—and after. Adler was not an everyman. He was a brainy thinker who was at home more in the style of the academic journal than in the style of a popular preacher. Some forty years after founding the movement, he described the development of his philosophy, in *An Ethical Philosophy of Life Presented in Its Main Outlines* (1918). The underlying principle for absolutely everything else he stood for was the inviolability of every human life, "that every human being is an end *per se*, worth while on his own account," as he put it.[46]

The system of thought (or call it religion) that Adler developed rested on the polarity of inviolable personality and sociality. But "sociality" needs to be construed very broadly. In *An Ethical Philosophy of Life*, Adler repeatedly used the word "collective" to describe the task and obligation that mankind faces. He also presented, in ascending order, the enterprises or groups that embody the collective spirit: the family, the vocations, the state, the international society, and religious fellowship. Each one of these enterprises or groups shows the same fundamental polarity of individual unit and larger network. But towering over everything else is the collective task of all mankind. That task is spiritual, and it creates the vast system of nodes at whose center individuals find themselves. The nodes are other individuals *now*, as well as individuals in the past and the future: it's one big web. "I, as an individual," he wrote, "am also inextricably linked up backward and forward with those who come before and those who are to come after. I cannot take myself out of this web. The task laid upon human society as a whole is also laid upon me. I am a conscious thread in the fabric that is weaving, conscious in a general way of the pattern to be woven."[47]

Was Ethical Culture a purely atheistic system of thought, or could it be considered a "religion?" Adler thought it could, as he explained in *A Religion of Duty* (1905). Instead of a god, you have duty, with the understanding that you remember "the cosmic significance of the moral law." But because we're talking about duty and the moral law, we're talking, once again, about social relations, and because we're talking about social relations, we're talking about cooperation. "The really strongest motive upon which we rely in modern times," he explained "is the social motive. A man must stay upon earth in order to be of use. The progress, the very existence of humanity depends on co-operation. All are bound to help one another."[48]

It would be a great exaggeration to suggest that Felix Adler and the branches of the Ethical Culture Society in various American cities exerted by themselves a transforming influence on the minds of huge numbers of Americans during the late nineteenth and early twentieth centuries—or, for that matter, at any time since the society was founded. If you were to take a representative selection of educated Americans in the era and ask them to list all the religious figures they considered to be involved in progressive reform movements, few, I imagine, especially non–New Yorkers, would think to name Felix Adler.

And yet his ideas were widely disseminated. You didn't have to read any of his books to know who he was and what he stood for. His primary means of communication was the public lecture—both at Ethical Society buildings and in huge public forums, such as Carnegie Hall and Standard Hall (in what is today Times Square). The *New York Times* followed his career closely, publishing well over a thousand articles on him during his almost sixty-year career. His lectures and activities were widely reported nationwide. Even the California newspapers kept tabs on what Professor Adler was saying and doing. Perhaps it could be taken as a sign of his prominence that he was not infrequently the object of ridicule. In 1897, for example, *Life* magazine poked fun at a "sermon" in which Adler decried discrimination against Jews in this country. Why poke fun? Because, the writer boldly stated, Jews are generally so unpleasant to be around that such discrimination is entirely justified. In the era of the Dreyfus scandal and despite proudly proclaiming that there is no race hatred in the United States, the editors even saw fit to include a degrading caricature of Adler. He's represented as a court jester, bearing the unmistakable stigmata of his "race": bald pate, unkempt beard, enormous ears and nose, and receding brow.[49]

Reform Judaism in the United States joined the struggle too. Many have claimed that social justice has been a central concern of Judaism from the very beginning. Starting in the last decades of the nineteenth century, the Reform movement began to speak of it in distinctly modern terms. A conference of rabbis in Pittsburgh in 1885 produced a short platform document that concluded with this paragraph: "In full accordance with the spirit of Mosaic legislation, which strives to regulate the relation between the rich and poor, we deem it our duty to participate in the great task of modern times, to solve, on the basis of justice and righteousness, the problems presented by the contrasts and evils of the present organization of society." The language here, to be sure, was vague, and anyone reading the platform in 1885 and subsequent years had to fill in the meaning of "the present organization of society." There could be no doubt that the phrase had something to do with industrial capitalism, but the rabbis were clearly being careful both to avoid sounding partisan and to issue a statement to which as many as possible could subscribe. Still, as anodyne as the paragraph appeared to be, it represented a bold move in its day. Before that time, debates in Reform Judaism generally centered on issues of theology and ritual practice. With the Pittsburgh Platform, even though there was plenty of negative reaction to it within the Jewish community, social justice began to enter the consciousness of Reform Jews in the United States.[50]

But Jewish involvement in affairs of social justice did not fully come into its own—or into the consciousness of non-Jewish Americans—until the first decade of the twentieth century. The Central Conference of American Rabbis, a Reform Jewish organization that had been around since 1889, began to get involved in social issues in 1908, when it threw its weight behind the movement to abolish child labor. The CCAR could hardly be described as radical in its politics, but it spent years formulating a social program, finally issuing a declaration of principles in 1918—six years after the Federal Council of Churches issued its Social Creed of the Churches. The document was remarkable less for its lofty ideas (the tepid statement that "the ideal of social justice has always been an integral part of Judaism" was about as exciting as it got) than for the specific nature of its recommendations: the signatories stood for a minimum wage, an eight-hour workday, the abolition of child labor, universal workmen's health insurance, and collective bargaining. The very willingness of the documents' authors to immerse themselves in the most concrete issues of the day already shows what a distance they had traveled from the attitudes of preceding generations of even Reform Jews. A *religious* body was willing to lend its authority to a detailed political program.[51]

In all likelihood, few Americans took notice of the CCAR's platform when it appeared in 1918. The figure who was undoubtedly the most visible Jewish advocate of social reform and justice, to Jews and non-Jews alike, was Stephen S. Wise (1874–1949). The son of a Reform rabbi and grandson of a chief rabbi of Hungary, Wise started out in the moderately conservative (lowercase *c*) B'nai Jeshurun Synagogue in New York City, and then went on to head a traditional Reform congregation in Portland, Oregon. In 1906, he returned to New York and over the next few years turned the Jewish world upside-down. The previous year he had been offered the pulpit at New York's Temple Emanu-El, quite possibly the most prestigious and visible synagogue in the country. In what some called a publicity stunt and others simply a passionate defense of principles, Wise had turned down the position on the grounds that the temple's board of trustees expected to exercise control over the content of his sermons. Not satisfied with politely declining Emanu-El's call, Wise wrote an open letter to Louis Marshall, chairman of the board of trustees, and published the letter as a pamphlet.[52] The issue was "freedom of the Jewish pulpit," and Wise set out the reasons why a rabbi must be at liberty to express himself on matters both theological and non-theological without being subject to censorship.

The next step was to establish a new synagogue, the Free Synagogue, as it would be called. In early 1907, Wise gave a series of six public addresses in which he explained the concept of the institution he had in mind. It would be Jewish, though both Jews and non-Jews would be welcome. Services were to be held on Sundays, as a concession to a world of commerce in which Saturday, like it or not, remained a business day and Sunday a day of rest (the two-day weekend, first introduced on a major scale by Henry Ford in the mid-1920s, was little more than a utopian dream at this time). Congregants would stand on an equal footing with one another, regardless of wealth or social position. It would be democratic, giving both the rabbi and the members freedom to express their views. And finally it would be dedicated to social justice.

For this purpose, Wise formed a Social Service Division. Years later, the head of that organization, Sidney E. Goldstein (1879–1955), described the original purposes of the division. Among them was "to further social movements and to advance social causes." If that sounded vague, he provided a long list of specific causes to which his organization would dedicate its energies. For example, "it should be among the first to fight child labor, discrimination, and the denial of human rights to every individual and to every group."[53] On this point, he was crystal-clear: the Free Synagogue would provide services not only to Jews but to anyone in need. As he explained, "Kingdom of God" is an ancient Jewish concept, and it is and has always been of this world. "It is not imposed upon us from above nor from below; it is our own creation and our own handiwork," he wrote. "We are the architects and the artisans of the social order in the midst of which we dwell."[54] Every synagogue, he believed, had an obligation to commit itself to "social action for the establishment of an ethical social order."[55] An ethical order embraced all humanity.

In 1910 and 1911, Wise, together with the pastors of the Church of the Messiah (Unitarian) and the Church of the Divine Paternity (Universalist), organized "union services," at which Jews and Christians worshipped together. Not surprisingly, the services brought angry opposition from many quarters. Wise found himself under fire even from prominent Jews who had initially supported the Free Synagogue. But the services were hugely popular, attracting enormous crowds. In December of 1910, Wise answered his critics in a sermon from his Free Synagogue "pulpit"—Carnegie Hall. Having defended at length the common goals of social reform to which the three congregations were dedicated, Wise came to the core of his message. It was all about cooperation, he said:

> Co-operation is the word of aspiration and of practice, too, in our age. Even in the world of affairs the most doctrinaire of individualists are beginning to admit that competition must be mitigated and modified by some measure of the spirit of co-operation. The question is,—shall we co-operate in all things save in the highest? The question is, as a venerable and cherished friend has written, whether one who regards in soberness the fact that synagogue and church face the same problem of leavening a community of which a fourth part are the children of Israel, with the ethico-religious ideals of the prophets of Israel, must not confess that it is too great a task for either to achieve separately as effectively as they can achieve it co-operatively.[56]

It should come as no surprise that Felix Adler inspired Rabbi Wise, who was almost a quarter-century Adler's junior. It should also come as no surprise that the two men had a sometimes troubled relationship over the years. To the outsider, especially to someone inclined to take the view that Ethical Culture is a little bit like a religion and that Wise's Reform Judaism was a little bit *not* like a religion, it would appear that there was far more that united them than that divided them. If you were looking for the most salient common factor, it would probably be the oratorical skill that both men possessed. They were said to be electrifying speakers. Newspaper accounts from the era describe the throngs that fought to gain entrance to their speeches. Classic photos of the two men convey something of the power they must have held over their audiences. Adler stares out at you with piercing blue eyes, almost bulging from their sockets as if to seize you, heart and soul (or the Ethical Culture counterpart of soul). Wise is seen in profile, gazing into space, his eyes asquint, straining, no doubt, to descry an object too distant for the vision of ordinary mortals. Let there be no doubt: enormous cooperative endeavors required the leadership of powerful individuals.

The Kingdom, Cooperation, and the Web

In a passage I quoted earlier, Walter Rauschenbusch referred to "the web of life." In a little book called *Dare We Be Christians* (1914), he wrote of how "the love for one man promptly widens out into the love of many and weaves more closely the web of social life."[57] In *An Ethical Philosophy*, Felix Adler wrote (in another passage I quoted earlier) about the "web" in which the individual finds himself linked to past and future. Toward the end of the book Adler stated that "the task of humanity in general" is "to spread the web of spiritual relations over larger and ever larger provinces of the finite realm."[58] Whether or not they used such words as "web" or "network," all religious figures who promoted social justice had elaborated a theology or secular philosophy that regarded the individual human being as connected by an intricate system of relations both to other human beings and to larger beings and forces.

The key in this broad movement was the connection with fellow human beings, and perhaps the most striking feature of it was how much it represented a *disruption* of existing religious practices and beliefs. What we're looking at here is a transition that many religious people underwent from an outlook that emphasized the individual, the individual's salvation, and the individual's relation with God to an outlook that ineluctably placed the individual in a network with all other individuals. Even for those who insisted that the new outlook was still religious, what distinguished it from, say, the one that underlay the universalist aspirations of the Catholic Church (*catholic* comes from a Greek word that means "universal," or "of the whole") is the logically necessary ecumenism that arose from it. By "ecumenism" here I mean "the whole world" (its Greek root means "inhabited," understood as applying to the known world) *not* as already unified under a single religion but with all its many different religions and systems of thought. This transition was especially pronounced among Jewish reformers, for conventional Jewish notions of social justice before the Progressive Era tended to center on *other Jews*, rather than on *all humanity*. When Stephen Wise invited clergymen of various Christian denominations to share his pulpit, it was not to thumb his nose at the established centers of Jewish clerical power; it was to give the public a concrete picture of religious individuals—Jews, Protestants, Catholics—who in casting a glance at their fellow human beings overlooked distinctions of faith and religious adherence. It meant, at least in the world of social relations, openly abandoning both the theology of Jewish election (the Jews as God's chosen people) and the then-prevailing notion of Jewish racial solidarity for a theology of universalism and a sociology of interracialism and transnationalism.

But for all those involved in the religious movement for social justice, with its emphasis on cooperation and interrelatedness, there was a strong push away from the conventional exclusive allegiance to one's own religion, denomination, or sect. Protestants especially carried the message of *all humanity*, rather than *all Christian humanity*, which meant that, if they initially belonged to a sect that promoted a theology of salvation for a chosen few, they had no choice but to reject that theology or at least somehow to suspend their commitment to it. The new theology taught that the kingdom of God is here on earth, that it is therefore secular, that its dominions extend over all mankind, that each of us is inextricably, cooperatively connected with our fellows, by divine decree, or at least with divine blessing. So, here was another realm where the individual, like it or not, was perched on a node at which lines from an immense network intersect.

Ever since the historian Richard Hofstadter published his classic *The Age of Reform: From Bryan to F.D.R.* in 1955, it's been conventional to view the Progressive Era (at least to a considerable extent) as the product of American Protestantism. Hofstadter was unequivocal in his belief: the Progressive mind, he wrote, "was pre-eminently a Protestant mind." It arose in rural

America, he said, though it created the greatest impact in the cities.[59] A quarter-century later, Robert M. Crunden, in *Ministers of Reform: The Progressives' Achievement in American Civilization, 1889–1920*, expanded on Hofstadter's statement, claiming that the entire Progressive Era was the handiwork of a group of prominent Americans who started out in Protestant homes, went through periods of doubt regarding not only their faith but also their direction in life, found a calling (whether it was settlement work or the presidency of the United States) and then infused that calling "with the religious and moral significance that the family environment had placed on the ministry a generation earlier."[60] There were many such prominent Americans, but for the sake of brevity Crunden drew up a short list of twenty-one figures to serve as the core in his book; they included Frank Lloyd Wright, Jane Addams, Upton Sinclair, William Jennings Bryan, and Presidents Theodore Roosevelt and Woodrow Wilson.

It's hard to argue with Crunden's claims about the figures he places in his Progressive pantheon. They certainly did start out Protestant, and in some (but decidedly not all) cases they undoubtedly brought a sort of Protestant morality (if we don't mind leaving the phrase a bit vague) to their various life missions. But I can't agree with the suggestion that the results, the practical proposals, or the actual outcomes that characterize the Progressive Era were somehow "Protestant" in nature—or for that matter Jewish or Catholic. On the contrary, the visions of the specifically *religious* reformers were hardly religious at all. Sheldon spoke the language of moderate socialism. Rauschenbusch spoke the language of a tamed and domesticated Marxism. Adler and Wise spoke languages that were virtually indistinguishable from each other, and let's not forget that Adler was allegedly not religious at all, in any conventional sense. By the time the Progressive Era came along, the principal religious denominations in the United States had already undergone a change that helped form the underlying social and political outlook for that era. However you reckoned it, whatever you wanted to call it, the outlook was secular and ecumenical. That outlook fundamentally transformed the relations between the individual, on one side, and all levels of social and political organization, on the other. That's the subject of the next chapter.

10 Citizen, Community, State

LATE IN 1901, you're browsing in a bookstore, and you come across a book with the unsensational yet intriguing title *The Life of the Bee*, published that year. Science interests you, and, thinking you've stumbled upon an entomology text, you pick up the volume, leaf through it, and, on a lark, purchase it.

The book is not at all what you expected. In fact, had you taken the time to read just the first two pages carefully, you would have learned right away what it was *not*. It was neither "a treatise on apiculture, or practical bee-keeping" nor "a scientific monograph on Apis Mellifica, Ligustica, Fasciata, Dorsata, etc., or a collection of new observations and studies."[1] The name of the author, Maurice Maeterlinck, means nothing to you at first, nor does the book shed any light on who he is. The book is a translation from the Belgian author's original French. Once you've read past the opening pages, you find yourself drawn into Mr. Maeterlinck's world, and not so much because of what the book has to say about bees. As you read the first two chapters, "On the Threshold of the Hive" and "The Swarm," you find yourself more and more tempted to think that this is really a book about *us*, humans.

In the final section of the first chapter ("On the Threshold of the Hive"), you read these words: "Let us not too hastily deduce from these facts conclusions that apply to man."[2] In the two pages leading up to this disingenuous admonition, the author had described the bee as "above all, and even to a greater extent than the ant, a creature of the crowd. She can live only in the midst of a multitude," he wrote (the translator, retaining the gender of *abeille* in French, gave the impression that all bees are female).[3] Isolated from the crowd, he added, the bee "will expire in a few days not of hunger or cold, but of loneliness."[4] *Loneliness?* These bees seem awfully human, even in these early pages of the book. Maeterlinck wrote about the "laws of the hive," saying that in them "the individual is nothing, her existence conditional only, and herself, for one indifferent moment, a winged organ of the race. Her whole life is an entire sacrifice to the manifold, everlasting being whereof she forms part."[5] In fact, immediately after the warning not to confuse bees with humans, Mr. Maeterlinck offers this astonishing reflection:

> The aim of nature is manifestly the improvement of the race; but no less manifest is her inability, or refusal, to obtain such improvement except at the cost of the liberty, the rights, and the happiness of the individual. In proportion as a society organises itself, and rises in the scale, so does a shrinkage enter the private life of each one of its members. Where there is progress, it is the result only of a more and more complete sacrifice of the individual to the general interest.[6]

It grows more obvious, especially in the following chapter, "The Swarm," which appears to represent the true core of the book. There, as earlier, whole passages seem to be drawn from an eighteenth-century European or American treatise on democratic government, though the author's point is precisely that bees do *not* enjoy the rights associated with such a government. Bees are governed by "the spirit of the hive." The spirit of the hive, Maeterlinck writes, "disposes pitilessly of the wealth and happiness, the liberty and life, of all this winged people."[7] Sacrifice to the community and cooperation are the essential ideas here, but these are ideas presented in oddly favorable terms. They are grounds for optimism. "It is to the future, therefore, that the bee subordinates all things; and with a foresight, a harmonious co-operation, a skill in interpreting events and turning them to the best advantage, that must compel our heartiest admiration."[8]

Cooperation Is Based in Science

The Life of the Bee went through many printings—at least four in its first year of publication—and attracted lots of attention. Some years later, partly on the strength of this work, Edwin E. Slosson included Maeterlinck, along with Bergson and others, as one of his "Twelve Major Prophets of To-day," in a series that ran in *The Independent* (which Slosson edited) and that was subsequently published as a book.[9] It was clearly not just the mesmerizing, often poetic prose in which *The Life of the Bee* was written that captivated readers. Virtually all those who wrote about it were in agreement on one point, namely that the book was not just about bees. Ernest Ingersoll, a well-known naturalist and science writer of the era, reviewed Maeterlinck's book for the *New York Times* shortly after its appearance. Though Ingersoll devoted plenty of space to bees, there appeared to be no doubt in his mind about what aroused our interest in the topic. Here were his opening thoughts: "Man has always been eager and has found it singularly pleasing to discover a reflection of himself in the 'lower' animals. Hence he has imagined a primitive condition in which they were as one with him, sympathizing, mutually understanding, and conversing together in equality of freedom from fear and pride."[10]

Individual rights versus those of the community seemed to be on the mind of everyone who read the book. Axel Emil Gibson, a writer based in Los Angeles, dropped all pretense of limiting himself to the terms and phrases that Maeterlinck himself had used, dishing up a salad of then-current political and social theory disguised as a summary of the book's ideas. Maeterlinck, Gibson wrote, "makes us acquainted with a system of life in which the individuals are prompted by a single impulse—the *collective will* of the commonwealth, to which every bee submits with an intensity that knows no fear. . . . Enjoyment, suffering, sexual instinct, struggle for existence—all the mastersprings of self-preservation are heedlessly thrown aside, or sacrificed on the altar of the collective welfare."[11] Not a single one of the key phrases in this passage, including even "sexual instinct," actually appeared in *The Life of the Bee*.

Any reader seeking more explicit support for the claim that evolutionary forces had produced a natural tendency toward cooperation among humans would have found it in a book that came out the year after Maeterlinck's. This one was originally written in English, though English was not the native language of the author. In 1902, the author carried far more name recognition internationally than did the Belgian-born amateur apiarist. It was Peter (or Petr) Kropotkin. To ordinary Americans, continually reminded in the popular press of the evils of the brutal Russian autocracy, on the one side, and of the frightening ideologies and political operatives it spawned, on the other, Kropotkin was a perfect object of fascination. He was Russian, he was politically radical (he was called, variously, an anarchist, a socialist, and a communist), and, though he had personally renounced his noble title, to the West he was always *Prince* Kropotkin. In 1902, he showed that he was also a naturalist, when he published *Mutual Aid: A Factor of Evolution*.

Like Darwin before him, Kropotkin had scientific credentials. He had traveled extensively in eastern Siberia and northern Manchuria in the 1860s, observing animal life while serving as a military officer. But the settings in which he made his observations were completely different from the ones in which Darwin made so many of his. Kropotkin was witness to animal behavior in vast, desolate regions where the individual's primary antagonist was the environment itself. Darwin, by contrast, saw animal behavior in densely populated areas where an individual's antagonists were often members of the same species. Darwin was frequently struck by an *intraspecific* struggle for existence, a struggle, that is, that pits members of the same species against one another (though he did not, like some of his followers, see this sort of struggle as universal). Kropotkin was struck by a struggle for survival against the elements and was drawn to conclude that, in more cases than not, individual members of the same species survive by *cooperating*, rather than by killing one another.

In the 1870s, Kropotkin began to develop the anarchist social views that would bring him international notoriety in subsequent decades. His zoological observations were partly responsible. So was a trip to the Jura Mountains in Switzerland, where he observed the phenomenon of voluntary mutual support among watchmakers (perhaps as important for the Swiss industry as the principle of interchangeable parts for the American). In Russia, he was arrested and imprisoned for his beliefs in 1874, and then, in 1876, he made a spectacular escape, fleeing his native land for Western Europe, where he would remain till the February Revolution in 1917.

In 1888, while living in England, Kropotkin picked up an issue of the literary monthly *The Nineteenth Century* and saw an article by Thomas H. Huxley, one of the most visible supporters of Darwin's theory of evolution. The title was "The Struggle for Existence in Human Society." Huxley was certainly not the first Darwinian to turn his attention to human society. But Kropotkin was horrified by two passages, the first about lower forms of animal life, the second about life among humans. Here was the first: "From the point of view of the moralist the animal world is on about the same level as a gladiator's show. The creatures are fairly well treated, and set to fight—whereby the strongest, the swiftest, and the cunningest live to fight another day. The spectator has no need to turn his thumbs down, as no quarter is given."[12] The second was specifically about man in the "primitive" state: "the Hobbesian war of each against all was the normal state of existence. The human species, like others, plashed and floundered amid the general stream of evolution, keeping its head above water as it best might, and thinking neither of whence nor whither."[13] Even setting aside the moral dimension of these statements—who would want to believe that humans are at bottom prepared to slaughter each other in a continual Hobbesian struggle?—Kropotkin found that his own empirical observations simply did not support Huxley's positions. So he took up his pen and wrote a series of responses, which the editors of *The Nineteenth Century* published between 1890 and 1896. These articles then became the individual chapters of *Mutual Aid*. Kropotkin obviously struck a chord, for Henry Drummond (whom we encountered in the last chapter) was already quoting the first of the *Nineteenth Century* articles in the *Lowell Lectures* (and Kropotkin returned the favor when *Mutual Aid* came out as a book, citing Drummond's book).[14]

The aim of *Mutual Aid* was simple, and the book, packed with evidence though it is, can be summarized very briefly. Kropotkin began with "animals" (meaning, of course, non-human animals), moved on to primitive forms of human life (first "savages," then "barbarians"), examined life in "the mediæval city," and finally turned to "ourselves" in the modern era. Everywhere he looked he saw confirmation of his fundamental finding, namely that competition among members of a species is injurious to that species, while mutual aid and sociability are the key to survival. The final chapters of the book, devoted to modern times, will probably strike today's reader as preachy and doctrinaire. Kropotkin had lots to say about then-modern political associations, labor unions, the workers' guild (*artel′*) in Russia, friendly societies, and, of course, socialism—anything to prove that people "naturally" tend to cooperate and that cooperation produces the best results for the group and its constituent individuals. Like Maeterlinck's bees, Kropotkin's humans—and all animals, for that matter—exist in a network (he used this word several times in his book), the network prepares the group for the future, and the result is a naturally justified optimism. What could be clearer in the book's final sentence? "In the practice of mutual aid, which we can retrace to the earliest beginnings of evolution," Kropotkin wrote, "we thus find the positive and undoubted origin of our ethical conceptions; and we can affirm that in the ethical progress of man, mutual support—not mutual struggle—has had the leading part. In its wide extension, even at the present time, we also see the best guarantee of a still loftier evolution of our race."[15] Modern biologists would likely agree generally with Kropotkin's claims about "mutual aid" in nature, though they might find those claims insufficiently substantiated and would certainly use updated terminology.[16]

Many years after the first edition of *Mutual Aid* was published, anthropologist and popular science writer Ashley Montagu, in the foreword to a revised and expanded edition, claimed that Kropotkin's book had always been in such demand that it was "constantly out of print." He named it "one of the world's great books."[17] It strangely received far less mention in the press than did *The Life of the Bee*, but, if we assume that Montagu was right—as he likely was, since he lived in the era when the book was going through so many printings—then it must have attracted plenty of attention from the American public.

The American Individual Finds a New Network

A classic history of the era we're looking at was *The Search for Order, 1877–1920*, published in 1967 by the late Northwestern University historian Robert H. Wiebe. If there's one social development that overshadows almost all others, in the view of Wiebe, it's the loss of what he called "island communities." Wiebe never really defined "island community," but it's clear that he had in mind small towns and small groups within towns whose members were joined through interests confined by geography and physical familiarity. The culprit behind the destruction of the communities was the corporation, or simply corporate wealth. The result, in Wiebe's eyes, was a widespread sense of dislocation, bewilderment, and even loss of freedom. In the end, what characterized the period was not so much the total victory of urban corporatism over old-fashioned community traditions as a tension between the two forces. As corporatism disrupted communities, Americans began to look for new ways to assert a sense of local autonomy (with the emphasis on *local*), as through progressive social causes (temperance, for example), Protestantism, and anti-immigrant sentiment.[18]

By the end of the first decade of the twentieth century, quite a few prominent writers in the United States felt that a dramatic shift had lately taken place in the relationship between the American individual and . . . well, something bigger than the individual. Exactly what that something bigger was depended on the writer. But many would disagree with Wiebe's assessment, and so would I. Not that the "island community" for anyone remained the essential constituent of American society in our era, but rather that new forces formed new and more far-reaching bonds—networks, as I've called them. Not that there wasn't a feeling of bewilderment and dislocation, but rather that larger communities of an entirely new sort were formed.

In *Social Control* (1901), Edward A. Ross (who wrote "The Causes of Race Superiority") argued that the complexity of modern society necessitates a form of artificial moral engineering that will bind the otherwise possibly unruly individual to the social order. He appears at first to disparage theories of mutual aid ("charming tales of the mutual aid of ants, beavers, and prairie dogs," as he puts it), having read several of Kropotkin's essays before they were published as chapters of his book.[19] And yet two considerations suggest that Ross regarded modern society as already powerfully bound together by forces that were not artificial. First, the model he uses at the very beginning of his influential book is essentially that of the network, as he likens the stresses and conflicts of modern society to the choices individuals must make instantaneously in order to preserve order by avoiding collisions "at the junction of crowded city thoroughfares." Back in the days of island communities, it's unlikely anyone would have described life among one's fellows as "the smooth running of social machinery" and likened it to traffic at a busy street corner in a big city.[20] And second, despite the contempt he displays for the theory of mutual aid, this often highly contradictory thinker rolls out an account of *sympathy*—which he defines as the "connective tissue" of social order—that is Darwinian to the core. For sympathy and altruism (in parallel with egoism, to be sure) emerge in the evolutionary development of the mammalian reproductive function.[21] Ross's aim in *Social Control* is to assert that modern society requires more than just a natural tendency toward altruism to keep it together; it requires artificial control as the force that maintains the critical balance between the individual and the social order. It's precisely the messiness of modern urban life—given, of course, the mingling of those superior and inferior races that Ross spoke of at the meeting in Philadelphia the same year *Social Control* was published—that necessitates the application of a man-made cohesive force.

In *The Promise of American Life* (1909), progressive journalist Herbert Croly wrote of "national Promise," "the national principle," and "collective responsibility" as occupying the pole opposite the individual in American

social life. The binding concept for Croly was the *nation*, which he defined as "a people in so far as they are united by traditions and purposes." He cited Bismarck (before his days as prime minister of Prussia and chancellor of Germany) as the source of this definition, which was odd, because Croly's idea was to draw a contrast between the American notion, based as it was on a "collective character" of long standing, and the European one, based on "political and social privilege."[22] He wrote of a "religion of human brotherhood," which gives rise to a "network of mutual loyalties and responsibilities woven in a democratic nation."[23]

In *Social Organization: A Study of the Larger Mind* (1909), University of Michigan sociologist Charles H. Cooley presented the individual human mind as intrinsically and organically linked to other minds—so much so, in fact, that the phrase "individual mind" was without meaning. There was only social mind, because "every thought we have is linked with the thought of our ancestors and associates, and through them with that of society at large."[24] So at the pole opposite the individual mind (a purely theoretical notion) lay the social mind (the only sort that exists), and at the pole opposite the individual person was social organization (whose source, naturally, was the social mind). In an earlier book, Cooley had written at length about sympathy, defined as "primary communication or an entering into and sharing the mind of someone else."[25] The approach was psychological, but Cooley's aim was to show the practical manifestations of sympathy and the social mind. These were, at the most basic stage, the "primary groups" of society (family, play-group, neighborhood, community group of elders), which Cooley called the "nursery of human nature."[26] The ultimate manifestation was "public will," which ideally served as the basis for human government.[27]

In 1910, the year before she died, Ellen H. Richards published *Euthenics: The Science of Controllable Environment*. The guiding light of American home economics called the pole opposite the individual several things: the community, the state, the social republic. Richards even called it "the race," but she always used race to mean "species," as in "human race." *Euthenics* was more an exhortation than a scientific description of factors that necessarily make us behave like cooperative beings, but Richards believed that historical circumstances in the new century were such as to make inevitable both cooperation and the subordination of the individual to a higher purpose. She even adopted a tone that must have struck many of her contemporaries as frighteningly socialistic. "But it is certain that the individual must delegate more or

less of his so-called rights for the sake of the race," she said, "and since the only excuse for the existence of the individual is the race, he must so far relinquish his authority." And this: "In the social republic, the child as a future citizen is an asset of the state, not the property of its parents."[28] The logic was just what you'd expect from Richards. We saw in chapter 6 that for her the home—together with the family living in it—was the basic social unit from which all else flowed. She never abandoned that belief: "The individual may be wise as to his own needs, but powerless by himself to secure the satisfaction of them. Certain concessions to others' needs are always made in family life. The community is only a larger family group, and social consciousness must in time take into account social welfare."[29]

In 1912, Bliss Perry, Harvard English professor, Walt Whitman scholar, and former editor of *The Atlantic Monthly*, published *The American Mind*. For Perry, at the pole opposite the individual was something he broadly called "fellowship." Perry expressed his views in supremely simple and down-to-earth terms:

> American men and women are learning, as we say, "to get together." It is the distinctly twentieth-century programme. We must all learn the art of getting together, not merely to conserve the interests of literature and art and society, but to preserve the individual himself in his just rights. Any one who misunderstands the depth and the scope of the present political restlessness which is manifested in every section of the country, misunderstands the American instinct for fellowship. It is a law of that fellowship that what is right and legitimate for me is right and legitimate for the other fellow also. The American mind and the American conscience are becoming socialized before our very eyes.[30]

These books all sold well and attracted a fair amount of notice among the reading public. But they certainly were not responsible for changing the public's attitude about the individual in relation to a larger, collective body. All four authors believed they were not only urging something for the future but also documenting something that had already taken place, or that was already taking place.

And they were right. Something certainly *had* changed by 1909, if not before. It would continue to do so over the next few years, and it was not the shift from island communities to mass dislocation and bewilderment.

Much of this story is already well known, and some of it we've seen in this book. As we saw in the previous chapter, by the first decade of the twen-

tieth century households and the individuals who ran them, except for the most rural, were linked to a network of standardized products and services. In chapter 2, we saw how the Public Health Movement pushed the American individual, especially the urban individual, into a network from which there was no escape. Once health had become a collective responsibility—and ordinary citizens of all ages were reminded every day that it had—you could no longer exist, sick or healthy, in isolation from your fellows.

The first decade of the twentieth century brought the most enormous expansion of federal regulatory power in the history of the republic, and 1906 was the summit year. The 59th Congress, at the end of the legislative year in June, enacted three pieces of legislation that transformed the relationship between individual citizens and the federal government. The Hepburn Act, or Railroad Rate bill, regulated shipping rates on railroads, outlawed certain unfair and preferential practices, and gave the Interstate Commerce Commission authority to inspect the books of shipping companies. The Pure Food and Drug Act, together with the Meat Inspection Act, gave the federal government the power to regulate the processing of food and to outlaw the production of adulterated food and drugs—patent medicines, especially.

The press at the time made much of the circumstance that the legal basis for these bills was the power that the Constitution gives Congress to regulate commerce between the states. This may very well be true, but equally clear in the press was that the Interstate Commerce Clause was being more broadly interpreted than ever before. To judge from reporting at the time, President Roosevelt, the 59th Congress, and the public wanted these measures. A triumphant editorial in the *New York Times* spoke favorably of what would cause many post-Reagan Americans to shudder: the "paternalism" inherent in the food and meat bills, of the "exaltation of the Federal power," and of "centralization" arising from "the desire and the will of the people themselves." Congress had acted "with a notable and altogether unaccustomed obedience to public opinion."[31] The villains from which the public needed protection here were reportedly big corporations and trusts—organizations with the necessary power and money to defraud and despoil innocent consumers. But in the case of the Pure Food and Drug Act and the Meat Inspection Act, what was really being protected was public health, as the *Times* editorial also pointed out. And so, as in the case of the entire Public Health Movement, once members of the public understood that an individual's problem was the community's problem, they were willing to take a portion of their individual autonomy and surrender it up to a governmental authority in exchange for the protection they believed that authority could offer them. When the protection took the form of *inspection*, then, as with the mandatory reporting of communicable diseases, the public was submitting to what has been called more recently (and often with bitter irony) *benevolent surveillance.* Once again, corporatism was in large part the new enemy, as in Wiebe's account, but if the *Times* got it right, then the upshot was not a retreat into new forms of localism but a willing embrace of a much larger community than ever before: the nation headed by a newly powerful, paternalistic federal government. Where Wiebe did get it right was in his description of the extremely limited reach of the federal government at the end of the nineteenth century, its responsibilities being limited essentially to "gathering income and appropriating funds."[32]

One measure of the American individual's changing relationship to the federal government was the evolution in the response to disasters in the first decade or so of the twentieth century.

Galveston, Texas

On September 8, 1900, a hurricane that the Weather Bureau had been tracking in the Caribbean made landfall on Galveston, Texas, a city of some 42,000 located on a thin coastal island in the Gulf of Mexico. The storm pounded the island for over eight hours, and by the time it was done much of the city lay in ruins. Buildings were upended, bridges were washed away, communication lines were severed, streetcar tracks were destroyed, trains stopped operating, and, by most accounts, between ten and twelve thousand people were killed. At this writing, the Galveston hurricane remains the worst natural disaster (measured in deaths) in American history.

The response—and reaction to the response—might surprise some of us over a century later. Texas requested of the federal government tents and rations, which the federal government sent. National guardsmen from several states were dispatched, mostly to keep order and prevent looting. At the request of Texas governor Joseph D. Sayers, the Treasury Department, the Lighthouse Board, and the Navy Department sent ships to provide communication between Galveston and the mainland. Later, as part of the larger rebuilding effort, the U.S. Army constructed a protective wall near the beach, but the purpose of the wall was to protect the Army's own Fort Crockett.

From the federal government, that was about it. And by the standards of the day it was apparently more than what was expected. Three days after the storm, the *New York Times* took an almost apologetic tone in its laudatory description of the response from Washington, as if readers might be indignant at *any* response. The editors also indicated that there should be limits to such a response but that those limits had been respected in the present case. "The request of Texas for National assistance in the matter of tents and rations for its homeless and the prompt response of the President were perfectly comprehensible," the editor assured readers. "The National Government was properly asked to give its aid and properly has done so. But the great bulk of assistance must come from the people. There has never been an event which has demanded a more generous outpouring of public generosity."[33] The same issue of the *Times* proudly reported a relief fund that New York City mayor Robert A. Van Wyck had established. The following day the *Times* was already reporting that citizens and businesses from around the country had sent a hundred thousand dollars and that contributions were continuing to pour in to Galveston.[34]

The mayor of Galveston set up a Central Relief Committee the day after the hurricane. The Red Cross helped solicit and distribute donations. Clara Barton herself, president of the American National Red Cross, arrived in Galveston about a week after the storm and stayed on till mid-November, carrying out relief work, reporting on conditions, and issuing personal pleas for contributions. In short, the vast bulk of assistance that Galveston received came from what later generations would call "the private sector."[35]

San Francisco

The famous earthquake struck San Francisco early in the morning on April 18, 1906. The story of what happened is well known. The bulk of the damage to the city was caused not by the shocks of the quake but by fire. It's impossible to know how all of the individual blazes started, but, to complicate matters, water mains were severed, and the fire department could not do its job. In addition, the army and the fire department attempted to create firebreaks by using dynamite to clear buildings away from the paths of the fires. No one in charge seemed to realize this was not a good idea. Those entrusted with this job were not trained to do it, and they did not use the correct materials. The result was further, extensive damage from fires caused directly by explosives. The death toll from the earthquake was revised upward periodically for over a century. Philip L. Fradkin, who published a book on the earthquake the year before its centennial, tells the story of how the estimate rose from 322 one year after the quake to somewhere around 3,000 today. During the era—in fact, all the way up to 1980—estimates remained in the hundreds. As to the total cost of physical damage, Fradkin writes, the high estimate that emerged in the era was a billion dollars (not adjusted for inflation).[36]

The federal government appropriated 2.5 million dollars, the funds being divided among various departments of the U.S. Army, which assisted in the relief effort. All other funds came from private sources. The Red Cross was involved, but even though the organization was meant to be in charge of receiving and disbursing relief funds, it ended up playing a relatively minor role in this respect. As Fradkin shows in his book, local officials dominated the aftermath of the quake and, to understate the case charitably, did not always put the city's interests first.

The quake occurred during the tenure of the same 59th Congress that would soon pass landmark regulatory legislation. Congress debated the notion of national aid for disaster relief. On May 2, exactly two weeks after the earthquake, Senator Francis G. Newlands of Nevada introduced a resolution on "financial aid in the restoration of San Francisco" and asked the Senate's consent that he be permitted to speak about the resolution. The remarks offer a fascinating snapshot of the peculiar moment at which Senator Newlands was speaking, because they show both that the idea of "national aid" was relatively new and that the country was poised to accept such an idea. They are also likely to strike us, today, with the modesty of their scope, when we compare what Newlands was proposing with what more than a half-century of federal disaster relief has taught us to expect in the early twenty-first century. Here's an excerpt:

> I believe that the restoration of San Francisco is a national matter, in which the people of all sections should participate through subscriptions to a private financial project, if that be practicable, or through national aid if practicable, or both combined, and I see no constitutional or practical difficulties in the way. . . . Here we have a dual sovereignty in this country—the sovereignty of the State and the sovereignty of the nation. I see no reason why when either sovereignty is in danger the other sovereignty should not rush to the rescue, within, of course, its constitutional powers. It is this mutual spirit of cooperation between the States and the National Government that will give us the prosperity which we seek. We are all bound together by the ties of amity and interest, and when interstate or foreign commerce is impeded by the paralysis of a port in a particular State the concern is national and is not confined to a particular State or to the port itself.[37]

The resolution he introduced included no provisions for massive direct aid to San Francisco. He was asking his fellow senators to discuss the practicality of either a "guaranty of credit" (essentially a large, low-interest loan) or an effort "to promote the organization of a great financial corporation" (essentially, as I take it, the issuance of bonds). And yet Newlands's remarks were fully in line with the spirit of the era, at least as the 59th Congress embodied that spirit. Interstate commerce, as a constitutional concept, provided the legal foundation for regulatory law. But in the everyday sense that Senator Newlands gave it, the phrase referred to a network that ineluctably bound together individuals, communities, and cities.

The Triangle Fire

The Triangle Waist Company ("waist" for "shirtwaist," a tailored blouse for women) was housed in floors eight through ten of the Asch Building, right off Washington Square, at the corner of Washington Place and Greene Street in Greenwich Village. Today it belongs to New York University and is called the Brown Building of Science. The company was owned by two immigrant Jews, Max Blanck and Isaac Harris. Most of the employees were also immigrants, either Jewish or Italian, and the vast majority of them were women. The fire broke out on March 25, 1911, a Saturday, when the number of workers (there was no confirmed count of those present) would have been slightly reduced because a small number of Jewish employees stayed home to observe the Sabbath. The fire started on the eighth floor. The whole incident lasted less than twenty minutes. In that time, 146 victims burned to death, asphyxiated from the smoke, or jumped to their deaths from windows. The owners, whose offices were located on the tenth floor (and one of whom had brought his daughters to work that day), survived by climbing to the roof, where they were rescued. The Triangle Waist Company had no fire sprinklers; it had a poorly designed fire escape (with window shutters opening out onto its balconies, blocking passage); doors to the stairways opened inward (so that when they were shut, a rush of people effectively sealed them); and the owners routinely kept at least some of these doors locked, presumably so that workers could not leave their shifts early, take smoking breaks, or steal without being detected.

Reaction was swift and massive. Newspapers across the country ran banner headlines about the catastrophe, with gruesome photographs of the carnage. New York papers reported extensively on the fire and its aftermath. Given the number of immigrant Jewish victims, the reaction was understandably intense in New York's Yiddish press. The socialist *Jewish Daily Forward*, champion of workers' rights since its founding in 1897, ran front-page stories for weeks. The editors knew their readers were angry, and they pulled no punches. On March 26, the day after the fire, an enormous banner headline announced the tragedy by screaming, "The Morgue Is Filled with Our Victims!"[38] Mass meetings were organized. Hundreds of people turned out to watch funeral processions and to visit the ghastly scene at Charities Pier, on 26th Street, where the victims' bodies were initially kept.

But the real story for us here is the reform effort that followed. There are two key figures in this effort. Who they were, the contrast in their backgrounds, and the fact of their collaboration are among the clearest bits of evidence that something truly extraordinary was taking place in this era. The first was Frances Perkins. *Washington Post* reporter David Von Drehle published the definitive history of the Triangle fire in 2003. He tells the story of Perkins's spectacular rise from a middle-class Congregationalist upbringing in Worcester, Massachusetts, to an undergraduate education at Mount Holyoke College, to settlement house work in Chicago, to a position with the Consumers' League in New York, and eventually to her Cabinet post (the first ever occupied by a woman) in FDR's administration, where she was secretary of labor for twelve years.[39] There are many recordings of Perkins's voice, and if you listen to one of them for only a few moments, you immediately hear the classic Brahmin notes in her speech. You also hear an eloquence and an unswerving but serenely expressed passion for social justice. As Von Drehle tells it, a history professor at Mount Holyoke who took students to observe conditions in factories taught Perkins about "seeing problems firsthand." She was moved by Jacob Riis's *How the Other Half Lives* and by Florence Kelley of the Consumers' League.[40] Collective action for the greater good was the theme of Perkins's entire adult life.

So persuasive and well-spoken was Perkins that she helped change the course of history after the fire. By pure chance, she was visiting a friend a couple of blocks away from the Asch Building as the fire broke out, and the sound of sirens led the two women to the site of the disaster, where they watched its final, horrible minutes. Perkins had already spent a few months as a lobbyist in Albany for the Consumers' League. When a "Committee on Safety" was formed, in the wake of the Triangle fire, to lobby the state legislature for factory reform, Perkins was placed on the committee. Von Drehle tells the amazing story of how she insinuated her way into the Tammany Hall political machine and successfully lobbied for a state investigating commission. The bill that created the commission was signed into law on June 30, 1911.[41]

The other figure was Dr. George M. Price, whom Von Drehle identifies only briefly as a member of the Joint Board of Sanitary Control. This committee, designed to represent employers, employees, and the public, had been organized in the summer of 1910, after a strike in the garment industries. It included two representatives of the Manufacturers' Protective Association, two representatives of the cloak-making unions, and three representatives of the public. Dr. Price was one of the two union representatives.[42]

But Price had a much more interesting past than just this. Very few historians know about it, and, as often as his name appeared in the English-language American press between the time of the Triangle fire and his death in 1942, I've seen only a single, garbled reference to anything he did before the turn of the century and only scattered references to his activities in the first decade of the twentieth century. His story could hardly have differed more sharply from Perkins's. Price was born in Poltava in the Russian Empire (today Ukraine), in 1864. As best I can tell, either Russian was his first language or he spoke Yiddish as a child but acquired native, educated fluency in Russian. He attended the prestigious gymnasium (high school) in his hometown. He came to New York in July of 1882, part of the mass immigration of Russian and Eastern European Jews to the United States that had begun the previous year. While many early Jewish immigrants in this wave came for political reasons, Price came to escape the poverty and persecution that were the lot of almost all Jews in Russia at that time.

There's virtually no record of what Price did for the first three years after his arrival. He apparently lived in the tenement neighborhoods of New York's Lower East Side. At the age of 21, he secured a job as sanitation inspector for New York City, and over the next ten years he worked and put himself through what was then called New York University Medical College, earning his M.D. in 1895. From that year until 1910, he worked for the city Department of Health. Then he took up his position on the Joint Board of Sanitary Control.

During the early 1890s, in addition to studying medicine, Price was busy leading the life of a transplanted Russian intellectual on the Lower East Side. He sent numerous articles back to St. Petersburg for publication in two Russian-language Jewish magazines, including a series on the Russian Jews in America. This series was published, also in St. Petersburg, as a book in 1893.[43]

In 1891, before the Russian book came out, it was translated into Yiddish and published in Odessa.[44] A notice for the Russian version weirdly appeared in a Philadelphia newspaper in 1895, the title misspelled almost beyond recognition.[45] Other articles had to do with various aspects of Jewish life in the United States. All this became available to American readers in the years after Price's death, when Leo Shpall, a Russian-born Jewish historian and teacher, published translations of Price's work and a list of his articles in *Publications of the American Jewish Historical Society.*

But one piece of the history has consistently been missed, because the documentation for it is so obscure. Price was the publisher of two Russian-language newspapers in New York. The first, *Russkii listok* (Russian leaflet), appeared for a brief time in 1892, and the second, *Russkie novosti* (Russian news), appeared for most of 1893. Both papers obviously had very limited circulations. Though they were ostensibly aimed at New York's Russian immigrants, it's clear from the contents that the readership was specifically Russian-*Jewish.* Virtually all newspapers designed for Jewish immigrants in this era were written in Yiddish, not Russian, since such a small percentage of new Jewish arrivals spoke or read Russian with any degree of proficiency (in fact, many Yiddish-speaking immigrants could barely read Yiddish). *Russkii listok* ran articles about immigration, Russian political issues, Jewish charities, and other topics of interest to recent Jewish immigrants. *Russkie novosti* was more overtly political. This is hardly surprising. The paper was edited by Jacob Gordin, soon to become the best-known Yiddish-language playwright of the era. As most people knew it, Gordin's career was carried out entirely in Yiddish. And yet, when he arrived in the United States in 1891 he was every bit the Russian-speaking Jewish intellectual, and Price was able to engage his services. The paper was filled with news items about Russia, but it also gave a picture of Jewish immigrant life in New York. If you look carefully at the names of the immigrants, both in ads and in news stories, you quickly see that Price and Gordin were dealing with many of the same people who would shortly become noted socialists and union activists on the Lower East side as well as in the broader American political scene: Isaac Hourwich (Yiddish journalist, future lawyer, economics professor, and Census Bureau statistician), Louis Miller (Yiddish journalist), Morris Hillquit (future founder of the Socialist Party of America), and Abraham Cahan (future editor-in-chief of the *Jewish Daily Forward*).

Such was the background of the gentleman who was sitting on the Joint

Board at the time of the Triangle fire. After the Factory Investigating Commission was formed, in June 1911, a lead investigator was needed, and legislative leaders picked Dr. Price. They couldn't have made a better choice. Over the next year or so, primarily in 1912, Perkins and Price sent teams into thousands of factories in the state of New York, the commission held public hearings, and Albany passed legislation that Von Drehle rightly describes as "unmatched to that time in American history": not only fire safety laws but a host of laws protecting the most vulnerable members of the state's workforce.[46] There was remarkably little opposition to the legislation when it was proposed in Albany. To judge from the remarks of Henry Morgenthau Sr., lawyer and real estate magnate, the time had simply come. At a hearing before the Committees on Labor and Industry of the New York State Senate and Assembly, he said:

> As we all know, this commission was organized as a result of the Asch Building fire in New York City. Like galley slaves chained to their benches, the poor creatures who were working in that building were cooped and locked in the rooms where they were employed, with not a chance for escape. A good many of us felt that the time had come for a change. I feel sure that any hardships that may be placed on the shoulders of the real estate men as a result of the legislation proposed here will be borne gladly if the proposed changes be beneficial to the working classes and tend to assure their safety.[47]

If Morgenthau, whose personal financial interests were at stake with the new legislation, was reflecting the sentiments of the American public, then we can surmise that what swayed opinion in favor of government regulation was the human dimension of the calamity: not only the victims—all disasters have victims—but the culprits in this case. In the Triangle fire, there was no impersonal force of nature at work but real, living men, whose faces were plastered across the city and the entire nation in the wake of the fire. Even if the time was not yet right for a full-blown federal program (that wouldn't come till 1950, with the first Disaster Relief Act), it certainly was right for stepping between ordinary citizens and the rich and powerful.

For a number of years, Price was in the news in connection with his support for regulatory reform and workmen's compensation. In 1913 he opened the Union Health Center, a clinic for members of the International Ladies' Garment Workers' Union (ILGWU). He continued to write books on factory safety, hygiene, and sanitation, but the bulk of his efforts for the remainder of his life went into the health center. As for Frances Perkins, her work for factory safety investigation was only one stretch on a continuum that led eventually to her central role in the creation of the entire New Deal, including especially the Social Security Act. How fitting that these two Americans spearheaded a reform effort that marked such a profound change in the attitude of the individual citizen toward a larger community, a change that signaled a willingness to accept benevolent surveillance from one or another level of government—the state, in this case.

George M. Price, as best we can tell, was fired by memories of the injustices inflicted on the Jewish people in his homeland as well as by the plight of his fellow immigrants in the sweatshops of New York City. To the extent (difficult to determine from the evidence we have) that he had been connected with the socialist politics of the labor union movement in the 1880s and 1890s, he was equally fired by a philosophical commitment to equality, fairness, and collective action.

As for Frances Perkins, no doubt the most eloquent expression of the urge that drove her to devote her career to social, political, and economic reform appears in a speech she gave at Social Security Administration headquarters in 1962, when she was 80 years old. Her topic was "The Roots of Social Security." The Social Security website features an audio recording and a transcript—modified and edited, since Miss Perkins appeared to be speaking, at least in part, extemporaneously. Here, in the transcript version (with a host of parenthetical asides deleted), is one small part of what she said:

> I suppose the roots—the idea that we ought to have a systematic method of taking care of the material needs of the aged—really spring from that deep well of charitableness which resides in the American people, and the efforts and the struggles of charity workers and social workers to handle the problems of people who were growing old and had no adequate means of support. Out of this impulse to be kind to the poor sprang, I suppose, a mulling of ideas about social insurance for the aged. But those people who were doing it didn't know that it was social insurance. They just kept thinking that something definite, something that people could look forward to, would be a great asset and a great assistance to them in their work. Even De Tocqueville, in his memoirs of his visit to America, mentioned [what] he thought was a unique state of mind of the American people: That they were so honestly concerned about their poor and did so much for them personally. It was not an organization; it was not a national action; it was not a State action; it was not Government. It was personal action that De Tocqueville mentioned as being charac-

teristic of the American people. They were so generous, so kind, so charitably disposed.[48]

Of course, what grew out of this "root" *was* a large government program, not simply the good works that flowed from innately charitable individuals, and Perkins was modestly deflecting attention from herself and the role she personally played. The guiding force as she appeared to see it was something that stemmed from the American people themselves, something that had been around for several centuries. But the speech was really about how that national character trait, together with a number of ideas that were at first purely academic, led to the establishment of colossal federal powers. Her idea seemed to be that this could never have happened without public support and that public support stemmed from the national character trait.

What happened in the first two decades of the twentieth century was still a far cry from Social Security, federal disaster relief, and all the federal programs that arose in the second half of the twentieth century. But it was also a far cry from an earlier era, when even in large urban centers individuals and households existed in a condition of far greater physical, social, and economic autonomy (those island communities). Wiebe thought the great network of coordination and cooperation came along during the Great War and immediately afterwards. The networks he saw were the network of communication and the network of the modern corporation. The war effort drew on capacities that were already there but gave them pervasiveness and permanence.[49] But existence within a network was the hallmark of the era, and it started much earlier than this. It was there in full force by the turn of the century, if not a decade or two earlier. With isolated exceptions, it became the expected way of life for all Americans. The first twelve or thirteen years of the new century showed especially that (again, with rare exceptions) you really had no choice in the matter: you were in, whether you liked it or not.

Conclusion

Who You Are

SO, THOSE RAILROAD TRACKS . . .

By 1913, if you're a reasonably informed American, you live in networks, and you are yourself a network. Networks are inside, outside, before, now, and henceforth. Almost nothing in life is comprehensible outside them.

Say you're a homemaker living in the Aqua Vista on Riverside Drive. Then you're one of the privileged female denizens of that tony neighborhood who, as a reporter for the *New York Times* put it, create a morning rush hour at the Riverside Exchange, "using the 'phone to give orders to the 'butcher and baker and candle-stick maker.'"[1] If you're her husband, then your business probably has you on the telephone, checking the ticker tape throughout the day, arranging for the passage of goods over vast transportation grids, and performing transactions over a literal mesh of wires and an immaterial mesh of radio signals. If you're a doctor, you spend your days making forays into the inner structure of the dozen or more human organisms that come to your office or that you visit at home, assessing the malign progress of microscopic beings that have found an entry point into those networks. Or if you're a shop-girl, elegant and poised behind the gleaming glass showcases at Arnold, Constable & Co. or similar establishment, as you proffer fashionable goods that can be found also in Podunk and Flagstaff, then you're a living cog in Christine Frederick's "highly complex machinery of distribution": if the goods can be found in Podunk and Flagstaff, they're standard.

Or what if you're an alumna of Simmons College, employed as the head of a hospital dining room? Then you use the interconnected technology of the most modern kitchen and the metropolitan commercial network to supply that kitchen. But you might also remember the words you read in the *Simmons Quarterly* a couple of years ago. The current Dean, Sarah Louise Arnold, had written about "the Task" that fell to all Simmons alumnae: "giving largely, generously, in return for what you are receiving."[2] As you fulfill the sacred task of your mentors at Simmons College, you've also established for yourself a position on a huge network of social service. Of course, not everyone is professionally or even personally engaged in social service, as you are. Your devotion to this Task stems from any number of elements in your character and your upbringing but also from a conscious choice you made after undergoing something of a personal transformation during your student years in Boston. If your professional sphere of activity, involving you as it does in the care of your fellow human beings, can be described as a sort of social network, in addition to being a commercial and technological network, it's because your position is expressly designed for just that. Presumably anyone in any era whose central task in life was to care for others—say, a member of a religious order devoted to providing comfort to the sick and the poor—could be described as existing in a social "network" of some sort. But by 1913, for non-rural Americans it had become almost impossible *not* to exist in a number of social networks whose bonds were more far-reaching and more powerful than similar forms of association had been in the past. The foundation for these networks was almost always some form of scientific knowledge, no matter how crude by later standards and no matter how crudely understood by ordinary people.

Take two conventional forms of association: *my people* and *my religious group*. Since the beginning of the nineteenth century (at the latest), *my people* in the Western world had been conceived in the organic terms that we find in romanticism and crude natural philosophy. When Johann Gottlieb Fichte delivered his "Addresses to the German Nation" to a French-occupied Prussia in 1807 and 1808, he filled his speech with botanical images designed to suggest in the minds of his listeners the natural affinity that he believed existed among Germans. If Germans shared certain characteristics, it was not only because of their history (which Fichte unabashedly distorted to suit his purposes) but also, apparently, because of a poorly understood process by which those characteristics are passed on from generation to generation. This sort of thinking formed a foundation for European nationalism.

But the modern conception of "race" provided an informed person with what appeared to be a solid, scientific basis for the claim that "my people" form a true, biological network. This was especially true in the era of modern genetics, after the turn of the twentieth century. Modern science had proved that something physical is actually passed from parents to offspring, establishing a material link. But it was true even before that, once Darwin had proposed a means, no matter how sketchy and incomplete, for envisioning the transmission of characteristics from one generation to the next. Even without the concepts of chromosomes and genes, this process of transmission had a more substantive feel to it than what you derived from merely noticing resemblances among family members over a number of generations. The network of race was something that extended over time, back into the past and ahead into the future. To those who regarded race as a force that determines character and behavior, individual human beings were inextricably linked with their ancestors and their offspring-to-be. The crude habit among genuine racists of associating their enemies with organic pathogens (how many times did Hitler refer to the Jews as "bacilli"?) is proof that the association of race with something-or-other "scientific" took hold in the popular imagination early on.

I'll leave it to anthropologists and historians of religion to suggest a basis for earlier feelings of solidarity among members of religious groups, numerous and disparate as those feelings and those groups were. But by 1913, a feeling of solidarity *within* the group frequently either existed side by side with, or was subordinated to, a feeling of solidarity with, a larger community. Most religious campaigns for social justice in this era did not target only followers of a single faith or sect. Many did not even include among their aims attracting new believers or strengthening the commitment of current believers. Rev. Maxwell in Charles Monroe Sheldon's novel is content to combat saloons and low wages without necessarily attempting to entice drunks and underpaid workers into his church.

The foundation for this view of religion? It's difficult to suggest a single, simple one. Again and again we see, among socially progressive religious leaders, a willingness to take the then-current social and political state of affairs in American cities—featuring the exploitation of workers, low wages, poor working conditions, unsuitable housing, drunkenness, in short, the ravages of industrial capitalism, as seen by critics of that economic system—and consider it *the* world in which a religious ministry is carried out. The secularism of this approach is of a piece with the scientific secularism of scholarship that was now interpreting the scriptural traditions of various religions and sects. Critical and historical analysis of texts, the refusal to insist that those texts were divine and inerrant, the introduction of empirical evidence outside the tradition, the acceptance of evolutionary theory—everything now seemed to be permitted in what had become for many an almost entirely earthbound discipline.

And so, once again, you're looking at a foundation in some sort of science. Early in the nineteenth century, G. W. F. Hegel had famously spoken of the Holy Spirit as the force under Protestantism (as a stage of development beyond Catholicism) that bound all mankind together.[3] But less than a century later, in the United States, many religious leaders had recourse to the same theory that led secular leaders to speak of a large, human family, namely the allegedly *scientific* theory that nature itself promotes cooperation.

The newer, secular forms of social network were founded in, or at least strongly supported by, scientific developments as well. *My fellow citizens*, or *residents of my city or town*, were bound together by the nature of the biological self. Susceptibility to infection and recognition that the avoidance of such infection required a collective effort created a network whose bonds were difficult to escape. Every time you saw a paper cup instead of a communal glass at a drinking fountain, every time you (a man) shaved, every time you (a woman) put on a skirt with a hemline above the ankle, you knew you were in the network. *My fellow citizens*, or *residents of my nation*, were bound together by the simple recognition that modern transportation and communication technology allowed the polity (municipal, state, federal government) to care for groups of individuals even in widely dispersed locales. Thanks to networks, news of the latest disaster could be broadcast around the country almost immediately, and supplies could be shipped by rail within days. Against possible disasters caused by human error or malfeasance, the network of government surveillance was there to allay the fears of citizens. *My fellow human beings* in the largest sense were bound together in part by a product of evolutionary development: the network of mutual aid and cooperation (if you believed in this). This network too was activated by the global communication network, which allowed for the rapid transmission of news and images. If it really was true that it's in the nature of individual members of your species to come to the aid of others, even if those others dwell thousands of miles away, then the communication network, bringing you news reports and images that were recent and fresh, had a way of placing you irresistibly in the network of aid and cooperation. Not that you necessarily *did* something in response, say, to reports of atrocities in the Congo Free State—but you were necessarily enmeshed in the reports and the atrocities.

Perhaps no network was as all-encompassing, as determining, as confining as the one created by standard time. It was physical, with its ubiquitous appurtenances: jewelers' chronometers, time balls, prominently displayed clocks, and most of all, personal watches. But it was also social. Henri Bergson really got this right, even if huge numbers of Americans didn't actually study his books. Unlike an international human rights campaign or a religious mission, which you could join or not, you had no choice here. There was an implicit *social* contract, to wit: in consideration of the surrender of my *free, deep self* (or some other way of saying, "freedom to live in my own temporal world"), I hereby agree to abide by standard time, which comes from the Naval Observatory ("telephoned down from God"), to my jeweler's chronometer, to my Waltham. Once the implicit contract was in place, there was no quitting, and it applied to virtually everyone. Stepping out of the time network—setting your watch wrong, choosing to ignore it and the other mechanical timekeepers you continually encountered during a routine day—could quickly bring palpable and even disastrous consequences: you missed that critical business meeting, you missed the beginning of a lecture by Bergson, you missed your train back from a forbidden tryst, or, as the conductor of the train, you caused a collision, with massive injuries and loss of life.

But you didn't have to read Bergson's *Time and Free Will* to wonder now and then about the individual, autonomous person you were, even as you occupied various nodal points on the network, where innumerable filaments stretch out and belay you fast to other such points. When you did turn your thoughts in this direction, what were you likely to think was *there*, inside you, that made you *you*?

If you kept up with the latest developments in psychology, as they were reported to the public, you knew there was that network of nerves and the brain, hard though it might be to think actual thoughts and at the same time imagine that those thoughts are coursing, in the form of electrical or chemical impulses, through chains of nerve cells. As its own system in your body, with its incalculable complexity, this network had to be unique to you. But, since psychology had offered something of a crossroads early in the century, you knew you had the option of conceptualizing your inner life as a relatively disembodied but highly dynamic realm of thoughts, drives, memories, and wishes. You understood that vast stretches of territory in that realm lay beyond (or beneath) your reach but that those stretches of territory were inextricably tied to stretches that lay *within* your reach. The two sections formed a system; they were interdependent. And, built as they were in part from the happenstances of your own life, they too, like your brain and nervous system, were unique to you. So, whether you were inclined to be an amateur neurophysiologist or an amateur psychoanalyst, there were plenty of solid reasons to conclude that you were your own unique, autonomous, individual, internally networked being.

And yet, if you stopped to think about it, you realized that your autonomy was strictly limited. The physiological "organic" explanation put you back in the world of biology, where, as you understood with particular clarity after the turn of the twentieth century, traits are transmitted *physically* from your parents to you. That network of nerves inside you, in its peculiar design and day-to-day functioning, may be unlike any other, and yet presumably it comes with a set of tendencies and characteristics that were already there at birth, thanks to the genes and chromosomes your parents passed along to you. And, under the "functional" explanation, the unconscious region of your mind contains desires and drives that are innate and common to all individuals in the species. Call it a "collective unconscious," with Carl Jung, or not; it still must be recognized as a property that networks you externally with your fellows.

So, what about autonomy? What about a truly private inner realm of freedom and *real duration*, a realm that *is* you?

In the end, there's not much to support the idea of individual autonomy during this era or afterwards. The optimism, or will to optimism, I've mentioned so often in this book arose precisely because of networks. The networked biological self, fending off enemies from without, thanks to the network of the public health campaign, holds out the promising prospect of long life for you and your children. The network of standard time and the networks of transportation and communication that it controls offer you a future of safety and efficiency. The networked home promises you a future of comfort and more leisure time. A host of social networks point you to a bright future of pride in your own people and cooperation among all people and peoples. The network of globalization ensures a future of increasing access to exotic and desirable products. But all these bright futures are purchased at a cost, and that cost is individual autonomy.

Toward the end of his Lowell Lectures, Henry Drummond devoted a long passage to "the Brain of Man." The description is both remarkably advanced and remarkably accessible for something written in the mid-1890s. Drummond resorted to the concept of the network:

> The Brain of Man is an elevated table-land of stratified nervous matter, furrowed by deep and sinuous cañons, and traversed by a vast net-work of highways along which Thoughts pass to and fro. The old and often-repeated Thoughts, or mental processes, pass along beaten tracks; the newer Thoughts have less marked footpaths; the newer still are compelled to construct fresh Thought-routes for themselves. Gradually these become established thoroughfares; but in the increasing traffic and complexity of life, new paths in endless multitudes have to be added, and bye lanes and loops between the older highways must be thrown into the system. The stations upon these roads from which the travellers set out are cells; the roads are transit fibres; the travellers themselves are in physiological language nervous discharges, in psychological language mental processes.[4]

And yet this language, describing what sounds like a self-contained system, leads directly into a passage that presents motherhood, therefore sympathy, therefore self-sacrifice and devotion, therefore connection with the outside social world. Drummond's entire book, don't forget, was about the vast cooperative network that is human society (though he doesn't actually use the word "network" in this connection).

He was right. In fact, he didn't know just how right he was. By 1913, twenty years after the Lowell Lectures were delivered, there were so many external networks of such vast reach and such confining power that it's difficult to imagine any conception of the individual as an even moderately autonomous being. That may not be a bad thing. If the networked human being has sacrificed some measure of autonomy in return for a host of networks, maybe those networks bring material and social benefits that outweigh the loss of autonomy.

To get a sense of how very different the new conception was from what it had been in the recent past, think back to the "Then!" house and the "Now!" house. It's an excellent model for the entire state of affairs. Let's say it's 1913 and you're a young, educated, urban-dwelling woman—a Simmons alumna, for example. The woman scrubbing clothes in front of the "Then!" house could be your grandmother. There's no need to repeat how her life differs physically from the life of her daughter (your mother), assuming her daughter is the matron of the "Now!" house. A child who grows up in the "Now!" house, a child such as you, will actually *be* like that house. In your own conception of yourself as an individual, you will be internally networked, just like the house, with its pipes that connect the kitchen with the upstairs and the downstairs. But the house in its belly holds a bundle of tentacles that reach out into the municipal services of your town or city. In the surrounding world—biological, social, commercial, cultural, cosmic—you stand on the nodes of clusters of filaments that stretch out across time and space. And just as the distant stations and junctions on the rail network define any randomly chosen entryway into that network as a kind of pure potentiality—you can go there, it beckons you—so the myriad nodes on your several networks beckon you. But more than that: they define and determine you.

NOTES AND INDEX

Notes

Preface

1. Alexis de Tocqueville, *Democracy in America*, trans. Henry Reeve, ed. Philips Bradley (New York: Knopf, 1960), 2: 98, 105, 106.

2. Ibid., 2: 109–10. John Kobler includes a couple of pages on the foundation and development of the American Temperance Society, in *Ardent Spirits: The Rise and Fall of Prohibition* (New York: G. P. Putnam's Sons, 1973), pp. 55–57.

3. Robert H. Wiebe, *The Search for Order, 1877–1920* (New York: Hill and Wang, 1967), chapter 3, "Crisis in the Communities" (pp. 44–75). I'll return to Wiebe in chapter 10.

4. Quoted in Tim Wu, *The Master Switch: The Rise and Fall of Information Empires* (New York: Knopf, 2010), pp. 5–6. The phrase appears in Tesla's article "The Transmission of Electrical Energy without Wires," originally published in *Electrical World and Engineer*, March 5, 1904.

5. Many thanks to Edwin DeLeon, Track Supervisor of the New York & Atlantic Railway, for the experience of a lifetime, when he let my son and me ride along, in a HiRail, on a routine inspection tour of the Bay Ridge branch, pointing to the exact place where the railway's tracks join the New York City subway system. Thanks also to Paul Victor, president of New York & Atlantic, for granting us permission to ride along.

Chapter 1

1. Alan M. Kraut discussed "better-baby contests" as part of a national eugenics movement in the 1920s. See *Silent Travelers: Germs, Genes, and the "Immigrant Menace"* (New York: Basic Books, 1994), pp. 253–54.

2. *New York Times*, 13 November 1921, p. E11.

3. Ibid., 16 November 1921, p. 6.

4. Ibid., 13 November 1921, p. E11.

5. Ibid., 9 October 1921, p. 25.

6. Mazÿck Ravenel, "The American Public Health Association, Past, Present, Future," in Mazÿck Ravenel, ed., *A Half Century of Public Health: Jubilee Historical Volume of the American Public Health Association* (New York: American Public Health Association, 1921), p. 21.

7. Stephen Smith, "A Half Century of Public Health," *American Journal of Public Health* 12, no. 1 (January 1921): 3–6. The quoted material appears on p. 5.

8. Stephen Smith, "The History of Public Health, 1871–1921," in *A Half Century of Public Health*, pp. 1–12. The passage on bone development appears on p. 3.

9. Smith, "A Half Century of Public Health," p. 5.

10. *New York Times*, 16 November 1921, p. 18. The reference to King Hezekiah and the "dial of time" is a paraphrase of Isaiah 38:8. God has announced, through Isaiah, that he has granted Hezekiah an additional fifteen years of life, which will allow the ailing King of Judah to see Jerusalem delivered from the Assyrians. For a sign, God says, "I will bring again the shadow of the degrees, which is gone down in the sundial of Ahaz [Hezekiah's father], ten degrees backward."

11. "Dr. Smith, 98, Guest of Health Show," *New York Times*, 16 November, 1921, p. 6.

12. Charles V. Chapin, "History of State and Municipal Control of Disease," in Ravenel, ed., *A Half Century of Public Health*, pp. 133–60. The quoted passage appears on pp. 159–60.

13. These are the findings of Clayne L. Pope, "Adult Mortality in America before 1900: A View from Family Histories," in Claudia Goldin and Hugh Rockoff, eds., *Strategic Factors in Nineteenth Century American Economic History* (Chicago: University of Chicago Press, 1992), pp. 267–96.

14. These figures are drawn from the Haines Tables, named for demographic historian Michael Haines and commonly considered as presenting the most authoritative historical vital statistics for the United States. The Haines Tables may be found in *Historical Statistics of the United States* (Cambridge, UK: Cambridge University Press, 2006). Online version (http: //hsus.cambridge.org): "Expectation of life at birth, by sex and race, 1850–1998" (Series Ab644–53:); and "Infant mortality rate," (Series Ab920–23). According to Indiana University historian James C. Riley, the Haines Tables contain some possible errors for the period 1870 to 1880, because the 1880 census authorities collected more complete information than those in 1870, leading Haines and others to show a surprising drop in expectation of life and rise in infant mortality for that period. Thanks to Riley for pointing this out in an e-mail to me, and for checking the accuracy of the account I've given here.

15. Chapin, "History of State and Municipal Control of Disease," pp. 158–59.

16. As reported in Ravenel, "The American Public Health Association, Past, Present, Future," p. 19.

17. For a short history of this table, see Shepard B. Clough, *A Century of American Life Insurance: A History of the Mutual Life Insurance Company of New York, 1843–1943* (New York: Columbia University Press, 1946), pp. 61–62.

18. Irving Fisher, *National Vitality, Its Wastes and Conservation*, report of National Conservation Commission, Senate document no. 676, 60th Congress, Second Session, 1909 (rpt. New York: Arno, 1976), p. 647.

19. "Working to Lengthen Man's Span of Life," *New York Times*, 7 March 1909, Sunday Magazine, p. 7.

20. Allan L. Benson, "Learning the Length of Life," *New York Times*, 16 May 1909, Sunday Magazine, p. 6.

21. *New York Times*, 23 May 1913, p. 13.

22. See *Vital Statistics Report for the Department of Health Annual Report for 1912*, at http: //www.tlcarchive.org.

23. Department of Commerce Bureau of the Census, *United States Life Tables 1910* (Washington, DC: Government Printing Office, 1916).

24. George Chandler Whipple, *Vital Statistics: An Introduction to the Science of Demography* (New York: John Wiley and Sons, 1919), p. vi.

25. Steven Mintz and Susan Kellogg write about the optimistic view of the American family that arose by the 1930s, when the family "was much less likely to be disrupted by the premature death of spouses or children." They list "declining death rates" and "rising life expectancies" as the source of this view, citing the work of demographic historian Peter Uhlenberg. But neither Mintz and Kellogg nor Uhlenberg explains the connection between vital statistics and the attitudes of ordinary people. See Steven Mintz and Susan Kellogg, *Domestic Revolutions: A Social History of American Family Life* (New York: Free Press, 1988), p. 131. Uhlenberg writes, "There is widespread agreement that mortality levels in a society constrain attitudes and feelings that parents have toward their infant children." But he offers nothing to explain the connection between the statistical figures he supplies and the attitudes and feelings of parents toward their children. See Peter Uhlenberg, "Death and the Family," *Journal of Family History* 5, no. 3 (1980): 313–20. The quoted passage appears on p. 314.

26. See Edwin O. Jordan, *Epidemic Influenza: A Survey* (Chicago: American Medical Association, 1927), pp. 214–15. Jordan gives 548,452 as the figure for total deaths from influenza in the United States for the last four months of 1918 and the first six months of 1919, and 309,930 for deaths from influenza in the final four months of 1918. The mortality figure for the first six months of 1919 would thus be 238,522. Mortality figures for the influenza epidemic have been widely debated. Many contemporary scholars think that the mortality rate was much higher than was believed during and shortly after the epidemic. A paper published in 2002, for example, following an international conference on the flu, held in Cape Town in 1998, puts the U.S. total at 675,000 and the worldwide total at close to 50 million, suggesting that even this last figure could be low by 100 percent. See Niall P. A. S. Johnson and Juergen Mueller, "Updating the Accounts: Global Mortality of the 1918–1920 'Spanish' Influenza Pandemic," *Bulletin of the History of Medicine* 76 (2002): 105–15, cited in Nancy K. Bristow, *American Pandem-*

ic: The Lost Worlds of the 1918 Influenza Epidemic (New York: Oxford University Press, 2012), p. 201n1. Bristow speaks of a fourth wave that struck in early 1920. Most historians discount the fourth wave, characterizing it as a new strain or locating it outside the United States. Bristow, however, claims that her own great-grandparents died from the 1920 wave in the United States. On the collective American amnesia regarding the pandemic, see Alfred W. Crosby, *America's Forgotten Pandemic: The Influenza of 1918* (Cambridge: Cambridge University Press, 1989), Afterword, "An Inquiry into the Peculiarities of Human Memory," pp. 311–25.

27. On influenza and other illnesses at the Paris Peace Conference, see Robert M. Crunden, *Ministers of Reform: The Progressives' Achievement in American Civilization, 1889–1920* (New York: Basic Books, 1982), pp. 253–56. Crunden sees Wilson as hobbled by illness of various sorts in the final years of his presidency.

Chapter 2

1. E. A. Schaefer, "Are We Near the Chemical Creation of Life?" *New York Times*, 15 September 1912, Sunday Magazine, p. 4. The popular press often spelled the professor's name "Schaefer" instead of "Schäfer."

2. No biologist or biochemist today would use this language to describe "life." A colloid is a liquid in which particles that are too large to dissolve are suspended. It's not entirely clear what Schäfer meant by "colloidal compounds." It's certainly true that living things contain the elements and the salts he lists. Salts can't be the substances that get suspended in colloids, since salts form solutions in water, and a solution is not the same thing as a compound. My best guess is that he's describing not organic compounds in general but protoplasm or simply *cells*, to the extent that these were understood by means of the relatively crude (by today's standards) microscopy available in 1912. In the aqueous medium inside a cell, there are indeed many molecules that exist in suspension, because, though they are hydrophilic (chemically attracted to water), they are too large to dissolve. Schäfer may also have had in mind simply the structures inside the cell that were visible to scientists at that time: chromosomes, for example, or organelles such as chloroplasts. The futuristic possibility Schäfer is holding out to his audience, I think, would be that of creating protoplasm in the laboratory. If this is what he had in mind, it's puzzling, to say the least, because this "doctrine of protoplasm," according to which protoplasm is (a) a single chemical compound and (b) the key to life, had long since been discredited by the time Schäfer gave his speech. Thanks to my colleague Gabriele Wienhausen and my daughter Eva Cassedy for helping to explicate this passage.

3. E. A. Schäfer, "The Nature, Origin and Maintenance of Life," *Science* 36 (1912): 289–312. This passage appears on p. 296.

4. "Say Life Problem Cannot Be Solved," *New York Times*, 6 September 1912, p. 4.

5. "Wallace Ridicules the Life Producers," *New York Times*, 7 September, 1912, p. 4.

6. Schäfer, "Nature, Origin and Maintenance of Life," p. 293.

7. Harold Brown Keyes, "Effect of Outdoor and Indoor School Life on the Physi-

cal and Mental Condition of Children," in Thomas A. Storey, ed., *Fourth International Congress on School Hygiene* (Buffalo, NY: Courier Co., 1913), 2: 125.

8. T. Mitchell Prudden, *Dust and Its Dangers* (New York: G. P. Putnam's Sons, 1890), p. 97. Mentioned in Nancy Tomes, *The Gospel of Germs: Men, Women, and the Microbe in American Life* (Cambridge, MA: Harvard University Press, 1998), p. 98.

9. "The Passing of the Beard," *Harper's Weekly* 47 (1903): 102. Cited in Tomes, *The Gospel of Germs,* p. 159.

10. William Inglis, "The Revolt against the Whisker," *Harper's Weekly* 51 (1907): 612–13. Mentioned in Tomes, *The Gospel of Germs,* p. 159.

11. "To Make Outdoor Sleeping Easy and Popular," *New York Times*, 26 May 1907, Sunday Magazine, p. 4.

12. "Sleeping and Sitting in the Open Air," National Association for the Study and Prevention of Tuberculosis, 1917, New York, p. 5.

13. The Fourth International Congress on School Hygiene, held in Buffalo, New York, in August of 1913, included an entire session on open-air schools. For example, I. Ogden Woodruff read a paper titled "Fresh Air Schools in New York City: A Comparative Study," filled with statistical data on the height, weight, and hemoglobin count of the schoolchildren studied. The best explanation he can give for the empirically observed improvement in health among children in open-air classes is that "somehow or other their general resistance is raised." *Fourth International Congress on School Hygiene*, ed. Thomas A. Storey (Buffalo, NY: Courier Co., 1913), 2: 90. On the open-air classrooms in New York City, see C.-E. A. Winslow, "Studies of Air Conditions in New York Schools," 2: 211–26.

14. H. W. Conn, *The Story of Germ Life* (New York: Appleton, 1897), pp. 9, 3.

15. Herbert W. Conn, *The Story of the Living Machine: A Review of the Conclusions of Modern Biology in Regard to the Mechanism Which Controls the Phenomena of Living Activity* (New York: Appleton, 1899), p. 80.

16. Ibid., p. 86.

17. James Ellis Humphrey, "Some Modern Views of the Cell," *Popular Science Monthly* 49 (1896): 602–14.

18. For example, Louis Agassiz and A. A. Gould, *Principles of Zoölogy: Touching the Structure, Development, Distribution, and Natural Arrangement of the Races of Animals, Living and Extinct* (1848; rev. ed., Boston: Gould and Lincoln, 1853), gave a basic account of cells, pp. 37–38. A. S. Packard, in *Zoology for High Schools and Colleges* (New York: Henry Holt, 1879), discussed cells, tissues, and organs, pp. 5–10.

19. George William Hunter, *A Civic Biology, Presented in Problems* (New York: American Book Company, 1914), pp. 47–57.

20. George Henry Lewes, *The Physiology of Common Life* (Edinburgh: William Blackwood and Sons, 1859), 1: 285.

21. Hunter, *Civic Biology,* p. 49.

22. Ibid., p. 317.

23. For a good, concise history of this period in American medicine, see James H. Cassedy, *Medicine in America: A Short History* (Baltimore, MD: Johns Hopkins University Press, 1991), chaps. 1–2 (pp. 3–66).

24. On the sanitarian phase, see Martin V. Melosi, *The Sanitary City: Urban Infrastructure in America from Colonial Times to the Present* (Baltimore, MD: Johns Hopkins University Press, 2000).

25. Robert H. Wiebe, *The Search for Order, 1877–1920* (New York: Hill and Wang, 1967), pp. 115–16.

26. Charles V. Chapin, "The End of the Filth Theory of Disease," *Popular Science Monthly* 60 (1901–2): 234–39. The quoted passage appears on p. 239.

27. James H. Cassedy, *Charles V. Chapin and the Public Health Movement* (Cambridge: Harvard University Press, 1962), p. 113.

28. Charles V. Chapin, *The Sources and Modes of Infection* (New York: Wiley, 1910), pp. 167–68. On the provenance of the list, see S. A. Knopf, "Tuberculosis, A Social Disease," *Bulletin of the Johns Hopkins Hospital* 17, no. 189 (December 1906): 393–405. A version of the list appears on p. 396, with an explanation of its provenance in a footnote.

29. Tomes, *The Gospel of Germs*, pp. 157–82.

30. Margaret C. Beer, "Hygiene Instruction in the Gardner School of Valparaiso," *Fourth International Congress on School Hygiene*, pp. 580–81. The quoted passage appears on p. 580.

31. Elie Metchnikoff, *The Nature of Man: Studies in Optimistic Philosophy*, ed. P. Chalmers Mitchell (New York: Putnam's, 1903), pp. 69–77.

32. Ibid., p. 253.

33. Ibid., p. 244.

34. On yogurt, see Elie Metchnikoff, *The Prolongation of Life: Optimistic Studies*, ed. P. Chalmers Mitchell (New York: Putnam's, 1908; rpt. New York: Arno, 1977), pp. 69 ff.

35. Metchnikoff, *The Nature of Man*, p. 255.

36. Ibid., pp. 259–60.

37. Pierre Flourens, in *De la longévité humaine et de la quantité de vie sur le globe*, 2nd ed. (Paris: Garnier, 1855), pp. 92–93, put it at 100. Wilhelm Ebstein, in *Die Kunst das menschliche Leben zu verlängern* (Wiesbaden: Bergmann, 1891), pp. 8–12, gave 70 as the figure.

38. Metchnikoff, *The Nature of Man*, pp. 277–78.

39. Metchnikoff, *The Prolongation of Life*, p. 327.

40. Ibid., p. 329.

41. Ibid., p. 331.

42. For the claim that life can be extended indefinitely, see ad in *New York Times*, 17 January 1908, p. 9. For the figure 140 (and similarly high figures), see untitled review, *The Critic* 43, no. 5 (November 1903): 391–92; Arthur E. McFarlane, "Prolonging the Prime of Life: Metchnikoff's Discoveries Show That Old Age May Be Postponed," *McClure's Magazine* 25, no. 5 (September 1905): 541–51 (quoted passage on p. 542); "Metchnikoff and Stedman," *New York Times*, 28 June 1908, p. 8; "The Span of Life," *New York Times*, 8 May 1909, p. 6; and Allan L. Benson, "Learning the Length of Life," *New York Times*, 16 May 1909, Sunday Magazine, p. 6.

43. Arthur B. Reeve, *Dream Doctor* (New York: Harper, 1914), p. 94.

44. Alexis Carrel, "On the Permanent Life of Tissues outside of the Organism,"

Journal of Experimental Medicine 15 (1912): 516–28. The quoted sentence appears on p. 516.

45. Ibid., p. 528.

46. *New York Times*, 2 May 1912, p. 8.

47. *Proceedings of the American Philosophical Society* 47 (1908): 677–96. The quoted passage appears on pp. 686–87.

48. Burton J. Hendrick, "On the Trail of Immortality," *McClure's Magazine* 40 (January 1913): 304–17. The quoted sentences appear on pp. 316–17.

49. For the story of the reception of Darwinism in scientific circles in the United States, see Ronald Numbers, *The Creationists: From Scientific Creationism to Intelligent Design*, expanded ed. (Cambridge, MA: Harvard University Press, 2006), pp. 15–19; and Edward J. Pfeifer, "United States," in Thomas F. Glick, ed., *The Comparative Reception of Darwinism* (1974; rev. ed., Chicago: University of Chicago Press, 1988), pp. 168–206.

50. L. T. Townsend, *Collapse of Evolution* (New York: American Bible League, 1905).

51. William Hanna Thomson, "The Mystery of Life and the Mystery of Man," *New York Times*, 5 November 1911, Sunday Magazine, p. 10.

52. "Hold to Evolution Theory. Scientists Deny Theologians' Statements That It Has Collapsed," *New York Times*, 7 February 1913, p. 2. "Has Evolution Collapsed?" *New York Times*, 23 February 1913, p. 96.

53. John M. Coulter, "The Religion of a Scientist," *Biblical World* 41, no. 2 (February 1913): 80–86.

54. An alumni publication article, "The Bergson Lectures," by W. T. Bush, was reprinted in *Columbia University Quarterly* 15, no. 3 (June 1913): 154–57. This article summarizes the English series ("The Method of Philosophy"). A summary of the French series, "Spirituality and Liberty," was given in a Poughkeepsie-based church journal, *The Chronicle* 13 (6 March 1913): 214–20. Both articles are reprinted in Henri Bergson, *Mélanges* (Paris: Presses Universitaires de France, 1972), pp. 978–89. The editors of this volume established a plausible list of dates for the two series, though they inadvertently transposed the titles.

55. "Students Flock to Bergson to Learn New Philosophy," *New York Times*, 27 August 1911, Sunday Magazine, p. 6.

56. *Chronicle*, pp. 218–19; Bergson, *Mélanges*, p. 988.

57. Henri Bergson, *Creative Evolution*, trans. Arthur Mitchell (London: Macmillan, 1911), pp. 285–86. Quoted in the *New York Times*, 27 August 1911, Sunday Magazine, p. 6.

Chapter 3

1. "Sex O'clock in America," *Current Opinion* 55, no. 2 (August 1913): 113. I've been unable to find where Reedy himself originally used this phrase.

2. Alice Bunker Stockham, *Tokology: A Book for Every Woman* (1883; rev. ed., Chicago: Sanitary Publishing Co., 1887), p. 157.

3. Ibid., p. 159.

4. John Cowan, M.D., *The Science of a New Life* (1869; rpt. New York: Cowan, 1874), pp. 112, 117.

5. Ibid., pp. 101, 118–19.

6. William Acton, *The Functions and Disorders of the Reproductive Organs in Childhood, Youth, Adult Age, and Advanced Life, Considered in Their Physiological, Social, and Moral Relations* (London, 1857; 6th ed., Philadelphia: Blakiston, 1883), pp. 212–13. Quoted in John Harvey Kellogg, *Plain Facts for Old and Young: Embracing the Natural History and Hygiene of Organic Life* (1877; rev. ed., Burlington, IA: Senger, 1891), pp. 473–74.

7. Rebecca Edwards, *New Spirits: Americans in the Gilded Age, 1865–1905* (New York: Oxford University Press, 2006), pp. 130–50.

8. Arthur B. Reeve, "The Dream Doctor," *Cosmopolitan* 55 (August 1913): 324–34. The quoted material appears on p. 325.

9. "Dreams of the Insane Help Greatly in Their Cure," *New York Times*, 2 March 1913, Sunday Magazine, p. 10. The passage appeared three years earlier in "Science Discovers Reality of Dreams," *New York Times*, 8 May 1910, Sunday Magazine, p. 14. It originally appeared in an article by Brill in the *New York Medical Journal*. This article then reappeared in Brill's *Psychanalysis* [*sic*]*: Its Theories and Practical Application*. The earlier *New York Times* article may well have been Reeve's source, since it contains another passage that appears in "The Dream Doctor." This second passage, which concerns the division of dreams into three classes, paraphrases a passage in Brill's *Psychanalysis*. Reeve's version is almost identical to the passage in the *Times*, so it is unlikely that the creator of Craig Kennedy used Brill's book or article as a source. For the two passages in Brill's book, see *Psychanalysis: Its Theories and Practical Application* (Philadelphia: Saunders, 1913), pp. 34, 42.

10. Reviewed in the *New York Times*, 1 June 1913, p. 56.

11. *Excessive Venery* was the title of yet another late-nineteenth-century marriage manual: Joseph W. Howe, M.D., *Excessive Venery, Masturbation and Continence* (New York: E. G. Treat, 1896).

12. Cowan, *Science of a New Life*, pp. 92–93.

13. Herbert W. Conn, *The Story of the Living Machine: A Review of the Conclusions of Modern Biology in Regard to the Mechanism Which Controls the Phenomena of Living Activity* (New York: Appleton, 1899), pp. 112–13.

14. Thomas Hunt Morgan, *Heredity and Sex* (New York: Columbia University Press, 1913), p. 72.

15. J. Arthur Thomson, "Solving the Problem of the Determination of Sex," *New York Times*, 20 October 1912, Sunday Magazine, p. 6.

16. Reported in *The Independent* 72, no. 3308 (25 April 1912): 910.

17. Prince A. Morrow, "Prophylaxis of Social Diseases," *American Journal of Sociology* 13 (July 1907): 20–33. The quoted passage appears on p. 26.

18. Ibid., pp. 21, 26.

19. Ibid., p. 27.

20. "Bibliography of Sex Hygiene: A Course for Teachers," *Educational Review* 56 (June–December 1913): 168–76.

21. Lyman P. Powell, "An Acute Problem for Parents," *Good Housekeeping* 53 (September 1911): 317–20; Havelock Ellis, "Dangers of Sexual Hygiene," *Good Housekeeping* 53 (October 1911): 456–59; Prince A. Morrow, "The Teaching of Sex Hygiene," *Good Housekeeping* 54 (March 1912): 404–7; Dorothy Dix (Elizabeth Meriwether Gilmer), "The Handicap of Sex," *Good Housekeeping* 57 (August 1913): 215–18.

22. The best source on this subject is an unpublished doctoral dissertation: Wallace H. Maw, "Fifty Years of Sex Education in the Public Schools of the United States (1900–1950): A History of Ideas," Ed.D. diss., University of Cincinnati, 1953. See pp. 88–89 for the period 1912–18.

23. "Pupils Told of Personal Purity," *Chicago Daily Tribune*, 28 October 1913, p. 2.

24. "Mails Closed to Lectures on Sex," *Chicago Daily Tribune*, 14 November 1913, p. 11; "Stumbling Block for Sex Hygiene Lectures," *Chicago Daily Tribune*, 21 November 1913, p. 13.

25. "Mrs. Young Wins; Re-elected Head of City Schools," *Chicago Daily Tribune*, 24 December 1913, p. 1.

26. "School Board Stops Teaching of Sex Hygiene," *Chicago Daily Tribune*, 8 January 1914, p. 1. For an account of the entire episode, including opposition from Catholic leaders, see Jeffrey P. Moran, *Teaching Sex: The Shaping of Adolescence in the 20th Century* (Cambridge, MA: Harvard University Press, 2000), pp. 50–55.

27. "Sex Hygiene for Schools Is Urged," *Chicago Daily Tribune*, 17 April 1911, p. 11.

28. On the integrated method of instruction, see Moran, *Teaching Sex*, pp. 101–6. On the period 1918 to 1929, see Maw, "Fifty Years of Sex Education," pp. 89–107.

29. Newell W. Edson, "Some Facts Regarding Sex Instruction in the High Schools of the United States," *School Review* 29 (October 1921): 593–602. See Moran, *Teaching Sex*, pp. 105–8.

30. W. Carson Ryan Jr., *School Hygiene: A Report of the Fourth International Congress on School Hygiene, Held at Buffalo, N.Y., August 25–30, 1913* (Washington, DC: Government Printing Office, 1913), pp. 51, 53.

31. Ellen Key, *Love and Ethics* (New York: Huebsch, 1911), p. 20.

32. Marie Carmichael Stopes, *Married Love, or Love in Marriage* (1918; rpt. New York: Eugenics Publishing Co., 1927), p. 58.

33. Ibid., pp. 83–84.

34. Virginia Woolf, *A Room of One's Own* (San Diego, New York, and London: Harcourt, 1989), p. 80.

35. Theodoor H. Van de Velde, *Ideal Marriage: Its Physiology and Technique*, trans. Stella Browne (New York: Random House, 1926), pp. 8, 10–11.

36. Ibid., p. 15.

37. Ibid., p. 141.

38. Ad in *New York Times Book Review*, 10 July 1960, p. 19.

39. James Reed told the story of the birth control movement in *The Birth Control Movement and American Society: From Private Vice to Public Virtue* (Princeton, NJ: Princeton University Press, 1978). For figures on the use of various devices and methods, Reed relied on data gathered by sex researcher Alfred Kinsey and his associates in the

1930s and 1940s. Reed gives a good account of these data, together with judicious warnings about their limitations. See pp. 123–28.

40. Marie Carmichael Stopes, in J. Arthur Thomson et al., eds., *The Control of Parenthood* (New York: Putnam's, 1920), pp. 207–22. The quoted passage appears on p. 207.

41. Ibid., p. 217.

42. Ibid., pp. 222.

43. For an account of the conference, see Stefan Kühl, *The Nazi Connection: Eugenics, American Racism, and German National Socialism* (New York: Oxford University Press, 1994), pp. 32–35.

44. Sanger cited Goddard's figures on the alarming number of "feebleminded and other defectives" in the United States in *Woman and the New Race* (New York: Brentano's, 1920), pp. 40–41. She cited Yerkes's figures on the high percentage of morons among drafted men in the U.S. Army in *The Pivot of Civilization* (New York: Brentano's, 1922), p. 263.

45. Sanger, *Pivot of Civilization*, p. 181.

46. Ibid., p. 271.

47. Ibid., p. 274.

48. Ibid., p. 189.

49. Havelock Ellis, "Eugenics and St. Valentine," *Nineteenth Century and After* 59 (1906): 779–87. The quoted phrases appear on pp. 781 and 786.

50. Ibid., p. 787.

51. Havelock Ellis, *The Task of Social Hygiene* (Boston: Houghton Mifflin, 1913), p. vi.

52. Sanger, *Pivot of Civilization*, p. 173.

Chapter 4

1. "Roosevelt Thrown as Platform Falls," *New York Times*, 24 March 1912, p. 1.

2. Morton Prince, M.D., "Roosevelt as Analyzed by the New Psychology," *New York Times*, 24 March 1912, Sunday Magazine, p. 1.

3. Morton Prince, *The Nature of Mind and Human Automatism* (Philadelphia: Lippincott, 1885), p. 8.

4. G. Stanley Hall, *Founders of Modern Psychology* (New York: Appleton, 1912), p. 252.

5. For this discussion of Helmholtz and nineteenth-century neurophysiology, I've borrowed heavily from my own article: "A History of the Concept of the Stimulus and the Role It Played in the Neurosciences," *Journal of the History of the Neurosciences* 17 (2008): 405–32.

6. Johannes Müller, *Zur vergleichenden Physiologie des Gesichtssinnes des Menschen und der Thiere* (On the Comparative Physiology of the Visual Sense in Man and Animals) (Leipzig: Cnobloch, 1826), p. 22. My translation.

7. Hermann von Helmholtz, *Handbuch der Physiologischen Optik*, in G. Karsten, ed., *Allgemeine Encyklopädie der Physik*, vol. 9 (Leipzig: Voss, 1867), p. 30. My translation.

8. Ibid., p. 443. Emphasis is in the original.

9. Ibid. p. 191.

10. Helmholtz, *Handbuch der Physiologischen Optik*, 2nd ed. (Hamburg: Voss, 1896), p. 595.

11. "Geniuses Hydrocephalous," *New York Times*, 12 May 1907, p. C1, includes Helmholtz among geniuses afflicted with hydrocephalus; and "Brain of Dr. M'Gee Weighs 1,140 Grams," *New York Times*, 18 September 1912, p. 7, includes Helmholtz in a list of great men whose brains were extraordinarily large. Helmholtz's weighed 1,440 grams, though topping the list was Russian novelist Turgenev, weighing in cerebrally at 2,012.

12. Charles Sherrington, *The Integrative Action of the Nervous System* (New Haven, CT: Yale University Press, 1906), pp. 236, 347.

13. Ibid., p. 233.

14. "Magic in the Brain," *Current Literature* 18, no. 3 (September 1895): 246–48.

15. "Functional Nervous Affections," on the work of neurologist Charles Édouard Brown-Séquard, then at Harvard, *Medical and Surgical Reporter*, 23 June 1866, p. 14. See also Leopold Putzel, *A Treatise on Common Forms of Functional Nervous Diseases* (New York: William Wood, 1880).

16. "The Health Congress," *New York Times*, 13 November 1874, pp. 1–3; "On Sexual Hygiene," Medical and Surgical Reporter, 8 June 1878, p. 38; "Little Done at Albany," *New York Times*, 7 May 1882, p. 1.

17. See T. L. Maddin, "The Neuron," *Medical and Surgical Reporter*, 16 May 1898, p. 78.

18. "Hypnotism the Cure-All," *New York Times*, 30 April 1899, p. 12.

19. Elwood Worcester, Samuel McComb, and Isador H. Coriat, *Religion and Medicine: The Moral Control of Nervous Disorders* (New York: Moffat, Yard & Company, 1908), pp. 6, 2.

20. See, for example, "Religion and Science at Work Together," *New York Times*, 5 January 1908, Sunday Magazine, p. 1.

21. Ray Stannard Baker, "The Spiritual Unrest," *American Magazine* 47, no. 2 (December 1908): 192–204. The quoted passage appears on p. 194.

22. Ibid., p. 194.

23. Edwin E. Slosson, Introduction to Henri Bergson, *Dreams*, trans. Slosson (New York: Huebsch, 1914), p. 9.

24. "Among the Authors," *New York Times*, 16 February 1913, p. 69. The *Columbia Spectator*, 12 February 1913, p. 5, reported twenty thousand ("rumor has it"), but this figure seems unlikely. For the seating capacity of Carnegie Hall when it opened, see T. Allston Brown, *A History of the New York Stage, from the First Performance in 1732 to 1901* (New York: Dodd, Mead, 1903), 3: 613. On the seating capacity of the lecture room in Havemeyer Hall, see "Columbia University," *Scientific American* 78, no. 13 (26 March 1898): 200–202. The author apparently rounded up to 325. I've counted 319 and see no evidence that the hall has changed.

25. "The Latest of Philosophers, Three Works Which Have Given Bergson Wide Repute Among the World's Thinkers," *New York Times*, 20 August 1911, Book Review, p. 503.

26. Henri Bergson, *Matter and Memory*, trans. Nancy Margaret Paul and W. Scott Palmer (New York: Macmillan, 1911), p. 157.

27. Ibid., pp. 190, 327, 239.

28. Henri Bergson, *Creative Evolution*, trans. Arthur Mitchell (New York: Henry Holt, 1911), p. 128.

29. "Students Flock to Bergson to Learn New Philosophy," *New York Times*, 27 August 1911, Sunday Magazine, p. 6.

30. James Gibbons Huneker, "The Playboy of Western Philosophy," *Forum* 49 (March 1913): 257–68. The quoted passage appears on pp. 258–59.

31. "The Latest of Philosophers." p. 503.

32. Documents from Columbia University, University Archives, Central Files (box 664, file 33).

33. W. T. Bush, "The Bergson Lectures," *Columbia University Quarterly* 15, no. 3 (June 1913): 154–57.

34. "Bergson Stands by Will," *New York Times*, 5 February 1913, p. 8; "Believes in Intuition," *New York Times*, 6 February 1913, p. 10; "Human Will Makes Energy," *New York Times*, 11 February 1913, p. 24.

35. E. E. Cummings, *Him* (New York: Boni and Liveright, 1927), pp. 59–62.

36. J. Brooks Atkinson, "A Play Misunderstood," *New York Times*, 19 April 1928, p. 23.

37. On sales of Freud's works in English, see Nathan G. Hale, Jr., *Freud and the Americans: The Beginnings of Psychoanalysis in the United States, 1876–1917* (New York: Oxford University Press, 1971), pp. 430–31.

38. J. B. Kerfoot, "Ye Latest Books," *Life* 62 (14 August 1913): 274.

39. Arthur B. Reeve, "The Dream Doctor," *Cosmopolitan* 55 (August 1913): 324–34. The quoted material appears on pp. 332–33.

40. Sigmund Freud, "The Origin and Development of Psychoanalysis," *American Journal of Psychology* 221, no. 2 (April 1910): 181–218.

41. H. W. Chase, "Freud's Theories of the Unconscious," *Popular Science Monthly* 78 (April 1911): 355–63.

42. "Freud's Discovery of the Lowest Chamber of the Soul," *Current Literature* 50, no. 5 (May 1911): 512–14.

43. Ibid., p. 513.

44. "Psycho-Analysis," *British Medical Journal* 2776 (14 March 1914): 597–99.

45. "How Psycho-Analysis Has Obsessed the World with Sex," *Current Opinion* 56 (June 1914): 441–42.

Chapter 5

1. For example, Charles Dunan, *Les Arguments de Zénon d'Élée contre le mouvement* (Paris: Félix Alcan, 1884); Paul Tannery, "Le concept scientifique du continu: Zénon d'Élée et Georg Cantor," *Revue philosophique de France et de l'étranger* 20 (1885): 385–410; Georges Noel, "Le mouvement et les arguments de Zénon d'Élée"; G. Milhaud, "Le concept du nombre chez les pythagoriciens et les Éléates"; Victor Brochard, "Les prétendus sophismes de Zénon d'Élée"; François Evellin, "Le mouvement et les partisans

des indivisibles"; Georges Lechalas, "Note sur les arguments de Zénon d'Élée," *Revue de métaphysique et de morale* 1 (1893): 107–23, 140–56, 209–15, 382–95, 396–400.

2. Dunan, *Les Arguments*, pp. 35–36. My translation.

3. French literary critic and diarist Charles Du Bos quotes Bergson's story about the moment of inspiration in his *Journal, 1921–1923* (Paris: Corrêa, 1946), pp. 63–65. Connor J. Chambers told the story, quoting from Du Bos's *Journal*, in "Zeno of Elea and Bergson's Neglected Thesis," *Journal of the History of Philosophy* 12, no. 1 (January 1974): 63–76.

4. Henri Bergson, *Essai sur les données immédiates de la conscience* (Paris: Félix Alcan, 1889), pp. 84–85. My translation.

5. Antoine Breguet, "L'unification de l'heure dans les grandes villes, par le moyen de l'électricité," *Le Génie civil: Revue générale des industries françaises et étrangères* 1 (1880–81): 9–11. Cited in Peter Galison, *Einstein's Clocks, Poincaré's Maps: Empires of Time* (New York: Norton, 2003), pp. 97–98.

6. M. W. de Nordling, "L'unification des heures," *Revue générale des chemins de fer* 11 (April 1888): 193–212. Quoted in Galison, *Einstein's Clocks, Poincaré's Maps*, pp. 98–100.

7. Galison, *Einstein's Clocks, Poincaré's Maps*, chapter 3, "The Electric Worldmap," pp. 84–155.

8. De Nordling, "L'unification des heures," p. 193.

9. Bergson, *Essai*, p. 94.

10. Ibid., pp. 103–4.

11. As reported in the *New York Times*, 19 August 1853, p. 1.

12. *New York Observer and Chronicle*, 25 August 1853, p. 31.

13. "More Slaughter by Railroad," *New York Times*, 13 August 1853, p. 4.

14. For the story of the P & W crash and its aftermath, see Ian R. Bartky, *Selling the True Time: Nineteenth-Century Timekeeping in America* (Stanford, CA: Stanford University Press, 2000), pp. 25–31.

15. "Time Light for Mariners," *New York Times*, 22 April 1910, p. 6.

16. Macy's display ad, *New York Times*, 21 November 1915, sect. 3, p. 1.

17. Michael O'Malley, *Keeping Watch: A History of American Time* (New York: Viking, 1990), pp. 139–40.

18. Bartky, *Selling the True Time*, p. 207.

19. "Daylight Bill Sent to President, Who Favors Its Adoption for U.S.; Effective at 2 A.M. March 31," *Washington Post*, 17 March 1918, p. 1.

20. See David S. Landes, *Revolution in Time: Clocks and the Making of the Modern World* (1983; rev. ed., Cambridge, MA: Harvard University Press, 2000), pp. 326–37.

21. For output figures, see ibid., p. 418. For sales and earnings figures, see the authoritative history of the company, Charles W. Moore, *Timing a Century: History of the Waltham Watch Company* (Cambridge, MA.: Harvard University Press, 1945), p. 50.

22. "Making Watches in America," *New York Times*, 26 June 1867, p. 5.

23. Landes, *Revolution in Time*, p. 344.

24. Display ad, *New York Times*, 2 February 1913, Part 9, p. 4.

25. "Bergson Stands by Will," *New York Times*, 5 February 1913, p. 8.

26. Charles H. Parkhurst, "In His Steps," *Bible Record* 9, no. 1 (January 1912): 6–11. The quoted passage is on p. 9.

27. W. T. Bush, "The Bergson Lectures," *Columbia University Quarterly* 15, no. 3 (June 1913): 154–57. The quoted material appears on pp. 256–57.

28. According to a report in the *Archives du Collège de France*, reproduced in Henri Bergson, *Mélanges* (Paris: Presses Universitaires de France, 1972), pp. 976–77. My translation.

Chapter 6

1. "The Woman Who Invented Scientific Housekeeping," *New York Times*, 6 July 1913, Section 7, p. 10.

2. Christine Frederick, *The New Housekeeping: Efficiency Studies in Home Management* (1912; rev. ed., New York: Doubleday, 1919), p. 204.

3. "Putting the American Woman and Her Home on a Business Basis," *American Review of Reviews* 44 (January–June 1914): 199–208. The quoted passage appears on p. 200.

4. Helen Louise Johnson, "The Meaning of Home Economics," *Harper's Bazaar* 43, no. 10 (October 1909): 1024–26.

5. Frederick, *The New Housekeeping*, p. 233.

6. The Riverside Station is correct; the electrical substation is an educated guess. See *Thirty Years of New York: Being a History of Electrical Development in Manhattan and the Bronx* (New York: Press of the New York Edison Company, 1913), pp. 115–16, 172.

7. Mrs. H. M. (Harriette Merrick) Plunkett, *Women, Plumbers and Doctors* (New York: Appleton, 1885), frontispiece. The images are reproduced in David P. Handlin, *The American Home: Architecture and Society, 1815–1915* (Boston: Little, Brown, 1979), p. 456.

8. Letty Anderson, "Fire and Disease: The Development of Water Supply Systems in New England, 1870–1900," in Joel A. Tarr and Gabriel Dupuy, eds., *Technology and the Rise of the Networked City in Europe and America* (Philadelphia: Temple University Press, 1988), pp. 137–56. Information on population supplied with water appears on p. 138.

9. For the history of indoor plumbing in the United States, see Siegfried Giedion's classic and hugely fascinating *Mechanization Takes Command: A Contribution to Anonymous History* (New York: Oxford University Press, 1948), pp. 659–712; David P. Handlin, *The American Home: Architecture and Society, 1815–1915* (Boston: Little, Brown, 1979), pp. 465–71; and Susan Strasser, *Never Done: A History of American Housework* (New York, 1982; rev. ed., New York: Holt, 2000), pp. 85–103.

10. For example, "A Cosey Little Cottage," *Art Amateur: A Monthly Journal Devoted to Art in the Household* 22, no. 3 (February 1890): 64–66. References to gas appliances appear on p. 66. Louis Stotz, author of *History of the Gas Industry* (New York: Stettiner Bros., 1938), p. 118, reports that a Philadelphia company began manufacturing gas ranges in 1879, but I've found no other references to the company or its ranges.

11. *Ladies' Home Journal* 10, no. 5 (April 1893): 31.

12. Ads for the home systems began appearing in magazines around 1912. See, for

example, "Vacuum on Tap," *The Independent* 72 (January 1912): xvi. Giedion includes a copy of a leaflet ad (company not identified), from 1910, in *Mechanization Takes Command*, p. 591. For the history of the Spencer Turbine Company, see the Spencer website: http: //www.spencerturbine.com/about-us/company-history.html. Thanks to vacuum cleaner historian (yes, there is such a thing) Charlie Lester, who supplied the phrase "vacuum cleaner in reverse," in an e-mail to me, 14 October 2004.

13. "The Doom of Dust," ad in *Scientific American* 94, no. 5 (3 February 1906): 120.

14. For the dates when various electrical appliances first made their appearances, see Strasser, *Never Done*, pp. 78–81; Witold Rybczynski, *Home: A Short History of an Idea* (New York: Viking, 1986), pp. 151–54; Ellen M. Plante, *The American Kitchen, 1700 to the Present: From Hearth to Highrise* (New York: Facts on File, 1995), pp. 214–17.

15. U.S. Bureau of the Census, Historical Statistics of the United States: Colonial Times to 1970 (Washington, DC: Government Printing Office, 1976), p. 827. Mentioned in Strasser, *Never Done*, p. 89.

16. I've based this estimate on figures in *Historical Statistics of the United States: Colonial Times to 1970*, http: //www.census.gov/prod/www/abs/statab.html, p. 783.

17. Herbert N. Casson, *The History of the Telephone* (Chicago: A. McClurg, 1910), p. 139.

18. Ibid., pp. 140–41.

19. On the dial telephone, see Edwin S. Grosvenor and Morgan Wesson, *Alexander Graham Bell: The Life and Times of the Man Who Invented the Telephone* (New York: Harry N. Abrams, 1997), pp. 164–65.

20. Casson, *History of the Telephone*, p. 154.

21. Ibid., pp. 158–59.

22. David Mercer tells a short version of the story in *The Telephone: The Life Story of a Technology* (Westport, CT: Greenwood, 2006), pp. 57–71.

23. Quoted in Tim Wu, *The Master Switch: The Rise and Fall of Information Empires* (New York: Knopf, 2010), p. 9. On the centralization of telephone service under Vail, see pp. 3–10 and 50–60.

24. William A. Alcott, *The Young House-Keeper, or Thoughts on Food and Cookery* (Boston: George W. Light, 1938).

25. Catherine Beecher, *A Treatise on Domestic Economy for the Use of Young Ladies at Home and at School* (Boston: Marsh, Capen, Lyon, and Webb, 1841).

26. Catherine Beecher and Harriet Beecher Stowe, *The American Woman's Home: or, Principles of Domestic Science* (New York: J. B. Ford, 1869).

27. Caroline L. Hunt, *The Life of Ellen H. Richards* (Boston: Whitcomb and Barrows, 1912), p. 181.

28. Ibid., p. 184.

29. Ibid., p. 185.

30. Ibid., p. 186.

31. Ellen H. Richards, *Food Materials and Their Adulterations* (Boston: Estes and Lauriat, 1886), p. 7.

32. Ibid., p. 10.

33. See "The Rumford Kitchen, Exhibit at World's Columbian Exposition, Chicago, 1893, Excerpts from *Report of the Massachusetts Board of World's Fair Managers,* Boston, 1894," http: //libraries.mit.edu/archives/exhibits/esr/esr-rumford.html#exterior.

34. C. H. Fowler and W. H. De Puy, *Home and Health and Home Economics: A Cyclopedia of Facts and Hints for All Departments of Home Life, Health, and Domestic Economy* (New York: Phillips and Hunt, 1880).

35. Ellen H. Richards, "Ten Years of the Lake Placid Conference on Home Economics: Its History and Aims," Lake Placid Conference on Home Economics, *Proceedings of the Tenth Annual Conference* (1908), p. 22. Quoted in Hunt, *Life of Ellen H. Richards,* p. 268.

36. Hunt, *Life of Ellen H. Richards,* pp. 286–90.

37. See Sarah Stage, "Ellen Richards and the Social Significance of the Home Economics Movement," in Sarah Stage and Virginia B. Vincenti, eds., *Rethinking Home Economics: Women and the History of a Profession* (Ithaca, NY: Cornell University Press, 1997), pp. 17–33. The history of the Boston School of Housekeeping appears on pp. 24–25.

38. Inventory, Simmons College School/Department of Household/Home Economics, Records, 1900–(1913–1969)–1972. The College Archives, Simmons College, Boston, Massachusetts, pp. 12–13. The dean of the college, Sarah Louise Arnold, told the history of household economics in an article she wrote for the tenth anniversary of the opening of the college: "The Teaching of Home Economics at Simmons College," *Simmons Quarterly* 2, no. 3 (April 1912): 1–12.

39. "Preliminary Announcement of Simmons College, Boston" (Boston: Geo. H. Ellis Co., 1902), p. 8.

40. Mary Caroline Crawford, "A Girls' College with a Practical Idea," *Ladies' Home Journal* 24, no. 9 (August 1907): 24.

41. Richards, "Ten Years of the Lake Placid Conference," p. 22.

42. Frederick explains this in *The New Housekeeping,* p. 36.

43. Christine Frederick, *Household Engineering: Scientific Management in the Home* (Chicago: American School of Home Economics, 1920); Frederick, *Selling Mrs. Consumer* (New York: Business Bourse, 1929).

44. Plante, *The American Kitchen,* pp. 110–13.

45. Quoted in Hunt, *Life of Ellen H. Richards,* pp. 287–88.

46. Lillian W. Betts, "The New Woman," *Outlook* 51, no. 15 (12 October 1895): 587.

47. Winnifred Harper Cooley, *The New Womanhood* (New York: Broadway Publishing Company, 1904), p. 19.

48. Ibid., p. 123.

49. Arthur M. Schlesinger, *Paths to the Present* (New York: Macmillan, 1949), p. 243.

50. Frederick, *The New Housekeeping,* pp. 21–22.

51. Ibid., pp. 208–9.

52. Plante, *The American Kitchen,* p. 139.

53. Frederick, *The New Housekeeping,* p. 195.

54. Ellen H. Richards, *Euthenics: The Science of Controllable Environment: A Plea for*

Better Living Conditions as a First Step toward Higher Human Efficiency (Boston: Whitcomb and Barrows, 1910), p. 59.

Chapter 7

1. The Steinway model X upright now belongs to my family. It was a wedding present to my wife and me from my parents, who purchased it from the grandson of Mr. Sherman in 1975. My principal source of information is a personal letter to me, dated February 1, 2007, from the late Henry Z. Steinway, great-grandson of the company's founder and the last member of the family to serve as company president. In addition, I used the 1911 edition of the *Encyclopaedia Britannica* for the possible provenance of materials about which Mr. Steinway was unsure. Other useful sources of information on piano construction from this era are Alfred Dolge, *Pianos and Their Makers: A Comprehensive History of the Development of the Piano from the Monochord to the Concert Grand Player Piano* (Covina, CA: Covina Publishing Company, 1911); "To Make a Piano," *Massachusetts Ploughman* 48, no. 1 (6 October 1888): 3; and Frederick S. Hall, "Great Industries of the United States, VII. The Manufacture of Musical Instruments," *Cosmopolitan* 38, no. 3 (January 1905): 353–64. Nicaragua and South America as sources of mahogany and rosewood are conjecture, based on newspaper reports from the period. On ivory in the Connecticut Valley: Richard Conniff, *From Combs to Keyboards: The Development of a Connecticut Valley Industry* (Essex, CT: Steamboat Dock, 1990).

2. Dolge, *Pianos and Their Makers*, p. 115.

3. Alfred E. Eckes Jr., and Thomas W. Zeiler, *Globalization and the American Century* (Cambridge, UK: Cambridge University Press, 2003), p. 18.

4. Ibid., pp. 32–36.

5. See Fran Beauman, *The Pineapple: King of Fruits* (London: Chatto and Windus, 2005), pp. 206–7.

6. Ibid., p. 213.

7. Ibid., p. 221.

8. Ibid., pp. 225–26.

9. *Harper's Bazaar* 43, no. 1 (January 1909): 117; *McClure's Magazine* 1 (January 1909): 133, 307.

10. Jennie June (Jane Cunningham Croly), *Jennie June's American Cookery Book* (New York: American News Company, 1866).

11. See, for example, Maria Parloa, *Miss Parloa's New Cook Book: A Guide to Marketing and Cooking* (Boston: Estes and Lauriat, 1881), pp. 287, 289, 293. There are six recipes in Fannie Merritt Farmer's *Boston Cooking-School Cook Book* (Boston: Little, Brown, 1896), but numerous recipes in her *New Book of Cookery: Eight Hundred and Sixty Recipes, Covering the Whole Range of Cookery* (Bedford, MA: Applewood Books, 1912), p. 5.

12. Marion Harland (Mary Virginia Terhune), *The Cottage Kitchen: A Collection of Practical and Inexpensive Receipts* (New York: Charles Scribner's Sons, 1883).

13. Marion Harland (Mary Virginia Terhune), *365 Desserts: A Dessert for Every Day in the Year* (Philadelphia: G. W. Jacobs, 1900).

14. Marion Harland (Mary Virginia Terhune) and Christine Terhune Herrick, *The Helping Hand Cook Book, with a Menu for Every Day in the Year, Together with Numerous Recipes* (New York: Moffat, Yard), pp. 87, 336.

15. *How We Serve Hawaiian Pineapple* (Honolulu: Hawaiian Pineapple Packers' Association, 1914)

16. Virginia Scott Jenkins, *Bananas: An American History* (Washington, DC: Smithsonian Institution Press, 2000), pp. 11–12. The source of the story about the Centennial Exposition and the tinfoil-wrapped bananas appears to be inventor and writer Frederick Upham Adams, who wrote an adulatory history of the United Fruit Company in *Conquest of the Tropics: The Story of the Creative Enterprises Conducted by the United Fruit Company* (Garden City, NY: Doubleday, Page, 1914). On pp. 21–23, Adams tells about visiting the exposition as a youngster with his father and then buying bananas at a fruit store in Philadelphia on the same day.

17. Adams, *Conquest of the Tropics*, pp. 82–84.

18. On the fruit companies and mergers, see Marcelo Bucheli, *Bananas and Business: The United Fruit Company in Colombia, 1899–2000* (New York: New York University Press, 2005), pp. 45–49.

19. Virginia Scott Jenkins, *Bananas: An American History* (Washington, DC: Smithsonian Institution Press, 2000), pp. 145–50.

20. Ibid., pp. 85–87.

21. Ibid., p. 161.

22. Ad in *McClure's Magazine* 62, no. 1 (November 1913): 185.

23. Susan Wagner, *Cigarette Country: Tobacco in American History and Politics* (New York: Praeger, 1971), p. 50.

24. On the invention of the cardboard matchbook, see Eric Burns, *The Smoke of the Gods: A Social History of Tobacco* (Philadelphia: Temple University Press, 2007), p. 137.

25. The identical story is told in Wagner, *Cigarette Country*, pp. 36–37; Iain Gately, *Tobacco: The Story of How Tobacco Seduced the World* (New York: Grove Press, 2001), p. 207; and Burns, *Smoke of the Gods*, p. 134.

26. Burns, *Smoke of the Gods*, p. 135. Burns gives no source for the figures.

27. Gately, *Tobacco*, p. 210.

28. U.S. Department of Commerce, *Report of the Commissioner of Corporations on the Tobacco Industry, Part III: Prices, Costs, and Profits* (Washington, DC: Government Printing Office, 1915), pp. 334–35.

29. Images of many of these packages may be found in Michael Thibodeau and Jana Martin, *Smoke Gets in Your Eyes: Branding and Design in Cigarette Packaging* (New York: Abbeville Press, 2000).

30. Ibid., p. 33.

31. Gately, *Tobacco*, p. 244.

32. H. Westendarp, "Ivory Production," *Current Literature* 22, no. 3 (September 1897): pp. 217–18.

33. Henry Morton Stanley, *In Darkest Africa, or the Quest, Rescue, and Retreat of Emin Governor of Equatoria* (New York: Charles Scribner's Sons, 1890), 1: 240. Quoted in

Conniff, *From Combs to Keyboards*, p. 78. The store of ivory was reported, for example, in the *Washington Post*, 5 April 1889, p. 2, and 6 April 1889, p. 1; *New York Tribune*, 6 April 1889, p. 1; *The Independent*, 41, no. 2106 (11 April 1889), p. 9; *New York Times*, 5 April 1889, p. 5. Sale of the ivory in Antwerp was reported in the *New York Times*, 24 November 1889, p. 6. For a much more skeptical account of the Emin Pasha expedition, see Adam Hochschild, *King Leopold's Ghost: A Story of Greed, Terror, and Heroism in Colonial Africa* (Boston: Houghton Mifflin, 1998), pp. 96–100.

34. Edward A. Berlin, *Ragtime: A Musical and Cultural History* (Berkeley: University of California Press, 1980), p. 123.

35. Ibid., pp. 123–24.

36. "Wilson Banned Ball Fearing Turkey Trot," *New York Times*, 21 January 1913, p. 3.

37. The earlier of the two articles is "On the Real Value of Negro Music," *New York Herald*, 21 May 1893. The second is "Music in America," *Harper's New Monthly Magazine* 90, no. 537 (February 1894): pp. 428–34.

38. "The Future of American Music," *Current Literature* 39, no. 2 (August 1905): 191–92.

39. "President Says Negro Makes American Music. May Furnish the Foundation of the True National School," *New York Times*, 15 February 1906, p. 7.

40. Richard Aldrich, "Indian and Negro Music," *New York Times*, 25 February 1906, Part Four, p. 1.

41. Natalie Curtis, "The Negro's Contribution to the Music of America: The Larger Opportunity of the Colored Man of Today," *Craftsman* 23, no. 6 (March 1913): 660–69.

42. Reproduced in Karl Koenig, *Jazz in Print* (Hillsdale, NY: Pendragon Press, 2002), pp. 103–4.

43. Quoted in "Black-Music Concerts in Carnegie Hall, 1912–1915," *Black Perspective in Music* 6, no. 1 (Spring 1978): 75.

44. "An American Minstrel," *Outlook*, 28 May 1919, pp. 140–41.

45. Peter C. Muir, *Long Lost Blues: Popular Blues in America, 1850–1920* (Urbana: University of Illinois Press, 2010), pp. 7–10. Some sources list the composer of "Baby Seals Blues" as Arthur Seals. See Francis Davis, *The History of the Blues* (New York: Hyperion, 1995), p. 59.

46. Muir presents this account in chapter 6, "Published Proto-Blues and the Evolution of the Twelve-Bar Sequence," *Long Lost Blues*, pp. 181–215.

47. Gordon Seagrove, "Blues Is Jazz and Jazz Is Blues," *Chicago Daily Tribune*, 11 July 1915, Part Eight, p. 8.

48. "The Offshore Pirate," in *Collected Stories of F. Scott Fitzgerald* (New York: Barnes and Noble, 2007), pp. 3–31.

49. See, for example, ads in *Chicago Defender*, 16 December 1922, p. 6, 16 June 1923, p. 20, 21 April 1923, p. 3; *New York Times*, 31 August 1923, p. 8.

50. For the story of remote recordings, see Tim Gracyk and Frank Hoffmann, *Popular American Recording Pioneers, 1895–1925* (New York: Haworth, 2000), pp. 155–56. See also Ross Laird and Brian Rust, *Discography of OKeh Records, 1918–1934* (Westport, CT: Praeger, 2004), pp. 3–6, 8–15.

51. Karl Hagstrom Miller, *Segregating Sound: Inventing Folk and Pop Music in the Age of Jim Crow* (Durham, NC: Duke University Press, 2010), pp. 180–84, 187–214.

52. For the best account of this concert and the genesis of "Rhapsody in Blue," see Howard Pollack, *George Gershwin: His Life and Work* (Berkeley: University of California Press, 2006), pp. 294–315. Thanks to Howard for his help with the paragraphs on Gershwin.

53. Alain Locke, ed., *The New Negro* (1925; rpt. New York: Touchstone, 1997), p. 216.

Chapter 8

1. Edward A. Ross, "The Causes of Race Superiority," *Annals of the American Academy of Political and Social Science* 18 (July 1901): 67–89. The quoted passages appear on p. 67. The article is discussed in Thomas F. Gossett, *Race: The History of an Idea in America* (1963; rpt. New York: Oxford University Press, 1997), pp. 168–71.

2. Ross, "The Causes of Race Superiority," p. 69.

3. Ibid,, p. 70.

4. Ibid., p. 76.

5. Ibid., p. 89.

6. For a list, see Gossett, *Race*, p. 280.

7. Gossett devoted an entire chapter to the topic of race and Social Darwinism, pp. 144–75.

8. Francis Galton, *Hereditary Genius: An Inquiry into Its Laws and Consequences* (London: Macmillan, 1869), p. 339.

9. Gossett covers Galton, the origin of eugenics, and its rise in the United States on pp. 155–59.

10. "Another Giant Departs," *New York Times*, 20 January 1911, p. 10.

11. Eugen Dühring, *Die Judenfrage als Racen-, Sitten- und Culturfrage* (Karlsruhe: H. Reuther, 1881), pp. 1–4.

12. Joseph Jacobs, *Studies in Jewish Statistics: Social, Vital, and Anthropometric* (London: D. Nutt, 1891).

13. Ibid., p. xxx (Appendix).

14. My crude estimate comes from searching the phrase "Jewish race" in ProQuest's *Historical New York Times* by decade, from the 1870s to the present, and simply using the number of articles that appear for each decade. I did not analyze the content of the articles or attempt to parse the meaning of the phrase in individual occurrences.

15. Theodore Roosevelt, *The Winning of the West*, vol. 1: *From the Alleghanies to the Mississippi, 1769–1776* (New York: G. P. Putnam's Sons, 1889), p. 331. On Roosevelt's racial attitudes toward the Indians, see Richard Slotkin, *Gunfighter Nation: The Myth of the Frontier in Twentieth Century America* (New York: Atheneum, 1992), pp. 29–62.

16. Adam Hochschild, *King Leopold's Ghost: A Story of Greed, Terror, and Heroism in Colonial Africa* (Boston: Houghton Mifflin, 1998), p. 233. Hochschild, acknowledging that reliable data are sparse, and having included outright murder, "starvation, exhaustion, and exposure," disease, and a "plummeting birth rate" as causes of death, is aware

that this figure represents a very rough estimate. See pp. 215–17 for a description of Morel's use of photography at protest meetings.

17. "Col. Williams's Charges. Stanley Says Blackmailing Has Been Attempted. A Letter to King Leopold, the Publication of Which Is Rather Late. Allegations of Bad Government on the Congo," *New York Times*, 14 April 1891, p. 1; "Williams in Middletown. He Prospered for a Time, but His True Character Was Learned," *New York Times*, 15 April 1891, p. 5. Hochschild tells the story of Williams (without mentioning these articles in the *Times*) in chapter 7, "The First Heretic," pp. 101–14.

18. (Edward) Harold Spender, "The Great Congo Iniquity," reprinted from *The Contemporary Review* in *Living Age* 250, no. 3239 (4 August 1906): 259–68. The quoted passage appears on p. 266.

19. Booker T. Washington, "Cruelty in the Congo Country," *Outlook* 78 (October 8, 1904): 375–77.

20. Mark Twain, *King Leopold's Soliloquy* (Boston: P. R. Warren, 1905), p. 40.

21. "The Negro—a Vassal or a Citizen," *Congregationalist and Christian World* 88, no. 17 (April 25, 1903): 583. Hillis's words are reported in "Dr. Hillis Demands Vote for the Negro. Denounces the Views of Mr. Cleveland and Dr. Abbott," *New York Times*, 18 May 1903, p. 6.

22. G. Stanley Hall, *Adolescence: Its Psychology and Its Relations to Physiology, Anthropology, Sociology, Sex, Crime, Religion, and Education* (New York: D. Appleton, 1904), vol. 2, chap. 18, "Ethnic Psychology and Pedagogy, or Adolescent Races and Their Treatment," pp. 648–748.

23. "Proceedings of the Thirteenth Universal Peace Congress (Continued)," *Advocate of Peace* 67, no. 2 (February 1905): 41–45. Gossett discusses Hall's racial attitudes in *Race*, pp. 154–55.

24. Édouard Drumont, *La France juive: Essai d'histoire contemporaine* (Jewish France: Essay on Contemporary History) (Paris: Blériot, 1885), p. 108.

25. Barrès, *Scènes et doctrines du nationalisme* (Paris: Félix Juven, 1902), pp. 152–53. This passage is partially quoted in Michael Marrus, "Popular Anti-Semitism," in Norman L. Kleeblatt, ed., *The Dreyfus Affair: Art, Truth, and Justice* (Berkeley: University of California Press, 1987), p. 59. Marrus stacks the deck by leaving out all reference to the final sentence.

26. "Vindex," "The Case of Captain Dreyfus," *Forum*, June 1897, pp. 448–62. The quoted material appears on pp. 450, 454–55.

27. "The Case of Capt. Dreyfus," *New York Times*, 15 October 1897, p. 6.

28. "The Jews," *New York Observer* 76, no. 5 (3 February 1898): 139.

29. "A Modern Tragedy," *Outlook* 83, no. 12 (July 21, 1906): 640–41.

30. Edward Alsworth Ross, "The Hebrews of Eastern Europe in America," *Century* 88, no. 5 (September 1914): 785–92. The article appeared in the book as a chapter with the title "The East European Hebrews," in *The Old World in the New: The Significance of Past and Present Immigration to the American People* (New York: Century, 1914), pp. 143–67. Alan M. Kraut has some good pages on conflicting attitudes toward Jews in the United States in *Silent Travelers: Germs, Genes, and the "Immigrant Menace"* (New York: Basic Books, 1994), pp. 136–65.

31. Mark Twain, "Concerning the Jews," *Harper's New Monthly Magazine*, 99, no. 592 (September 1899): 526–35.

32. Burton J. Hendrick, "The Great Jewish Invasion," *McClure's Magazine* 28, no. 3 (January 1907): 307–21.

33. Burton J. Hendrick, "The Jewish Invasion of America," *McClure's Magazine* 40, no. 5 (March 1913): 125–65.

34. For example, Jacob Rader Marcus, *United States Jewry, 1776–1985: The Germanic Period, Part 2* (Detroit, MI: Wayne State University Press, 1993), p. 177; and Leonard Dinnerstein, *Antisemitism in America* (New York: Oxford University Press, 1994), p. 61.

35. James Weldon Johnson, *Along This Way: The Autobiography of James Weldon Johnson* (New York: Viking, 1933), p. 341.

36. "Negro Troopers in Riot," *New York Times*, 5 July 1919, p. 5.

37. Lothrop Stoddard, *The Rising Tide of Color against White World-Supremacy* (New York: Scribner's, 1920), p. 5.

38. Ibid., p. 90.

39. Ibid., p. 220.

40. According to Kenneth T. Jackson, in *The Ku Klux Klan in the City, 1915–1930* (New York: Oxford University Press, 1967), p. 129.

41. Kevin Boyle, *Arc of Justice: A Saga of Race, Civil Rights, and Murder in the Jazz Age* (New York: Henry Holt, 2004), 141–43.

42. *The International Jew: The World's Foremost Problem* (Dearborn, MI: Dearborn Independent, 1920–22), 2: 20.

43. Neil Baldwin, *Henry Ford and the Jews: The Mass Production of Hate* (New York: PublicAffairs, 2001), pp. 172–73.

44. Adolf Hitler, *Mein Kampf* (Munich: Verlag Franz Eher Nachfolger, 1925–27), 2: 298. The most widely available English translation renders the words slightly differently. See Adolf Hitler, *Mein Kampf*, trans. Ralph Manheim (New York: Houghton Mifflin, 1943), p. 639.

45. See article in the *New York Times*, 31 July 1938, p. 1.

46. E. G. Pipp, *The Real Henry Ford* (Detroit: Pipp's Weekly, 1922), p. 21. Cited in Robert Singerman, "The American Career of the *Protocols of the Elders of Zion*," *American Jewish History* 71, no. 1 (September 1981): 72.

47. For the extremely complicated story of Brasol and the various translations of the *Protocols*, see Singerman, "The American Career," 48–78. Brasol's translation appeared as part of a book: *The Protocols and World Revolution: Including a Translation and Analysis of the "Protocols of the Meetings of the Zionist Men of Wisdom"* (Boston: Small, Maynard, 1920). The translation used in the *Dearborn Independent* was the brainchild of Harris Ayres Houghton, a doctor who worked for the U.S. War Department, but it was published, without his name, as *Præmonitus præmunitus* ["Forewarned is Forearmed"]: *The Protocols of the Wise Men of Zion* (New York: Beckwith, 1920).

48. "Proof That the 'Jewish Protocols' Were Forged," *New York Times*, 4 September 1921, Sect. 7, p. 1.

49. E. J. Dillon, *The Inside Story of the Peace Conference* (New York: Harper and Brothers, 1920), p. 12.

50. *The Protocols and World Revolution*, p. 124.

51. Ibid., p. 149.

52. *The International Jew*, 1: 166. My emphasis.

53. Ibid., 2: 138.

54. F. M. Dostoievsky, *The Diary of a Writer*, trans. Boris Brasol (New York: G. Braziller, 1949). For the phrase *status in statu*, see pp. 645–50.

55. Baldwin, *Henry Ford and the Jews*, pp. 144–46.

56. Ibid., pp. 204–40.

57. Burton J. Hendrick, "The Jews in America," *World's Work* 45 (November 1922–April 1923): 266–86, 373.

58. Ibid., pp. 144, 266.

59. Ibid., p. 377.

60. Boyle, *Arc of Justice*.

61. David E. Lilienthal, "Has the Negro the Right of Self-Defense?," *Nation* 121, no. 3155 (23 December 1925): 724–25. Mentioned in Boyle, *Arc of Justice*, p. 301.

62. "1,500 Hail Attack on Race Isolation," *New York Times*, 4 January 1926, p. 7.

63. "Doctors in Harlem Hear Dr. O. H. Sweet," *Chicago Defender*, 9 January 1926, p. 2.

64. Alain Locke, ed., *The New Negro* (1925; rpt. New York: Touchstone, 1997), pp. 7, 11.

65. Ibid., p. 14.

66. Ibid., p. 411.

67. The classic statement of this principle is Ernest Gellner's definition of nationalism: "In brief, nationalism is a theory of political legitimacy, which requires that ethnic boundaries should not cut across political ones, and, in particular, that ethnic boundaries within a given state . . . should not separate the power-holders from the rest." See *Nations and Nationalism* (Oxford, UK: Blackwell, 1983), p. 1.

Chapter 9

1. Abbott published the speech in *Outlook* 96, no. 12 (19 November 1910): 639–41.

2. Francis A. Henry, "The Critical Study of the Scriptures," *Princeton Review* (July–December 1883): 294–320. The quoted passage appears on p. 294.

3. Ibid., p. 295.

4. Ibid., p. 320.

5. In an excellent article on the reception of Strauss's *Life of Jesus*, Erik Linstrum names a number of predecessors to Strauss in the tradition of describing scriptural stories as mythic. See "Strauss's *Life of Jesus:* Publication and the Politics of the German Public Sphere," *Journal of the History of Ideas* 71, no. 4 (October 2010): 593–616.

6. D. H. Lawrence, *Sons and Lovers* (New York: Mitchell Kennerley, 1913), p. 280. I told the same story in *Dostoevsky's Religion* (Stanford: Stanford University Press, 2005), p. 42

7. The syllabus was printed in "Professor Briggs's Inaugural Address," *The Independent* 43, no. 2200 (29 January 1891): 16.

8. "Charles A. Briggs," *The Independent* 74, no. 3367 (12 June 1913): 1323.

9. Lyman Abbott, *The Life and Literature of the Ancient Hebrews* (Boston: Houghton Mifflin, 1901), pp. 9–10.

10. "Dr. Abbott on Traditions," *New York Times*, 15 May 1897, p. 3.

11. "The Bible as Literature. Dr. Lyman Abbott Concludes His Lectures on Higher Criticism," *New York Times*, 30 January 1899, p. 2.

12. "Dr. Abbott on St. Paul," *New York Times*, 22 November 1897, p. 8.

13. "The Bible as Literature," p. 2.

14. "Rabbis Censure New York Jewish Seminary," *New York Times*, 4 July 1904, p. 5.

15. Quoted in "Full Text of the Papal Syllabus," *New York Times*, 4 August 1907, Part Three, p. 4.

16. Joseph Jacobs, "The Religion of Israel," *New York Times*, 4 December 1910, Literary Section, p. 18.

17. "Dr. Wise on the Bible," *New York Times*, 31 December 1923, p. 5.

18. Paul S. Boyer, "*In His Steps:* A Reappraisal," *American Quarterly* 23, no. 1 (Spring 1971): 60–78.

19. Charles M. Sheldon, *In His Steps: "What Would Jesus Do?"* (Chicago: Advance Publishing, 1898), pp. 23–24.

20. Walter Rauschenbusch, *Christianity and the Social Crisis* (New York: Macmillan, 1907), pp. 64, 161.

21. Ibid., pp. 26–28.

22. Ibid., pp. 56–59.

23. Ibid., p. 60.

24. Walter Rauschenbusch, *A Theology for the Social Gospel* (New York: Macmillan, 1917), p. 142.

25. Rauschenbusch cited Kant in a footnote to *A Theology for the Social Gospel* (p. 139, n. 1). Kant's statement of the "practical imperative" is from *Groundwork of the Metaphysics of Morals.* See Immanuel Kant, *Werke*, ed. Wilhelm Weischedel (Frankfurt am Main: Suhrkamp, 1956–64), 7: 61 (my translation). He writes of the kingdom of God, man as an end in himself, and the categorical imperative as the highest good in the *Critique of Practical Reason.* See Kant, *Werke*, 7: 259, 263, 266.

26. Shailer Mathews, *The Social Teaching of Jesus: An Essay in Christian Sociology* (New York: Macmillan, 1897), pp. 53–54.

27. "The Kingdom of God; A Symposium," *Biblical World* 12, no. 1 (July 1898): 12–19.

28. Shailer Mathews and Gerald Birney Smith, eds., *A Dictionary of Religion and Ethics* (New York: Macmillan, 1921), p. 254.

29. Harry F. Ward, *The Social Creed of the Churches* (New York: Abingdon Press, 1914), pp. 6–7.

30. On the Federal Council of Churches, see Susan Curtis, *A Consuming Faith: The Social Gospel and Modern American Culture* (Baltimore, MD: Johns Hopkins University Press, 1991), pp. 142–44, 177–78.

31. Frederick D. Smith, "The Forward Movement," *New York Times*, 4 June 1911, Sunday Magazine, p. 14.

32. "Forward Movement Ends Its Campaign," *New York Times*, 25 April 1912, p. 12.

33. "The Religious Movement," *New York Times*, 26 April 1912, p. 10; and Clarence A. Barbour, ed., *Making Religion Efficient* (New York: Association Press, 1912), p. 7.

34. *Messages of the Men and Religion Movement*, vol. 2: *Social Service* (New York: Funk and Wagnalls, 1912), p. 18.

35. Barbour, *Making Religion Efficient*, p. 8.

36. "See 33 Evils in Slums," *Washington Post*, 16 February 1912, p. 2.

37. "Hard Hitters, These Experts," *Los Angeles Times*, 15 March 1912, p. 18.

38. "Unite in Oak Park for Forward Move," *Chicago Daily Tribune*, 4 November 1911, p. 8.

39. John A. Hutchinson, *We Are Not Divided: A Critical and Historical Study of the Federal Council of the Churches of Christ in America* (New York: Round Table Press, 1941), p. 30.

40. Charles S. Macfarland, *Spiritual Culture and Social Service* (New York: Fleming H. Revell, 1912), pp. 81, 83, 88.

41. John Fiske, *Through Nature to God* (Boston: Houghton Mifflin, 1899), pp. 105, 122.

42. Macfarland, *Spiritual Culture*, p. 83.

43. Henry Drummond, *The Lowell Lectures on the Ascent of Man* (New York: James Pott, 1894), pp. 240–41.

44. Ibid., pp. 233–34.

45. Ibid., p. 18.

46. Felix Adler, *An Ethical Philosophy of Life Presented in Its Main Outlines* (New York: D. Appleton, 1918), pp. 6–7.

47. Ibid., p. 243.

48. Felix Adler, *The Religion of Duty* (New York: McClure, Phillips, 1905), pp. 91, 102.

49. *Life* 30, no. 784 (23 December 1897): p. 554.

50. On the Pittsburgh Platform and the response to it, see Michael A. Meyer, *Response to Modernity: A History of the Reform Movement in Judaism* (New York: Oxford University Press, 1988), pp. 268–70.

51. On the CCAR and its development of a social program, see ibid., pp. 288–89. The text of the declaration from the era may be found in *Annals of the American Academy of Political and Social Science* 85, no. 174 (September 1919): 115.

52. Wise himself told the story and reprinted the bulk of the pamphlet in *Challenging Years: The Autobiography of Stephen Wise* (London: East and West Library, 1951), pp. 30–40. For another account, see Melvin I. Urofsky, *A Voice That Spoke for Justice: The Life and Times of Stephen S. Wise* (Albany: State University of New York Press, 1982), pp. 49–58.

53. Sidney E. Goldstein, *The Synagogue and Social Welfare: A Unique Experiment (1907–1953)* (New York: Bloch Publishing Company, 1955), p. 48.

54. Ibid., p. 185.

55. Ibid., p. 186.

56. "Union Meeting of Synagogue and Church," in Stephen S. Wise, *Free Synagogue Pulpit: Sermons and Addresses by Stephen S. Wise*, vol. 2 (New York: Bloch Publishing

Company, 1910), pp. 155–70. The quoted passage appears on p. 169. For the most complete account of the union services, see Robert D. Shapiro, *A Reform Rabbi in the Progressive Era: The Early Career of Stephen S. Wise* (New York: Garland Publishing, 1988), pp. 219–31.

57. Walter Rauschenbusch, *Dare We Be Christians* (New York: Pilgrim Press, 1914), p. 32.

58. Adler, *An Ethical Philosophy*, p. 340.

59. Richard Hofstadter, *The Age of Reform: From Bryan to F.D.R.* (New York: Knopf, 1955), p. 203.

60. Robert M. Crunden, *Ministers of Reform: The Progressives' Achievement in American Civilization, 1889–1920* (NY: Basic Books, 1982), p. 277.

Chapter 10

1. Maurice Maeterlinck, *The Life of the Bee*, trans. Alfred Sutro (New York: Dodd, Mead, 1901), pp. 3–4.

2. Ibid., p. 32.

3. Ibid., p. 30.

4. Ibid., pp. 30–31.

5. Ibid., p. 31.

6. Ibid., p. 33.

7. Ibid., p. 40.

8. Ibid., p. 110.

9. Edwin E. Slosson, "Maurice Maeterlinck," *The Independent* 70, no. 3257 (4 May 1911): 933–45. The book was *Major Prophets of To-day* (Boston: Little, Brown, 1914).

10. Ernest Ingersoll, "An Epic of Bees," *New York Times*, 31 August 1901, p. BR 3.

11. Axel Emil Gibson, "Maurice Maeterlinck and the Bees," *Arena* 27, no. 4 (April 1902): 381–86. The quoted passage appears on pp. 382–83.

12. Thomas H. Huxley, "The Struggle for Existence in Human Society," reprinted in Petr Kropotkin, *Mutual Aid: A Factor of Evolution* (New York, 1902; rpt. Boston: Extending Horizons Books, 1955), pp. 329–41. The quoted passage appears on p. 330.

13. Kropotkin, *Mutual Aid*, p. 332.

14. Henry Drummond, *The Lowell Lectures on the Ascent of Man* (New York: James Pott, 1894), p. 239; Kropotkin, *Mutual Aid*, p. xiv.

15. Kropotkin, *Mutual Aid*, p. 300.

16. Today, with decades' more observation and with more sophisticated methods at their disposal than Kropotkin had, biologists speak of "inclusive fitness," by which they mean the fitness of an individual to produce its own offspring *plus* that individual's fitness to produce genetically related offspring by acts of altruism toward other closely related members of its own species. *Kin selection* is the name for the type of natural selection that favors altruism of this sort. In addition, modern biologists speak of "reciprocal altruism," a phrase that refers to an individual's willingness, at a risk to itself, to help a nonrelated individual, in the expectation that that individual will return the favor, at a

risk to *itself.* For instance, if two unrelated male lions, each at the risk of sacrificing his own life, take turns protecting the pride (social group) from other marauding males, they will increase their own fitness—so long as neither one cheats and both continue to cooperate and reciprocate. Finally, "mutualism" refers to a form of cooperation where both individuals benefit at little or no cost to themselves. Cleaner fish (a type of fish) pick off and eat parasites and dead skin from larger predatory fish, which, in exchange for the favor, provide nourishment to the cleaners (in the form of parasites and dead skin) and refrain from eating them. Neither fish risks much in the arrangement, so this is a form of mutualism. Or, to return to lions, if two unrelated males fight marauders *together*, not by turns, the males can be said to be practicing mutualism (because an individual cannot succeed on its own). Thanks to my colleague, evolutionary biologist Lin Chao, for explaining and clarifying these concepts, for supplying the hypothetical example of the male lions, and for checking the accuracy of this note.

17. Ashley Montagu, "Foreword," in Kropotkin, *Mutual Aid* (unnumbered pages).

18. Robert H. Wiebe, *The Search for Order, 1877–1920* (New York: Hill and Wang, 1967), chapter 3, "Crisis in the Communities," pp. 44–75.

19. Edward Alsworth Ross, *Social Control: A Survey of the Foundations of Order* (New York: Macmillan, 1901), p. 5. For an excellent analysis and historical account of Ross's theory, see Dorothy Ross, *The Origins of American Social Science* (Cambridge: Cambridge University Press, 1991), pp. 229–53.

20. Ross, *Social Control*, pp. 1–2.

21. Ibid., pp. 7–8.

22. Herbert Croly, *The Promise of American Life* (New York: Macmillan, 1909), pp. 265–66.

23. Ibid., p. 453.

24. Charles Horton Cooley, *Social Organization: A Study of the Larger Mind* (New York: Charles Scribner's Sons, 1909), pp. 3–4.

25. Charles Horton Cooley, *Human Nature and the Social Order* (New York: Charles Scribner's Sons, 1902), p. 102.

26. Ibid., p. 24.

27. Ibid., pp. 395–419.

28. Ellen H. Richards, *Euthenics: The Science of Controllable Environment: A Plea for Better Living Conditions as a First Step Toward Higher Human Efficiency* (Boston: Whitcomb and Barrows, 1910), pp. 132, 133.

29. Ibid., p. 40.

30. Bliss Perry, *The American Mind: The E. T. Earl Lectures* (Boston: Houghton Mifflin, 1912), pp. 236–37.

31. "The Federal Power Exalted," *New York Times*, 30 June 1906, p. 6.

32. Wiebe, *Search for Order*, p. 31.

33. "The Galveston Disaster," *New York Times*, 12 September 1900, p. 6.

34. "Whole Country Sends Aid," *New York Times*, 13 September 1900, p. 2.

35. On the Galveston storm and the response to it, see David G. McComb, *Galveston: A History* (Austin: University of Texas Press, 1986), pp. 121–49.

36. Philip Fradkin, *The Great Earthquake and Firestorms of 1906: How San Francisco Nearly Destroyed Itself* (Berkeley: University of California Press, 2005), pp. 74–75, 188–91.

37. See http://oac.cdlib.org/view?docId=hb3k40057z;NAAN=13030&doc.view=frames&chunk.id=div00001&toc.depth=1&toc.id=div00001&brand=oac4.

38. "Der morg iz ful mit unzere korbones!" *Forverts (Jewish Daily Forward)*, 26 March 1911, p. 1.

39. David Von Drehle, *Triangle: The Fire That Changed America* (New York: Grove Press, 2003), chap. 8, "Reform," pp. 194–218.

40. Ibid., pp. 195–96.

41. Ibid., pp. 206–12.

42. Henry Moskowitz, "The Joint Board of Sanitary Control in the Cloak, Suit and Skirt Industry of New York City," *Annals of the American Academy of Political and Social Science* 44 (November 1912): 42–43.

43. G. M. Prais (Price), *Russkie evrei v Amerike* (Russian Jews in America) (St. Petersburg: A. E. Landau, 1893).

44. G. M. Prays (Price), *Di Yuden in Amerika* (Odessa: Be-defus Aba Dukhno, 1891).

45. "Received: Erzei v. Ameriki. By George M. Price, M.D. New York. Published in Petersburg. Price, 1 ruble," *Times and Register* 30, no. 26 (28 December 1895), p. 510.

46. Von Drehle, *Triangle*, pp. 213–15.

47. As quoted in "Factory Reform Urged," *New York Times*, 20 February 1913, p. 7.

48. "The Roots of Social Security by Frances Perkins," http: //www.ssa.gov/history/perkins5.html.

49. Wiebe, *Search for Order*, pp. 293–97.

Conclusion

1. "When the Rush Hours Come in New York's Telephone System," *New York Times*, 27 September 1908, Sunday Magazine, p. 7.

2. Louise Arnold, "After College—What?" *Simmons Quarterly* 1, no. 4 (April 1911): 1–4.

3. In *The Philosophy of History*. G. W. F. Hegel, *Werke in zwanzig Bänden*, ed. Eva Moldenhauer and Karl Markus Michel (Frankfurt am Main: Suhrkamp, 1970): 12: 495–96.

4. Henry Drummond, *The Lowell Lectures on the Ascent of Man* (New York: James Pott, 1894), pp. 285–86.

Notes

Abbott, Lyman, 188–90, 195, 198, 218–19, 228; "The Bible as Literature" (lecture series), 224–25; and higher criticism, 224–25; on religion of service, 218; and Social Gospel Movement, 228
Acton, William, 47. *See also* sex manuals
Addams, Jane, 245
Adler, Felix, 218–19, 238–40, 242–43, 245. Works: *An Ethical Philosophy of Life*, 238–39, 243; *A Religion of Duty*, 239. *See also* Ethical Culture
Agassiz, Louis, 40
Alcott, Louisa May, 127
Alcott, William A., 127
Aldrich, Richard, 164–65
altruism, 236–37, 252, 302–3n16; reciprocal (in evolutionary theory), 302–3n16
American Experience Table, 10–11, 14
American Federation for Sex Hygiene, 54. *See also* sex education; sex hygiene
American Home Economics Association, 131. *See also* home economics
American Public Health Association (APHA), 4–9; *A Half Century of Public Health*, 5–8, 15; Jubilee meeting, 4–9, 15–16; Vital Statistics section, 9. *See also* Public Health Movement
American Social Health Association, 54. *See also* sex hygiene
American Social Hygiene Association, 54. *See also* sex hygiene
American Society of Sanitary and Moral Prophylaxis, 52, 54. *See also* sex education; sex hygiene
American Temperance Society, xvi
American Tobacco Company, 153–54
American Vigilance Association, 54
American Watch Company. *See* Waltham Watch Company
anti-kissing campaign, 29
Anti-Semitic League of France, 192. *See also* Dreyfus Affair
anti-Semitism, 182, 192–99, 202–10, 215
appliances, household, 122–24
Aristotle, 95–97; *Physics*, 95–96
Arnold, Sarah Louise, 268
Association for the Study and Prevention of Tuberculosis, 22
Atkinson, (J.) Brooks, 85
AT&T, 126
attire, women's, 6; short skirts, 6, 20–21

bacteria, 6, 21, 23, 33–34. *See also* bacteriology; germs; germ theory of disease; Public Health Movement
bacteriology, 23, 28, 30–36, 127. *See also* bacteria; germs; germ theory of disease; Public Health Movement, bacteriological phase
Baker, Ray Stannard, 77
bananas, 149–51
Barnet, Richard J., 144
Barrès, Maurice, 193–94; *Scènes et doctrines du nationalisme*, 193–94
Bartky, Ian R., 106, 109
Barton, Clara, 257
Battle Creek Sanitarium, 46
Beard, George M., 75; *American Nervousness: Its Causes and Consequences*, 75
Beecher, Catherine, 127. Works: *The American Woman's Home*, 127; *A Treatise on Domestic Economy*, 127. *See also* Stowe, Harriet Beecher
Beecher, Henry Ward, 224
Bell Telephone, 124
benevolent surveillance, 256, 264
Benson, Allan L., 11–12
Bergson, Henri: Columbia University lectures, 42–43, 78–84, 85–86, 92, 97–98, 113–15, 247, 283n54; on death, conquest of, 42–43, 82, 83; on deep self vs. superficial self, 80, 83, 102–3, 271; on evolution, 42–44, 81, 82; on freedom of will, 80, 82–83, 115; on intuition, 42, 81, 82–83, 114–15; on mind as independent of brain and nervous system, 43, 78–84; on real duration, 79–80, 83, 102–3, 114–15, 272; on scientifically measured time, 44, 79–80, 92, 97–98, 101–3, 115, 271; on social life, 102–3; on "vital impulse" (*élan vital*), 42, 81, 82; Zeno's Paradoxes of Motion and, 97–98. Works: *Creative Evolution* (*l'Évolution créatrice*), 43–44, 65, 81–83, 86; *Matter and Memory* (*Matière et mémoire*), 79–81; *Time and Free Will* (*Essai sur les données immédiates de la conscience*), 79–80, 98, 102–3, 271
Berlin, Edward A., 162–63
Berlin, Irving, 163, 173; *Alexander's Ragtime Band*, 163
Berlin Conference (on Africa), 158–59
Bernstein, Herman, 204, 206
Betts, Lillian W., 135
Bible (Hebrew Bible and New Testament), 219–29; inerrancy in, 223; miracles recounted in, 223. *See also* documentary hypothesis; higher criticism
Bible, Hebrew, 222–23. *See also* documentary hypothesis; higher criticism
Bible League of North America, 40
Billings, John S., 12
biological self, 17–44, 115, 124, 140–41, 270. *See also* network, biological self as; network, biological self as part of
biology, xviii, 18, 26, 33–35, 272
birth control, 60–65
birth, registration of, 9–11. *See also* life, expectation of; infant mortality; vital statistics
Bismarck, Otto von, 158, 253; Berlin Conference (on Africa), 158–59
Black Plague. *See* venereal disease
Blanck, Max, 259. *See also* Triangle Waist Company, fire
blues, 160–74; ballad, 167; definition, 161–62; origin, 161; twelve-bar form, 167–68
B'nai Jeshurun Synagogue (New York City), 241
Bolshevik Revolution, 201, 205
Bolshevism, 201, 204
Bond & Son, 106–7
Bonsack, James Albert, 153
Boston Fruit Company, 151; Great White Fleet, 151. *See also* bananas
Boston School of Housekeeping, 131, 134. *See also* Simmons College, Household Economics, Department of

Boveri, Theodor, 50
Boyle, Kevin, 212
Bradford, Perry, 171; "Crazy Blues," 171–72
Brasol, Boris: and Henry Ford, 204–6; on Jewish "state within a state," 204–6; translator of Dostoevsky, *Diary of a Writer*, 206
Breguet, Abraham-Louis, 99
Breguet, Antoine, 99–100
Breguet, Louis-François-Clément, 99
Breguet (watch manufacturer), 99
Breuer, Josef, 88
Briggs, Charles A.: and higher criticism, 222–24; tried by Presbyterian Church, 223–24
Brill, A. A., 49, 86–87, 284n9. *See also* Freud, Sigmund, *Interpretation of Dreams*
British Association for the Advancement of Science, 17
British Eugenics Society, 61
Brown, Helen Gurley, 35
Bryan, William Jennings, 41, 212, 245
bunny hug (dance), 162
Bush, Wendell T., 114

Cahan, Abraham, 207, 262. *See also Jewish Daily Forward*
cakewalk (dance), 162–63
Carrel, Alexis, 19, 36–39, 197; general vs. elemental death, 37–38; immortality of tissues, 36–39. *See also* life, prolongation of; Metchnikoff, Elie
Casson, Herbert N., 124–25
Castle, Irene and Vernon, 163, 169
Catholic Church, Catholicism, 225–26, 244, 270
cells, xviii, 19–20, 24–26, 33–34; doctrine, 24–26, 36; extending life of after death of organism, 18–19. *See also* organs; tissues
Census Bureau, 12–13
Central Conference of American Rabbis (CCAR), 240–41; declaration of principles, 240–41
Chapin, Charles V., 7–8, 9–10, 15, 28–29. *See also* Public Health Movement
Charcot, Jean-Martin, 72, 74–75, 76
Chase, Harry W., 88–91
Chiquita Brands International, 150. *See also* bananas
cholera, 4, 7, 53
chromosomes, 24–25, 50–52, 269, 272
Churchill, Winston, 144
cigarettes, 151–57; advertising, 152–57; Camel (brand), 151–52, 156; Chesterfield (brand), 156; Fatima (brand), 154; Lucky Strike (brand), 156; Pall Mall (brand), 155–56; Philip Morris (brand), 153–54; rolling machines, 153; Turkey Red (brand), 154–55. *See also* tobacco
Civil War, 111, 118, 224
Clef Club Orchestra. *See* Europe, James Reese
Cleveland, Grover, 189–90
clocks. *See* watches and clocks
clubs, women's, 135–36, 140
collectivity, 44
colloidal compounds, 18, 280n2. *See also* Schäfer, Edward A.
color perception, 70–72; trichromatic theory of, 70. *See also* Helmholtz, Hermann von; Müller, Johannes; Young, Thomas
Commission on the Church and Social Service, 235
Committee on Diphtheria Bacilli in Well Persons (Charles V. Chapin), 29
Congo, 143, 157–60, 186–91, 215–16, 271
Congo Reform Association, 186, 189–91
Conn, Herbert W: *The Story of Germ Life*, 23; *The Story of the Living Machine*, 24, 50
Connecticut River basin: ivory trade in, 157, 160
Conservative Judaism, 225
Consumers' League, 260
continence (sexual), 45–49, 53–54, 58, 59
contraception. *See* birth control

Cooley, Charles H.: *Social Organization*, 253
Cooley, Winifred Harper: *The New Womanhood*, 135–36
cooperation, xvii, 14–16, 235–45, 247–51, 265, 270; in Ethical Culture, 239; in Protestantism, 235–38; in Reform Judaism, 240–43. *See also* network, of cooperation
Coriat, Isador H., 76–77
Coulter, John M., 41, 56
Cowan, John, 46–47, 49. *See also* sex manuals
Crawford, Mary Caroline, 132–33
Croly, Herbert: *The Promise of American Life*, 147, 252–53
Croly, Jane Cunningham, 147; *Jennie June's American Cookery Book*, 147, 149
Croton Aqueduct, 119, 126
Crunden, Robert M.: *Ministers of Reform*, 245
Cummings, E. E.: *Him*, 84–85
Curtis, Natalie, 165

Damrosch, Walter, 173
Dana, James Dwight, 40
Darrow, Clarence, 212–13. *See also* Sweet, Ossian
Darwin, Charles, 19, 21, 219–20, 230, 236–37, 249, 252, 269. Works: *The Descent of Man*, 40; *On the Origin of Species*, 39–40, 219. *See also* evolution, theory of; natural selection
Darwinism. *See* evolution, theory of
Daylight Saving Bill. *See* Standard Time Act
Dearborn Independent (newspaper), 202–10. *See also* Ford, Henry
death: accidental vs. natural, 33–34, 38; conquest of, 36–39, 43–44; general vs. elemental, 37–38; rate, 5; registration of, 9–11. *See also* birth, registration of; Carrel, Alexis; immortality; Metchnikoff, Elie; vital statistics
Dempsey, Jack, 3
Dennett, Mary Ware, 60
Dennison, Aaron Lufkin, 111
Detroit, 201–2, 211–13
Detroit Stove Works, 122
Dewey, Melvil, 130
diaphragm (birth control device), 61
Dillon, E. J., 204–5
diphtheria, 4, 7
Disaster Relief Act, 263
disasters, 256–65. *See also* Galveston, hurricane; San Francisco, earthquake; Triangle Waist Company, fire
Dix, Dorothy (Elizabeth Meriwether Gilmer), 55
documentary hypothesis, 222. *See also* higher criticism; Wellhausen, Julius
Dole, Charles F., 190
Dole, James Drummond, 146, 148–49, 190
Dole Corp., 146
Dolge, Alfred, 143
domestic science. *See* home economics
Dostoevsky, Fedor, 206; *Diary of a Writer*, 206
Doyle, Arthur Conan, 189
Dreyfus, Alfred, 191–99
Dreyfus Affair, 191–99, 240
Drummond, Henry, 236–37, 250, 272; *The Lowell Lectures on the Ascent of Man*, 237, 250, 272
Drumont, Édouard, 192–93; *La France juive*, 192–93. *See also* Anti-Semitic League of France; anti-Semitism; Dreyfus Affair
Du Bois, W. E. B., 177; "The Negro Mind Reaches Out," 214–16; *The Souls of Black Folk*, 177. *See also The New Negro*
Dühring, Eugen, 182–83, 193, 203
Duke, James Buchanan, 153
Dunan, Charles, 97
dust (agent of disease), 21, 123. *See also* Public Health Movement, sanitarian phase
Dvořák, Antonín, 164

ebony, 143
Eckes, Alfred E., Jr., 144
ecumenism, 244–45
Edward VII, King, 155
Edwards, Rebecca, 47
efficiency, 116, 133, 134, 136–38, 140, 233–34. *See also* Frederick, Christine
Ehrlich, Paul, 31
Einstein, Albert, 99
electricity, 122–23, 126
Elgar, Edward, 173
Eliot, Charles W., 54–55, 57. *See also* sex education; sex hygiene
Eliot, George (Mary Ann Evans), 221
Ellis, Havelock, 55, 63–64. Works: *Studies in the Psychology of Sex*, 58; *The Task of Social Hygiene*, 64
Emin Pasha (Eduard Schnitzer), 159–60
Emmanuel Church, Protestant-Episcopal, 76
Emmanuel Movement, 76–78
Esterhazy, Ferdinand Walsin, 192
Ethical Culture, 218–19, 238–40, 243. *See also* Adler, Felix
eugenics, 61–65, 181–82
Eugenics Publishing Company, 61
Europe, James Reese, 165–66; Clef Club Orchestra, 165–66; Society Orchestra, 169
euthenics. *See* Richards, Ellen Henrietta Swallow
evolution, theory of, 18, 31, 81, 179, 231, 236–37, 270; and cooperation, 248–52; public attitudes toward, 40–41. *See also* Darwin, Charles; natural selection

Factory Investigating Commission, 263
Farmer, Fannie, 148; *Boston Cooking-School Cook Book*, 149
February Revolution (Russia), 249
Federal Council of Churches, 232, 235, 240; "Social Creed of the Churches," 232, 240
Fichte, Johann Gottlieb: "Addresses to the German Nation," 268
Field, Marshall, 137
filth theory of disease, 27–28. *See also* Public Health Movement, sanitarian phase
Fisher, Irving, 11, 22; *National Vitality, Its Wastes and Conservation*, 11
Fisk Jubilee Singers, 161
Fiske, John, 236–37; *Outlines of Cosmic Philosophy*, 236; *Through Nature to God*, 236
Fitzgerald, F. Scott, 170–71, 201. Works: *The Great Gatsby*, 201; "The Offshore Pirate," 170–71
Flemming, Walther, 24
flu. *See* influenza pandemic of 1918–19
Ford, Henry, 202–10; *Dearborn Independent*, 202–10; *The International Jew*, 202–3
Ford Motor Company, 202
Foster, Allyn K., 234
Foster, Stephen, 164
fox-trot (dance), 163, 169
Fradkin, Philip L., 257–58
France, Anatole 189
Frederick, Christine, 116–19, 127, 129, 133, 136–38, 234; Efficiency Kitchen, 116–17, 130; *The New Housekeeping*, 117, 234. *See also* home economics; scientific management
Free Synagogue, 218, 241–42; Social Service Division, 241–42. *See also* Wise, Stephen S.
Freud, Sigmund, 48–49, 67–68, 80, 83, 84–92; on childhood sexuality, 88–89; at Clark University, 69, 87–88, 190; on dreams, 48–49, 86–89; on impulses (drives, instincts), 87–89; and psychoanalysis, 88–92; on repression, 87, 89; on sexuality, 48, 87–92; on unconscious, 87–92, 272. Works: *Interpretation of Dreams*, 49, 86–89; *Three Contributions to the Sexual Theory*, 88
Friedan, Betty, 118

Friml, Rudolf, 173
Fundamentalism, 41

Galison, Peter, 99, 101
Galton, Francis, 61, 63, 181–83; *Hereditary Genius*, 181–82
Galveston, Texas, hurricane, 256–57
Garrison, William Lloyd, 46
Garvey, Marcus, 214; pan-Africanism of, 214–15
gas (coal, for heating and lighting), 122, 126; ranges, 122
Geddes, Patrick, 51
Gellner, Ernest: definition of nationalism, 299n67
genes, xvii, 269, 272
genetics, 40, 50–52, 181, 269
germs, 20–23; and aging, 32–33; and facial hair, 20–22; and short skirts, 20–21. *See also* bacteria; bacteriology; germ theory of disease; Public Health Movement
germ theory of disease, 23, 24, 25, 29–30, 34, 122. *See also* bacteria; bacteriology; germs; Public Health Movement
Gershwin, George, 172–73. Works: "Rhapsody in Blue," 172–73; "Swanee," 173
Gibson, Axel Emil, 248
Gilbreth, Frank and Lillian, 136
Gilmer, Elizabeth Meriwether. *See* Dix, Dorothy
Gladden, Washington, 228, 232. *See also* Social Gospel Movement
globalization, 144–45, 172–73
Goddard, H. H., 63
Goldman, Emma, 60
Goldstein, Sidney E., 242
Goodman, Benny, 169
Good Samaritan, parable of, 226
Gould, Stephen J., 63
gonorrhea, 52–53
Gordin, Jacob, 262
Gospel(s), 220–21, 236; Luke, 226; Matthew, 227
Gossett, Thomas F.: *Race: The History of an Idea in America*, 180–81
Grand Central Palace, 3
Grand Central Terminal, 3, 113–15
Graves, Philip, 204
Great War, 15, 78, 144, 172, 265
Greenfield Village (Detroit), 202
Greenwich Observatory, 100–101; Prime Meridian, 101, 108–10, 113
Griffith, D. W.: *Birth of a Nation*, 201
grizzly bear (dance), 163
Guilfoy, William H., 13

Haines, Michael: Haines Tables, 278n14. *See also* infant mortality; life, expectation of; vital statistics
Hall, G. Stanley, 69, 190; *Adolescence*, 190
Handy, W. C., 162, 168. Works: "The Memphis Blues," 167–69; "St. Louis Blues," 168; "Yellow Dog Blues," 168
Harland, Marion. *See* Terhune, Mary Virginia
Harlem, 213–14; as race capital, 214. *See also* Harlem Renaissance
Harlem Renaissance, 174, 213–17
Harris, Isaac, 259. *See also* Triangle Waist Company, fire
Hawaiian Pineapple Company, 146. *See also* pineapples
Hays, Arthur Garfield, 213
Health Week (New York City, 1921), 3–4
Hearst, William Randolph, 35
Hegel, G. W. F., 270
Heifetz, Jascha, 173
Helmholtz, Hermann von, 69–73, 83–84, 92; *Handbook of Physiological Optics*, 71; idealism of, 71–72
Hendrick, Burton J., 37–38, 197–99, 207–10, 216. Works: articles on "Jewish invasion," 197–99, 207; *The Jews in America*, 207–10
Henry, Francis, A., 219–20, 222
Henry, Hubert-Joseph, 192
Hepburn Act, 255
Herbert, Victor, 173

Herrick, Christine Terhune: *Helping Hand Cook Book*, 148. *See also* Terhune, Mary Virginia
Herzl, Theodor, 196
higher criticism, 219–26, 229. *See also* Abbott, Lyman; Briggs, Charles A.; documentary hypothesis; Wellhausen, Julius
Hillis, Newell Dwight, 190
Hillquit, Morris, 262
Hitler, Adolf, 62, 203, 269; *Mein Kampf*, 182, 203
Hochschild, Adam, 187, 296–97n16; *King Leopold's Ghost*, 187
Hofstadter, Richard: *The Age of Reform*, 244–45
home (social institution), 116–19. *See also* house (physical structure); network, home as
home economics, 127–34, 136; origin of phrase, 130–31. *See also* Frederick, Christine; housekeeping, scientific; Parloa, Maria; Richards, Ellen Henrietta Swallow; Simmons College
Hooke, Robert, 24
Horace Mann School, 23
Hourwich, Isaac, 262
house (physical structure), 119–26; bathroom, 121, 123; kitchen, 120–21, 123, 134; plumbing, 120–22. *See also* home (social institution); network, house as
household economics. *See* home economics
housekeeping, scientific, 116–19, 127–30. *See also* Frederick, Christine; home economics; Parloa, Maria; Richards, Ellen Henrietta Swallow; Simmons College
How We Serve Hawaiian Pineapple, 148
Huneker, James Gibbons, 82
Hunter, Alberta, 171
Hunter, George William: *A Civic Biology*, 25–26
Huxley, Thomas H., 249–50
hygiene, personal, 28–30, 34, 53, 127; school instruction in, 29–30. *See also* Chapin, Charles V.; Public Health Movement; sex hygiene
Hylan, John F., 3
hypnotism, 74–77
hysteria, 74–75

idealism, 71–72, 77
immortality, 5, 43, 83, 229; of tissues, 36–39. *See also* Bergson, Henri; Carrel, Alexis
inclusive fitness (in evolutionary theory), 302–3n16
individual, 251–65, 267–74; autonomy of, 84, 115, 138–40, 272–74; and collective networks, 251–54; and federal government, 254–65. *See also* network, individual as
individualism, xvi
infant mortality, 7–9, 11, 13–14, 30. *See also* life, expectation of; mortality; vital statistics
influenza pandemic of 1918–19, 15–16, 279–80n26
Ingersoll, Ernest, 248
Institution for the Insane, Ward's Island, 49
International Congo League, 190. *See also* Congo
International Ladies' Garment Workers' Union, 263
island communities. *See* Wiebe, Robert H.
ivory, 143, 157–60. *See also* Congo

Jacobs, Joseph, 182–83, 226
jazz, 160–74; definition, 161–62; origin, 161, 168–70
Jesus, 218, 220–22, 226–31, 235–36. *See also* Social Gospel Movement
Jewish Daily Forward, 207, 262; on Triangle fire, 259–60
Jewish Theological Seminary, 225
Jews. *See* race

Johnson, Helen Louise, 118, 134
Johnson, James Weldon, 199, 212
Joint Board of Sanitary Control, 261–63
Josephus, 221
Judaism (religion), 225, 229
June, Jennie. *See* Croly, Jane Cunningham
Jung, Carl, 92, 272; collective unconscious, 92, 272

kahal (of Jewish community), 205
Kant, Immanuel, 69; 230–31; categorical imperative, 230–31; *Critique of Practical Reason*, 231; on kingdom of God, 231
Kelley, Florence, 260
Kellogg, John Harvey, 46–47. *See also* sex manuals
Kellogg, Susan, 279n25
Kennedy, John F., 180
kephir, 32
Kerfoot, J. B. (John Barrett), 86–87, 90
Key, Ellen: *Love and Ethics*, 58; *Love and Marriage*, 58
kingdom of God, xviii, 229–31, 233–34, 242, 244. *See also* Kant, Immanuel; Mathews, Shailer; Rauschenbusch, Walter; Social Gospel Movement
kin selection (in evolutionary theory), 302–3n16
Koch, Robert, 4, 23, 28
Kodak (portable camera), 187, 189
Kropotkin, Peter, 248–52, 302–3n16; *Mutual Aid*, 249–52
Ku Klux Klan, 201–2, 212

lactic acid, 32
Lake Placid Conference on Home Economics, 130–33. *See also* home economics
La Libre Parole (newspaper), 193. *See also* Drumont, Édouard
Landes, David S., 110–12
Langley, Samuel P., 107
LaRocca, Dominic "Nick," 170, 173; "Livery Stable Blues," 170; Original Dixieland Jazz Band, 170
Lawrence, D. H.: *Sons and Lovers*, 221–22
League of Anti-Semites (Germany), 182. *See also* anti-Semitism; Marr, Wilhelm
League of Medical Freedom, 55
Leopold II (king of Belgium), 158–59, 186–89, 199. *See also* Congo
Lewes, George Henry: *The Physiology of Common Life*, 26
Lewis, Sinclair: *Babbitt*, 22
life expectancy. *See* life, expectation of
life, expectation of, 5–16, 30. *See also* infant mortality; mortality; vital statistics
life insurance industry, 10–12, 14. *See also* American Experience Table
life, prolongation of, 5–6, 9, 15, 18–19, 30–39. *See also* Carrel, Alexis; Metchnikoff, Elie
Liggett & Myers, 154
Lilienthal, David E., 212–13
Lillie, Frank R., 41
"Livery Stable Blues." *See* LaRocca, Dominic "Nick"
Locke, Alain, 214–16; editor of *The New Negro*, 213–14
Lodge, Oliver, 19
Loeb, Jacques, 41
longevity. *See* life, expectation of; life, prolongation of
Loubet, Émile, 192
Low, Seth, 72
Luce, Henry, 144
lynchings, 199, 211

Macfarland, Charles S., 235–38; *Spiritual Culture and Social Service*, 236
McKinley, William, 145
Macy Time Star, 108, 114. *See also* time ball
Maeterlinck, Maurice, 246–48; *The Life of the Bee*, 246–48, 251
management, scientific. *See* scientific management

Manassas Industrial School for Colored Youth, 164
Mannes, David, 165
Manufacturers' Protective Association, 261
Marr, Wilhelm, 182, 192. *See also* League of Anti-Semites (Germany)
marriage manuals. *See* sex manuals
Marshall, Louis, 206, 241
Marx, Karl, 233
Mathews, Shailer, 41–42, 228, 231, 232; on kingdom of God, 231; poll on evolution, 41. *See also* Social Gospel Movement
Meat Inspection Act, 255
Men and Religion Forward Movement, 232–35; *Making Religion Efficient*, 233–34; *Messages of the Men and Religion Movement*, 233–34
Mendel, Gregor, 25, 51, 64, 181–82
mental illness, functional vs. organic conceptions of, 74–78
Metchnikoff, Elie, 19, 30–38, 48; old age as disease, 30–36, 48; optimism, 30–36; orthobiosis, 34. Works: *The Nature of Man*, 31–34; *The Prolongation of Life*, 31–34. *See also* Carrel, Alexis; life, prolongation of
Metropolitan Transit Authority, New York, xix. *See also* subway, New York City
miasma (sewer gas), 27–28, 122
microbes. *See* bacteria; germs
Miller, Karl Hagstrom, 172
Miller, Louis, 262
mind: as independent of nervous system, 74–92; neurophysiological view of, 68–74, 271. *See also* network, mind as; New Psychology
Mintz, Steven, 279n25
mitosis, 24
Moderwell, Hiram K., 166
Montagu, Ashley, 185–86, 251; *Man's Most Dangerous Myth*, 185
Morel, Edmund, 159, 186–88
Morgan, J. P., 232
Morgan, Thomas Hunt: *Heredity and Sex*, 50–51
Morgenthau, Henry, Sr., 263
Morrow, Prince A., 52–55, 155. *See also* sex education; sex hygiene; venereal disease
mortality, 7–8, 10–11, 14–15. *See also* infant mortality
Moskowitz, Henry, 218
Müller, Johannes, 70–71; law of specific energy of sensory nerves, 70–71
Muir, Peter C., 166–68
Muller, Robert E., 144
Murphy, Frank, 212
Music School Settlement for Colored People, 165
mutual aid, 34, 249–52, 270. *See also* Kropotkin, Peter; network, mutual aid as
mutualism (in evolutionary theory), 303n16

NAACP (National Association for the Advancement of Colored People), 212–13, 218
National Conservation Commission, 11
National Conservatory of Music, 164
nationalism, 215–16, 268
natural selection, 31–32, 302–3n16. *See also* Darwin, Charles; evolution, theory of
Naval Observatory, 107–8, 113–14, 271. *See also* time ball; time, standard
Negroes. *See* race
Negro spirituals, 161
nervous system, xviii, 18–19, 68–74, 91–92, 271–72. *See also* mind, as independent of nervous system; network, nervous system as; neurophysiology
network, xvi, xvii–xviii, 267–74; archaic past as, 92; benevolent surveillance as, 270; biological self as, 39, 92, 140–41; biological self as part of, 29–30; body as, xviii, 51; circulatory system as, 25–26; communication,

270–71; community as, 140–41; consumer products as, xvii, 142–74; of cooperation, 243–45, 265, 270–71, 273; evolutionary, 52; federal regulatory power as, 254–65; home as, 127–41; house as, xviii, 119–26, 139–41, 274; individual as, 274; of individual in Ethical Culture, 238–39; mind as, xviii; municipal services as, 27; mutual aid as, 34, 250–51, 270–71; nervous system as, 69–74, 83–84, 92, 271–73; piano as hub of, 142–45; Public Health Movement as, 16, 30, 255–56, 270; race as, 91, 185, 191, 193–94, 216–17, 269; railroad, 101; sewers as, 27; sexuality and, 57–58, 64–65; social, 29, 58, 185, 268–72; standard time as, xvii, 44, 84, 104–15, 271; telephone system as, 124–26; transportation, xviii, 270; watch as hub of, 113–15

neurasthenia, 75

neurophysiology, xviii, 69–74, 91–92, 97, 115, 271–72. *See also* mind, as independent of nervous system; nervous system

New England Kitchen of Boston, 130

New Harmony community (Indiana), 46

Newlands, Francis G., 258–59

The New Negro, 174, 213–17. *See also* Du Bois, W. E. B.; Harlem Renaissance; Locke, Alain

New Psychology, 67–69, 77–78, 82, 83, 92. *See also* mind, as independent of nervous system

Newton, Isaac, 70

New Woman, 134–36

New York Academy of Medicine, 40

New York City Department of Health, 12–13

New York Times: annex building, 113–14

Noquet, Paul, 67

Nordling, M. W. de, 100–101

North Harlem Medical Society, 213

oekology. *See* Richards, Ellen Henrietta Swallow

Okeh Records, 171–72, 174. *See also* blues, jazz

old age as disease, 30–36. *See also* Metchnikoff, Elie

Old Testament. *See* Bible, Hebrew

O'Malley, Michael, 109

open-air classes, 20, 29

optimism, 14–16, 43, 140–41, 247, 250; about expectation of life, 14–16, 30–36. *See also* Metchnikoff, Elie

organs, xviii, 24–26, 33–34. *See also* cells; tissues

Original Dixieland Jazz Band. *See* LaRocca, Dominic "Nick"

Osborn, Henry Fairfield, 41

Owen, Richard, 5

Owen, Robert, 46

Owen, Robert Dale, 46

Paderewski, Ignace, 160

Paris Peace Conference, 15, 204

Parkhurst, Charles H., 114

Parloa, Maria, 130, 148. *See also* home economics

Pasteur, Louis, 4, 23, 28

Paul (Apostle), 224–25

Pentateuch. *See* Torah

perfect baby contest, 3

Perkins, Frances, 260–65; lobbyist for factory reform, 260–61; "The Roots of Social Security," 264; and Social Security Act, 264; work for factory safety investigation, 263–64. *See also* Triangle Waist Company, fire

Perry, Bliss: *The American Mind*, 254

phagocytes, phagocytosis, 32–33

pianos, 142–44, 157, 160. *See also* network, piano as hub of; Steinway & Sons

pineapples, 145–49; Hawaiian canned, 146–49

Pipp, E. G., 204

Pittsburgh Platform. *See* Reform Judaism

Pius X, Pope, 225–26; Papal Syllabus on higher criticism, 225–26
plague, 7
Plante, Ellen M., 134, 137–38
Plato: *Parmenides*, 95
Plunkette, Harriette Merrick, 120–22; "Then!" house and "Now!" house, 120–21, 125–26, 138–39, 273–74; *Women, Plumbers and Doctors*, 120–22
Plymouth Church (Brooklyn), 190, 224
Poincaré, Henri, 99
Presbyterian Church, 223–24
preventive medicine, 4–6. *See also* Public Health Movement
Price, George M., 261–64; lead investigator for Factory Investigating Commission, 263; *Russkii listok* (newspaper), 262; *Russkie novosti* (newspaper), 262; series on Russian Jews in America, 261–62. *See also* Triangle Waist Company, fire
Prime Meridian, 101
Prime Meridian Conference, Washington, DC, 100–101, 109
Prince, Morton, 67–69, 74; *The Nature of Mind and Human Automatism*, 68
Progressive Era, 38, 234, 244–45
prostitution, 52–53, 58, 155, 235
Protestantism, 228–29, 238, 244–45, 251, 270
Protocols of the Learned Elders of Zion, 203–5, 208
protoplasm, 24–25, 280n2
Prudden, T. Mitchell, 21
psychoanalysis, 88–92. *See also* Freud, Sigmund
psychology, 68–69, 71–72, 74–77, 92, 271–72
public health. *See* Public Health Movement
public health campaign. *See* Public Health Movement
Public Health Movement, xvii, 7, 9–10, 13–14, 23, 26–30, 34, 255–56; bacteriological phase, 28–30, 122; sanitarian phase, 27–28, 122–23, 150. *See also* bacteria; bacteriology; Chapin, Charles, V.; dust (agent of disease); germs; germ theory of disease; hygiene, personal; network, Public Health Movement as
Pure Food and Drug Act, 255
Pushkin, Alexander, 99; *Eugene Onegin*, 99, 145

Quackenbos, John D., 75–76

race, 177–217, 269; Anglo-Saxon, 184; and evolutionary theory, 180–81; and Harlem Renaissance, 214–17; Indians (Native Americans) as, 183–84; Jews as, 182–85, 195–96, 269; Negroes as, 178 85; scientific foundation of concept of, 180–85; and transnational groups, 184–99, 213–17, 269. *See also* network, race as; racism
race records, 171–72
Rachmaninoff, Serge, 173
racism, 180, 269. *See also* race
radio, xviii
ragtime, 160–74; definition of, 161–62; origin of, 161–62; syncopation in, 166, 169
railroads, 98–112; crashes, 104–5. *See also* network, railroad; Railroad Standard Time
Railroad Standard Time, 106–9. *See also* railroads
Ramón y Cajal, Santiago, 72–74
Rauschenbusch, Walter, 228–32, 243, 245; on kingdom of God, 229–31. Works: *Christianity and the Social Crisis*, 228–31; *Dare We Be Christians*, 243. *See also* Social Gospel Movement
Ravenel, Mazÿck P., 4–6
reciprocal altruism. *See* altruism, reciprocal
Red Cross, 257–58
Red Summer (1919), 199–200, 211

Reedy, William Marion, 45, 47; "Sex O'Clock in America," 45, 47, 90–91
Reeve, Arthur B., 35, 47–49, 86–87, 284n9; "Dream Doctor," 35, 47–49, 86, 90, 284n9
Reform Judaism, 240–43; Pittsburgh Platform, 240
religion, 219–45. *See also* higher criticism; kingdom of God; Social Gospel Movement
"REMEMBER THESE THINGS," 29
remote recordings, 171–72
Renan, Ernest: *La Vie de Jésus* (*The Life of Jesus*), 221–22
repression. *See* Freud, Sigmund
Richards, Ellen Henrietta Swallow, 127–35, 139–40; and environment, science of, 128; euthenics, 129; *Euthenics*, 253–54; and home economics, 128–31; oekology, 129; Rumford Kitchen, 130; and scientific housekeeping, 128–30; and women's education, 128. *See also* Boston School of Housekeeping; home economics; scientific management; Simmons College
Richards, Robert Hallowell, 128
rights: civil, 191; human, 185–99, 216–17
Riis, Jacob, 183–84, 260; *How the Other Half Lives*, 183–84, 260
Riley, James C., 278n14
Rockefeller, John D., 232
Rogers, James A., 174
Roosevelt, Franklin Delano, 260
Roosevelt, Theodore, 66–69, 145, 164–65, 184, 245; *The Winning of the West*, 184
Ross, Edward A., 177–79, 196, 252; *Social Control*, 252
rubber, 158
Rubinstein, Anton, 160
Ruth, George Herman "Babe," Jr., 3

Salvation Army, 232
San Francisco, earthquake, 257–59
Sanger, Margaret, 60, 62–63. Works: *The Pivot of Civilization*, 62–63; *Woman and the New Race*, 62–63
sanitary engineering. *See* sanitary science
sanitary science, 9, 120, 122, 127, 133. *See also* Public Health Movement, sanitarian phase
sanitation, 4–6
Sapiro, Aaron, 206
Sayers, Joseph D., 256
scarlet fever, 7
Schäfer, Edward A.: "The Nature, Origin and Maintenance of Life," 17–20, 24, 26, 38, 68–69, 74, 280n2
Schechter, Solomon, 225
Schleiden, Matthias, 24–25
Schlesinger, Arthur M., 136
Schnitzer, Eduard. *See* Emin Pasha
Schwann, Theodor, 24–25
scientific management, 127, 134, 136, 141. *See also* Frederick, Christine; Richards, Ellen Henrietta Swallow; Taylor, Frederick Winslow
Scopes, John, 25; "Monkey Trial," 25, 212
Scriptures. *See* Bible
Seagrove, Gordon, 168–69
Seals, H. Franklin: "Baby Seals Blues," 167
Sears, Roebuck, 112
secularism, 269–70
Self-Winding Clock Co., 113, 115
Seligman, Isaac N., 218
servant problem, 133–34
sewer gas. *See* miasma
sewers, 27, 122
sex education, 52–58, 235; emergency vs. integrated, 56–57; *Good Housekeeping* series on, 55. *See also* sex hygiene
sex (gender) determination, law of, 49–52
sex hygiene, 52–58, 63, 235. *See also* sex education
sex manuals, 45–50, 53–54, 57, 59–60. *See also* Acton, William; Cowan, John; Kellogg, John Harvey; Stockham, Alice Bunker
sexuality, 45–65; as independent of reproduction, 58–61; Victorian

attitudes toward, 45–47. *See also* birth control; continence, law of; Freud, Sigmund; network, sexuality and; sex education; sex hygiene; sex manuals; venereal disease
sexual reproduction, 18
sexual selection, 63
Shapp, Leo, 262
Sheldon, Charles Monroe, 226–28, 245, 269; *In His Steps*, 226–28, 269. *See also* Social Gospel Movement
Sherman Antitrust Commission, 153
Sherrington, Charles: *The Integrative Action of the Nervous System*, 73–74
Simmons College, xiv, 131–33, 267–68, 273; Household Economics, Department of, 131–33. *See also* home economics
Sinclair, Upton, 245
Slosson, Edwin E., 78, 247–48; "Twelve Major Prophets of To-day," 247–48
smallpox, 7, 9
Smith, Frederick D., 232
Smith, Mamie, 171; "Crazy Blues," 171
Smith, Stephen 5–6, 9, 30
Smith, Theobald, 29
Social Darwinism, 181–83
social disease. *See* venereal disease
social evil. *See* prostitution
Social Gospel Movement, 228–35. *See also* Gladden, Washington; Mathews, Shailer; Rauschenbusch, Walter; Sheldon, Charles Monroe
socialism, 245, 250
Social Security, 264–65
Society for Birth Control and Progress of Race, 62
Spanish-American War, 144
Spanish Flu. *See* influenza pandemic of 1918–19
Spencer, Herbert, 236
Spender, Edward Harold, 188
standardization, 136–38
standard time. *See* time, standard
Standard Time Act, 109–10
Stanley, Henry Morton, 159–60, 187; *In Darkest Africa*, 159–60
Stanton, Elizabeth Cady, 46
Steffens, Lincoln, 78
Steinberg, Saul, 86
Steinem, Gloria, 118
Steinway & Sons, 293n1. *See also* pianos
Steinway, Henry Z., 293n1
stimulus, 70–73, 92
Stockham, Alice Bunker: *Tokology*, 45–47. *See also* sex manuals
Stoddard, Lothrop, 200–201; *The Rising Tide of Color*, 200–201
Stopes, Marie Carmichael, 58–65; and eugenics, 61–65. Works: *Love's Creation*, 59; *Married Love*, 58–59
Stowe, Harriet Beecher, 127; *The American Woman's Home*, 127. *See also* Beecher, Catherine
Strauss, David Friedrich, 220–22; *Das Leben Jesu* (*The Life of Jesus*), 220–21
subconsciousness. *See* unconscious
subway, New York City, xviii–xx
suffrage, Negro, 189–90
Sumner, William Graham, 61
Sunday School Associations, 233
Survey Graphic (magazine), 214
Swallow, Ellen Henrietta. *See* Richards, Ellen Henrietta Swallow
Sweet, Gladys, 211–13
Sweet, Henry, 212
Sweet, Ossian, 211–13
syncopation, 165, 170, 173. *See also* blues; jazz; ragtime
syphilis, 52–53

Taft, William, 66
Tammany Hall, 260–61
Tarbell, Ida, 77
Taylor, Frederick Winslow, 127, 133, 136, 234; *Principles of Scientific Management*, 136, 234. *See also* scientific management
Teachers College of Columbia University, 22–23

telegraph, 107
telephone, 124–26; etiquette associated with, 125. *See also* network, telephone system as
telephone girls, 124–25
Temple Emanu-El (New York City), 241
Terhune, Mary Virginia, 147–48; *The Cottage Kitchen*, 148; *Helping Hand Cook Book*, 148, 149; *365 Desserts*, 148. *See also* Herrick, Christine Terhune
Tesla, Nikola, xviii, 277n4
Thomson, J. Arthur, 51
Thomson, William Hanna, 40
time ball, 100, 110, 271; *See also* time; Western Union
time: daylight saving, 109–10; distribution by telegraph, 107–10; and motion, science of, 127, 133, 136; standard, xvii, 98–103, 106–12, 271; zones, 101, 104, 107–10. *See also* network, standard time as; Railroad Standard Time; time ball; watches and clocks
tissues, xviii, 24–26, 33–34. *See also* Carrel, Alexis; cells; organs
tobacco: Bright, 152, 154; Burley, 152; domestic, 151–52, 156; Egyptian, 154; Turkish, 151–52, 154, 156. *See also* cigarettes
Tocqueville, Alexis de, xvi–xvii, 264–65
Tomes, Nancy: *Gospel of Germs*, 23, 29
Torah, 220, 222
Townsend, Luther, 40
transnational groups. *See* race
Triangle Waist Company: fire, 259–63. *See also* Perkins, Frances; Price, George M.
tuberculosis, 4, 7, 21–23, 53, 58; open air and, 22–23, 29
Tulsa, Oklahoma, race riot, 200
turkey trot (dance), 163
Twain, Mark (Samuel Langhorne Clemens), 188–89, 196; "Concerning the Jews," 196; *King Leopold's Soliloquy*, 189
typhoid fever, 7, 9, 53
typhus, 7
Tyre, William H.: *Panama: A Characteristic Novelty*, 166

Uhlenberg, Peter, 279n25
unconscious, 66–67, 76–77, 87–92. *See also* Freud, Sigmund
Union Theological Seminary, 222–24
United Brands, 150
United Fruit Company, 150; as Banana Trust, 150
United States Public Health Bureau, 3

vacuum cleaners, 122–23, 290–91n12
Vail, Theodore N., 126
Van Dyke, Henry, 188
Van Wyck, Robert A., 257
Velde, Theodoor H. van de: *Ideal Marriage*, 59–60
venereal disease, 52–58, 62; conspiracy of silence regarding, 52–53. *See also* sex education; sex hygiene; sexuality
Victoria, Queen, 155
"Vindex," 194
Virchow, Rudolf, 24
vision, faculty of, 70–72. *See also* color perception; Helmholtz, Hermann von; Müller, Johannes; Young, Thomas
vital force, 19
vital statistics, 9–14, 279n25. *See also* birth, registration of; death, registration of; life, expectation of
Von Drehle, David, 260–61, 263

Wallace, Alfred Russel, 19
Waltham Watch Company, 111–14, 271. *See also* watches and clocks
Walton, Lester A., 166
Wanamaker, John, 137, 188–89, 232
Wand, Hart A.: "Dallas Blues," 167
Washington, Booker T., 164, 177, 188–90
watches and clocks, 99–115, 271; American, 110–12; interchangeable parts in, 110–11; per capita ownership, 112. *See also* network, watch as hub of; Waltham Watch Company

waterworks, 121
Webb, Jack, 154
Wellhausen, Julius, 222, 229. *See also* documentary hypothesis; higher criticism
Western Union, 107–8; time ball, 107–8
Whipple, George Chandler, 13–14
Whiteman, Paul, 173; Palais Royal Orchestra, 173; "Rhapsody in Blue" premiere, 173
Whitney, Eli, 111
Wiebe, Robert H., 28, 251–52, 256, 265; on island communities, xvii, 251–52, 265
Wild West shows, 144
Williams, George Washington, 187
Wilson, Teddy, 169
Wilson, Woodrow, 15, 109–10, 163, 245, 280n27
Wise, Stephen S., 218, 226, 241–45; on cooperation, 242–43; Free Synagogue, 218, 241–42; Social Service Division, 241–42
women: equality with men, 118, 131, 135. *See also* New Woman
Women's Educational and Industrial Union (Boston), 131
Woolf, Virginia: *A Room of One's Own*, 59
Woolsey, John M., 58
Worcester, Elwood, 76–77; *Religion and Medicine*, 76–77
World War I. *See* Great War
Wright, Frank Lloyd, 245
Wu, Tim, 126

yellow fever, 4, 7, 53
Yerkes, Robert M., 63
YMCA (Young Men's Christian Association), 231–33
yogurt, 32
Young, Ella Flagg, 55–56
Young, Thomas, 70

Zanzibar, 143, 159. *See also* Congo
Zeiler, Thomas W., 144
Zeno of Elea, 95–99, 102; Paradoxes of Motion, 95–99, 115. *See also* Bergson, Henri
Zionism, 196, 215
Zola, Émile, 192, 194, 196; "J'accuse!", 192, 194. *See also* Dreyfus Affair